MODERN NAVAL COMBAT

Above: The Invincible class aircraft carrier HMS Ark Royal.

Above: The Ohio class ballistic missile submarine USS Florida.

MODERN
NAVAL COMBAT

DAVID MILLER • CHRIS MILLER

a Salamander book
Published by Salamander Books Limited
LONDON • NEW YORK

A Salamander Book Credits

Published by
Salamander Books Ltd.,
52 Bedford Row,
London WC1R 4LR
United Kingdom.

© Salamander Books Ltd., 1986

ISBN 0 86101 231 3

Distributed in the United Kingdom by
Hodder & Stoughton Services,
PO Box 6, Mill Road,
Dunton Green, Sevenoaks,
Kent TN13 2XX.

All correspondence concerning the content of this volume
should be addressed to the publisher.

Editor: Bernard Fitzsimons

Designer: Mark Holt

Colour artwork: Tony Gibbons, Terry Hadler, Ray Hutchins,
Janos Marffy, Maltings Partnership, Tony Payne, TIGA

Line profiles: John Jordan, Maltings Partnership

Diagrams: TIGA

Filmset by Modern Text Ltd.

Colour reproduction by Melbourne Graphics

Printed in Belgium by Proost International Book Production, Turnhout

The Publishers wish to thank wholeheartedly the many organizations
and individuals in the defence and naval construction industries,
and the armed forces of various nations, who have been of
considerable help in the preparation of this book.

The Authors

David Miller is a serving officer in the British Army, a career which has taken him to Singapore, Malaysia, Germany and the Falkland Islands and which has included service in the Royal Corps of Signals, several staff jobs at Army headquarters and the command of a regiment in the UK. He has contributed numerous articles to technical defence journals on subjects ranging from guerilla warfare to missile stategy and is the author of *An Illustrated Guide to Modern Submarines* (1982) and *An Illustrated Guide to Modern Sub Hunters* (1984) and a contributor to *The Vietnam War* (1979), *The Balance of Military Power* (1981) and *The Intelligence War* (1983), all published by Salamander Books.

Chris Miller is a former lieutenant in the Royal Navy. His naval career included appointments to anti-submarine frigates and to the staff of a flag officer at one of the main NATO maritime headquarters, teaching at the School of Navigation and extensive involvement in wargames and tactical simulators. Since leaving the Navy he has been employed in the off-shore oil industry.

Below: The Kiev class aircraft carrier Minsk photographed in the western Pacific shortly after starting her deployment with the Soviet Pacific Fleet.

Contents

Below: A pair of F-14 Tomcats prepare to launch on combat air patrol from USS Saratoga (CV 60) under way in the Mediterranean in February 1986.

Foreword

This book is about naval combat in the late 1980s and the next decade. Designed to give the reader both an overview of the subject and a detailed description of weapons, equipment and tactics in one comprehensive volume, it ranges in scope from the recently refurbished World War II battleships of the US Navy, through aircraft carriers, cruisers, destroyers and frigates, to the increasingly important but still little understood world of the submarine, and places them all in their tactical and technological context.

Unseen and unheeded by the majority of laymen, and generally unpublicised by the navies themselves—still the 'Silent Services' in most nations—the world's fleets patrol the oceans constantly, frequently coming within very short distances of each other. Unlike the better known land confrontations, such as those on the inner German border between the Warsaw Pact and NATO, on the Chinese-Vietnamese border and on the 'Green Line' between Greek and Turk in Cyprus—the oceans have no clear-cut demarcation line to separate the opposing sides. Instead, apart from a narrow band along the coast, ships and fleets on the high seas can intermingle, the degree of separation depending solely on the skill and determination of their captains. Indeed, more than one collision between Soviet and US Navy ships has provided evidence, if any were needed, of the closeness of the watch that navies keep on each other.

Reference is made throughout this book to the South Atlantic War of 1982 between the United Kingdom and Argentina. No apologies are made for this repitition, as that war was an event of the greatest significance in naval affairs. On land, army tactics and equipment have been tested repeatedly since the end of World War II. Medium-intensity conflicts such as those in Korea, Indo-China and the Middle East, and low-intensity conflicts in Asia, Africa and South America have kept land forces in a state of constant practice. Similarly, air combat experience has accumulated steadily, with consequent feedback to the planners and designers. At sea, however, while there have been regular patrols and exercises and occasional though relatively low-level confrontations, there have been few conflicts involving more than a handful of ships.

The South Atlantic War on the other hand depended on sea power. The Argentinians could not have captured the Falkland Islands and South Georgia, nor could the British have recaptured them, without the use of ships on a large scale. Without ships, in fact, the British could not have got anywhere near their South Atlantic colonies, given their distance from the nearest friendly air base on Ascension Island and the fact that the Argentinians had occupied the only airfield on the Falklands. At the same time, because the Argentinian mainland air bases were within range, if only just, British carrier-borne airpower was essential to the prosecution campaign.

Of wider significance was the fact that the war in the South Atlantic was the first for many years during which warships had been exposed to true combat conditions, and this proved to be a true eye-opener, with the British losing three modern warships and a major landing ship, and the Argentinians a cruiser and a submarine (both elderly) and some smaller units. Missiles and aircraft were used, both taking their toll, and each side menaced the other with its submarines. The subsequent analyses have proved of value to every navy in the world. The bigger navies have had a major strategic role for many centuries, and they have not infrequently been the ultimate arbiters of victory. Their physical reach, however, was confined to the range of a gun until carrier-borne aircraft gave them the ability to strike inland. Through the 1940s and 1950s that reach was increased as aircraft became faster and longer ranged, but this capability was confined to the US fleet, although other navies such as the British and French had a tactical strike capability. The nuclear-powered submarine, however, and the submarine-launched ballistic missile have changed all that. Now the navies with such submarines can strike at any target in the world from virtually anywhere in the world's oceans.

Alone among the world's navies, the Soviet Navy has continued to expand since the end of World War II, it's growth unremitting both in types and numbers as well as in sophistication, capability and global reach. In the 1950s it was a coastal force equipped with surface warships heavily influenced by Italian designers, and submarines directly descended from the German designs of 1945,

Below: In April 1986 a Royal Navy task group sets off on a round-the-world deployment. The destoyer Manchester and the frigates Beaver and Amazon, seen here with the destroyer Southampton and the frigate Brazen plus a support tanker and a fleet replenishment ship, took part in Global 86, which included participation in the joint US and Allied Rimpac 86 exercises.

but today it is one of the two pacesetters, with ships which are second to none, in capability, design and sophistication.

Nevertheless, the Soviet Navy has never fought a fleet action; their engagements in World War II were confined to individual ship actions, and even those were on a very limited, purely coastal scale. As the South Atlantic War showed, even such an experienced body as Britain's Royal Navy can forget some of the major lessons of 40 years ago and their is no doubt that their ships and weapon systems were found wanting in certain respects. How much more deficient may be the Soviet ships, when even there most senior officers now have no personal memory of actual combat in a ship at sea?

The United States Secretary for Defense, Casper Weinberger, summed up the attitude of the major naval powers in his Annual Report to the Congress for Fiscal Year 1987 when he said:

'As an island nation and a senior partner in a global alliance system, the United States needs a strong navy to support its forward defense strategy. In peacetime the navy helps maintain an American military presence in forward areas where we have vital interests to safeguard. These routine overseas deployments provide tangible evidence of our commitment to preserving international stability and security. In times of crisis, naval forces are often dispatched to trouble spots, both to support friends and allies and to deter aggression against them. Should deterrence fail, these forces would serve among the lead elements in our forward defense strategy, which emphasises an active defense of Europe and the Eurasian littoral regions. In their wartime role, naval forces would be called on to protect friendly shipping from air or sea attacks, to deprive enemy forces of access to strategic areas and to protect power against targets at sea or on land.'

If there were to be another global conflict then one of the major areas of conflict would be at sea. Indeed, such a war might well start at sea and could even be decided there. The intention of this book is to show what forces might be involved, what equipment, sensors and weapons might be used, and how they would all be tied together to achieve their tactical and strategic purposes.

Many of the ships may look outwardly similar to those of 40 years ago, but they are designed differently, use different weapons and have sensors with capabilities undreamt of at the end of the last global conflict. This book explains just how different they are.

Above: Naval deployments and exercises are closely monitored by the potential opposition: here the Soviet carrier Minsk comes under scrutiny by crewmen on the deck of a US Navy carrier.

Below: The South Atlantic War of 1982 saw the first real naval combat for many years. HMS Coventry was just one of the ships lost in what proved a truly eye-opening conflict.

Naval Technology

Below: Even the smallest warships are able to incorporate command and control centres with tactical displays and weapon control consoles for missiles and torpedoes.

Introduction

By the end of World War II the nations involved had a fairly clear idea of the requirements for navies. In the case of the Western combatants it was naval power which had enabled the Allies to ferry supplies and reinforcements across the Atlantic to reinforce the United Kingdom and then to invade continental Europe, and to gradually strangle the power of Imperial Japan in the Pacific. And in the Soviet Union, although naval power had not played a major role in that campaign, it was clear to the military planners that if they were to challenge the West on a global scale then they needed naval power of their own.

The naval nations were also in general agreement about the ideal composition of their fleets and the types of ships which should go to make them up. In the surface combatant category there were aircraft carriers, battleships, cruisers, destroyers, escort vessels and light attack craft, together with masses of ships and craft developed for the amphibious warfare role, as well as a few types which were slightly harder to classify.

Aircraft carriers had finally achieved the status of capital ships during the course of the war, and as well as two basic types—the fleet carrier of 20,000 tons or more and the light fleet carrier of less than 20,000 tons—there were also some wartime conversions known as escort carriers. The majority of carriers belonged to the US Navy or the Royal Navy, although by the end of the decade France had one and Canada two light fleet carriers (both ex-British).

Many battleships still existed in 1945, but it was generally agreed that the day of the all-big-gun heavily armoured capital ship was over. The existing fleets were divided between the USA and the United Kingdom, although France had two battleships and South American navies had a few.

Battle-cruisers, of which a very few were still in service, had been conceived in the early 1900s as ships with the firepower of battleships and the speed of cruisers, but at the cost of protection, so they represented a rather unsatisfactory compromise. As a class battle-cruisers had a very chequered career, and the Royal Navy (which had conceived the type) had some spectacular disasters, including the loss of no fewer than three battle-cruisers at Jutland in 1915 and the loss of the *Hood*, sunk by the German fast battleship *Bismarck* in 1941. The Royal Navy was, therefore, very happy to scrap its last remaining battle-cruiser in the late 1940s.

The US Navy had designed several classes of battle-cruiser over the years but never actually built any until the very end of the era when they produced the two ships of the Alaska class (34,250 tons), which were commissioned in 1944 and 1945. These saw brief service in World War II, then spent some time in reserve before being scrapped in 1961; with that the day of the of the battle-cruiser was considered to be at an end.

Next in order of size and importance came the cruiser, a term which denoted a self-sufficient fighting ship with long range, high speed, adequate protection and substantial armament, and which, although inferior to the battleship, was superior to all other types of warship. Cruisers ranged in size from 5,000 tons displacement armed with six 6in guns (eg, the British Leander class) to the US Navy's 20,950-ton Des Moines class with nine 8in and 12 5in guns. Most cruisers had some armour protection, usually of the order of 4in (10cm) over the boiler and engine rooms. All had a mass of smaller anti-aircraft weapons and most carried torpedo tubes, but ASW sensors were rarely carried. Their role was as escorts to carrier battle groups or major convoys, or to act independently to patrol the ocean highways. There were large cruiser fleets throughout the world, and in many navies they were the largest ships in service.

By far the most common type, however, was the destroyer, the maid-of-all-work in every fleet, whose roles ranged from forming the outer screen for carrier battle groups through acting as ASW escorts for convoys to carrying out independent missions requiring high speed and dash. Most ships categorized as destroyers were at of least 1,000 tons displacement, with the largest about 3,000 tons. Main armament was usually four or six

Left: Frigates, such as the Brazilian Navy's Niteroi class, have become the most widely used of modern warships, though with far greater capabilities than their World War II counterparts.

Below: Air power is a fundamental element of modern naval strength: these Yak-38 Forgers on the after end of Kiev's flight deck typify the innovative approach of Soviet naval design and technology.

Right: Designed for anti-submarine warfare in the unforgiving waters of the North Atlantic, the Canadian Iroquois class destroyers feature variable-depth sonar at the stern and a hangar for two CHSS-2 Sea King helicopters. A planned upgrade will replace the existing 5in gun and Sea Sparrow missiles with a 76mm gun and vertically launched Standards and add a Phalanx CIWS, plus new engines, radars and EW equipment.

guns of 4in (102cm) to 5in (127mm) calibre with a number of anti-aircraft weapons. All had torpedo tubes and some form of ASW weapon such as the British 'Hedgehog' or depth-charges, and virtually all had a variety of ASW sensors. There were many hundreds of destroyers in service throughout the world.

The description 'frigate' had originated with the French Navy in Napoleonic times and was later adopted by the British as well, only to lapse in the 1880s. During World War II, however, the term was revived by the British to describe a ship which was in some ways a utility destroyer and whose primary role was ASW, but which was capable of other escort duties as well. The US Navy used the term 'destroyer escort' to describe ships in the category. In general, the Royal Navy's World War II frigates were of 1,000-1,500 tons displacement and armed with up to four guns and a variety of ASW weapons and sensors.

At the lower end of the scale of warships came the small escort vessels of 500-1,000 tons displacement, which had been produced in very large numbers during the war, especially by the USA, the United Kingdom and Canada. These served as ASW escorts to large, slow-moving convoys and conducted inshore patrols and the myriad other minor tasks required of a fleet. They were designated corvettes or sloops in most navies.

Finally, there was a miscellany of fast attack boats of 40-100 tons displacement. Armed with light guns and torpedoes these were designated patrol boats by the US Navy and motor torpedo boats by the Royal Navy; again, there were many hundreds in service around the world.

There had been many amphibious operations during the war—in the Mediterranean, along the Northern coast of Western Europe, and in the Indian and Pacific Oceans — and even the Soviet Navy had undertaken several, although none on the scale of the D-Day landings or the US operations against Japanese-held islands. To cope with these demands a huge armada of amphibious warfare craft had been produced, often by converting existing vessels. In many cases, however, entirely new specialized designs had been produced, including such types as landing-ships, tank (LSTs), the smaller landing-craft, tank (LCTs) and the much more sophisticated landing platform, dock (LPD).

Submarines had been involved in violent and wide-ranging campaigns in both the Atlantic and Pacific, where enormous tonnages of surface shipping were sunk along with many submarines. The diesel-engined, torpedo-armed submarine reigned supreme, and the great majority of the boats in service showed little improvement over the slow-moving, low-endurance submersibles at sea in 1939. Just as the war was ending, however, the German Type XXI demonstrated how streamlining and increased power could be used to attain very much higher submerged speeds, but even these fine boats were still compelled to return to the surface regularly to recharge their batteries.

At the end of World War II, then, the naval scene appeared to be fairly straightforward. The day of the battleship and battle-cruiser was clearly over, and their role as the lynchpins of the fleet had been assumed by the aircraft carrier. Only the American and British navies had sizable carrier fleets and they were clearly determined to stay in the business, building ever larger carriers, while a few other navies had one or at most two carriers each. There were large numbers of cruisers, whose postwar role was a little unclear, and there were vast numbers of destroyers, frigates and corvettes whose obvious role was escorting carriers and combating the ever-growing threat of the submarine.

The two great navies were those of the USA and the United Kingdom, two nations whose global responsibilities could only be met by the deployment of large fleets. The German and Japanese fleets had been totally destroyed or taken over as war booty, while the Soviet Navy was relatively small and had a role which confined it to the coastal waters of the USSR. The remaining fleets were small and of little global strategic consequence.

Surface Ship Types

In the years since the end of World War II the distinctions between the various types of surface warship have tended to blur as new weapons have and improved sensors have allowed entirely new capabilities to be conferred on even the smaller vessels. The traditional roles have not disappeared, however, and in the following pages subsequent developments of each major type are outlined under the appropriate heading.

AIRCRAFT CARRIERS

In the immediate postwar period those navies with aircraft carriers concentrated on coming to terms with jet aircraft. Much development work went into the aircraft themselves and their engines, but the ships, too, needed change, and there were three crucial inventions: the steam catapult, the deck-landing mirror, and the angled flight-deck.

The US Navy was determined to have its own nuclear role and produced first the North American AJ-2 Savage and then the Douglas A-3 Skywarrior, both of which were designed to carry atomic bombs, which at that time weighed some 12,000lb (5,450kg) although they were soon reduced to under a quarter of that weight. Much bigger aircraft carriers were needed to carry such bombers, and this led to the Forrestal class (78,000

tons) and then to the nuclear powered Enterprise (89,600 tons) and Nimitz (91,400 tons) classes, together with the non-nuclear Kitty Hawk class (82,000 tons); by the mid-1980s the US Navy had 14 aircraft carriers in service, with a further three nuclear powered ships under construction.

The other major aircraft carrier operator, the Royal Navy, peaked in operational capability and effectiveness in the mid-1960s with some excellent carriers (*Ark Royal*, *Eagle*, *Victorious* and *Hermes*) whose air wings consisted of such useful types as the McDonnell F-4 Phantom and de Havilland Sea Vixen fighters, the Blackburn Buccaneer long-range attack aircraft and the Fairey Gannet for airborne early warning (AEW). A crisis arrived, however, when requirements for a new carrier, the new and expensive Type 82 escorts and new aircraft coincided, and the defence budget proved incapable of accommodating them all. The new CVA-01 carrier design was cancelled, and it appeared for a while that the Fleet Air Arm would be restricted to helicopter operations, but agreement was obtained to build the three ships, originally described as 'through-deck cruisers' but later properly designated light aircraft carriers, of the Invincible class (19,812 tons) now in service.

The French Navy spent the first few postwar years with just one ex-Royal Navy and two ex-US light fleet aircraft carriers, but then had two built to its own design in the late 1950s. These ships, *Clemenceau* and *Foch* (32,780 tons), have served the French very well and will be replaced in the 1990s by two nuclear powered aircraft carriers (the de Gaulle or PAN-1 class).

It is in the USSR, however, that some of the most surprising developments have taken place,

Above: The Forrestal class aircraft carrier USS Saratoga (CV 60) in the Mediterranean with the US Sixth Fleet. The four Forrestals, built in the 1960s, will serve on to 2005, having undergone Service Life Extension Program refits.

Below: HMS Hermes last of the traditional British fleet carriers, enters Portsmouth harbour at the end of the 1982 South Atlantic war. The 12° ski-jump enabled Sea Harriers and Harriers to operate at maximum payload.

starting with the *Moskva* (18,000 tons), a specialized helicopter-carrying ASW cruiser, and followed by the Kiev class (38,000 tons). The Soviet Navy is clearly carrying out a long-term plan to develop a fully capable air arm of its own, and as this is a completely new field for them, they are unfettered by traditional practices and out-of-date ideas. The *Kiev* introduced many novel ideas, and it is certain that the new nuclear-powered Kremlin class CVNs will continue that process.

Smaller navies have traditionally purchased surplus aircraft carriers from either the US or British navies, and the Indian, Argentinian and Brazilian navies continue to operate such vessels. The Spanish and Italian navies, however, have recently produced their own light aircraft carrier designs, and both ships were in the process of working up by 1986. These light carriers are based on the use of helicopters and of V/STOL aircraft, which currently means the British Aerospace Sea

Harrier, and will be very attractive to a navy either seeking its first aircraft carrier or needing to replace its existing carriers.

BATTLESHIPS AND BATTLE-CRUISERS

In the immediate postwar years the older battleships and battle-cruisers were scrapped, although the Korean War revived the need for shore bombardment and all four US Navy battleships saw service there before being returned to mothballs in 1954-58. By 1960 the only battleships left were the four US Iowas, the British *Vanguard*, and the French *Jean Bart* and *Richelieu*. The British and the French, however, consigned these last remaining capital ships to the scrapyards and the Iowas were left in reserve, objects of curiosity and considered to be museum pieces. The shore bombardment role reappeared during the Vietnam War and *New Jersey* was reactivated during 1967-69 before being put back into reserve once more, and the battleship story might well have ended there had it not been for the apearance of the Soviet Kirov class in the late 1970s.

The Soviet Navy has undergone a most remarkable expansion during the postwar years under the inspired guidance of Admiral Gorschkov, one of the greatest naval administrators in history, who envisaged a Soviet Navy which could at least hold its own with the navies of the West, if not actually attain superiority. Both the numbers and the maximum size of Soviet ships increased dramatically, and from the mid-1960s onward the Soviets, rather than follow the patterns established in other countries, started to produce original concepts of their own and in a number of fields became the pacesetters.

One startling demonstration of their innovative approach was the appearance in 1977 of the *Kirov*, by far the biggest surface warship

Above: USS New Jersey (BB 62) leaves Pearl Harbor for an operational deployment off Vietnam on September 11, 1968. The four Iowa class battleships have served the US Navy well.

other than aircraft carriers built since the end of World War II. Of 28,000 tons displacement, fast, long-ranged, relatively unprotected and with a heavy anti-ship missile armament, the *Kirov* was in some ways a totally new concept, but one bearing a strong relationship with the battle-cruisers of a previous era.

Faced with this new Soviet threat the US Navy decided to refurbish and recommission all four of its Iowa class battleships, which were still in excellent condition and which are now in the process of being returned to service. A very ambitious plan to replace the after 16in turret with a large flight-deck has been shelved, mainly on cost grounds, in favour of a less drastic and much cheaper alternative, but with nine 16in guns plus eight Tomahawk and 16 Harpoon launchers, coupled with high speed and heavy armour protection, these are still very formidable ships. Indeed, their armour makes them relatively immune to anti-ship missiles, and while it seems very doubtful that any new battleship of the size and complexity of the Iowas will be built, nobody had expected the Soviet Navy to build something like the *Kirov*.

CRUISERS

The masses of cruisers left over from the war sufficed the great majority of navies well into the 1960s, except for the USSR, the first of whose 14 Sverdlov class cruisers (17,200 tons full load displacement) was commissioned in 1951. The Sverdlovs, the last all-gun cruisers to be built, were in effect the end of the traditional line, being followed in the Soviet

Navy in the 1960s by the Kynda class, which combined a gun armament with eight SS-N-3 anti-ship missiles, in the 1970s by the Kresta and Kara classes, and in the 1980s by the Slava class.

Each class carried the latest guns and missiles and an ever-increasing array of sensors, and their size has steadily increased in consequence: the Kynda displaces 5,550 tons, the Kresta I 7,600 tons, the Kara 9,700 tons and the Slava 12,500 tons, while length has grown from the Kynda's 465.8ft (142m) to the Slava's 613.4ft (187m). In 1986 there were 39 cruisers in service with the Soviet Navy, of which 12 were the remaining ships of the Sverdlov class.

The US Navy had vast numbers of cruisers left over from the war and there was little new construction until the late 1950s when the USS *Long Beach* (CGN 9), of 17,525 tons, was completed. The world's first nuclear powered surface warship, she was also the first to have a guided-missile main battery, and from then on there was a steady stream of nuclear powered guided-missile cruisers: *Bainbridge* (8,592 tons), commissioned in 1962, *Truxtun* (9,127 tons), commissioned in 1967, two Californias (9,561 tons), commissioned in 1974 and 1975, and four Virginias (10,000 tons) commissioned 1976-80. The US Navy has also produced a series of non-nuclear powered cruisers, the Leahy class (5,670 tons) commissioned 1962-64 and the Belknap class (8,200 tons) commissioned 1964-67.

By the early 1970s the benefits of nuclear powered ships — primarily their long range and the reduction they allowed in fleet trains — were starting to be offset by their enormous capital costs, and when faced with a bid for a numerically large class of cruisers to take the Aegis system the US Congress insisted that the oil-fired Spruance design rather than the nuclear powered Virginia be used as the starting point. The result, the Ticonderoga (CG 47) class, is a series of extremely effective ships with outstanding air defence and air direction capabilities, and at least 27 are to be built, making it one of the most significant of all contemporary warship designs.

Intended essentially for the anti-air mission, but with some surface and ASW capabilities as well, these cruisers will act as screens for carrier task groups. The US Navy currently possesses nine nuclear powered and 23 conventionally powered cruisers, with another 23 Ticonderogas due to join the fleet between 1987 and the mid-1990s.

Other navies have tended to allow their cruiser fleets to waste away, especially the Royal Navy, which had no fewer than 60 cruisers at the end of World War

Representative cruiser classes

Ticonderoga (USA)

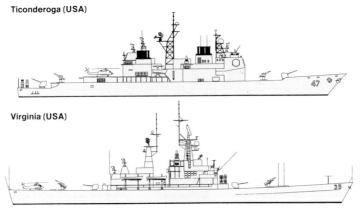

Virginia (USA)

Suffren (France)

Type 82 *Bristol* (UK)

Andrea Doria (Italy)

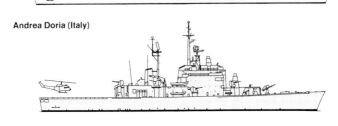

Slava (USSR)

Kara (USSR)

Kirov (USSR)

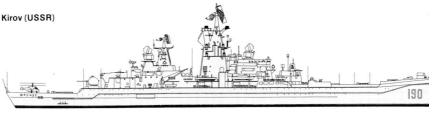

Ticonderoga (9,530 tons). This class is designed around the Aegis system. AA armament is two Mk 26 launchers for Standard SM-2 (MR) SAM, plus two 30mm Mk 15 CIWs; surface weapons are eight Harpoon SSM and two 5in Mk 45 DP guns; ASW armament is Asroc (Mk 26 launcher), six torpedo tubes and two LAMPS III helicopters.

Virginia (11,500 tons). These CGNs are designed as CVN escorts. Primary AA weapon is Standard SM-2 (MR) (Mk 26 launchers), with two Mk 15 CIWS to be fitted later. Surface weapons are two 127mm DP guns and eight Harpoon SSM. ASW systems are Asroc (Mk 26 launcher), six torpedo tubes and one LAMPS I helicopter.

Suffren (6,090 tons). Designated destroyers, these are cruiser-sized warships. AA system is French Masurca SAM plus two 20mm AA guns; there are four MM.38 Exocet SSMs and two 100mm DP guns, but ASW weapons are limited to two torpedo launchers; there are no on-board helicopter facilities, a major weakness.

Bristol (7,100 tons). Designed as escort for CVA-01, the Type 82 has not been a great success. AA systems are Sea Dart, four 30mm AA and four 20mm AA guns, but the only surface weapon is a 4.5in DP gun and the only ASW weapon is an Ikara missile system; there are no torpedo tubes nor is there an on-board helicopter.

Andrea Doria (7,300 tons). Air-capable escort cruisers with strong ASW capability. AA armament is Standard SM-1 (ER) SAM (Mk 10 launcher) and six/eight 76mm AA Guns in Dardo system. ASW weapons are six torpedo tubes and four AB 212 ASW helicopters. There are no dedicated surface warfare weapon systems.

Slava (12,500 tons). Built as a safeguard against failure of the Kirov class. AA armament comprises eight SA-N-6 and two SA-N-4 SAM launchers and six 30mm CIWs; surface weapons are 16 SS-N-12 (with Helix-B for OTH targetting) and two 130mm DP guns; ASW systems are ten torpedo tubes and two RBU-6000.

Kara (9,700 tons). Designed for ASW, these were the first large cruisers since the Sverdlov class. AA armament is two SA-N-3 and four SA-N-4 SAM launchers, plus four 30mm CIWS. There are four 76mm guns mounted amidships, and ASW systems are ten torpedo tubes, two RBU-6000 and one Hormone-A ASW helicopter.

Kirov (2,800 tons). *Kirov* and *Frunze* are much bigger than Western cruisers and are best described as battle-cruisers. Weapon and sensor fits differ, but the latest, *Frunze*, has an AA armament of 12 SA-N-6 and 16 SA-N-9 SAM launchers, and eight 30mm CIWS. Her surface weapons are 20 SS-N-19 and two 130mm DP guns; ASW weapons are one RBU-6000, two RBU-1000, eight torpedo tubes and three Hormone/Helix-B helicopters.

There is some dispute about correct descriptions for warship classes, with the categories of cruiser, destroyer, frigate and even corvette frequently overlapping, but the ships shown above all have a full load displacement of over 6,000 tons and may be described collectively as cruisers. They have large hulls and can accommodate a good mix of weapon systems and sensors: all have high/medium-altitude SAM systems and all except the Type 82 and Suffren have small calibre CIWS. Not all have guns of over 100mm calibre—a deficiency not likely to be repeated following the lessons of the 1982 South Atlantic War—nor do they all have SSMs, though all have plenty of space and modern SSM such as Exocet take up little room. Some have very light ASW armament.

almost invariably being ships which have some capability in all fields but are outstanding in none—something like the Chinese Luda class (3,900 tons), which has missiles, guns, ASW rocket launchers and depth-charges, but neither a good anti-air nor an adequate anti-surface capability, while its ASW effectiveness is minimal.

The US Navy has probably poured the most resources into this area and, at least until the 1986 round of budget cuts, it had the most ambitious future plans. The backbone of the escort fleet is the Spruance class of 31 ships, which are optimized for the ASW mission, plus the four very similar ships of the Kidd class, originally ordered by the Shah of Iran and constructed on Spruance hulls, but with a more general capability conferred by their two twin Mk 26 launchers firing Standard SAMs and Asroc ASW missiles. The Shah was deposed before they could be delivered and they were eventually bought for the US Navy, making a very useful addition to the fleet.

The remaining US destroyers are the 10 Coontz class and 23 Charles F Adams class ships, most of which are due to be given a DDG mid-life upgrade, but the USN's plans now centre on the Arleigh Burke (DDG 51) class, 29 of which are planned, and which will be followed by 30 of an Improved Arleigh Burke design, with better electronics and machinery and—most importantly—the helicopter facilities omitted from the original design.

The US Navy also has a large fleet of 116 frigates, the oldest of which, the Bronstein class (2,690 tons), date back to 1963. The biggest group comprises the 52 large Oliver Hazard Perry (FFG 7) class vessels of 3,585 tons displacement, equal in size to many other navies' destroyers. Armed with Harpoon SSMs, Standard SAMs, one 76mm gun and one Phalanx 20mm CIWS, and equipped with two LAMPS III ASW helicopters, these capable ships have also attracted orders from Spain and Australia.

II but only 23 by 1953 and just five in 1963. Today the Royal Navy officially has no cruisers at all, although the sole Type 82 destroyer, HMS *Bristol*, is, at 7,100 tons, every bit as large as the Soviet Kynda and US Navy Leahy class cruisers. France has one modern cruiser and Italy two, while Peru and Chile each have two of World War II vintage.

DESTROYERS AND FRIGATES

There is currently little international agreement on the classification of warships in the 2,000-6,000 ton range. At the end of the war there was a fairly clear system, with a descending order in tonnage and size from cruiser through destroyer to frigate and corvette, but today there is no such logic. The Royal Navy, for example, designates the 4,100-ton Type 42 class ships as destroyers, but the larger Type 22s (4,900 tons) are frigates, while the NATO system for Soviet warships classifies the Kynda class (5,560 tons) as cruisers but the 8,000-ton Udaloys are destroyers.

In the US Navy escort ships of 10,000 tons (the Virginia class), classified in the 1970s as frigates, are now designated cruisers, while the Spruance class (7,810 tons) are classified as destroyers and the Ticonderoga class, on an identical hull but with a greater displacement (9,600 tons), are cruisers.

To add to the confusion the French Navy used to rate ships such as the Type C 67 (5,745 tons) as corvettes, but then re-rated them as frigates, although they were then given 'D' (destroyer) rather than the logical 'F' (frigate) pennant numbers. Nor have the French dropped the designation corvette, having rated the new Type C 70 (4,170 tons) as such, although these too have 'D'

Above: Vitse-Admiral Drozhd one of four guided-missile cruisers (Raketny Kreyser) of the Soviet Navy's Kresta I class. Main armament is four SS-N-3B SSMs, two SA-N-1 launchers, four 57mm AA guns and four Gatling CIWS; an ASW helicopter is carried.

Below: USS Long Beach (CGN 9), the first nuclear propelled US warship, following her 1980 modernization. The massive bridge structure originally carried bill-board fixed arrays but these were removed in the refit, and Standard SAMs have replaced Terriers.

pennant numbers. Rather than try to devise a new and more logical system—and thus almost certainly add to the confusion — the ship designations used here are those given by the respective navies, or by NATO in the case of Warsaw Pact warships, however illogical they may be.

The problem facing virtually all navies is that the price of even small warships has soared and arguments over quality versus quantity have become more acute than ever. A hull of about 4,000 tons is as much as most navies can afford, in terms both of finance and manpower and of construction and dockyard facilities. However, these medium-sized ships are required to fulfil a number of roles and to be able to deal with airborne threats, surface-skimming missiles, other surface warships and submarines.

As a result, some navies have tried to produce general-purpose escorts capable of meeting all these threats, the outcome

Below: HMAS Hobart (D 39), one of three Charles F Adams class destroyers procured by the Royal Australian Navy in 1964-67. All were modified in the early 1970s and are currently undergoing yet another update to enable them to serve through to the next century.

The Soviet Navy built a large number of destroyers as part of the great postwar naval expansion plan, and 44 members of the Skory, Kotlin, SAM Kotlin, Kanin and Kildin classes remain in service, with others in reserve. Then, in the years 1963-72, came the Kashin class (4,500 tons), the first major warships to be powered exclusively by gas turbines; 13 of the original model are still in service, along with six of the Modified Kashin class. There was then a long gap until the Sovremennyy (7,900 tons) and Udaloy (8,000 tons) classes were laid down in 1976 and 1978 respectively. The Sovremennyys are optimized for the surface and anti-air roles and have a heavy missile and gun armament, as well as carrying one Ka-32 Helix helicopter. The Udaloys are optimized for the ASW role and use a totally different hull design from that of the Sovremennyys, in marked contrast to the practice of Western navies, which tend more and more to economise by using common hulls for different weapons and sensor fits to meet different roles. Current examples include the US Ticonderoga/Spruance, French Georges Leygues/Cassard and Dutch Kortenaer/Jakob van Heemskerck variations. Six Sovremennyys and eight Udaloys were in service by 1986, with at least two more of each class building.

The Soviet Navy also has a large number of frigates, pre-eminent among which is the Krivak class, 33 strong by 1986 with one more building. Virtually all Western frigates are designed as convoy—especially merchant convoy—escorts, but this role is not really required in the Soviet Navy and most frigates, particularly those of the Krivak class, are therefore designed as escorts for task groups.

The Royal Navy emerged from World War II with a large fleet of destroyers and frigates, most of which had ASW as their primary function. In a major programme in the 1950s large numbers of the destroyers were converted into specialized ASW ships and redesignated frigates, while the destroyer line continued with the Daring class (3,699 tons) and then the County class. The latter were commissioned in the 1960s, and at 6,200 tons displacement were as large as many cruisrs in other navies, such as the contemporary US Leahy (5,670 tons) and Soviet Kynda (5,550 tons) classes.

Next to appear was the *Bristol* (7,100 tons), the sole example built of the proposed Type 82 class, which had been intended as escorts for the planned aircraft carrier CVA-01. The latest Type 42 destroyers (4,100 tons), known initially as the Sheffield class, are designed for the area air defence of a task

Representative ASW ship classes

Spruance (USA)

Bremen (West Germany)

Broadsword (UK)

Georges Leygues (France)

Maestrale (Italy)

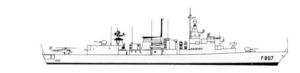

Kortenaer (Netherlands)

Udaloy (USSR)

Hatsuyuki (Japan)

The eight principal ASW classes in the major navies show some interesting similarities. All rely on helicopters and torpedoes as their main ASW weapons, except for the Spruance and Hatsuyuki which have the extra range conferred by Asroc, while the Udaloy also has two RBU-6000 rocket launchers. All have hull- or bow-mounted sonars, while most have VDS and some have or are about to get towed arrays. **All have reasonable surface capabilities, with guns and anti-ship missiles, and all have short- or medium-range surface-to-air missiles, but close-in gun defence systems range from four 30mm Gatlings on the Udaloy to single 40mm mounts on Broadsword and Kortenaer, though the last two are scheduled to receive the Dutch Goalkeeper system shortly. Size varies considerably, with the** two largest (Spruance and Udaloy) **coming, not surprisingly, from the two largest navies, while the smallest is the Maestrale, a consequence of the Italian Navy's more limited habitability requirements. Obviously, the greater the size the more comprehensive the weapon and sensor fits, and the better the balance between air, surface and sub-surface capabilities.**

Spruance (8,040 tons). Very large for the designation destroyer, these ships are heavily armed, and displacement has exceeded the planned 6,800 tons. ASW weapons include Asroc, ASW torpedoes and SH-2F or SH-3B ASW helicopters. Bow-mounted sonar is SQS-53A and SQR-19 towed array will be fitted.

Bremen (3,750 tons). Based on the Dutch Kortenaer design, the Bremen class frigates are optimized for Baltic conditions. ASW weapon systems comprise Mk 32 torpedo tubes and two Westland Lynx Mk 88 helicopters, while the bow-mounted sonar is the German-designed DSQS-21B(Z) with electronic stabilization.

Broadsword (4,900 tons). The Type 22 has been developed through three batches, of which the third is illustrated, though ASW armament is the same in all versions, comprising six 12.75in STWS.1 torpedo tubes and one or two Westland Lynx helicopters armed with the widely used Stingray ASW torpedoes.

Georges Leygues (4,170 tons). Principal ASW ships of the French Navy, the Type C70s are designated corvettes. ASW armament is L5 torpedoes and two Westland Lynx helicopters; sonars are the bow-mounted DUBV-23 and the DUBV-43 VDS, the latter being replaced by towed arrays in the last four ships.

Maestrale (3,200 tons). Eight Maestrale class frigates have been built to a design developed from that of the Lupo class. ASW armament consists of two 21in (533mm) tubes for A.184 torpedoes and two AB 212 ASW helicopters, while sonar fit comprises the hull-mounted DE 1160B and the variable depth DE 1164, both by Raytheon.

Kortenaer (3,786 tons). ASW element of the Dutch EASTLANT task groups, these ships have four tubes for Mk 32 324mm ASW torpedoes and carry one or two Westland Lynx helicopters; sonar is the hull-mounted SQS-505. This successful design is in service with the Netherlands, Greek and West German navies.

Udaloy (8,200 tons). Latest Soviet ASW ships, these destroyers have two RBU-6000 ASW rocket launchers, eight 21in (533mm) torpedo tubes and two Helix-A ASW helicopters. A large LF bow sonar and a VDS are the principal ASW sensors. It is possible that a towed array will be fitted in due course.

Hatsuyuki (3,700 tons). The leading ASW element of Japan's growing destroyer fleet, the Hatsuyukis are armed with Asroc, six 324mm torpedo tubes and one HSS-2B helicopter (licence-built Sea King). Current sonar is the hull-mounted OQS-4, but the US SQR-19 towed array is to be fitted to all ships.

group. They have a mixed gun and missile armament, and the latest to be constructed (Batch 3) have been stretched by some 51ft (16m) in overall length to accommodate better weapons systems and to improve speed and seakeeping.

For some years the Royal Navy's frigate fleet centred on the very successful Type 12 (2,560 tons) and the even more effective follow-on Leander class (2,700 tons), which incorporate helicopter facilities, variable-depth sonar and long-range radar. The Leander design was in production for ten years, with many improvements embodied in the various batches, and in addition to the Royal Navy's 23 Leanders a total of 20 are in service with the navies of Australia (two), Chile (two), India (six), New Zealand (four) and the Netherlands (six Van Speijk class). The Royal Navy also took delivery of eight Type 21 or Amazon class (3,250 tons) frigates, the first Royal Navy warships for many years to have been designed by civilian naval architects.

Successor to the Leander class is the Type 22 (4,200 tons Batch 1; 4,900 tons Batch 3), and like the Type 42 destroyers, the design of later examples has been stretched and considerably altered in appearance; 14 have been ordered. The successor class is the Type 23 frigate, the first of which had been ordered by the beginning of 1986. There has been considerable

Above: A Kashin class guided missile destroyer of the Soviet Navy. This was the first major warship class to have all gas turbine propulsion, one of a number of firsts by modern Soviet Navy designers, who have shown no fear of innovation.

controversy over this design, the arguments centring on the efforts to reconcile the lessons of the South Atlantic war with the problem of keeping expenditure within the limits set by a very restricted national defence budget. The Royal Navy's 1986 front-line strength in these two classes was 13 destroyers, with 44 frigates and four building.

The Japanese Maritime Self-Defence Force (JMSDF) has built up a remarkable destroyer and frigate fleet by following a clear policy of constant improvement in a succession of interrelated classes. Destroyer development is following two separate mission-oriented lines, one for air defence/surface warfare and the second for ASW, and the destroyers tend to be large, handsome, well armed and equipped with very comprehensive electronics, as would be expected from a nation with such a strong electronics industry.

Of the 34 destroyers in JMSDF service in 1986 the main current designs were the Hatsuyuki (3,800 tons) and Hatakaze (4,600 tons) classes. All the more recent destroyer classes have excellent helicopter facilities, with the

Above: Evertsen (F 819), one of six Van Speijk class ASW frigates built for the Royal Netherlands Navy in the 1960s. Based on the British Leander design, they have since undergone numerous modifications, including the funnel IR suppressor caps.

surprising exception of the very latest air defence type, the Hatakaze class, but this appears to be a temporary aberration and one unlikely to be repeated. Japanese frigates are of less than 2,000 tons displacement and include 18 ships of four classes in service, the latest being the Yubari class (1,690 tons). These ships are also well equipped for their size, although none of them carries a helicopter.

The French Navy is steadily becoming more important in international maritime matters, not least in the field of destroyers, where it has a great tradition of imaginative and effective design, and, like the Japanese, the French have followed a policy of gradually improving a fairly large number of small classes. They have also begun to produce separate anti-air and ASW designs, the latest

Below: The unique profile of the Netherlands Tromp (F 801), with the huge SPS-01 3D radome (known as Kojack) above the bridge and bifurcated funnel. Well-armed and with a good sensor fit, both Tromp and her sister De Ruyter serve as flagships.

being the Georges Leygues (ASW) and Cassard (AA) classes, which use the same hull with two different weapon/sensor fits. The total number of destroyers in service in 1986 was 19. French frigates (avisos) tend to be somewhat different in concept from those of other navies, being built with the colonial policing role very much in mind and being rather small but very well armed and with long ranges. There were 25 in service in 1986, with more building.

The Italian Navy also has a long history of large, effective destroyer designs, and has produced a series of classes since the war. The four destroyers currently in service include two of the very impressive Audace class (4,400 tons). There are also 16 frigates of four classes in service, the latest of which, the Maestrale (3,040 tons), is well armed and equipped and, like all Italian ships, exceptionally fast.

The other navy with a significant fleet in this area is that of the Netherlands, which had produced a series of exceptional designs in order to be able to operate three balanced task groups as part of NATO's EASTLANT command. Initially, the Dutch built six British-designed Leander class frigates as the van Speijk class (2,835 tons), following them with two large and very powerful frigates of their own design, the Tromp class (4,308 tons), which are equivalent in every way to the destroyers of other navies.

An attempt to agree a collaborative venture with the British having failed, the Dutch then produced the Kortenaer class (3,630 tons), of which they have built ten for themselves and two for Greece, while a further six have been produced to a slightly modified design in West Germany as the Bremen class (3,600 tons). Two anti-aircraft frigates under construction in 1986, the Jakob van Heemskerck class (3,750 tons), mount specialized anti-aircraft weapons and sensor fits on the Kortenaer hull, and a further four frigates of the new 'M' class (3,050 tons) were on order.

The Royal Canadian Navy built a series of very adventurous and unusual frigate designs in the 1950s and 1960s, of which 19 remain in service, and four equally unusual destroyers of the DD 280 class (4,700 tons) in the early 1970s. There was then a complete gap in shipbuilding, primarily as a result of budgeting problems, and many of these ships are now very elderly. At last, however, a new Halifax class (4,254 tons) of six destroyers has been announced, to be commissioned between 1989 and 1992.

China produces its own destroyers and frigates, many still based on Soviet designs, and a number have been exported. Some other nations have produced their own frigates, including Denmark (two Peder Skram class, 2,720 tons, and three *Niels Juel* class, 1,320 tons); Belgium (four Wielingen class, 2,820 tons); Spain (six Descubierta class, 1,479 tons, and five Baleares class, 4,177 tons); the Federal Republic of Germany (four Hamburg class, 4,680 tons); and Norway (five Oslo class, 1,745 tons).

A large number of destroyers and frigates are in service with the smaller navies, most being export versions of other nations' designs and the majority originating from the United States, the Soviet Union, the United Kingdom, France, Italy, Spain and China. One interesting trend, however, is that some Western shipyards are offering destroyer and frigate designs specifically for export, because the home navy designs are either too complex or too expensive (and frequently both) for Third World navies' needs. Thus, the West German MEKO series, the French F2000 and the British Vosper Thornycroft series of frigates are in service with several foreign navies, but not with their own.

CORVETTES

A recurring theme in this book is the expense of modern warships. Many smaller navies find themselves unable to afford even the smaller destroyers or frigates, and there has been a consequent revival of interest in the corvette, usually of about 500-1,000 tons displacement, which represents an intermediate type between the frigate on one side and the fast attack craft on the other.

The corvette went out of fashion after World War II, but has been the subject of a revival in recent years, not only because of its relative cheapness but also because of the appearance of lightweight guns, missiles and sensors which enable a fairly heavy equipment and weapon fit to be installed in a light hull. The Finnish Navy's Turunmaa class, for example, manages to mount a 120mm gun, two 40mm

Representative AA ship classes

Arleigh Burke (USA)

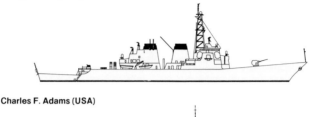

Charles F. Adams (USA)

Type 42 Batch 3 (UK)

Cassard (France)

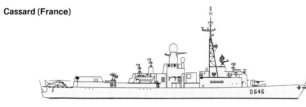

Audace (Italy)

Jacob van Heemskerck (Netherlands)

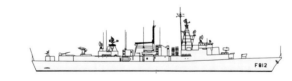

Sovremennyy (USSR)

Hatakaze (Japan)

The air threat at sea was considered in a rather casual manner by many navies in the 1960s and 1970s, but a growing realization of the threat was rudely reinforced by the British experiences in the 1982 South Atlantic War, where three major warships and one critical logistics ship were lost to air action. The threat comes from direct attack by aircraft and from missiles, the latter being launched by aircraft, other surface warships or submarines. Some anti-ship missiles require a third element in the control loop, such as a targeting helicopter, but many are now autonomous and once launched find their own way to the target, fighting their own EW battles on route. This major threat has given rise to the return not only of ever-increasing AA armament

Arleigh Burke (8,400 tons). New Aegis destroyers armed with Mk 41 VLS with a capacity of 90 missiles (SAM, SSM and Asroc). SAM is Standard SM-2 (MR) and two Mk 15 CIWS will be fitted. Surface weapons are Tomahawk, Harpoon and 5in Mk 45 gun. ASW weapons are Asroc and six torpedo tubes, but no helicopter is carried.

Charles F. Adams (4,825 tons). Now somewhat elderly, these ships serve in the US, West German, and Australian navies. They have single Mk 11 or 13 launchers for 34 Standard SM-I (MR) SAM, a surface armament of Harpoon and two 5in Mk 42 DP guns, while ASW weapons are Asroc and six torpedo tubes. There are no helicopter facilities.

Type 42 Batch 3 (4,775 tons). Latest stretched version of RN air defence/air warning destroyer. AA weapon is the tested Sea Dart SAM (22 carried), but the only close-in defence is two Oerlikon 20mm AA guns. Surface weapon is one 4.5in DP gun and ASW systems are six torpedo tubes and one Lynx helicopter.

Cassard (4,300 tons). Built on George Leygves hull, these are specialized AA ships. AA weapons are one Mk 13 launcher for 40 Standard SM-1 (MR) SAMs and two Sadral PDMS. Surface weapons are eight MM.40 Exocet and a 100mm DP gun. ASW systems are two torpedo launchers and one Lynx helicopter.

Audace (4,400 tons). Typical Italian large destroyers with good helicopter facilities. AA armament is one Mk 13 launcher for 36 Tartar/Standard SAMs and four 76mm guns in Dardo CIWS. Surface armament is two 127mm DP guns and there are six torpedo tubes. Two AB 212 ASW helicopters are carried.

Jacob van Heemskerck (3,750 tons). Specialized AA ships built on Kortenaer hulls. AA armament is 40 Standard SM-1 (MR) on Mk 13 launcher, NATO Sea Sparrow PDMS and Goalkeeper CIWS. Surface weapons are eight Harpoon SSM, and the only ASW weapons are eight torpedo tubes. There are no guns or helicopters.

Sovremenny (7,900 tons). Large surface and AA destroyers with very limited ASW capability. AA weapons are SA-N-7 (44 missiles) and four 30mm CIWS. Surface weapons are eight SS-N-22 (with Helix helicopter for OTH targetting) and two 130mm DP guns. ASW systems are limited to four torpedo tubes and two RBU-1000.

Hatakaze (4,600 tons). Latest in a long series of Japanese destroyers optimized for AA/surface warfare. AA weapons are Tartar SAM (40 missiles) and two Vulcan/Phalanx CIWS. Surface weapons are Harpoon SSM (eight tubes) and two 127mm DP guns. ASW weapons are Asroc and six torpedo tubes. No helicopter is carried.

on all warships, but also of the specialized AA ship. Some, like the Dutch Jacob van Heemskerck and the French Cassard classes, are being built on ASW hulls, while others are designed and built from the keel up specifically for the purpose. Undoubtedly the most sophisticated AA ships are the US Navy's Ticonderoga class, but the Arleigh Burke class destroyer is only marginally less capable.

and two 20mm cannon, depth-charge racks and anti-submarine rockets on a 770-ton hull. And Vosper Thornycroft corvette designs, a number of which have been sold to a variety of navies, include the Mark 9, which mounts a 70mm gun, one 40mm and two 20mm cannon, an ASW rocket launcher and a Seacat SAM launcher on a 780-ton hull.

The most successful exponent of such designs is, without a doubt, the Soviet Navy, which has produced a series of capable light combatants. The Nanuchka III class vessels (660 tons), for example, are armed with six SS-N-9s, two twin SA-N-4 launchers, a 76mm gun and a 30mm Gatling CIWS, while the Tarantul IIs, slightly smaller at 580 tons, mount four SS-N-22s, a quad SA-N-5, a 76mm gun and two 30mm Gatling CIWS, and both are capable of a top speed of 36 knots. The Pauk class uses the Tarantul hull, but is optimized for the ASW role and powered by diesels rather than gas turbines; it does not have SSMs, but is armed with an SA-N-5 launcher, a 76mm gun and a 30mm Gatling CIWS, together wth an ASW armament of four torpedo tubes, two RBU-1200 rocket launchers, and two depth-charge racks.

These small warships, heavily armed as they may be, are by no means the complete answer to problems of size and cost. No gain is ever obtained without penalty, and in the case of corvettes and fast attack craft a heavy weapon and sensor fit is only feasible at the expense of speed, range and seakeeping qualities.

FAST ATTACK CRAFT

Smallest of the combatant classes are the Fast Attack Craft (FACs), the successors to the Motor Torpedo Boats (MTBs), Motor Gun Boats (MGBs) and Patrol Torpedo (PT) boats of World War II. Several hundred are in service with many navies, some with conventional hulls and others with hydrofoils, and although they had been around

Above: Landing Craft Air-cushion LCAC-1 enters the well-deck of USS Pensacola (LSD 38), an Anchorage class Landing Ship Dock. Western navies have been slower to utilize the capabilities of air-cushion vehicles in amphibious warfare than the Soviets.

for a long time, these FAC did not achieve international prominence until 1967, when an Egyptian Osa sank the Israeli destroyer *Eilat*. This action demonstrated that the missile had given these craft a hitting power previously inconceivable.

Below: Ivan Rogov, a 13,000-ton large landing ship (Bolshoy Desantnyy Korabl) of the Soviet Navy. She has two flight decks for her four Hormone-C helicopters, and the stern ramp gives access to a docking well which accommodates three ACVs.

Below: USS Welch (PG 93), a patrol combatant of the 235-ton Asheville class, one of two such ships leased to the Colombian Navy in 1983. Armed with one 76mm and one 40mm gun and four machine guns, the Ashevilles have a top speed of over 40 knots.

Among current boats, for example, the Israeli Romat class (488 tons) mounts four Gabriel and four Harpoon SSMs, while the West German Type 148 (265 tons) has four MM38 Exocet missiles and a 76mm gun.

AMPHIBIOUS WARFARE SHIPS

The major navies found themselves at the end of World War II with an enormous number of amphibious warfare craft, the majority of which were either scrapped or sold to the smaller navies. For many years the only navies to retain a significant capability in this area were the US Navy and the Royal Navy, with the French Navy some way behind. The US Navy was able to mount a major amphibious landing at Inchon in 1952, and the British and French carried out a rather smaller operation at Suez in 1956; thereafter there were only a few very minor landings until the British operation to retake the Falkland Islands in 1982, when virtually the whole of the Royal Navy's remaining amphibious warfare fleet was mobilized.

The major developments in amphibious warfare have been the introduction of the helicopter, the air-cushion vehicle and the V/STOL aircraft, all of which have helped ease the problems involved in the critical and most vulnerable initial stage of a landing operation. These led the US Navy to develop new assault ships, first the Iwo Jima class (18,825 tons) and then the very large and capable Tarawa class (39,300 tons), of which seven of the former and five of the latter are in service. The Tarawa class can accommodate various mixes of CH-53 Sea Stallion and CH-46 Sea Knight helicopters, plus AV-8A/B Harriers, together with four large and six small landing craft and a reinforced US Marine Corps battalion.

In amphibious warfare as in so many other areas, the Soviet Navy has developed a global capability which, although not yet equalling the US Navy in either numbers or effectiveness is strong and growing with every year. The Soviet fleet curntly consists of 17 Ropucha class LSTs (3,800 tons), 14 Alligator class LSTs (4,700 tons) and 43 Polnochny class LSMs (800 tons). Their most impressive ships, however, are the two Ivan Rogov class LPDs (13,000 tons), each of which carries a battalion of Soviet Naval Infantry together with two ACVs (Air Cushion Vehicles), a number of landing craft and some helicopters.

Most other navies have a limited amphibious capability, which usually consists of a small number of LPDs and a slightly larger number of LSTs and LCTs. Only the USA and the USSR have an ACV capability, with the Soviet Navy currently far ahead of the US Navy in this respect.

Surface Warship Design

The design of a surface warship, like that of any weapon system, is inevitably the result of a number of compromises. The ship must accommodate the necessary sensors, weapons, propulsion machinery and crews; and it must be capable of allowing these to be used effectively in the weather conditions and survive in the combat environment specified in the operational requirement.

The task of the warship designer is, quite simply, to fit everything in, and to satisfy a host of competing demands: the weapons specialists require the heaviest possible firepower with the largest possible magazines; the command element needs the greatest number of sensors, all sited to achieve the greatest possible range, and with all the displays concentrated in a spacious, ergonomically designed Combat Information Centre (CIC); the marine engineers want the largest volume for power systems, not only to drive the ship as fast as possible over the greatest possible distances, but also to power everyone else's electrical and electronic equipment; the budget controllers demand the smallest possible hull, to keep costs down; the construction engineer requires a design that can be built easily, preferably in existing yards; finally, but by no means least, the crew must be adequately accommodated. The emphasis placed on each requirement varies from nation to nation and can change for reasons ranging from recent combat experience to simple changes of nautical style or fashion.

MONOHULLS

In general, the monohull retains it supremacy principally because it is cheaper, well understood and considered to give the best all-round performance. There is still considerable scope for refinement, however, and one of the major current debates centres on the possible advantages of hulls which are shorter but much broader in the beam than those currently used. The main embodiment of this at the moment is in the British Osprey class design, but the only ships to use it are four fishery protection vessels constructed at the Frederikshavn Dockyard in Denmark (three for Burma and one for Denmark). These patrol ships have a displacement of 550 tons and a beam-to-length ratio of 1:4.76 rather than the more usual 1:9 or more.

Beam-to-length ratios for current designs in other navies include 1:9.35 for the Soviet Slava class cruisers, 1:8.8 for the British Type 42 Batch 1 destroyers, and 1:9.9 for Georges Leygues class (C 70ASW) destroyers. The US Navy, however, appears to be following the trend towards beamier ships with the new Arleigh Burke (DDG 51) class destroyers, which have a beam-to-

Above: The Soviet Krivak class frigate is considered by Western experts to be a skillful balance of design features, resulting in a ship with a good blend of capabilities relative to its displacement.

Below: The Oliver Hazard Pery class hull exhibits a typical, traditional beam: length ratio (in this case 1:9.9). There is pressure in some navies to adopt a shorter, much beamier hull.

length ratio of 1:7.9, compared to the 1:10.2 of the Spruance and Ticonderoga designs. It is claimed that the reduced ratio gives better seakeeping qualities as well as improved manoeuvrability and an increase in usable space— the Osprey class vessels, for example, are able to accommodate much larger helicopter decks than is usual on a 505-ton displacement.

Modern design and construction techniques have enabled shipbuilders to produce very efficient structures for surface warships, though one major problem is the demand for equipment, especially sensors and antennas, to be located as high as possible, mainly to increase range. This demand, which is coupled in gas-turbine ships with an inescapable requirement for large downtakes and uptakes, increases topweight, raising the metacentric height and reducing stability unless the superstructure can be lightened in compensation.

One response to this conflict which achieved some popularity in the 1960s was the use of lightweight aluminium alloys in the upperworks, but the disastrous fire and extensive damage that ensued when USS *Belknap* (CG 26) collided with USS *John F Kennedy* (CV 67) on November 22, 1975, brought this solution into some disrepute. Hostility to the idea was heightened by some very loose and

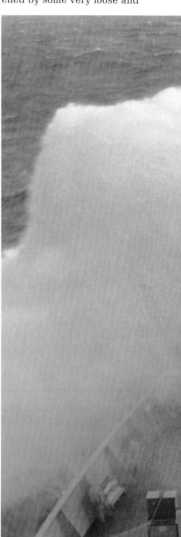

ill-informed comment in the immediate aftermath of the loss of the Type 42 destroyer HMS *Sheffield* during the 1982 South Atlantic war, and in view of the importance of the subject it is worth noting the findings of the British Ministry of Defence: *There has been comment on the use of aluminium in the construction of ships. The facts are that aluminium was used in the superstructure of the Type 21 class frigate and to a small extent in a few other classes, but not in the Type 42 destroyers, such as HMS Sheffield. In addition, aluminium is sometimes used for non-structural bulkheads, ladders and ventilation trunking. By use of aluminium it is possible to make significant savings in the weight of ships above the waterline, but it has been recognised that this metal loses strength in fires and therefore its extensive use in the construction of RN warships was discontinued several years ago. Nonetheless, there is no evidence that it has contributed to the loss of any vessel.* (The Falklands Campaign: The Lessons, HMSO, London, December 1982, Cmnd 8758; p19 para 220).

Related to the question of the ship's structure is the need to update weapon and sensor fits at fairly frequent intervals to keep pace with technological advances, some of which can have a dramatic impact on the

ship's capabilities. US designers have made a deliberate attempt to build in such adaptability by making large, spacious superstructures (in for example, the Spruance class destroyers and the Oliver Hazard Perry class frigates) as well as giving the ships hulls that are slightly larger than necessary in the first instance. An alternative approach is taken in the MEKO FES system, where all weapons and sensors are installed in standard containers with

Below: A view over the bow of a warship in the North Atlantic. The bulwarks and breakwater visible on the foredeck are obvious necessities even in such a relatively modest swell.

Above: In the open sea the considerable pounding and slamming leads to torsional stress on the hull and can result in damage to rigidly mounted fittings as well as discomfort for the crew.

standard interfaces, which enable changes to be effected quickly and relatively easily throughout the ship's life.

SEAKEEPING

A discussion of hull design cannot exclude consideration of seakeeping qualities, in which the major factors are pitching, slamming, wetness and rolling. Weather and sea states can make the oceans a hostile environment, and as conditions

worsen they can lead initially to crew discomfort, then to equipment malfunction and damage, and ultimately to structural damage; limitations in choice of speed and heading and the curtailment of helicopter operations may be followed by the ship's inability to carry out its combat role, or even to its foundering. It is essential, therefore, that hull design should incorporate features which will enhance the ship's seakeeping qualities, though some can only be achieved by compromise, and almost all will be costly. Further, the beneficial effects of one feature will sometimes work to the detriment of another.

Length, fullness of load waterline, draught and bow flare all affect pitching. Length is one of the most important characteristics and in general terms the longer the waterline the less will be the pitching motion. The fullness of the load waterline is also a factor, especially forward, and while increasing draught will reduce the pitching motion it obviously affects on the ship's ability to clear shallow ground. Pitching particularly affects helicopter operations and can be the most significant constraint in a seaway. Such effects can be at least partially reduced by siting the helicopter landing spot as near to the centre of the ship as possible, rather than

Hull stresses

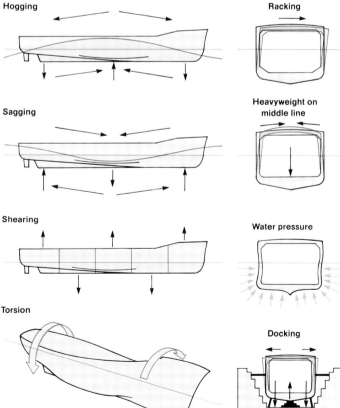

Hogging

Sagging

Shearing

Torsion

Racking

Heavyweight on middle line

Water pressure

Docking

Above: Anyone embarked on a ship notices the creaks and groans made by the hull as it moves through even the calmest sea. These diagrams show some of the stresses placed upon a ship's hull

which lead to such noises. The designer of any vessel must achieve a balance, in this case between exessive rigidity, or stiffness, on the one hand and excessive flexibility on the other.

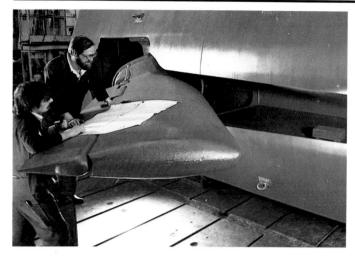

toward the stern as was the fashion in the 1960s and 1970s.

Weather deck wetness is an important considertion, though slightly less so today when gun turrets and missile launchers are essentially unmanned and the superstructure is rather more extensive. Nevertheless, excessive wetness can have a deleterious effect on vital operational functions such as helicopter operations or the ship's ability to steam into a head sea. Wetness depends primarily upon freeboard, though bow and stern design are also important—a well-known example is that of the British battle-cruiser HMS Hood, whose quarterdeck was virtually unusable at any significant speed due to the volume of water being shipped — but a balance must be struck between height and stability. Bows can incorporate breakwaters (as, for example, on the Soviet Slava class cruisers, where one is used to protect the twin 130mm turret) or bulwarks forward as on the British Type 22 frigates and the US Navy's Spruance destroyers.

For the Georges Leygues class the French designed a heavily raked bow but then had to reduce the sheer forward in order to give the 'A' gun turret an adequate field of fire directly ahead. This may have had an adverse effect on seakeeping, however: from the fifth of the class it is intended to raise the bridge by one deck level in order to alleviate the problem of seas breaking over the foredeck and obscuring the view from the bridge in heavy weather.

While bow sheer and flare can be used to reduce foredeck wetness, they may increase weight and reduce stability. Bow design also has to consider the installation of bow sonars, when a heavy rake is necessary to carry the anchors well forward of the sonar dome, but bow flares such as that on the Soviet Udaloy class destroyers must be considered somewhat exaggerated.

Rolling has a major influence on crew effectiveness and weapon performance, and in particular on helicopter operations. In this case, however, the answer is relatively straightforward in that active fins can be fitted which will reduce

rolling by 50 per cent or more on virtually all course headings at speeds above about 10 to 12 knots. As always, there is a penalty, in this case weight and space for the installation.

MULTIHULLS

Hull design is naturally evolving as new techniques and research are brought to bear, and the traditional long, narrow monohull is under challenge not only by the shorter, beamier monohull. There are air cushion vehicle (ACV) combatants in production which are considerably faster than monohulls and competitive with them in moderate sea states, though they still suffer from relatively poor performance in very bad weather. Such craft offer particular advantages in amphibious warfare, being employed in that role by the USSR, the USA and Iran, and because of their low underwater noise signatures and high speeds ACVs are undergoing trials to access possible applications in coastal anti-submarine and minehunting roles.

Catamaran hulls are fast, quiet and good in a seaway; they also have large deck areas and lower

Above left: Folding-fin stabilizers are fitted to modern warships to give better sea-handling and to provide a steadier platform for weapons and sensors. This is a British Brown Brothers model.

Above: The potential combination of high speed and substantial payload offered by hydrofoil craft is vividly represented in this painting released by the US Department of Defense in 1985.

Above: The Soviet Navy has devoted more resources than any other to hovercraft development and has several classes in service, most of them being used to support amphibious landings.

Below: USS Ticonderoga (CG 47), showing her SQS-53 bow sonar. The lower part of the dome is made of rubber and is flooded when at sea, resulting in much better power transference characteristics.

noise signatures than monohulls. The US Navy has operated three large catamarans for some years: the USS *Hayes* (3,860 tons), an oceanographic research vessel, and two Pigeon class (3,411 tons) submarine rescue vessels. However, the first twin-hull warship is being built by the Royal Australian Navy in the form of a Bay class 170-ton minehunter, whose two hulls are each 101.7ft (30.8m) long and 9.85ft (3m) in beam, and are separated by 9.85ft (3m). While the US catamarans have been successful and the Australian design holds great promise the idea is not spreading fast. Doubts remain over the suitability of multihulls for use as major warships, one particular concern being their ability to cope with asymmetric damage in the event of only one of the hulls being hit.

WING-IN-GROUND-EFFECT

Finally, there is the Wing-In-Ground-effect (WIG) machine, which utilizes a well-known aerodynamic principle to fly at considerable speed just clear of the sea's surface. A great deal of research has been done in the Federal Republic of Germany, but no serious proposals for a production machine have yet emerged. There have, however, been persistent reports of WIG machines being deployed in the USSR, one type having ten turbojet engines and being capable of lifting some 900 troops. Potential applications include surveillance patrols, minesweeping and ASW, where high transit speeds would be of particular value in reaching reported contacts rapidly.

Below: A US official Department of Defense impression of the Orlan class wing-in-ground effect (WIG) machine which is under development by the Soviet Navy on trials in the Caspian Sea.

WEAPON AND SENSOR FITS

The types and numbers of weapon systems that need to be fitted into a warship seem to be constantly increasing, although periodically some new development alleviates some of the problems for a while. A good example of this is the new US Mk 26 launcher system, whose ability to handle several different types of missile removes the requirement for separate launchers and magazines. Ideally, surface warships should have weapons to engage enemy aircraft, missiles, surface ships

Above: The MEKO multi-purpose standard ship system has been developed by the West German shipbuilding firm of Blohm and Voss. In this system weapons and electronics systems are installed

and submarines, both effectively and at long range. This is, however, impossible without compromise and the designer is faced with three choices: build a multi-purpose design to optimize overall combat capability; build specialized designs to optimize capability in a specific field; or build a bigger ship.

The multi-purpose design clearly has its attractions in that it gives the navy concerned some capability in each area, but the unavoidable result is that the design is not particularly effective in any one. This could be said to apply to the MEKO 360 type *Aradu* (3,360 tons) delivered to Nigeria, which is heavily armed for

MEKO 360 function unit installation

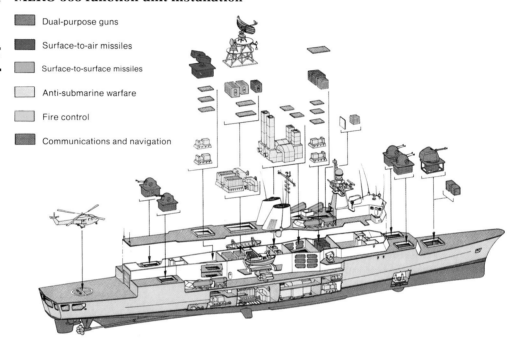

- Dual-purpose guns
- Surface-to-air missiles
- Surface-to-surface missiles
- Anti-submarine warfare
- Fire control
- Communications and navigation

in standardized function unit containers. Such units are easy and cheap to construct and install and can be removed easily for refurbishment or replacement by newer items.

its size but does not have the anti-air capability of a British Type 42 destroyer, nor the ASW capability of a Type 22 frigate.

The second choice, mission specialization, is particularly attractive at the destroyer/ frigate level, where it is proving exceptionally difficult to combine the anti-air and ASW roles in a combat-effective way. As a result, and as we have already seen, a growing number of navies are utilizing the same hull for two different types of armament, while others, such as the Soviet Navy with its Sovremennyy and Udaloy classes, and the Royal Navy with its Type 22 and Type 42, build separate

Below: A busy scene at the Blohm and Voss yard in Hamburg, with no fewer than five MEKO 360 destroyers fitting out prior to delivery to overseas countries. F 89 (centre) is the Nigerian Aradu.

hulls for the differing roles. Such specialization usually means that a greater number of hulls are required, along with more port facilities and greater support costs and more specialized manpower, and also that a tactical grouping must usually include both types of ship.

The problems of sensors is related to that of weapon systems. Even greater numbers of sensors must be carried for air, surface and sub-surface surveillance, weapon system control, electronic counter-measures and counter-counter-measures, and for navigation and communications purposes. All except sonar require antennas which generally need to be as high as possible for maximum range. Collectively these antennas represent considerable weight, and if placed too high they will raise the metacentric height and reduce stability.

This proved to be a particular problem with the French Cassard (C 70/AA) design where the combination of sensors necessary for the AA function and the trunking required for the gas turbines as fitted to the Georges Leygues proved to be impossible to accommodate without unacceptable penalties in seakeeping and stability. The only operationally acceptable solution was to convert to an all-diesel propulsion system (CODAD) in order to enable the sensors to be fitted. The Dutch, faced with the same problem, kept the Kortenaer's COGOG propulsion system in the Jakob van Heemskerck AA frigate, but gave up the 76mm gun, a sacrifice the French were obviously not prepared to make.

The final choice, to build bigger ships, is clearly at odds with cost considerations, which are of increasing importance. However, smallness is only achieved at the expense of capability. The Belgian Wielingen (2,283 tons) frigate design, for example, is a very ingenious compromise in many ways but has no facilities for a helicopter, which most navies now consider to be essential for the ASW mission. The somewhat

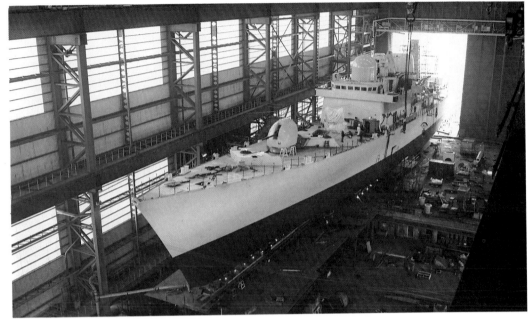

Above: Modern methods have speeded up ship construction. Here HMS Edinburgh, a Royal Navy Type 42 Batch 3 destroyer, is fitting out in the construction hall at Cammel Laird's Birkenhead.

larger Soviet Krivak (3,900 tons) is a widely admired design, but even so the Krivak I and II cannot accommodate a helicopter either, a deficiency only overcome in the Krivak III by halving the number of 3in gun turrets and removing the quadruple SS-N-14 battery altogether, as well as some other more minor changes.

So, if smallness means compromise, and compromise leads to unacceptable operational penalties, then the only answer is a larger hull. Such inexorable growth is illustrated in the British case by the progression from the Leander class of 2,450 tons through the Amazon class (3,259 tons) to today's Broadsword class of 4,200 tons (Batch 1) or 4,950 tons (Batch 3), a doubling of displacement for ships with a similar role over a 20-year

Below: The burgeoning number of sensors required for the operation of modern warships is apparent on this Soviet Kashin class destroyer, with its multitude of electronic and optronic devices.

period. Similarly, in the US Navy the Sherman class (4,200 tons) of the mid-1950s was succeeded by the Adams class (4,825 tons) and today's Spruance class (7,810 tons), an increase of 85 per cent.

PROTECTION

One effect of protracted periods of peace is that memories of combat conditions grow dim as men with actual combat experience become fewer, and so there is an insidious deterioration in standards and a revision of priorities because the realities of battle have been forgotten. Nowhere does this apply more strongly than in protection and damage control in warship design, where peacetime priorities tend to be on high-visibility facilities such as weaponry and sensors, machinery and accommodation, with protection coming a poor fifth. However, the critical and sometimes fatal effects of hits by Argentinian missiles and bombs on Royal Navy ships during the 1982 South Atlantic war has led to an urgent reconsideration of protection criteria and priorities in many navies. The most obvious form of damage is the result of direct hits by shells, missiles or bombs, but a near miss can be almost as destructive, and underwater shock and fires can also have devastating effects.

The result of a direct hit was made only too clear on May 4, 1982, when the Royal Navy Type 42 destroyer HMS Sheffield, on anti-air picket duty, was attacked by two Exocet missiles launched by two Argentinian Navy Super Etendard aircraft. One missile struck and entered her amidships, and after four-and-a-half hours, during which her ship's company fought fierce fires while engulfed in thick, black, acrid smoke, the commanding officer reluctantly gave the order to abandon ship; she finally sank in heavy seas

Frunze internal volume allocation by function

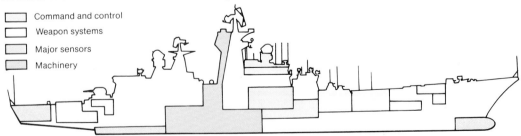

- Command and control
- Weapon systems
- Major sensors
- Machinery

Above: This section shows the probable allocation of volume to major systems on board the Soviet battlecruiser Frunze. The unmarked areas are not empty, but devoted to many other require- ments such as accommodation (never luxurious on a Soviet wasrship) and the storage of fuel, ammunition, spares, food, water and other consumables. The designers' skills lie in working out the allocation of space to give a balance of capacity, performance and sustainability which comes nearest to meeting the operator's requirements. Naturally, different navies reach different solutions.

while under tow on May 10.

The effect of a near miss was illustrated when, during the Vietnam war, the USS *Worden* (CGN 18) was the target of a totally accidental 'blue-on-blue' attack by a Shrike anti-radar missile. The Shrike performed exactly as designed, detonating very close to the ship's main radar antenna some 80-100ft (25-30m) above the bridge. As a result, the *Worden* lost all electrical power, communications and lights for 30 minutes, and even then she was only 40 per cent combat-effective and had to be withdrawn for shipyard repair.

As regards fires, there were certainly examples during the South Atlantic War. There have, however, been others, notably that on November 22, 1975, when the cruiser USS *Belknap* (CGN 26) was devastated by fire after a collision in the Mediterranean with the aircraft carrier USS *John F Kennedy*. The Soviet Navy has had its problems, too: one spectacular and tragic example occurred on August 30, 1974, when the Kashin class destroyer *Otvazhny* caught fire in the Black Sea off the Crimean coast and, following a subsequent explosion, became a total loss. Some 300 members of her crew were killed in one of the worst ever peacetime maritime disasters. In fact, the disaster control and passive protection on board Soviet warships must be open to question, not only because of their record of mishaps (especially with submarines) but also because of their lack of actual combat experience in warships larger than destroyers since before World War I.

The Royal Navy's most devastating experience in the Falklands was of direct hits by missiles and bombs, and as a result consideration is now being given by various navies to the renewed use of armour protection in warship construction, at least for the more vulnerable areas. However, since armour plating weighing about 560lb/sq ft (2,540kg/m²) is needed to defeat a 1,000lb (454kg) bomb, the effect on displacement is obvious. The US Navy's Arleigh Burke (DDG 51) class is reported to have "unusual hull hardness, particularly around the ship's vital zones", which might refer to an advanced form of armour, such as the British Chobham tank armour or, more probably, to Kevlar. Even if massive protection is ruled out on either cost or weight grounds, there seems to be no reason why the inside of the more vulnerable compartments could not be coated with a protective material such as Kevlar, which would at least minimize the effects of shrapnel and fragmentation.

A further form of passive protection is the dispersion and possibly the duplication of the ship's vital functions. The present practice of centralizing virtually all command, weapon

and sensor functions in one comprehensive Combat Information Centre (CIC) usually located, for convenience, immediately below the bridge is far from ideal in combat. As a first step, the primary CIC should be sited below water level, and any ship of significant size should have an alternative, permanently activated command centre, physically removed as far as possible from the first.

Below: Radar ghosting and blind arc effects can be cured by applying radar absorbent material (RAM) or installing absorber screens, as on the foremast of this British County class destroyer.

Distributed data processing is also necessary, together with a replicated data base to ensure that the ship's systems cannot be totally disabled by one hit on a solitary mainframe computer. Similar considerations apply to the machinery spaces, and it is essential that propulsion units are distributed and not concentrated in such a way that one hit can totally immobilize the ship.

Nuclear, chemical and biological (NBC) warfare protection also needs to be built in, both in the form of a citadel and by the use of effective wash-down facilities. Further, it is now becoming clear that hardening against electro magnetic pulse (EMP) is essential

Above: Fighting fires on RFA Sir Galahad after the Argentinian bombing attack during the 1982 war. The lessons learnt during this war forced all navies to reexamine their damage control capabilities.

if a warship is to continue to operate in a nuclear environment.

Finally, surface warships cannot expect to be totally hidden from every sensor that an enemy might deploy, but there is still no justification for the continued failure to take steps to reduce the ships' radio frequency (RF) and infra-red (IR) signatures. Just as stealth technology is now being applied to advanced aircraft, it is essential that warships should reduce the current level of radar, radio and IR echoes, both by design and by limiting RF and radar emissions.

The last word on this subject can be taken from the Royal Navy's report on its experience in the South Atlantic, where *Sheffield* was by no means the only ship to suffer extensive fire damage.

Some important lessons have been learned about the rapid spread of fire and smoke in ships, and about the use of materials which can prove hazardous in fires. Cabling fitted in older ships can prove inflammable; this hazard will greatly reduce in new ships. Urgent studies are now in hand aimed at improving the survivability of existing ships and incorporating lessons in future designs. Examples of measures which will be taken include improved fire zones; changes to the design of watertight doors and hatches; the provision of more escape hatches; making bulkheads more smoke-tight; the resiting of fuel tanks; reductions in inflammable materials; and additional fire pumps, breathing apparatus and personal breathing sets. (op cit, p19, para 221.)

Ship Propulsion

There have been significant changes in surface warship propulsion over the past 30 years. Until recently the oil-fired steam turbine was the most widely used means of propulsion for naval surface vessels above about 2,000 tons displacement, but such systems have relatively poor power-to-weight ratios and are inefficient users of internal volume. Moreover, such power units are comparitively complex, are slow to develop full power from a cold start, and require large numbers of well trained personnel to operate and maintain them. Consequently, when alternative means of propulsion became available the straightforward steam plants were quickly replaced; they are now rarer in new construction, though the Soviet Navy continues to install them in ships such as the Kiev class aircraft carriers and Sovremennyy class destroyers. The latter have pressure-fired, automated steam propulsion plants with an estimated power output of 110,000shp, giving a maximum speed of some 33 knots.

NUCLEAR POWER

Steam plants are still used in conjunction with nuclear reactors for the propulsion of large surface ships. Nuclear propulsion solves several problems, its most important benefit being that it does not need constant refuelling and significantly reduces the requirement for replenishment from a fleet train. The Nimitz class CVNs, for example, each with two pressurized-water-cooled reactors, are estimated to be able to steam for between 800,000 and one million nautical miles between core replacements, though they still need to be replenished every 16 days with aviation fuel for the air wings. The smallest nuclear-powered surface warship currently in service is the cruiser USS *Bainbridge* (CGN 25), of 8,592 tons displacement, though there is no technical reason why nuclear propulsion units could not be fitted to smaller ships, and the way forward may be shown by the French Rubis class SSNs, which are powered by comparatively small reactors.

An important factor in the use of nuclear reactors, however, is expense. There is no doubt that the installation and protection of nuclear plant is costly, and while no precise costing of a specific nuclear plant is available, the overall cost of a recent US Navy nuclear-powered aircraft carrier, USS *George Washington* (CVN 73), has been stated to be $3,280 million at FY83 prices, a figure which does not include the cost of the air wing. However, the US Congress insisted that the US Navy's Aegis system

should be mounted in a Spruance-type, gas-turbine-powered hull rather than a nuclear powered Improved Virginia hull for cost reasons.

A different view has been taken by the French, who estimate that nuclear propulsion for their new generation of aircraft carriers (PAN-1 class) has added 20 per cent to the ships' construction costs, but this is more than offset, in their view, by the fact that over the 30-year life of the ships the saving in expensive fuel oil (which would have to be paid for in US dollars) will be greater than the cost of the nuclear fuel plus the extra cost of the installation.

Pressurized-water reactors used in surface warships generate saturated steam at relatively low pressures and temperatures. The associated steam turbine plant is, therefore, rather bulky and the tremendous gain in the ship's endurance is, to a certain extent, offset by the reduced power and consequent lower speed. The French PAN-1, for example, is officially stated to have a power output of 83,000hp, giving a maximum speed of 27 knots, which compares poorly with the maximum speed of 32 knots on a power output of 126,000shp achieved by the current Clemenceau class.

The power problem can be solved in two ways, one being to introduce an additional means of propulsion. The Soviet Navy's Kirov class battle-cruisers have nuclear propulsion units with an output of approximately 90,000hp, which enables them to attain no more than 24 knots, and to achieve the speeds considered necessary they use a novel combined nuclear and steam (CONAS) system, in which the secondary oil-fired propulsion is used to boost top speed to 32 knots. If CONAS is feasible, then there seems to be no reason why a combined nuclear and gas (CONAG) installation should not also be feasible, with gas turbines giving the necessary boost for maximum speeds, but no such arrangement has yet been tried.) The alternative is simply to build much larger ships to contain the size of nuclear installation necessary. Either course is very expensive, but the only apparent alternative is to do as the French have done and accept the slightly lower speed.

One particular advantage of nuclear propulsion is that there is no need for the space-consuming uptakes, downtakes and fuel tanks needed for the combustion of fossil fuels, a problem which particularly applies to gas turbines.

GAS TURBINES

One very important area of development is that of gas turbine propulsion, and ships as big as the British Invincible class aircraft carriers (19,500 tons) are now powered exclusively by such means. Gas turbines have good power-to-weight ratios and

Rolls-Royce Olympus TM3 gas turbine module

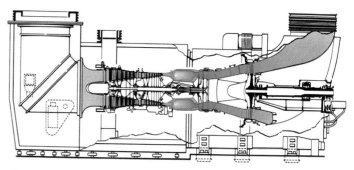

Above: A typical marine gas turbine installation comprises a gas generator, free power turbine, acoustic enclosure, cascaded air-inlet bend, fire protection and ancilliaries. This is the Rolls-Royce

Olympus TM3 package, widely used by Western navies. The module is 30ft (9.17m) long, 8.7ft (2.64m) wide and 12ft (3.71m) high; weight is 30.35 tons and max power output is 29,600hp (22MW).

Above: A General Electric LM-2500 gas turbine is removed from the destroyer Comte de Grasse (DD 974). Gas turbines are now widely used due to their small volume and ease of changing.

Below: The intakes and exhausts for the four LM-2500 gas-turbines on USS John Young (DD 973). Gas turbines require large, space-consuming trunking, which also adds to the top weight.

high peak power outputs, and are capable of rapid starts that are not possible with other means of propulsion; the Dutch Kortenaer class frigates, for example, can accelerate from a standing start to 30 knots in just 75 seconds on the power of their Rolls-Royce Olympus main engines.

A typical gas turbine package in a frigate comprises a marine gas-generator and free power turbine, an acoustic enclosure, a cascaded air inlet bend, anciliaries and a fire protection system, all mounted on a steel baseframe. The gas generator module is usually derived from an aircraft power-plant, modified with a new low-pressure compressor, a combustor specially designed to minimize particulate emissions, a

new casing and a revised mounting system. These changes are not as major as they sound and the proven technology of the aero-engine still forms the basis of the marine derivative. The power turbine, which transmits the power to the propeller shaft, is normally rigidly mounted as part of the permanently installed equipment and is connected to the gas generator by a flexible bellows.

Gas turbine powerplants do not of themselves occupy a large volume, but their air intake and exhaust requirements are considerable and much valuable topspace (and weight) must be devoted to air downtakes and exhaust uptakes. This has serious repercussions on medium-size ship design, where there is already a

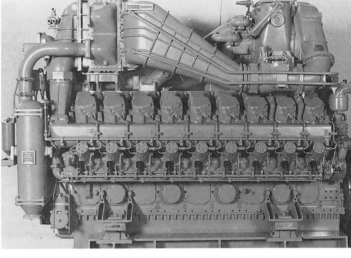

struggle to try to fit everything necessary on the superstructure, without threatening the stability of the ship.

Gas turbines are expensive in first costs, and since they cannot reverse they require either a reversing gearbox or a controllable propeller. The latter has a quicker response than a fixed-blade system, but is some 5 per cent less efficient when moving ahead.

Gas turbines are installed in various combinations with other gas turbines, or with other types of engine. The first to be used, and still the most frequently encountered, is combined gas or gas (COGOG), in which one or two high-power engines are installed for boost running in combination with one or two of rather lower power and fuel consumption for cruise running; the installation is such that only one type can be used at a time. A typical installation is that in the Dutch Kortenaer class, which involves two Rolls-Royce TM3B Olympus (50,000shp) for high speed and two Rolls-Royce RM1C Tynes (8,000shp) for cruising.

The other combination, combined gas and gas (COGAG), again consists of a combination of two engines on the same shaft, but in this case both types can be switched in together to give a really high power output when required. This arrangement is being used on the last seven of the Royal Navy's Type 22 frigates, which have two Rolls-Royce Spey SM1A (37,540shp) and two Rolls-Royce Tyne RM1C (9,700shp). It is also being used on the Japanese Hatakaze class destroyers, which will have two Rolls-Royce Olympus TM3B and two Rolls-Royce Spey SM1A.

DIESEL PROPULSION

Diesel engines are much used in small combatants, although they have relatively heavy maintenance demands and their removal for overhaul can be difficult. Nevertheless, the diesel is making something of a comeback and is now being fitted in larger warships such as frigates and destroyers. Such

Above: An alternative LM-2500 gas turbine installation powers the water jets on the patrol hydrofoil USS Hercules (PHM 2). Some 90,000gal (341,000lit) per minute are pumped through when foilborne at the full speed of 50 knots.

Below: Gas turbines cannot be reversed, so ships are fitted with either a reversing gearbox or controllable-pitch propellers. The latter are around five per cent less efficient than fixed-pitch propellers but respond faster.

Above: Diesel engines are widely used in marine applications in both surface ships and submarines, and are currently making something of a comeback. This is the British Paxman Valenta Mk2 (18RP200), an 18-cylinder model.

ships, with displacements in the region of 2,000-4,000 tons, must be capable of maximum speeds of about 30 knots and have a range in excess of 4,000nm. For such applications the diesel offers a relatively low specific fuel consumption over the whole power regime, the use of fixed-pitch propellers, and much simpler reduction gearing than that required by gas turbines. Initial capital costs are low and so, too, are running costs, especially if recycled lubricating oil can be used as fuel. Against this, the diesel engine has a high noise level and suffers from a certain amount of vibration, necessitating mounting on properly damped rafts and good acoustic insulation.

The US Navy's T-AGOS ships, designed for towing SURTASS arrays, are required to be able to steam to their patrol areas at 11 knots and then carry out a 90-day patrol at their towing speed of 3 knots. In the latter regime the propulsion system obviously needs to be as quiet as possible, and they use a diesel-electric system, in which four Caterpillar CAT D398 diesels, each rated at 860hp at 1,200rpm, drive four KATO 857kVA ac electric motors feeding a common bus. Propulsion power is derived through silicon-controlled rectifiers driving two General Electric dc propulsion motors, each driving a fixed-pitch propeller. There is no reduction gearing, and careful acoustic insulation and fixed-pitch propellers give a very low noise signature.

COMBINATIONS

Some combinations have already been mentioned, but various others are in use or under development, usually with the intention of reconciling the different propulsion requirements for high speed and cruising. Combined diesel or gas turbine (CODOG) utilizes diesels for cruising up to about 18 knots, giving good endurance, while the gas turbine is used for quick getaways and higher speeds. The German Navy selected this system for its Type 122 frigates in perference to the all-gas turbine COGOG system used in the Kortenaer class from which they were developed.

The French Navy's successful Georges Leygues class destroyers are powered by two SEMT-Pielstick 16-cylinder PA6V280 diesels of 10,400bhp and two Rolls-Royce Olympus TM3B gas turbines of 52,000bhp in a CODOG system, but the AA variant (Cassard class) instead uses an all-diesel combined diesel and diesel (CODAD) installation, using four SEMT-Pielstick engines driving fixed-pitch propellers through a reduction gearbox and twin shafts. At its mean displacement of 4,000 tons the C 70AA is

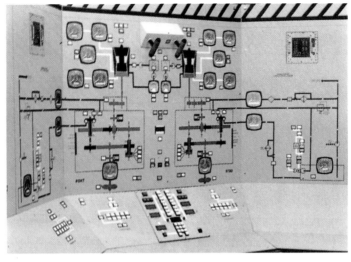

expected to have a maximum continuous speed of 29.6 knots, a flat-out speed of 30.2 knots, a range of 5,000nm at 24 knots and a cruising range of 8,200nm at 17 knots. The CODAD system has greatly reduced the need for trunking, thus releasing space and topweight for sensors and weapon systems.

Yet another combination is being installed in the Royal Navy's Type 23 frigates, the first of which is now under construction. The operational requirement called for ultra-low

Above: A Vosper Thornycroft engine control console for the new Type 23 frigate. Modern machine and control technology has drastically reduced the number of highly trained crew once required to man warships' engine rooms.

noise levels at very low speeds when the towed-array sonar is deployed, high efficiency and economy at cruise speeds, and rapid availability of high power—the so-called drift-or-sprint mode. This stringent requirement is being met by the combined

diesel-electric and gas turbine (CODLAG) system, an integrated propulsion system of diesel-electric drive and gas turbine boost using twin-shaft propulsion with fixed-pitch propellers.

Diesel generator sets provide power through a converter to a direct-drive dc electric motor on each of the two shafts for the slow-speed silent mode, for manoeuvring and for reverse, while for high speeds either one or both Rolls-Royce Spey SM1 boost gas turbines are started and each drives its respective propeller through a double-reduction gearbox. The gearbox contains an SSS clutch in its output shaft and when electric drive is in use the gearbox is isolated and the gear lubricating system pumps stopped to minimize noise yet further. The ship is driven astern using the diesel-electric drive with the gas turbine declutched, thus overcoming one of the problems inherent in gas turbine propulsion. This makes an interesting comparison with the diesel-electric drive for the US Navy's T-AGOS ships, which have a similar very quiet, low speed requirement, but do not have to be capable of the high speeds needed for normal warship operations.

Royal Navy Type 23 frigate CODLAG propulsion system

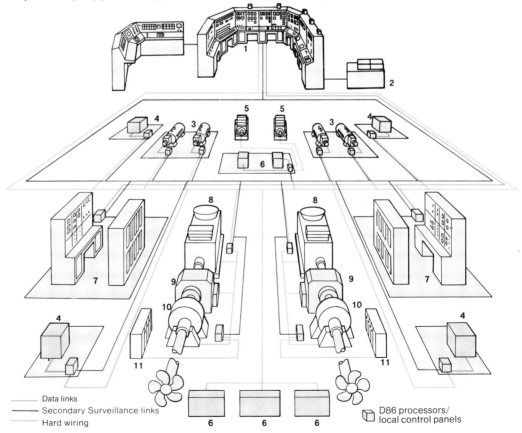

Data links
Secondary Surveillance links
Hard wiring

D86 processors/local control panels

Above: The combined diesel, electric and gas turbine propulsion system for the new Type 23 frigates uses diesel-powered electric motors at low speeds, with two Rolls-Royce Spey gas turbines for boost power. Integrated control and surveillance is carried out by a distributed microprocessor-based

system, and propulsion is controlled by a single lever per shaft with all control functions performed automatically, including declutching the turbines to comply with ahead or astern orders. Ship's service electrical systems are provided by two motor generator sets to ensure high-quality supply.

1 Ship control centre
2 Printers
3 Diesel generators
4 Chilled water plant
5 Motor generator sets
6 Auxiliary machinery
7 Switchboard and secondary controls
8 Gas turbines
9 Gear boxes
10 Electric motors
11 Convertors

Submarine Design and Propulsion

The ship types discussed above have all retained their basic role in the postwar period, and although their weapons and sensors have changed and the size of individual ships has grown, they remain recognizable descendants of their wartime predecessors. The submarine, on the other hand, has changed almost beyond recognition, both in size and performance and much more significantly, in role as well.

During World War II, Germany almost succeeded in cutting the vital Atlantic supply line from North America to Europe and on several occasions brought the UK to the brink of starvation. In the Pacific, too, the US Navy won a great underwater victory against the Japanese, reducing their merchant fleet to a critical level, and until the mid-1960s the primary strategic role of the submarine was, as it has been since 1917, to attack hostile naval surface vessels and maritime logistic traffic. This role still exists to a certain extent, but the evolution of submarine-launched ballistic missiles (SLBMs) and submarine-launched cruise missiles (SLCMs) has brought a further and even more important strategic role, that of striking directly at targets in the enemy's homeland.

The USSR, while developing SSBNs like those of other navies, has also paid great attention to special cruise-missile submarines (SSGN/SSG). These were produced specifically to counter the US Navy's aircraft carrier groups and their nuclear-capable strike aircraft. The Americans have avoided the need for such a submarine type by developing missiles such as Tomahawk and Harpoon, which can be launched from a standard 21in torpedo tube, thus making virtually every submarine a potential cruise missile carrier.

The third main role of the submarine is the traditional one of attacking other submarines and surface shipping. Without a doubt, the most effective submarine killers are the nuclear powered attack submarines (SSNs), although conventionally powered submarines are also very capable in this role. These diesel-electric submarines continue to thrive, and some 550 are operational with 39 navies in the attack role, in general patrol duties and in clandestine special duties.

Only the five most advanced navies can currently afford the increasing expense of nuclear-powered submarines, although Spain is giving serious consideration to nuclear propulsion for her next generation of attack submarines, and of those presently operating nuclear submarines only the US and French navies have an apparent intention to go all-nuclear, with the Soviet, British and Chinese navies all retaining conventional boats in production.

The world's largest submarine

fleet is that of the Soviet Union. As a nation the Russians have long been impressed by sheer size, and their latest Typhoon class SSBNs (29,000 tons) are the biggest submarines ever built. By 1986 four of these giants were in service, together with three Delta IVs, at least 14 Delta IIIs, four Delta IIs and 18 Delta Is. A number of the older Yankee class boats remain in service as SSBNs, but some have now been converted to the SSN and SSBN roles, while the very few elderly Hotel class SSBNs and Golf class SSBs that

Below: US official artist's impression of a Soviet Navy submarine facility. Such drawings, based on satellite pictures, have in the past turned out to be exceptionally accurate.

Above: The modern, sophisticated control room of USS Ohio is in stark contrast to the array of pipes, analogue meters and manually operated valves found on submarines only 20 years ago.

remain in service are almost certainly employed in a tactical rather than a strategic role.

The Soviet SSGN/SSG fleet is also large, comprising three boats of the Oscar class (14,000 tons), 17 Charlies and 29 Echos, together with 16 of the diesel-electric Juliett class SSGs. In fleet submarines (SSNs) the Soviet Navy appears to have no fewer than three classes under construction simultaneously, yet another indication of the enormous scope of its defence programme. There are sixty-nine SSNs in service of seven classes.

Finally, the Soviet Navy has the world's largest fleet of diesel-electric submarines, with some 150 in service, many quite elderly, but the Tango class (3,900 tons) and the latest Kilo class (3,200 tons) being both ultra-modern and very capable.

The US Navy's submarine fleet is less numerous than that of the Soviet Union, but includes some very powerful and capable classes. The latest SSBNs, those of the Ohio class (18,700 tons), mount 24 SLBMs, the largest payload of any SSBN. Eight Ohios are in service, together with 31 of the Franklin and Lafayette classes, and 12 of the latter have been converted to take the Trident 1 (C-4) missile, the remainder still carrying the older Poseidon (C-3).

The US SSN fleet is centred on the Los Angeles class (6,900 tons), of which it is intended that more than 50 should be in service by the end of the century. There are also 37 members of the Sturgeon class (4,640 tons) and 13 of the Thresher class (4,470 tons), as well as a number of one-off boats such as the *Lipscomb, Narwhal* and *Seawolf,* and the remaining boats of the now elderly Skipjack and Skate classes. Alone among the major navies the US Navy has announced an intention to go all-nuclear and the only operational diesel-electric boats remaining are the three units of the Barbel class (2,894) tons.

The United Kingdom has four Resolution class SSBNs with Polaris missiles, which will be replaced in the 1990s by four new Trident submarines. Building of SSNs has continued steadily, with HMS *Conqueror* holding the distinction of being the only nuclear powered attack submarine

Diving a conventional submarine

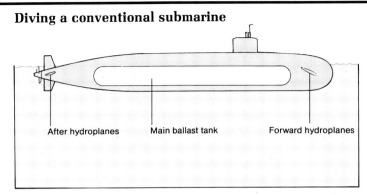

After hydroplanes   Main ballast tank   Forward hydroplanes

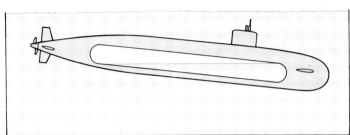

Above: USS Dolphin, a research submarine, has a cylindrical hull, closed at either end by hemispherical bulkheads. She is used for deep-diving, acoustic and oceanographic experiments.

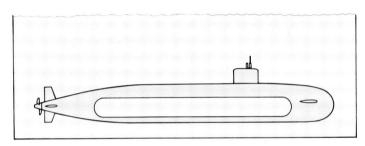

Above: To start the dive (top) the submarine's forward and after hydroplanes are set to 'dive' and main vents are opened to allow the main ballast tanks to start flooding. Descending at too steep an angle is somewhat dangerous, so the descent is checked (centre) by setting the after hydroplanes to 'rise'; the boat then levels off. Finally (bottom), when the main ballast tanks are full the main vents are closed, the hydroplanes set to horizontal and the auxiliary and compensating tanks are employed to trim the boat. At higher speeds the effect of the hydroplanes is more marked in the dive and ballast tankage is often much reduced. Nuclear powered attack submarines operate on similar principles, but the tank arrangement and procedures are slightly different.

to have sunk a hostile warship. There are 15 SSNs of four classes in service, the latest being the Trafalgar class (5,208 tons) of four units with one building and one on order. The Royal Navy still makes very good use of conventional submarines; there are 15 currently in service, and the first of the new Upholder class (2,400 tons) was ordered in 1985.

The French Navy has six SSBNs in service and two SSNs, having decided for political reasons to build SSBNs first rather than starting with SSNs as the USA, USSR and UK had done. The rest of the fleet comprises four Agosta class (1,725 tons), nine Daphne class (1,038 tons) and two Narval class (1,635 tons), all conventional diesel-electric boats. China has three SSBNs

and three SSNs, all of her own design, about which very little is known and more than 100 diesel-electric boats, virtually all of Soviet design but of Chinese construction. Of the remaining navies many have a small number of submarines, mostly of US, Soviet, French, German or British design.

DESIGN

Almost as important as the advent of nuclear propulsion has been the revolution in submarine hull design pioneered in the 1950s by the USS *Albacore* (AGSS 569). The long, narrow hulls of the time were proving unable to cope with the increased power becoming available and under certain circumstances, particularly at speeds of over 10 knots, control could be lost altogether—the USS *Nautilus* (SSN 571), for example, despite its nuclear powerplant, could not exceed 23.3 knots underwater. The diesel-electric powered *Albacore*, however, with a teardrop hull shape derived from those of airships, a cruciform tail empennage and a single propeller, achieved a sustained underwater speed of 26 knots in her original form and later, with contra-rotating propellers and silver-zinc batteries, became capable of an astonishing 33 knots.

Not surprisingly, the *Albacore* set the general pattern for all subsequent hull designs, though contemporary pressure hulls are slimmer, because a parallel mid-body is almost as efficient if the forward and after ends are properly designed, and a tubular body is, of course, much easier and cheaper to construct.

Surfacing a conventional submarine

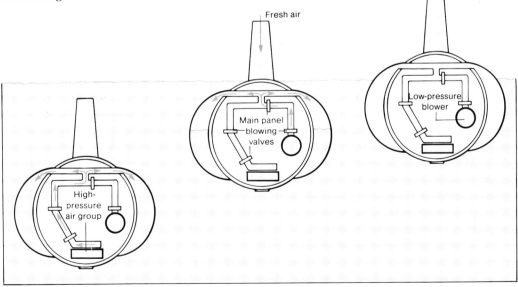

Fresh air

High-pressure air group

Main panel blowing valves

Low-pressure blower

Above: An ascent from depth is difficult to control, so conventional submarines normally come to periscope depth before blowing tanks and surfacing. The main ballast tank is blown gradually (left) using high-pressure air, until the boat is at periscope depth, at which point (centre) atmospheric air is sucked in through the schnorkel tube. It is then compressed by a low-pressure blower or air pump and then used to blow out the remainder of the main ballast. This has the effect of bringing the submarine fully to the surface (right). More modern boats use their higher speed and more effective control surfaces to bring the boat close to the surface before blowing ballast.

The design of any weapon system is inevitably the result of a number of compromises, but that of submarines is beset by a number of particularly difficult problems. The most basic of these is that a submerged submarine must have neutral buoyancy, and every element in the craft has an effect upon this. Diving depth is obviously a crucial tactical consideration, because depth provides shelter, especially if the submarine can go deep enough to exploit the acoustic properties of the sea to thwart ASW detection devices, and gives a safety margin in high speed manuoeuvres. Actual details are highly classified, but open-source figures for selected SSNs giving a general indication of normal operating depths for comparative purposes are: US Los Angeles class 1,475ft (450m); Soviet Victor III class 1,300ft (400m); French Rubis class 980ft (300m). Depth performance is becoming more important as the ASW threat increases and is naturally leading to extensive research and development into materials.

Considerable research effort is being devoted to the subject of hydrodynamic efficiency. Laminar flow has been tried, offering apparent drag reductions of over 50 per cent, but putting the theories into practice has been thwarted so far by the impurities of seawater. Streamlining has been the rule

since the German World War II Type XXII boats, but great attention is now being paid to the actual nature of the surface of the submarine. Special hull paints can reduce friction, allowing either increased speeds or reduced power requirements for a given speed, while releasing polymers around the hull is also used to increase the submarine's speed for short periods.

It has been reported that the exteriors of Soviet submarines are coated with a compliant covering derived from research into marine animals such as dolphins and killer whales, which combines suction and boundary-layer pressure equalization. Further development based on the same research may lead to devices to modify shapes to match the boat's speed by, for example, progressively retracting the hydroplanes or changing the shape of the fin as speed increases. These researches may also account for the very interesting shape of the latest Soviet submarines, which have bulbous bows similar in shape to the front end of a whale, while their sails are not only smaller than those on Western submarines but also less angular in shape and merged rather more smoothly into the hull rather like the fins of marine animals.

Manoeuvrability is obviously of great importance to a

submarine and again the *Albacore* had a great influence on all subsequent designs. The short hull improved manoeuvrability very considerably over the then current long, narrow designs, and during trials the *Albacore* was able to turn at 3°/sec, a substantial improvement over contemporary submarines of that era but a figure probably exceeded by current types.

The major control surfaces are the hydroplanes. Most nations use bow-mounted hydroplanes placed as far forward as practicable, but the US Navy and some others, such as Japan and France, use fin-mounted planes. While these may offer advantages for manoeuvrability, hydroplanes need to be capable of rotation to the vertical for breaking through ice, if it is operationally necessary to operate in the Arctic. The Los Angeles class are accordingly suffering from a serious tactical limitation now that under-ice operations have become necessary to counter the growing Soviet use of the Arctic, especially by SSBNs, and US Secretary of Defense Weinberger has recently announced that the planes will be moved to the bows on future Los Angeles class SSNs.

Virtually all modern submarines have cruciform tail empennages with horizontal and vertical control surfaces. In the

US Los Angeles and Ohio classes the horizontal hydroplanes are fitted with vertical endplates, both to improve control and as housings for hydroplanes. The latest Swedish Näcken and Dutch Walrus classes, however, have an indexed, X-shaped empennage; this configuration is less liable to physical damage since it does not protrude beyond the outer edge of the hull, but because of the complex relationship between steering and diving functions it requires computer-aided operation.

The submarine captain's greatest enemy is sonar and apart from tactical methods of avoiding sonar detection there are some passive measures which can be implemented at the design stage. The first is to limit size, since a smaller submarine is a more difficult target, but it is very difficult to fit the required mass of weapons and sensors into a small hull. The next step is to shape the contours of the hull in such a way that the sonar beams are diffused, following the example of the stealth technology now being applied to aircraft. Finally, anechoic (sound-absorbing) tiles can be used to coat the most critical parts of the submarine. These tiles are already in use on Royal Navy submarines and on the latest Soviet submarines (one type has the NATO designation Cluster Guard). They are also due to

Left: Fin-mounted hydroplanes offer several advantages: good submerged control, damage avoidance — especially when coming alongside — steadiness at periscope depth, and the avoidance of flow noise near the very sensitive bow sonar.

Below: Fin-mounted hydroplanes also have drawbacks, including making surfacing through the ice much more difficult. Therefore in future US submarines will return to the traditional bow-mounted planes.

are not only the world's fastest submarines, being capable of better than 42 knots, but also the deepest diving, with estimates of their maximum depth ranging from 2,000ft (600m) to 3,000ft (960m). Titanium is a very difficult material to weld, although the Soviets, for a long time world leaders in metallurgy, seem to have managed it, but it has the invaluable advantage of being non-magnetic and consequently undetectable by devices such as airborne MAD and bottom-laid coils. Some years ago the West Germans attempted to achieve similar results by using non-magnetic steel for their Type 205, 206, and 207 submarines, which were intended primarily for service in the shallow waters of the Baltic, but while early corrosion problems have long since been resolved the idea has not been extended to larger designs.

be installed in the US Navy's next generation of attack submarines.

CONSTRUCTION

The US Navy has used a series of high yield (HY) steels for submarine construction; all classes since the Thresher have been made of HY80. (The number gives the yield stress in lb/sq in, so HY80 has a yield stress of 80lb/sq in (5.624kg/cm².) It was at one time planned to build the Los Angeles class of HY130, although in the event HY80 was used. However, it is hoped that the HY130

will be developed to an acceptable standard in time for use in the later units of the US Navy's next SSN class.

In other nations there is also much research and development into stronger materials. The Japanese use NS-90 in their latest Yuushio class, while the new French Marel high-tension steel, claimed to give a 50 per cent increase in diving depth, is being used in the latest French and Dutch submarines. The USSR has continued to use steel for the majority of its submarines, but at least two classes (Alfa and Mike) are known to be built of titanium. The Alfas

Above: An Alfa class SSN, showing how the fin shape used by Soviet designers is lower and more blended into the hull than that on Western designs. Like all Soviet submarines except the Yankee and Delta class SSBN's the Alfas have bow-mounted forward hydro-planes.

Below: Submarine construction is becoming an ever more sophisticated and expensive undertaking. This is the General Dynamics yard at Groton, with an Ohio class SSBN (left) and a Los Angeles class SSN (right) in final stages of completion, and a second SSBN in the hall.

PROPULSION

Although there have been many advances in submarine design and construction, particularly in hull shape, there can be no doubt that the greatest single advance in postwar submarine technology is the advent of nuclear propulsion, which has released the submarine from being forced to make regular forays to the surface to recharge

Pressurized-water nuclear propulsion system layout

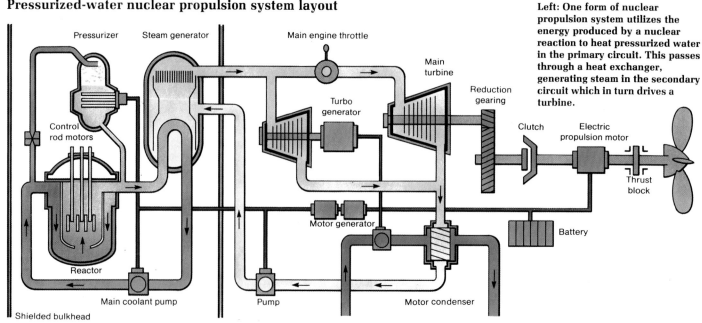

Left: One form of nuclear propulsion system utilizes the energy produced by a nuclear reaction to heat pressurized water in the primary circuit. This passes through a heat exchanger, generating steam in the secondary circuit which in turn drives a turbine.

its batteries and replenish its air supplies. In addition, nuclear propulsion confers virtually limitless range: the US Navy's Ohio class SSBNs, for example, are fitted with General Electric S8G nuclear reactors which have a core life of some nine years between refuellings.

All British and US nuclear powered submarines use pressurized-water reactors (PWRs), in which water acts as both coolant and moderator; this is a tried and tested technique and has proved exceptionally reliable in service. In such a system water passes round the primary circuit, making several passes through the nuclear reactor and thence to a steam generator. This coolant in the primary circuit (water) has to be kept at a high pressure to prevent it boiling and itself turning to steam, achieved by including a pressurizer in the primary circuit, and steam at the top of the pressurizer is used to compensate for changes in coolant volume as the reactor inlet and outlet temperatures vary.

The heat energy is transferred in the steam generator from the water in the primary circuit to unpressurized water in the secondary circuit, which then becomes steam and passes through the secondary circuit to the turbine. Having driven the turbine, the steam goes into a series of condensers, becoming water once again, and then returns in liquid form to the steam generator to recommence the cycle. The PWR condensers use seawater as a heat sink and require a constant throughput, maintained either by the forward motion of the submarine or, at slow speeds, by the use of pumps.

The operation of a PWR requires considerable auxiliary power, mainly to operate the circulation pumps in the primary circuit and the electrical heater elements in the pressurizer. The system can be designed to utilize

natural circulation resulting from the thermal gradient set up by the nuclear reaction, but at higher power levels the pumps still have to be switched in. Some systems, in an effort to minimize noise and vibration, use several pumps which can be selectively activated according to the power level. Whatever the system, however, all these pumps create noise which is detectable by suitable sensors.

Various other coolants have been tried. The USS *Seawolf* (SSN 575), launched in 1955, was fitted with an S2G liquid-sodium cooled reactor, which gave a much more efficient heat transfer but was very trouble-

Below: A nuclear reactor core is installed in a French nuclear powered ballistic missile submarine at the DCAN shipyard in Cherbourg. The French nuclear programme has been remarkably successful and apparently trouble-free.

some in service, and after two years this plant was replaced by a pressurized-water cooled reactor. Liquid metal cooling seems to be the only way to obtain smaller, lighter plants, and the Soviet Alfa class is generally agreed to have a liquid-metal cooled reactor in a fully automatic, unmanned engine room, leading to considerable savings in reactor shielding.

A particular problem for nuclear powered boats is that of machinery-generated noise, especially from gearing and rotating machinery such as pumps which, as described above, must be kept running, especially in PWR systems. In most Western boats machinery is mounted on rafts in an effort to isolate the vibrations from the hull. Turbo-electric drive was tried in the USS *Lipscomb* (SSN 685), which is still in service, but it has not been repeated in other boats, and direct drive

with twin contra-rotating propellers of different sizes was utilized in the USS *Jack* (SSN 605), but was unsuccessful and was removed. Free circulation is used in USS *Narwhal* (SSN 671) with apparent success, as it is now used in the S8G reactor in the Ohio class SSBNs.

The final item in the drive-train is the propeller, which is one of the major causes of noise, and one of the most readily identifiable features of individual submarines. Modern submarine propellers have up to seven blades, usually of a scythe shape, and are designed to be run at very low revolutions. The latest British Trafalgar class SSNs, however, are reported to use pump-jets, in which a ducted multi-bladed rotor turns against stator vanes, thus virtually eliminating cavitation noise, although rotating noises will probably still exist, albeit somewhat attenuated.

The Soviet Navy is examining a variety of other means of propulsion, and is reported (*Jane's Fighting Ships*, 1984/85) to be using both magneto-hydrodynamic (MHD) generators and electrodynamic thrust (EMT), both of which dispense with propellers to eliminate cavitation and mechanical noise and reduce wake turbulence. MHD involves the use of an open tube, filled with seawater and surrounded by a ferro-liquid in a sealed sleeve; a pulsating magnetic field causes sympathetic vibrations in the ferro-liquid, setting up a travelling wave, which results in the water in the open tube being pumped out at the rear, imparting forward thrust to the submarine.

This method of propulsion, bearing similarities to the electro-osmosis process, requires a great deal of electrical power and would probably be capable of moving the submarine only at slow speeds. Nevertheless, if an SSBN were to use normal propeller drive for

the relatively rapid transit to and from the patrol area, MHD could be very valuable for moving in a virtually undetectable slow-speed cruise. One theory concerning the enormous size of the Soviet Navy's Typhoon class SSBN is that there are two parallel pressure hulls within the outer casing, and that one of these pressure hulls contains a large nuclear plant required to generate the enormous power necessary for MHD propulsion.

EMT employs a different technique. A line of electro-magnets is set up on the centre-line of the vessel and banks of electrodes are mounted down on either side of the ship; electric current is passed through the electrodes, setting up a magnetic field, and the action between the two magnetic fields results in forward motion. The USSR and Japan are both reported to be experimenting with this system.

Above: A large, five-bladed fixed-pitch propeller fitted to a Type 209 submarine. Note the very complex shaping of the blades, designed to minimize cavitation, but maximize propulsive efficiency.

Diesel-electric submarines are far cheaper to build than nuclear submarines, far less complicated to operate, and free from the political problems associated with nuclear propulsion. However, their inherent problem is that they must surface to run their diesels and recharge their batteries, a process which requires about 3.5lb (1.58kg) of oxygen for every 1lb (0.45kg) of fuel oil. In very few submarines are the diesels connected directly to the propeller shafts; rather, the propellers are normally run off the batteries at all times, even on the surface, where the diesels recharge the batteries while the latter continue to run the propellers.

Above: The 9.84ft (3m) diameter propeller fitted to the Italian Nazario Sauro has seven blades of a significantly different shape from those of the Type 209 on the left. It is made of Sonoston alloy.

Other systems have been tried. Professor Helmuth Walther proposed a closed-cycle system using high-test hydrogen peroxide (HTP), and some experimental U-boats were completed just before the end of World War II. One scuttled example, *U-1407*, was raised by the Royal Navy, taken to the UK and commissioned as HMS *Meteorite*. It was used to develop the system and subsequently the Royal Navy constructed two submarines using the Walther cycle, HMS *Explorer* and *Excalibur*, but these proved very hazardous in service, to the extent that HMS *Explorer* was known to her crew as HMS *Exploder*.

Closed-cycle systems are under constant consideration. The

Brayton cycle uses inert gases such as argon, helium or xenon as working fluids and was an unsuccessful competitor as an engine for the US Navy's Advanced Lightweight Torpedo (ALWT). Another device, the Stirling piston engine, was under serious consideration for the Royal Swedish Navy's Vastergotland class (now under construction), but was eventually rejected. It should be noted that in any of these systems a fundamental consideration is that if they should give off a gaseous exhaust there is then a problem of disposal, especially at depth.

Another system with apparent potential for use in submarines is the fuel cell. In such a device two chemicals are combined in the presence of a catalyst, the resulting reaction, which is usually fairly violent, being used for the direct production of electricity. Efficiency is high (up

Walther exchange process

Below: The search for an alternative to the air-breathing diesel engine for submarines has lasted for many decades. Nuclear power is very expensive and has political constraints. The German Professor Walther experimented in the '30s-'40s with a hydrogen peroxide (H_2O_2) closed-cycle system, where disintegrated H_2O_2 was fed into a

combustion chamber and burned with injected fuel. The only by-product, CO_2, was expelled outside the hull where it was absorbed by the sea water, leaving no trace of the submarine's passage. After the war several navies experimented with the Walther cycle, but no operational boat was built.

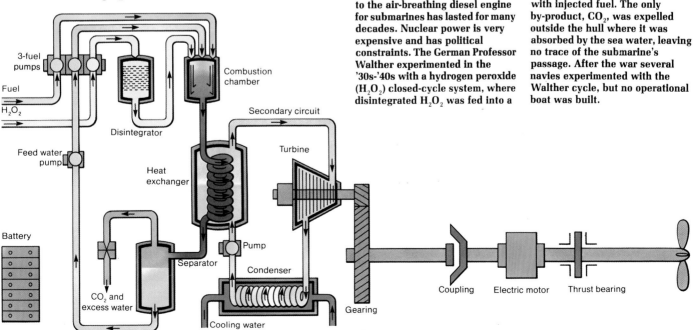

to 70 or 80 per cent in some cases), there are no severe heat dissipation problems, and in many cases (eg, lithium/peroxide cells) the product is pure, potable water.

Batteries are heavy and space-consuming. Lead-acid batteries are cheap, simple to produce and relatively easy to maintain. Silver-zinc and silver-cadmium batteries are lighter and smaller, more efficient, but much more expensive and need more careful handling. Apart from constant research into new types of battery, much development effort is being put into improving the performance of lead-acid batteries, for example, by changing the electrolyte underwater to get rid of poisoned electrolyte.

SSBNs

The first true ballistic missile submarines were those of the Soviet Navy's diesel-engined Golf class (SSB), which mounted three SS-N-4 missiles vertically in their fins. The next type, the Hotel, also had fin-mounted missiles and it was not until the apearance of the Yankee class in 1966 that the Soviets had purpose-built SSBNs equivalent to those in the West. Even so, the Yankee I's SS-N-6 had a comparatively short range, which meant that these boats had to deploy close to the US mainland to cover targets such as SAC bases.

The Yankee strength is decreasing as boats are converted to other roles to keep within the SALT II limits, and the sole Yankee II carries the experimental SS-NX-17. The next class, the Delta, is now in its fourth major modification—the Delta I had 12 SS-N-8, the Delta II 16 SS-N-8, Delta III 16 SS-N-18 and the Delta IV 16 SS-N-23—

Typhoon class possible internal layout

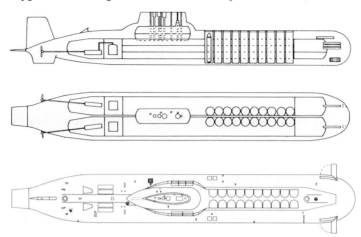

Above: There has been much speculation in the West about the internal layout of the Soviet Typhoon class SSBN. These diagrams show the most widely held view: that there are two

pressure hulls, each containing 10 missiles, a nuclear reactor and ancilliaries, with a further pressure vessel on top housing the command centre. All three are enclosed by a streamlined outer hull.

having grown in the process from 10,000 tons submerged to 13,600 tons. The members of the latest Typhoon class (29,000 tons), carry 20 SS-N-20 SLBMs ahead of the fin. Soviet SSBN design lagged behind that of the West for some years, the early types showing evidence of hasty conversion, and even the recent Deltas carry their missiles in an ungainly whaleback which is very poorly matched to the fin and will undoubtedly be very noisy at any speed.

The Typhoon is an interesting design which has been discussed at length in the West. The consensus view is that it has two parallel hulls joined

Below: A significant US picture of a Soviet Delta IV firing an SS-N-23 from a gap in the Artic ice. It would take the Delta IV some 15 minutes to fire all its missiles if it remained in one spot.

together and surrounded by an elliptical outer hull; it is even suggested that the hulls may simply be two modified Yankee or Delta hulls. This should make for a very spacious interior, which could be used for extra crew, for longer patrols, for additional equipment, or, as discussed below, an esoteric propulsion system.

The Typhoon appears to have been specifically designed for under-ice deployment, and has demonstrated the ability to launch at least four missiles simultaneously, whereas all other SSBNs fire their missiles in a ripple, which could take up to 15 minutes in the case of the older types and during which they are very vulnerable. One interesting note on the Typhoon is that her first commanding officer was awarded a very high decoration at the end of his tour of command; so high and rare, indeed, that he was the first

recipient since World War II, though the reasons for the award can only be a matter of speculation.

The US Navy has just two classes of SSBN in service: 31 of the virtually identical Lafayette and Franklin classes, 12 of which have been fitted to take 16 Trident I missiles while the remainder retain their 16 Poseidons; and a growing number of the Ohio class, which mount 24 Trident missiles abaft the fin, not in the whaleback necessary on all other Western SSBNs, but in a very neat and hydrodynamically efficient installation. Another significant feature of the Ohio class boats is that they are powered by the S5G natural-circulation nuclear reactor system, developed from that tested in the *Narwhal* (SSN 671).

British and French SSBN designs are conceptually similar to the US Navy's Lafayette/Franklin classes, with 16 missiles carried abaft the fin. The size of the boats is also remarkably similar, their submerged displacements and lengths ranging from Lafayettes' 8,250 tons and 425ft (129.5m) to the Resolutions, 8,500 tons and 425ft (129.5m) and *Le Redoutable's* 8,940 tons and 422.1ft (128.7m). The French have now produced six SSBNs, with a gradual improvement in each case, while the Royal Navy has not built any since the four Resolution class were finished in the late 1960s. There will, therefore, inevitably be substantial changes in design in the four new British Trident boats. Finally, China is building its own SSBNs, two were operational by the end of 1986 with a further four to follow.

In terms of design and operational concept the Yankee, Delta, Lafayette/Franklin, Resolution and Le Redoutable classes have a lot in common, and it is only with the advent of the Typhoon and Ohio classes

Current SSBN types

Hotel class (USSR)

I 377ft (115m), 8 tubes
II 427ft (130m), 16 tubes

Yankee class (USSR)

I 427ft (130m), 16 tubes
II 427ft (130m), 24 tubes

Delta class (USSR)

I 460ft (140m), 12 tubes
II 508ft (155m), 16 tubes
III 508ft (155m), 16 tubes

Typhoon class (USSR)

558ft (170m), 20 tubes

Lafayette/Franklin classes (USA)

425ft (130m), 16 tubes

Ohio class (USA)

560ft (170m), 24 tubes

Resolution class (UK)

425ft (130m), 16 tubes

Le Redoubtable class (France)

425ft (130m), 16 tubes

Xia class (China)

400ft (122m), 14 tubes

Above: The range of present types of SSBN, including those operated by the British, French and Chinese navies. Only a proportion of the total will be on active patrol at any one time.

that there has been a divergence. The Typhoon is huge and there seems no reason why next-generation Soviet SSBNs should not be even bigger if all they are required to do is to cover the relatively short distance to the Arctic ice-cap. The Ohio is a less radical design than the Typhoon and is, in effect, a logical progression of the Lafayette/Franklin class, bigger, longer, quieter and with more missiles. It will be interesting to see details of the Chinese SSBN, and to see what effect the new type of liquid metal-cooled nuclear reactor now fitted to the Rubis class SSNs will have on the design of the next generation of French SSBNs.

SSGNs

The Soviet Navy's submarine-launched cruise missile (SLCM) programme originated in the 1950s as a response to the threat posed by the US Navy's aircraft carrier task groups. Some crude conversions of Whiskey class patrol submarines were followed by the first purpose-designed classes, the nuclear powered Echo class (SSGN), and the diesel-electric Juliett class (SSG); 29 Echo IIs armed with eight SS-N-12 and 16 Julietts with four SS-N-3A were still in service by the beginning of 1986. In both classes the missiles are mounted in bins stowed flush with the hull casing, the bins being raised for launching once the boat has surfaced. Indentations behind each launcher which act as blast deflectors generate a lot of

Below: A most unusual surface rendezvous on the high seas between a Victor III SSN (foreground) and an Oscar class SSGN, participating in an exercise in 1985 in the North Atlantic.

underwater noise, but the missiles are fired from a range of about 200 miles (322km), well beyond the normal ASW screen. Such a range necessitates external assistance to achieve over-the-horizon targeting; initially this was provided by pairs of Bear-D reconnaissance aircraft, but the complexity involved in coordination, and the vulnerability of the aircraft, prevented this from being a very effective system, and it is believed that satellites are now used. The system also requires a large radar on the launch submarine, with the antenna—NATO designation Front Door or Front Piece—mounted at the forward end of the fin.

The first Charlie class SSGN appeared in 1968 and these boats are smaller, quieter, faster and exhibit much greater hydrodynamic efficiency than those of the Echo class. The

missile bins are all mounted forward of the fin, totally flush with the hull, and the SS-N-7 SLCM is fired underwater and does not need an aircraft in the control loop. The later Charlie class boats have lengthened bow sections, suggesting that they may be fitted with the SS-N-15 ASW missile. The next to appear was the Oscar class (18,000 tons), huge boats armed with 24 SS-N-19s and featuring an exceptionally wide beam of 60ft (18.3m). The missile bins are in the casing, but the great girth probably stems from the use of double hulls, making this class, like the Typhoons, very difficult to destroy.

The Soviet Navy has developed an SLCM similar to the Harpoon, which is launched from a standard 21in torpedo tube, and which will obviously be deployed on SSNs. Nevertheless, it would appear

Oscar class SSGN

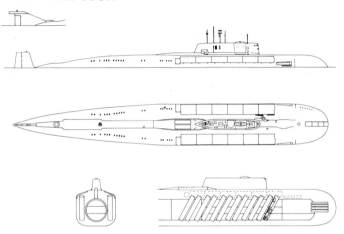

Above: The Oscar class SSGN carries 24 SS-N-19 cruise missiles, housed in bins at a fixed elevation of about 40° and mounted outside the pressure hull. There are six doors, each covering two missile bins. Inset above the side elevation is the rudder of the second and third boats of the class, with much greater chord and capped by a tubular housing, possibly for a towed array.

that Soviet SSGN development will continue, though there appears to be no intention in any Western navy to produce such a specialized type of submarine.

SSNs

The oldest SSNs in US Navy service are the five Skipjacks, which are small and handy but lack advanced sonar systems. The Permit and Sturgeon classes which followed are larger, carry a more sophisticated sonar outfit and fire Subroc, though as there was no increase in power, speed in these classes fell to 28kt. The latest US SSNs are those of the Los Angeles class, which showed a 50 per cent increase in displacement over their predecessors. Not only do they have more advanced sensors and fire control equipment— both of which are now being retrofitted to the 14 Permits and 37 Sturgeons—they have also restored the speed lost since the Skipjack class of the 1960s.

Soviet Navy operating procedures have in the past made it unlikely that there would be surface task groups against which US SSNs could concentrate (although with the advent of the Kiev and Kremlin class aircraft carriers and the Kirov class battle-cruisers the Soviets seem to be generating such targets) and US SSNs are therefore designed for three primary roles: ASW hunter-killer, independent forward area attack and reconnaissance, and the protection of task groups and convoys.

Nuclear propulsion is a relatively noisy way of powering a submarine, particularly at high speeds, but successive US designs have shown a steady improvement in this respect, and in the Los Angeles class particular attention has been paid to quietness, the large hull making it easier to cushion the machinery. The increase in speed also reflects the tactical

requirement for the defence of carrier task groups against Soviet SSGNs, and all US SSNs except the Skipjacks are being fitted with Harpoon missiles to give them a new capability against surface units.

The Soviet Navy still retains a number of the elderly and unreliable November class SSNs in service, but the principal current type is the second-generation Victor, which has a much improved hull form, greater diving depth, a much quieter propulsion system and a submerged speed of about 30kt. The 16 Victor Is were followed by six Victor IIs, which were 15.4ft (4.7m) longer and capable of carrying the SS-N-15, and the Victor III, longer still and with an unusual cylindrical housing on top of its rudder, which may be associated either with a towed array or with an advanced propulsion system. Finally, there are no fewer than three new types of Soviet SSN, the Mike, Sierra and Akula classes: the Sierra and Akula appear to be logical developments of the Victor III, but the Mike has a somewhat

differently shaped hull and fin and lacks the large bullet found on the fins of both the Sierra and the Akula classes.

The Royal Navy has produced a series of highly effective SSNs, of which all but the *Dreadnought* remain in service, similar but by no means identical to American SSNs. The main design features are that the hulls tend to be fuller and to taper at a greater angle, particularly at the stern, than those of the US boats, and the forward hydroplanes are mounted at the bow rather than on the fin, while a conformal sonar array is used at the bow, rather than the US sphere, allowing the torpedo tubes to remain in the bows. The drive system on the latest Trafalgar class employs hydrojets rather than propellers to cut down on cavitation noises.

The French Rubis class SSNs are much smaller than other SSNs, mainly because of the liquid-cooled nuclear reactor. The actual design of the boat is not unusual, however, being basically a modified version of the conventional Agosta.

Los Angeles class weapons and sensors

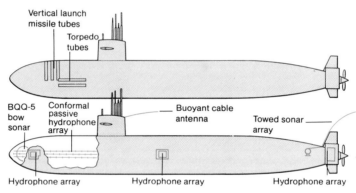

Above: The US Navy's Los Angeles class SSN is probably one of the most expensive defence programmes ever, but is also very successful and an excellent investment. Top view shows the armament of the later boats:

21in torpedo tubes mounted amidships on each side and three rows of four vertical launch tubes for Tomahawk cruise missiles. The lower drawing shows the bow sonar, conformal hydrophone and towed sonar arrays.

CONVENTIONAL SUBMARINES

Conventional submarine development is currently at a very interesting stage, with many existing boats becoming due for replacement, notably the ex-US Balao, Tench and Guppy types, the British Porpoises and Oberons, the French Daphnes and the Soviet Whiskeys and Romeos. There are a number of designs on offer, such as the British Type 2400, the French Agosta, the Italian Sauro, the Dutch Walrus, the Swedish Näcken and the West German IKL and Thyssen designs, while further designs in production but unlikely to be offered for sale abroad include the Japanese Yuushio and the Soviet Kilo and Tango classes.

Conventional submarines fall into three main categories. The first is the coastal or shallow-water submarine of 400-600 tons, epitomized by the German Type 205/206 and the Italian Toti classes. These have proved effective little boats, but obviously suffer from limitations in range, torpedo reloads and sensor capacity. Next are those of 900-1,300 tons, including the German Type 209, Yugoslavian Sava and the Swedish Näcken and Sjoeormen classes, again of limited endurance and carrying capacity, which are found in the smaller navies with medium-range roles, though it is interesting that the Swedish Näcken class is one of the finalists in the Australian submarine competition. The majority of current types are of 1,600 tons or more, such as the British Type 2400, Dutch Walrus and Soviet Foxtrot, Kilo and Tango classes, the last being the largest non-nuclear submarine design at 3,700 tons.

No one design or nation stands out as significantly different from the rest, and operational requirements are remarkably

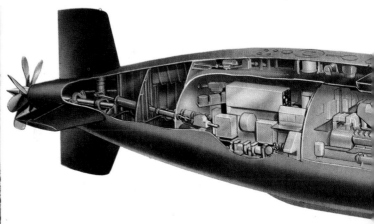

Left: Soviet Victor III, showing the intriguing bullet on the rudder. This may house a towed array or it could be, as some authorities claim, a new form of silent propulsion system.

Left: The Netherlands has produced a very effective diesel-electric submarine type in the Zwaardvis class. A point of interest is the large dielectric cover for the bow sonar.

Above: Successor to the Los Angeles class will be the Sea Wolf (SSN 21) class. These boats will be quieter than the Los Angeles, carry more weapons and have much improved under-ice capability.

similar in many respects. Of the three latest designs in the West, for example, the Japanese Yuushio is 249.25ft (76m) long with a surfaced displacement of 2,200 tons, while the figures for the British Type 2400 are 230.5ft (70.25m) and 2,125 tons and for the Dutch Walrus 220ft (67m) and 2,350 tons. All three have an armament of six 21in torpedo tubes and a submerged speed in the vicinity of 20 knots.

One interesting point is that the number of countries capable of producing their own

submarines is growing rapidly. The traditional manufacturers have been the UK, USA, USSR, France. Germany, Italy and Sweden, and these have been joined by Argentina, Turkey, Yugoslavia, Denmark, Spain, China and North Korea. On the other hand, this is one area where the USA has no capability whatsoever. The last operational diesel-electric submarine built in a US shipyard was the *Bonefish,* launched on November 22, 1958 and when there was a brief spate of

interest in another conventional class in the later 1970s it was a West German yard that made the offer.

THE FUTURE

Perhaps the overriding factor in future submarine design will be that of cost, the inevitable end product of steady growth in size and complexity, even of conventional diesel-electric submarines, apart from those designed for restricted waters such as the Baltic. Despite many resolutions to produce smaller, cheaper designs, this seldom happens, and the major research efforts are now concentrating on making submarines quieter, faster and deeper diving. Quietness does not make a submarine undetectable, but it does make the searcher's work much harder, probably forcing

him to use active sonar and reveal his position.

Possibly the greatest potential breakthrough would be to find a propulsion system which would free the non-nuclear submarine from the surface. It seems unlikely that there will be any major advances in battery design, although a process of continual refinement will obviously take place. Closed-cycle engines and fuel cells both have possibilities, although a practical system in either field has yet to appear. Nevertheless, there does seem to be a reasonable prospect of viable fuel cells for submarines by the mid-1990s. Nothing is known of Soviet developments in this area, but in view of their huge investments in submarine technology there is no reason to think that they will be behind the West in this field.

Below: Despite its growing fleet of nuclear powered attack submarines the Royal Navy has decided to go ahead with the new Upholder (Type 2400) class of diesel-electric submarines to replace its very

successful Oberon and Porpoise classes. The first of the new class has been ordered; they will be very sophisticated and consequently very expensive boats.

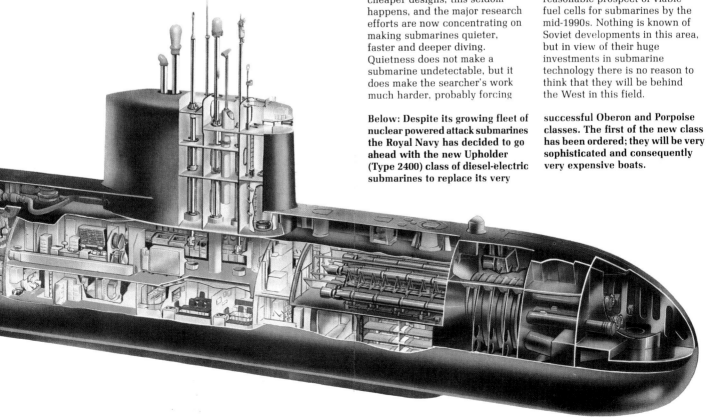

Weapon Systems

There is more discussion of naval armament than any other element of warship design, since in all but a very few cases the weapons are the ships' *raison d'être*. A surface warship needs to be able to engage and defeat other surface warships, submarines and aircraft, but the sensors and weapons systems needed for all these roles would require a very large hull and entail an almost prohibitive cost. The majority of warships are, therefore, optimized for one particular regime, and rely on other members of a task group for an overall balance of capabilities.

Warships' weapons are a manifestation of national design philosophies, although initial impressions of combat capability may sometimes be misleading. A study of contemporary surface warships indicates that the Soviet Navy gives top priority to weapon systems, followed by propulsion, electronics, endurance and, finally, habitability, while most Western naval staffs appear to give top priority to electronics, with habitability, weapon systems, propulsion and endurance being subordinate.

Soviet naval weapons, however, tend to be very obvious, and the Soviet Slava class cruisers, for example, positively bristle with weaponry, their most striking visual feature being eight twin SS-N-12 launchers lined up either side of the bridge. A twin 130mm gun turret is mounted forward, while air defence armament comprises eight SA-N-6 and two SA-N-4 launchers, together with six 30mm Gatlings, and ASW systems include two quintuple torpedo tubes, two RBU-6000 rocket launchers and a Hormone-B helicopter. The nearest US equivalent in size and role is the USS *Virginia*, whose surface weaponry includes two 5in Mk 45 single gun turrets and two quad

Above: Despite the apparent sparseness of weapon systems on their decks, the US Navy's Virginia class cruisers carry DP and CIWS guns plus AA, anti-ship and anti-submarine missiles.

Harpoon launchers, all in small, neat installations dwarfed by the superstructure. Air defence armament consists of two twin Mk 26 launchers for Standard missiles and two 20mm Phalanx CIWS, while the ASW fit includes Asroc, also fired from the Mk 26 launchers, two triple Mk 32 torpedo tubes, and two ASW helicopters in a hangar under the flight-deck. Every bit of deck space on the Soviet ship

is occupied, while the equivalent US cruiser has large areas of what appears to be totally free deck, but the Virginia class ships are every bit as well armed as the Slava and have more reloads, a design feature which may reflect the different concepts of a future conflict, the Soviets aiming for an all-out, short-lived onslaught while the US expects a more protracted campaign of resistance.

Perhaps the second most vexed subject is the balance of armament, and in particular whether the emphasis should be on guns or on guided missiles. Guided missiles are now used in every sphere of naval warfare

against air, surface and sub-surface targets, and they provide rapid response, heavy firepower and far greater ranges than guns. However, most require some form of electronic guidance system, and may thus be susceptible to electronic countermeasures (ECM). The gun, on the other hand, has a much shorter range and, in general terms, delivers a lighter punch, but is virtually immune to ECM. Further, it can be

Below: The only navy planning to equip its carrier aircraft with strategic missiles is the French; the ASMP-armed Super Etendard, shown here during trials, will become operational in 1988.

used to fire warning shots, something quite outside the capability of the missile.

BALLISTIC MISSILES

At the end of World War II naval forces were, as they had always been, primarily concerned with combat on the high seas. Heavy guns could be fired at inshore targets up to ranges of about 25 miles (40km) and carrier-based aircraft were capable of strikes further inland, though seldom more than 100 miles (160km), and there it ended. By the 1950s, however, the US Navy had strike carriers operating the AJ-1 Savage, which was capable of carrying of Mk 5 atomic bomb with a yield well in excess of the 20kT released in the Nagasaki and Hiroshima attacks. This capability, which improved rapidly through the 1950s and 1960s, caused major concern in the Soviet Union and helped spark off its major attack submarine programmes.

The next phase in this expansion of navies' traditional roles came with the ballistic missile submarine. The first true SSBs were the Soviet Navy's diesel-engined Golf class boats armed with three fin-mounted SS-N-3 missiles, but the US Navy moved a quantum jump ahead with the Ethan Allen class armament of 16 Polaris. Since that time the submarines and missiles have improved dramatically, with today's Ohio class SSBNs carrying 24 Tridents and the Soviet Typhoon class SSBNs having a weapon load of 20 SS-N-20.

Few weapon systems in history

have combined more dramatic technological innovations than the bold concept for a submarine-launched ballistic missile, formulated by Admiral W F Rayborn and a team from the Lockheed aerospace corporation. Two vital and far-reaching decisions taken at the very start of the project were to use a solid propellant and to expel the missile from a vertical tube while submerged, but the Polaris project introduced many other novel technologies: lightweight ablative reentry vehicles, miniaturized inertial guidance, miniaturized nuclear and thermonuclear warheads, cold-gas launch techniques, submarine inertial navigation systems and submarine noise reduction to name but a few. When Polaris reached operational status in November 1960 it changed the nature of strategic warfare and deterrence, and subsequent improvement programmes have taken the US Navy from Polaris to Poseidon and now to Trident I (C-4) and Trident II (D-5).

The Soviet Navy programme started with the SS-N-4, a missile so large that it could only just be fitted into a Zulu V class submarine between the keel and the top of the fin. Liquid fuelled and surface launched, it was of limited value and was quickly succeeded by the SS-N-5, still mounted in the fin, but able to be launched while the submarine was submerged. The next missile, SS-N-6, was small enough to be installed within the hull and 16 were carried by the first Soviet purpose-built SSBN, the Yankee class, which equalled the capability of

Left: The 1960s saw the introduction of a new strategic element of sea power, the submarine-launched ballistic missile. First Western type in service was the Polaris shown.

Below: Five navies have SLBMs. Two—the US and Soviet—are developing a first-strike, counter-force capability, but the other, much smaller fleets can only have a second-strike, counter-value role.

SUBMARINE-LAUNCHED BALLISTIC MISSILES (SLBM)

Country	Missile Type	Range		cep		Warhead			Guidance System	IOC	Submarine Type	Number of SSBNs on 1 Jan 86	Number of Missiles per SSBN
		nm	km	nm	m	Type	Number per Missile	Yield (MT)					
USA	Trident C-4	4350	8056	0·25	463	MIRV	10	0·1	Inertial	1979	Ohio	4	24
											Lafayette/Franklin	12	16
	Poseidon C-3	2500	4630	0·25	463	MIRV	8	0·4	Inertial	1971	Lafayette/Franklin	19	16
UK	Polaris A-3	2500	4630	0·5	926	MRV	3	0·2	Inertial	1967	Resolution	4	16
France	MSBS M-20	1860	3445	0·54	1000	Single	1	1	Inertial	1976	Le Redoutable	5	16
	MSBS M-4	2160	4000	0·5	926	MRV	6	0·15	Inertial	1985	L'Inflexible	1	16
USSR	SS-N-6 Mod 2	1300	3000	1	1856	Single	1	1	Inertial	1967	Yankee-I	20	16
	SS-N-6 Mod 3	1600	3000	1	1856	MRV	2	0·2	Inertial	1974			
	SS-N-8 Mod 2	4800	9100	0·84	1560	Single	1	0·8	Stellar-Inertial	1974	Golf-III	1	6
											Hotel-III	1	6
											Delta-I	18	12
											Delta-II	4	16
	SS-N-17	2100	3900	0·75	1410	Single	1	1	Inertial	1977	Yankee-II	1	12
	SS-N-18 Mod 3	3300	6500	0·74	1370	MIRV	7	0·2	Stellar-Inertial	1976	Delta-III	14	16
	SS-N-20	4800	8900	0·35	640	MIRV	9	0·5	Stellar-Inertial	1982	Typhoon	3	20
	SS-N-23	4800	8900	0·35	640	MIRV	10		Stellar-Inertial	1985	Delta-IV	1	16
China	CSS-N-3		2800	n.a.	n.a.	Single	1	2 (?)	Inertial	1983	Daquingyu	1	12

Western boats for the first time. A further step was taken with the SS-N-8 whose range on tests of 4,800nm far exceeded that of any other SLBM, and with SS-N-9 Mod 3 the Soviet Navy at last had a MIRVed missile. The SS-N-18, the next operational missile, has virtually all the capabilities of the American Trident II, but attained them a decade earlier, and its range of 4,300nm in its Mod 2 version is such that it can threaten the USA from almost any part of any ocean in the world. The latest operational missiles are the SS-N-20 and SS-N-23, each with a range of 4,800nm, now at sea in the Typhoon and Delta IV class SSBNs respectively.

All SSBN/SLBM systems are essentially similar, differing only in detail. The ballistic missile system comprises five basic subsystems: the submarine, the navigational system, the fire control system, the missile and the launch system. The SSBN is essentially a sea-mobile launch pad, providing transport and protection from the elements and hostile action for the missiles up to the moment of launch. As part of this function the submarine subsystem provides the other subsystems with electrical, hydraulic and pneumatic power, together with temperature and environmental control, and overall systems monitoring.

The navigation subsystem is responsible for determining the precise position, velocity and attitude of the submarine, and for transmitting this data continuously to the fire control subsystem. The principal means of achieving this is by use of the ships inertial navigation system (SINS), which records every

Above: A simulated launch on board the US Navy's ballistic missile submarine Ohio. Such launch exercises can occur at any time during SSBN patrol, keeping the crews at a peak of readiness.

Below: A time-delay picture shows the multiple independently targetable reentry vehicles (MIRVs) from a Trident missile reentering the atmosphere en route to impact on the US

Below: The missile tubes on USS Ohio, opened in port for the replacement of their Trident I missiles. Ohio carries 24 missiles. The Soviet Typhoon class boats 20, and most other SSBNs 16.

Kwajalein missile range. MIRVs enable a single missile to attack a number of widely separated targets, and the new manoeuvrable reentry vehicles (MARV), will give SSBNs a counter-force capability.

movement of the submarine with reference to a stable platform, and which can be updated by external inputs such as optical and LORAN fixes.

The fire control subsystem has to prepare and fire the submarine's missiles in the minimum possible time. Its essential functions are to set up the missile guidance system inertial platform, to determine true launch bearing, to store and compute target data, and to pass data to the missile guidance computer.

The launch subsystem is designed to store, protect and eject the missiles. The missiles are enclosed in capsules stowed inside shock-protected water-tight launch tubes. Some systems use high-pressure air to eject the missile, while others have a steam generator: in either case the result is a flameless ejection from the launch tube.

The missile is ejected with some force, and when approximately 90ft (27.43m) clear of the tube the first stage motor ignites and the missile is propelled through the surface and far out into the atmosphere. When it has been expended the first stage separates and falls away, and the second stage motor takes over, followed by a third stage on the latest SLBMs such as Trident, SS-N-20 and SS-N-23. During the powered flight phase the missile navigation subsystem is continuously measuring linear accelerations on the basis of its inertial system and altering the trajectory to counteract any unwanted accelerations caused by outside forces.

When it reaches the correct velocity, position and altitude for the assigned targets, the bus carrying the reentry vehicles (RVs) separates from the final stage of the main body of the missile and continues its flight, releasing individual RVs according to predetermined instructions fed to the missile computer just prior to launch. In the terminal phase the warheads reenter the atmosphere at a steep angle, the ablative material with which they are coated absorbing the heat generated by friction with the atmosphere.

The first SLBMs had just one reentry vehicle each, but as the technology developed it became possible to place several warheads—multiple reentry vehicles, or MRVs—on each missile, all being aimed at the same target, but improving the probability of actually hitting the target on the shotgun principle. The next refinement was multiple independently-targetable reentry vehicles (MIRVs), which as their name implies could be directed at different targets by being released from the bus at different points. The latest device is the manoeuvrable reentry vehicle (MARV), which contains a device to steer it precisely onto its targets, so that

its accuracy is independent of the launch accuracy or the precision of the deployment operation in space.

Missile warhead accuracy is assessed in terms of circular error probable (cep), the radius in nautical miles of a notional circle, centred on the point of aim, into which 50 per cent of all warheads launched will fall. In early SLBM systems the missile's navigation system could be no more accurate than the SINS on whose inputs it depended, and early single and multiple RVs had poor ceps, but refinement of both SINS and missile systems has resulted in a marked improvement. Whereas Polaris had a cep of 0.5nm Poseidon RVs have a cep of 0.3nm and those of Trident I still better 0.25nm. Soviet RVs were originally even less accurate than those of the USA (SS-N-5 2.0nm, SS-N-8 0.84nm and SS-N-18 Mod 2 0.76nm) but have since caught up; the cep of SS-N-20, for example, is 0.34nm. As long as these SLBM warheads remained fundamentally inaccurate they could only be used in a counter-value role—that is, they were aimed at cities and other area targets—but the advent of MARVs, with accuracies measured in tens of feet, will completely change the situation and there is a strong possibility that SLBMs will, within the next few years, assume a counter-force as opposed to a counter-value role. It is calculated, for example, that the Mk 600 MARV

to be fitted to Trident 2 will have terminal guidance capable of achieving a cep of 0.07nm, a step with deep significance for the balance of power.

The other nations with SSBN/SLBM systems are the United Kingdom, France and China. The current British Polaris SLBMs were remotored in the early 1980s, and given a new front end of entirely UK origin designated Chevaline, reported to carry six MRVs with a nominal yield of 40kT each. The older French SSBNs carry the M-20 missile, but the latest boats to join the fleet carry the new M-4 with six 150kT MIRVs. The Chinese SSBNs, of which only two are believed to be in service, are armed with the CSS-N-3 SLBM, but no details of warheads have yet been made public.

The UGM 93-A Trident I (C-4) missile design requirement emphasized range. An aerospike is extended after launch to create the aerodynamic effect of a sharp, slender nose, reducing drag by some 50 per cent and, allied to a third-stage motor and improved fuel, increasing range to 4,350nm, compared with the 2,500nm of Poseidon.

To overcome inherent SINS inaccuracies the Trident I's Mk 5 navigation system incorporates stellar updating for the inertial navigation system: the stellar sensor takes a star sight during the post-boost phase, allowing corrections to be made to the flight path, enabling the eight

Below: The table shows that the number of missiles is not a true indicator of the strategic balance and that factors such as the number of RVs, their yield and EMT must also be considered.

Above: Latest fruit of a very successful national nuclear weapon programme is the French MSBS M 4 missile, seen here immediately after firing from the test submarine Gymnote. Launched

at the behest of President de Gaulle, the French programme has resulted in a nationally developed and controlled triad of nuclear weapons, but the sea-based element is the most viable.

Below: Latest operator of SLBMs, the Chinese Navy deploys at least one SSBN armed with the CSS-N-3 missile, seen here after an underwater launch. No picture of the SSBN has been released.

THE USA/USSR SLBM STRATEGIC BALANCE: (a)

Country	Missile	Submarine				Re-Entry Vehicles (RV)		Effective Megatons (b)	
		Type	Number in Fleet	Missiles per SSBN	Total missiles	RVs per missile (c)	Total number of RVs	Yield per RV (MT) (d)	EMT
USA	Trident C-4	Ohio	6	24	144	10	1440	0·1	455
		Lafayette/Franklin	12	16	192	10	1920	0·1	607
	Poseidon C-3	Lafayette/Franklin	19	16	304	8	2432	0·04	486
Total			37		640		5792		1548
USSR	SS-N-6	Yankee-I	20	12	240	1	240	1	240
	SS-N-8	Golf-III	1	6					
		Hotel-III	1	6	292	1	292	0·8	261
		Delta-I	18	12					
		Delta-II	4	16					
	SS-N-17	Yankee-II	1	12	12	1	12	1	12
	SS-N-18	Delta-III	14	16	224	7	1568	0·2	701
	SS-N-20	Typhoon	3	20	60	9	540	0·5	382
	SS-N-23	Delta-IV	1	16	16	10	160	0·5	113
Total			63		844		2812		1709

Notes: (a) Figures given are for inventory totals of submarines, ie, the total number of submarines in the fleet, as of January 1, 1986; numbers actually available are many fewer. The US Navy has 66 per cent of Ohio SSBNs and 50 per cent of Lafayette/Franklin SSBNs at sea at any one time. The USSR, historically, has an average of just 13 SSBNs at sea.

(b) Effective Megatons (EMT) reflects the damage against soft point targets or area targets such as cities. The effect at a specific point distant from Ground Zero is proportional to the cube-root of the yield, while the area affected is proportional to the square of the distance. Thus:
$$\text{EMT} = (\text{Yield})^{2/3} \quad \text{BUT, where Yield} \quad 1\text{MT then EMT} = (\text{Yield})^{1\cdot2}$$

(c) Where missiles carry MIRVs the average load has been taken.

(d) Yield = Raw Yield per RV.

Mk 4 RVs, whose W-76 warheads have a yield of 100kT each, to achieve the reported cep of 0.25nm (457m), which may be reduced to 0.12nm (229m) in future.

Trident I was designed to be similar in payload and accuracy to Poseidon, but to have much greater range to allow the use of larger patrol areas, while Trident II is designed to have much greater accuracy. The resulting missile is longer—45.8ft (13.96m) compared to 34.08ft (10.4m) — and marginally greater in diameter, and is capable of carrying 14 RVs, though the SALT II agreement limits them to ten. The Mk 5 RV has a yield of 475kT and a cep of 0.19nm, but the Mk 600 MARV may be carried in due course, and the Mk 5 is quoted as being designed to take different warheads "tailored to the target assignment". Trident II is scheduled to equip 20 US Navy Ohio class SSBNs and the four new UK SSBNs. Each US SSBN will have 20 missiles, each with ten RVs, giving a total war load of two hundred RVs.

The Soviet Navy has two new SLBMs: the SS-N-20 on the Typhoon class and the SS-N-23 on the Delta IV. Little is known of SS-N-23 except that, somewhat surprisingly, it is liquid fuelled, and that it has greater throw-weight and accuracy than the SS-N-18 fitted to the Delta IIIs. It carries up to seven MIRVs. The SS-N-20 is a three-stage solid-fuel missile with a design range of 4,800nm carrying between six and nine RVs. On October 21, 1982, the first Typhoon class SSBN conducted a simultaneous launch of four SS-N-20s.

CRUISE MISSILES

The original naval strategic missile was the US Navy's Regulus, designed for use by both surface ships and submarines, which saw fleet service in the 1950s and 1960s before being superseded by Polaris. The Soviet Navy has had cruise missiles for many years, but these were limited by range to a tactical role. In the 1970s, however, the US Navy began development of a strategic cruise missile counterpart to the SLBM, since cruise missiles were not covered by existing amrs limitation agreements, and the resulting BGM-109 Tomahawk is now in wide service with the US fleet; a similar missile, the SS-N-21, is in Soviet service.

Tomahawk was originally intended for installation aboard ships in an armoured box launcher and for launch from standard 21in submarine torpedo tubes. This target was achieved and the Tomahawk is now being deployed, the eventual plan being that it will be carried by the refurbished Iowa class battleships, the nuclear powered cruiser Long

Tomahawk attack profile

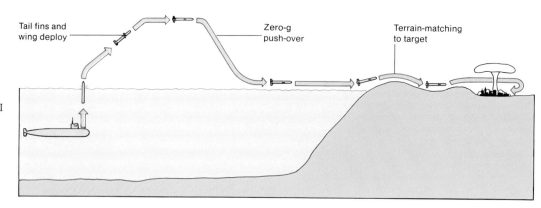

Tail fins and wing deploy

Zero-g push-over

Terrain-matching to target

Above: The US Navy's Tomahawk SLCM is launched vertically as shown, or from torpedo tubes. A lanyard starts the boost motor, which propels the missile up through the surface, whereupon the tail fins and wings deploy and the cruise engine starts. The missile at once does a zero-g push-over to avoid radar detection and descend to very low altitude before heading for land. TERCOM compares the terrain profile with stored data when crossing the coastline for the first positional fix.

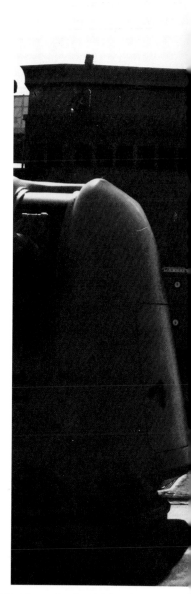

Above: A submarine-launched Tomahawk immediately after leaving the water and prior to the deployment of the wing and tail surfaces. Such missiles give SSNs a stategic attack capability.

Right: A surface-launched Tomahawk leaves its armoured box launcher on board the Spruance class destroyer USS Merrill (DD 976) during trials of the new system in 1981.

Beach (CGN-9), the conventionally powered cruisers of the California, Virginia and Ticonderoga (from CG-52 onward) classes, the Spruance and Arleigh Burke class destroyers, and most of the Los Angeles (SSN-688) class SSNs. The earlier Los Angeles boats will use Tomahawk in the torpedo-tube mode, with 12 missiles per boat, but following a reappraisal by the US Navy SSN-721 and subsequent boats will have 15 vertical launch tubes for Tomahawk in the bow casing between the outer and inner hulls, avoiding a reduction in torpedo capacity and causing no interference to other systems.

When fired from a submarine Tomahawk is expelled from the launch tube hydraulically. When a lanyard some 33ft (10m) long

runs taut, it fires a rocket boost motor which burns for about seven seconds to drive it in a 50+ degree climb up through the surface and into the atmosphere, where the wings and tail extend and the gas turbine is started up. The missile then noses over to avoid radar detection and begins its cruise toward the target, travelling at very low level at about Mach 0.7. Guidance is inertial until land is reached when the terrain comparison (TERCOM) system starts comparing the ground below with data on magnetic tape fed in from the submarine, immediately prior to launch.

TERCOM does not operate continuously, as that could alert defences and attract countermeasures, but switches on when crossing the coast and

at other selected reference points to update the inertial system, which remains in command throughout. The missile can be programmed to approach the target from any direction to confuse defences, and its accuracy is astonishing, cep being approximately 33 yards (30m); payload can be either high explosives or the W-80 nuclear warhead, which has a 200-250kT yield. Operation from surface ships is identical, except that launch is direct from a Mk 143 armoured box launcher, but in most ships the long-term plan is to install Mk 41 vertical launch systems.

The Soviet Navy is producing similar systems, the smallest of which is the SS-N-21, designed like Tomahawk to be fired from standard 21in torpedo tubes.

Possible platforms for this missile include all recent SSNs, including those of the Victor III, Akula, Mike and Sierra classes, as well as the Yankee class former SSBNs. According to data available by early 1986, the SS-N-21 is slightly larger than Tomahawk, with a range of the order of 1,620nm, but the second Soviet naval SLCM, the SS-NX-24, is much bigger, with a length of around 40ft (12m) and a diameter of 4.1ft (1.25m), while the sharply swept wings have a span of 19.5ft (5.94m). Another of the Yankee class SSBNs is being converted to a trials platform for this new SLCM, which will probably become operational in 1987/88. Both systems are likely to be as accurate as their US counterparts, and could presumably also have either nuclear or conventional

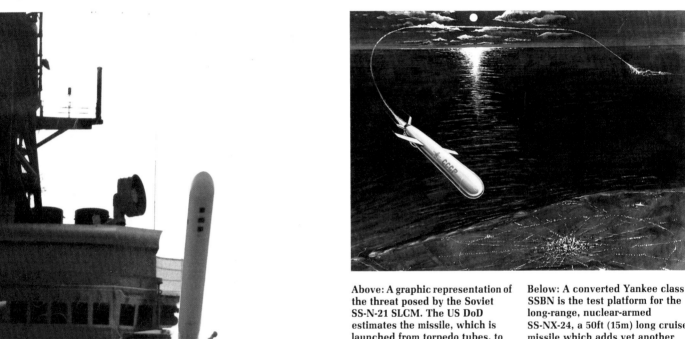

Above: A graphic representation of the threat posed by the Soviet SS-N-21 SLCM. The US DoD estimates the missile, which is launched from torpedo tubes, to have a range of 1,620nm (3,000km).

Below: A converted Yankee class SSBN is the test platform for the long-range, nuclear-armed SS-NX-24, a 50ft (15m) long cruise missile which adds yet another dimension to the Soviet threat.

warheads: given sufficiently accurate guidance systems, the latter could pose a significant non-nuclear threat.

ANTI-SHIP MISSILES

More, perhaps, than any other, naval forces have concentrated on missile development for both offensive and defensive purposes and there can be little doubt that naval missiles have been developed to a higher point than those used in any other form of warfare. The first significant demonstration of the power of anti-ship missiles came in 1967, when the Israeli destroyer *Eilat* was sunk by an SS-N-2 fired from an Egyptian Navy patrol boat. The impression formed then was reinforced in 1982, when Argentinian naval aircraft using Exocet missiles to attack British ships succeeded in sinking HMS *Sheffield*.

In its shipborne form the Exocet is used by many navies and a British County class destroyer was damaged off the Falklands by an Exocet launched from a naval mounting, albeit sitting on a wheeled trailer near Port Stanley. Since the end of that war Exocets have been used in the Middle East Gulf War and a number of very large merchant ships have been hit.

Despite the worldwide publicity generated by the loss of HMS *Coventry* and the merchant ship *Atlantic Conveyor* to single hits, a sober assessment indicates that more Exocets were foiled than reached their target and that the hit on HMS *Glamorgan* did only very limited damage. Further, the Exocets used by Iraq in the Gulf War have rarely put the ships completely out of action. Exocet, like many other ASMs, is subsonic and the latest fast-reaction SAMs and CIWS guns

should be able to defeat it under most circumstances. However, the new generation of ASMs, such as the Soviet SS-N-19, have speeds of up to Mach 2.5 and may well strain current defence systems beyond their limits.

An incoming Exocet flying at a height of 7-10ft (2-3m) and a speed in excess of Mach 0.9 should be detected by a warship's surveillance radar at a range of some 10nm, or approximately 60 seconds before impact. Radar tracking would be initiated at a range of 3.4nm, with 20 seconds to go, and a missile such as Seawolf launched when the incoming round was 2nm distant, or about

10-13 seconds before impact. This is a short enough timescale and requires fully automated control; indeed, it was reported from the South Atlantic that ships' crews were only alerted that an attack was imminent when the Seawolf missiles were launched; without the computer that would have been just too late. However, an SS-N-19 travelling at Mach 2.5 and at the same sea-skimming height would substantially reduce the time available to the defences—first acquisition at 10nm would be only about 19 seconds before impact.

The Soviet Kirov class battle-cruiser mounts 20

SS-N-19s in vertical launch tubes on the foredeck, while the Soviet cruisers tend to carry their anti-ship missiles in deck-mounted tubes set at about 20°; in neither case does it appear that reloading at sea is possible. The SS-N-19 has an estimated range of some 310 miles (500km) and a speed in the region of Mach 2.5, and external target detection and designation by aircraft is probably combined with on-board inertial guidance and homing systems.

The US Navy's principal anti-ship missile, the RGM-84A Harpoon, has a turbojet cruise engine and its flight profile is much lower than that of the

Above: An Exocet anti-ship missile levels off in the cruise after launch from the French Navy frigate D'Estienne d'Orves. The two launch tubes are mounted either side of the funnel.

Below: MM.40 Exocet is launched from a French Navy warship. Longer and heavier than the earlier MM.38, the MM.40 has much greater range—38nm (70km) compared to 23nm (43km). The

Exocet showed its capabilities in the South Atlantic war of 1982, when both air- and land-launched missiles scored hits on British ships. Air-lanched Exocets have also been used in the Gulf war.

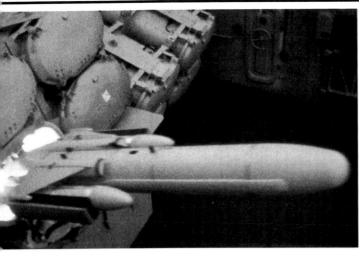

Above: The OTO Melara Otomat anti-ship missile has a range of 50nm (92km) and a 440lb (200kg) warhead. The Mk 2 is used in the Teseo system and is mounted in several Italian warships.

Below: McDonnell Douglas Harpoon Block 1C anti-ship missile is fired from a canister launcher on board the cruiser USS *Leahy* (CG 16) in June 1985. More than 3,000 Harpoon have been delivered.

Above: Anti Navire Supersonique (ANS) is being developed jointly by Aerospatiale of France and MBB of West Germany as the next-generation anti-ship missile system. The market is potentially huge.

SS-N-19, but with a final manoeuvre phase to evade CIWS defences. No data inputs are required from the ship after launch and a computer guides the missile to the vicinity of the target, where a frequency-agile homing radar takes over for the final phase.

Anti-ship missiles now form an essential part of the armament of virtually all surface warships, but none of the systems has been tested in a full-scale ship-to-ship engagement.

SURFACE-TO-AIR MISSILES

By the early 1960s it had become clear that a layered defence was necessary for ships at sea, with ship-based aircraft forming the outer layer, long-range area defence missiles providing the intermediate layer and a mixture of short-range missiles and guns providing the final point defences. One irony of the present situation is that the success of the defences in forcing attacking aircraft to fly very low and launch their missiles from a great distance has presented the ship with an even more difficult target to deal with, and there has been a resurgence of interest in the gun, which offers considerable advantages as a component of a point defence system. However, a new threat is that of saturation attacks by high-altitude, supersonic cruise missiles, fired in a heavy ECM environment and diving very steeply and very fast on to the target.

One of the most widely used of contemporary area defence SAMs is the US Navy's Standard. Both RIM-66 Standard Medium Range and RIM-67 Standard Extended Range are fitted with conventional high explosive warheads and either point-detonating or proximity fuzes, and while the latter has separate solid-propellant booster and sustainer rocket motors, the former has a single dual-thrust motor. All electronic circuits are solid-state and powered by a dry battery, which has reduced warm-up time from Tartar's 26 seconds to just

one second; very good ECCM is built in, and the system is constantly being upgraded.

The initial Standard Missile-1 (SM-1) is still in use in many ships, but the current Standard Missile-2 (SM-2) includes such improvements as a monopulse receiver; an inertial reference unit for mid-course guidance; a two-way telemetry link for missile position reporting, target position updating and guidance correction; a digital computer; and a new semi-automatic terminal guidance receiver. The inertial reference unit enables the missile to navigate itself to the vicinity of the target, where the semi-active radar homer takes over, giving a very energy-efficient trajectory, and a coupled autopilot for improved performance against diving, weaving targets. Standard SM-2 also has an anti-ship capability.

The Soviet Navy has long been an exponent of air defence missile systems: the SA-N-1 Goa, for example, became operational in 1961 and is still in service in five classes of destroyer and cruiser. The most recent air defence system is based on the SA-N-6 missile and arms the Kirov class battle-cruisers and Slava class cruisers. The missile has a single-stage solid-fuel motor giving a range of 75nm and a speed of Mach 3, and is armed with either 200lb (91kg) of high explosives or a nuclear warhead. The Kirov class ships each have 96 SA-N-6 missiles in 12 vertical launchers, each with an eight-cell magazine. The SA-N-6 is capable of engaging cruise missiles.

Naval point defence missile systems have to combat very fast, close-range, low-flying or steep-diving aircraft or missile targets—a very difficult proposition, but one which has resulted in numerous systems being produced around the world. The US Navy fielded the Basic Point Defence Missile System (BPDMS) in the 1960s using the Sparrow III missile launched from a modified eight-

Above: A Standard SM-2 (ER) missile is launched from the cruiser USS Ticonderoga (CG 47). Standard replaced the earlier Tartar, Talos and Terrier SAM systems in its SM-1(MR), SM-2(MR) and SM-1(ER) versions respectively, and has proved very successful. The SM-2ER also has an anti-ship capability.

Surface-to-air missiles

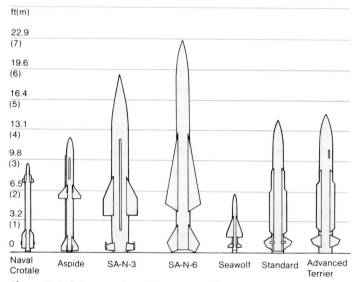

Above: A vital element of a modern ship's armament is its air defence missile system. preferably backed by a gun-based Close-In Weapon System (CIWS). Due to the inherited range limits on surveillance radars on ships at sea, such missiles must have rapid response and high acceleration and manoeuvrability, while fore control must be automated: human responses are too slow.

cell Asroc launcher mounted on a modified 3in/50 gun carriage. This was a fairly crude device and has been succeeded by the very successful NATO Sea Sparrow, based on BPDMS but incorporating numerous major improvements. The RIM-7H-5 missile has folding fins and is installed in the compact and lightweight Mk 29 launcher.

The greatest improvement is the Hughes Mk 23 target acquisition and fire control system, which combines L-band

Left: The French Naval Crotale air defence missile system is derived from the successful land-based system. Like many modern naval SAMs is has a secondary anti-ship capability.

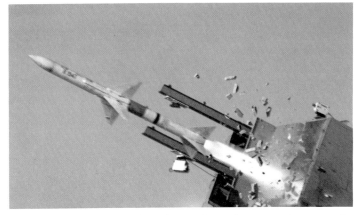

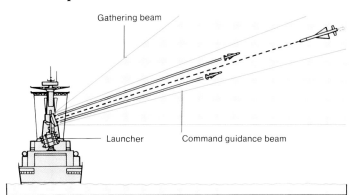

Seawolf operation

Gathering beam

Launcher

Command guidance beam

Above: Sea Sparrow launch. Both the Basic Point-Defence Missile System (BPDMS) and the later NATO Sea Sparrow system use versions of this missile, which has an extremely rapid response time and semi-active radar homing.

Below: The US Navy's Improved Point Defence Surface Missile System comprises the Mk23 target acquisition and fire control system whose display is seen here and an eight-round NATO Sea Sparrow launcher.

Above: The principal elements of the Seawolf system, which is equally effective against missiles diving onto the ship and surface skimmers, are shown here. Seawolf uses command-to-line-of-sight guidance with radar

differential or TV tracking and radio command. Error signals proportional to the missile deviation from the datum are processed, and coded correction signals are sent to the missile to return it to the correct flightpath.

pulse-Doppler radar with an IFF system capable of tracking 54 targets simultaneously. A total of 53 USN ships are being fitted with NATO Sea Sparrow, together with frigates belonging to Belgium, the Netherlands, the Federal Republic of Germany, Denmark, Italy, Norway and Spain. The Japanese Navy is also procuring this system.

Soviet Navy point defence missile systems are the SA-N-5, a navalized version of the man-portable SA-7 Grail, and the SA-N-8 mounted on the Udaloy class destroyers. One of the most advanced of all anti-missile systems is the British Seawolf, which can be installed in warships of as little as 1,000 tons displacement, and whose

entire operational sequence is automatic and timed in milliseconds. The Seawolf has destroyed an incoming 4.5in shell during tests but, more importantly, it did very well under actual combat conditions in the South Atlantic war. Sea-wolf is currently deployed in six- or four-canister launch units with manual reloading, presumably to avoid the weight and complexity of an automatic system, and is also available in a twin standard ISO 6m container installation. A vertical launch installation is under development.

GUNS

Advocates of missile armament became so powerful in some

navies that there was very strong pressure in the 1960s and 1970s to do away with guns altogether, and some warships appeared with only a token gun armament—the British Type 22 Batch 1 frigates, for example, had just two 40mm guns—but the folly of such a proposition has been shown repeatedly, and the need for at least one effective gun is now accepted. Fortunately, modern naval guns are highly automated and very compact; the US Navy's 5in/54 calibre Mk 45, for example, weighs 25 tonnes and fires 20 rounds per minute, and none of the six crew is in the turret.

One of the most successful Western guns is the Italian OTO Melara single 76mm, which is in

Above: The Italian OTO Melara 76mm/62 naval gun, seen here on a test rig, has been adopted by at least 35 navies. Its rate of fire is variable between 10 and 85 rounds per minute.

service with 35 navies. The weapon's firing rate is variable between 10 and 85rds/min and it can fire 80 rounds without reloading. It fires a 14lb (6.5kg) shell to a maximum range of 17,498 yards (16km), and total installation weight is 7.5 tonnes. OTO Melara are developing a new shell which has the same weight and ballistic performance as the present shell, but with much greater lethality, being filled with 630gm of cast Compound Three explosive and 4,660 0.2gm tungsten spheres. A proximity fuse detonates the shell some 26ft (8m) from the target.

By far the largest gun currently in service in any navy is the US Navy's 16in/50, of which nine are mounted in three triple Mk 7 mounts on each of the Iowa class battleships. These have a range of some 41,622 yards (38,060m) firing a high-capacity projectile weighing 1,900lb (862kg), of which 154lb (70kg) is the HE payload, or 40,185 yards (36,746m) with an armour piercing shell. Some 18,000 war rounds are currently available, and although the production line is still in existence it would require some six months to reactivate. Effective as they are, it is highly unlikely that guns of this calibre will ever be made again.

Both the Soviet Army and the Soviet Navy have long traditions of effective gun design, producing weapons which have excellent range coupled with accuracy and good payload. The Soviet Navy has never allowed itself to be seduced by the all-missile lobby; all its major warships have at least one gun turret and new designs are constantly appearing. The somewhat elderly 130mm/60 Model 1953/56, for example, which is installed in twin turrets on ships such as Kotlin class destroyers and Sverdlov class cruisers, has a range of 18,600 yards (17km) firing a 59.5lb (27kg) shell at 15rds/min. There is, however, a newer 130mm twin installation fitted in the *Frunze* (one turret), Slava class (one turret) and Sovremennyy class (two turrets), which is fully automatic and water-cooled, indicating a very high rate of fire—possibly as much as 30-35rds/min. There is also a recent type of 100mm gun in a single turret mounted on Udaloy class cruisers and the battle-cruiser *Kirov*.

Apart from reducing weight and increasing automation, designers have managed to squeeze ever greater range out of the gun. Much work has been devoted to investigating rocket-assisted projectiles (RAPs), particularly in the US in the 1960s and early 1970s, and some results were encouraging, with

OTO Melara 76mm/62 Compact feeding and loading system

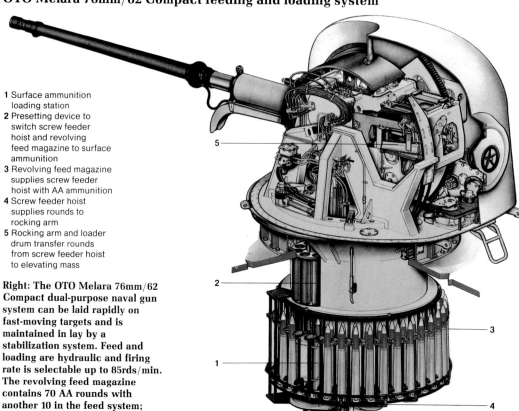

1 Surface ammunition loading station
2 Presetting device to switch screw feeder hoist and revolving feed magazine to surface ammunition
3 Revolving feed magazine supplies screw feeder hoist with AA ammunition
4 Screw feeder hoist supplies rounds to rocking arm
5 Rocking arm and loader drum transfer rounds from screw feeder hoist to elevating mass

Right: The OTO Melara 76mm/62 Compact dual-purpose naval gun system can be laid rapidly on fast-moving targets and is maintained in lay by a stabilization system. Feed and loading are hydraulic and firing rate is selectable up to 85rds/min. The revolving feed magazine contains 70 AA rounds with another 10 in the feed system; ammunition used for surface targets is manually loaded.

the 5in round giving an increase in range from 14,000 yards (12,800m) to 22,000 yards (20,117m); but, as always, there are penalties. In this case not only was accuracy reduced, but the weight of explosive fell from 7.9lb (3.58kg) for the standard round to just 3.5lb (1.59kg) for the RAP, even though the latter's total weight was 55lb (24.9kg) as opposed to 42.6lb (19.3kg). No RAP is in current naval use.

The threat from air attack and sea-skimming missiles has given rise to a requirement for CIWS for last-ditch defence, in which extremely fast reaction times and a heavy volume of fire are

essential. The US Navy's answer is the Mk 15 Phalanx, which incorporates the M61A1 20mm six-barrel Gatling gun into a very intelligent, fully automatic closed-loop control system; both the outgoing projectile and the incoming missile are tracked by radar and the angular error is used to correct the next burst as the system seeks constantly to eliminate the difference. Accuracy increases as the target approaches, reaching a peak at about 550 yards (500m). The training rate is 100°/sec and elevation is 86°/sec between limits of +80° and -25°. The system is completely self-

contained with a pair of radar transmitters sharing a common antenna in a housing on top of the gun unit. Ammunition is the Mk 149 depleted-uranium sub-calibre round, 1,000 of which are housed in a magazine beneath the fire unit, and effective range is 450-1,500 yards (410-1,370m). Phalanx has proved highly successful in service and was bought as a matter of operational urgency by the Royal Navy for installation in the Invincible class aircraft carriers following the 1982 South Atlantic war.

Another stand-alone CIWS is Goalkeeper, whose seven-barrel GAU-8/A 30mm Gatling gun has a rate of fire of around 4,200rds/min and which follows a similar general concept. Goalkeeper systems are being installed in Kortenaer class frigates and have also been ordered by the Royal Navy.

Below: The triple 16in guns mounted by the US Iowa class battleships are likely to remain the largest in service for the foreseeable future. Each barrel is 50 calibres long and weighs around 104 tons.

Below: The Mk15 Vulcan/Phalanx 20mm Close-In Weapon System is completely self-contained and has proved a great success. It is widely used in the US Navy and large numbers have been sold to other navies.

Creusot-Loire 100mm Compact system

1 Mount power supply box
2 Compressed air supply panel
3 Mount maintenance unit
4 Elevation motor
5 Train motor
6 Mount electronics box
7 Armature shunt box
8 Compressed air supply
9 Water cooling unit
10 Hydraulic power unit
11 Converter unit
12 Magazine captain's box
13 Secondary magazine (special ammunition)
14 Ammunition cost
15 Main magazine (conventional ammunition)
16 Electrical junction box
17 Remote control cabinet
18 Processing cabinet

——— Electrical circuit
——— Water supply
——— Hydraulic circuit

Above: The Creusot-Loire 100mm Compact dual-purpose gun has a double water-cooled barrel with a life of more than 3,000 rounds, despite the 90rds/min rate of fire. Total installation weight is only 17 tons.

Below: The Creusot-Loire 100mm Compact, seen here on the fore-deck of a D'Estienne d'Orves class frigate, is being developed with the French Navy's Cassard class anti-aircraft destroyers in mind as potential platforms.

Above: The Goalkeeper is a fully automatic and self-contained CIWS jointly developed by Hollandse Signaalapparaten and General Electric. It uses the seven-barrelled GAU-8/A 30mm Gatling gun.

The Soviet Navy has produced two CIWS, which it obviously finds very satisfactory as they are installed in many different ships. There is a twin 30mm/65 mounting in a fully automatic turret, which has a range of some 3,280-4,370 yards (3,000-4,000m) and a combined firing rate of about 1,000rds/min. This weapon is usually associated with the Drum Tilt fire control radar and sometimes with the Muff Cob. There is also a six-barrel 30mm Gatling design, similar in many ways to the US Phalanx but using a separately mounted Bass Tilt radar. Nevertheless, it is an extremely neat installation and is fitted to at least 20 classes of

Soviet warship ranging in size from the big *Kiroc* class battle cruisers to fast attack craft as small as 210 tons.

ANTI-SUBMARINE WEAPONS

The archetypical World War II ASW weapon, the depth-charge, is rarely used by surface ships, since to allow a modern submarine within launcher range—about 2 miles (3.2km)—would be very hazardous. However, depth charges are still used by some surface warships, as well as by ASW aircraft and helicopters, and two current examples are the British Mk 11, which contains 180lb (81.6kg) of Torpex, and the Chilean AS-228.

The other World War II weapon, the ASW mortar, is still used in some navies. The British Squid and Limbo are installed in a number of ex-Royal Navy ships

Bofors proximity-fuzed ammunition anti-missile operation

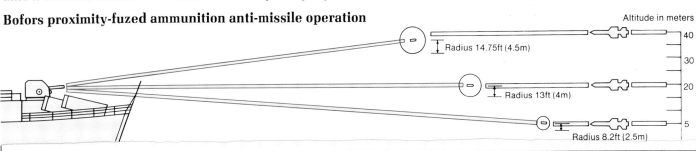

Altitude in meters

Radius 14.75ft (4.5m)
Radius 13ft (4m)
Radius 8.2ft (2.5m)

40
30
20
5

Above: One method of dealing with incoming anti-ship missiles is by direct fire from high-performance gun systems. The cross-sectional area of the missiles is small—that of Exocet, for example, is only some 149sq in (962cm²)— and to

engage such a target head on, especially one at near supersonic speed just above wave level, and at a safe distance from the ship, is a major undertaking. Nevertheless, several systems have been produced which are able to meet the

requirement, among them the Phalanx, Goalkeeper, Spanish Meroka and Soviet ADMG-630 Gatling. This diagram shows the triggering radius for the Bofors PFHE Mk 2 ammunition fired by the Breda Twin 40mm/70 gun used

in the Dardo CIWS, which must be minimized to adjust to sea-clutter, a factor which is more critical the nearer the target ASM is to the wavetops, and one which demands an exceptionally accurate proximity fuze.

and are also to be found on some postwar ships such as the Vosper Mk 1 corvettes of the Ghanaian Navy. The Italian Navy also uses the Menon mortar in some of its frigates.

ASW rocket launchers are more effective and capable of longer ranges, and the Swedish firm of Bofors produces launchers based on its 375mm rocket. The rocket weighs some 507lb (230kg), with a 176lb (80kg) hexotonal warhead, and has an effective range to 100ft (30m) depth of 1,728-3,964 yards (1,580-3,625m). The launch tubes are grouped in four on earlier models and in pairs on the latest, while the French firm of Creusot-Loire produces a six-barrel launcher under licence from Bofors. These systems are used by a large number of navies.

The Soviet Navy produces a series of 250mm and 300mm rocket launchers which are installed on virtually every surface warship. The 250mm bomb is estimated to weigh between 396lb and 441lb (180-200kg), of which the warhead could be expected to account for about 150lb (68kg). Designated RBU or MBU, these systems have a numerical suffix which denotes their range in metres—RBU-2500, for example, has a range of 2,734yd (2,500m)—and the barrels are assembled in combinations varying from as few as five to as many as 16. The RBU-6000, one of the latest 300mm systems, has automatic reloading and is installed on most new-build ships. The RBU-1000, also 300mm, is a six-barrelled weapon fitted on the quarter deck of larger ships such as Kirov and the Kresta class and appears to be designed to attack acoustic torpedoes as they begin their terminal drive towards the ship's propellers.

Far more effective, but with major political implications and therefore possible tactical limitations, is the nuclear depth bomb, exemplified by the US B57 Mod 1, whose yield is variable between 5kT and 10kT. This can be deployed on the S-3 Viking, P-3 Orion and SH-3 Sea King in US service and on similar aircraft and helicopters with the British, Netherlands and West German forces. This may be the only weapon which could have any significant effect against some of the latest submarines, with their dramatically strengthened hulls.

Mines have a major role in anti-submarine warfare, though the threat posed by moored and bottom-sitting mines may be limited by the mine-warning devices now carried by most submarines. Potentially more effective is the US Navy Captor (encapsulated torpedo), which is designed exclusively for attacking submarines and consists of a Mk 46 Mod 4 torpedo housed in a tube. It can be laid by submarines, aircraft

Anti-submarine missiles

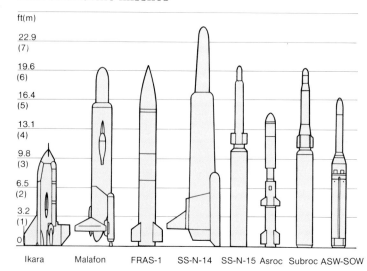

Above: A crucial ASW problem is that of delivering torpedoes to distant targets. Under their own power torpedoes are too slow and limited in range and are liable to detection, and one answer is to convey the torpedo to the vicinity of the target by means of either a rocket or a winged, turbojet-powered delivery vehicle. Such missiles normally drop the torpedo by parachute.

Above: ASW rocket launchers are installed on most Soviet Navy warships; this is one of two RBU-6000s on a Petya II class frigate. The figure in the designation gives the range in meters.

Below: US Navy RUR-5A Asroc is launched from an eight-cell Mk 112 launcher. Range is estimated to be between 1.25 and 6.2 miles (2-10km); payload is a Mk 46 acoustic homing torpedo.

and surface ships and sits on the ocean floor monitoring all passing maritime traffic using passive sonar with a range of about 3,000ft (1,000m), gated to exclude surface traffic. On identification of a submarine target the active sonar is switched on, optimum launch time is computed and the torpedo is launched. No IFF is fitted, so friendly submarines must be kept clear of any Captor minefields. Virtually all submarines are fitted with special detectors to warn them of mines in the vicinity.

To overcome the problem of reaching the target submarine before it can itself attack its hunter, a number of stand-off weapons have been developed to deliver a depth-charge or torpedo by means of a carrier missile or rocket. The US Asroc (Anti-submarine rocket) consists of a Mk 46 acoustic homing torpedo with a strap-on rocket motor and either a 971lb (44kg) explosive or a W44 1kT nuclear device (the nuclear warhead is for US Navy versions only). Similar weapons are made in France (Malafon), Australia (Ikara) and the USSR (FRAS-1/SS-N-14). Ranges are not great; for example, that of Asroc is estimated to be 1.25-6.2 miles (2-10km).

The US Subroc (submarine rocket) and Soviet SS-N-15/16 provide submarines with a similar capability, and are fired underwater from standard torpedo tubes before driving to the surface and then up into the air. Both SS-N-16 and Subroc have nuclear warheads, in the latter case the W55 with a yield reported to be approximately 1kT (there is no alternative HE warhead).

The US Navy intends to produce a common successor to Subroc and Asroc, known as the Anti-Submarine Warfare—

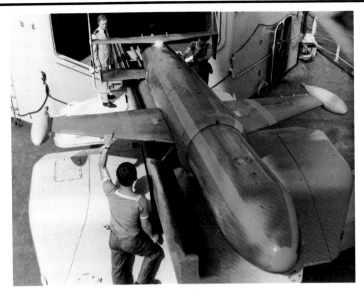

Above: The French Malafon ASW weapon system consists of a winged vehicle and a homing torpedo. It is launched by two booster rockets, which cut out after a few seconds, then glides to the target.

Above right: ASW-SOW (Anti-Submarine Warfare—Stand-Off Weapon) is an encapsulated torpedo which floats to the surface where the rocket motor ignites and propels it to the target area.

ASW-SOW attack profile

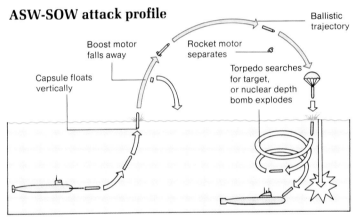

Above: ASW-SOW gives submarines a stand-off capability against other submerged submarines. Launch is from a torpedo tube and control fins steer it to the surface, where both end caps are

jettisoned and the rocket motor fires. The missile follows a ballistic trajectory, dropping the rocket motor before being lowered to the water by parachute. Payload is an Advanced Lightweight Torpedo.

Stand-Off Weapon (ASW-SOW). This is designed to combat the threat posed by such submarines as the Soviet Akula, Mike and Sierra classes, and estimates of its range vary from 35 to 100 miles (56-160km). Vertically launched from surface ships or expelled from standard 21in submarine torpedo tubes, the system comprises a common missile carrying either the Advanced Lightweight Torpedo (ALWT) or a nuclear depth-charge. The latter would almost certainly be a new common device to replace the US Navy's current W55, B57 and W44 nuclear warheads.

SUBMARINE WEAPONS

After World War II virtually all submarine guns were discarded, and for several decades the only weapon available to attack and patrol submarines was the torpedo, with the frequent result that very advanced and sophisticated SSNs and SSBNs have been at sea with torpedoes little better in performance than those of World War II, and some actually of wartime manufacture.

The recent history of the torpedo has been extraordinary, with vast sums being expended by many nations on some extremely expensive and not infrequently abortive development programmes. Even now, after all that expenditure, the current generation has a top speed no better, and possibly even worse, than that of its quarry. The US Mk 46, for example, has a speed of 40 kt, less than that of the Soviet Alfa class, making a stern chase completely out of the question.

The problem of lack of speed and range for torpedoes has been partially answered for surface ships by the use of helicopters and stand-off

Left: A US Navy Subroc powers away from the surface, its launch submarine hidden in the depths below. Range is around 35 miles (56km) and the warhead is a W-55 1kT nuclear depth bomb.

delivery systems, and in the case of submarines by Subroc, but there is still a need for a much faster torpedo. The US Advanced Capability (ADCAP) programme for the Mk 48 torpedo will raise its speed to 55 kt, and the British Tigerfish is reported to be capable of a similar speed, while the next-generation British torpedo, Spearfish, uses a gas turbine and a pump-jet to attain even higher speeds.

Another serious problem is that submarines in general, and Soviet submarines in particular, are becoming much bigger, and some are being constructed with double hulls, making them much stronger and more survivable, and even the smaller conventional submarines are being constructed of stronger materials in order to improve diving depth. At the same time, the general tendency among ASW forces has been to use lightweight torpedoes, both on aircraft and surface ships, and such weapons have necessarily limited warhead weight. The US Navy Mk 46 torpedo, for example, which is in widescale use among Western navies, has a warhead weighing just 99lb (45kg), which compares somewhat poorly with the 588lb (267kg) warhead on the Mk 48 or the 330lb (150kg) warhead on the French L5.

One answer is simply to make bigger torpedoes, but this results in space problems for submarines and payload problems for airborne ASW platforms, particularly helicopters, so some form of improvement such as a directed-energy (hollow-charge) warhead would appear to be required, the only apparent alternative being the use of nuclear warheads, which has serious political implications.

Torpedo guidance systems vary considerably. The US Navy's Mk 46, for example, has an active-passive homing head and either follows the target's radiated noise or, if the target is silent, switches to active sonar.

The US Mk 48 Mod 3 uses command guidance by wire in the mid-course part of its run, utilizing a two-way link so that it can send sonar information back to the launching submarine; it then switches to an active-passive terminal homing head.

The British Stingray guidance system is even more complex. On launch an active/passive sonar transducer works in the passive mode, before changing to the active mode automatically as soon as there is any indication that the target has become aware that it is under attack. Guidance wires link the torpedo to the launching submarine, and, as with the US Mk 48 Mod 3, not only are commands fed to the torpedo but sonar data information is also passed back to the submarine.

In general terms, however, the capabilities of current torpedoes lag behind those of the sonars that support them: they are slow, lacking in range, very noisy and, in many instances, unreliable as well. Reports of the 1982 South Atlantic war, for example, abound with stories of both the Royal Navy and the Argentinian Navy suffering from torpedo malfunctions.

The USSR and some other nations are experimenting with electric motors; at the moment these produce torpedoes which are quiet, but slow and lacking

Sub-Harpoon attack profile

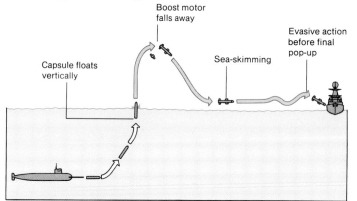

Above: The encapsulated Sub-Harpoon fits standard 21in torpedo tubes, from which it is ejected at 50ft/sec (15.24m/sec). Control fins steer it to the surface, where end caps are jettisoned, the rocket

in range, and improved performance can only be obtained by increasing the battery power, which means bigger torpedoes, or reducing warhead size, which could mean lack of effectiveness. Torpedo sonar, too, needs to be improved

Below: Multi-million dollar, highly automated nuclear submarines still depend upon the skill and muscle-power of the crew to strike down torpedoes in the cramped confines of the torpedo flat.

fires and the missile takes off. The rocket is dropeed after three seconds, the turbojet starts and the missile descends to its sea-skimming mode for the approach to the target area.

and the US Defense Advanced Research Projects Agency (DARPA) is working on this, possibly heading toward a torpedo with on-board signal processing coupled with a two-way fibreoptic link to the parent submarine. A further project is

Below: The devastating effect of a Marconi Tigerfish wireguided torpedo on the hulk of one of the Royal Navy's County class destroyers, HMS Devonshire, during trials.

to adopt such a system for use with ASW aircraft, by using a fibreoptic link from the torpedo to an air-dropped buoy containing a radio uplink to the aircraft.

Recently, a variety of new weapons has made submarines capable of nuclear or conventional strikes against targets far inland. The submarine-launched cruise missile has been around for some years and, as described earlier, the Soviet Navy has long had specialized boats to carry them.

The US Navy took a different approach and instead of developing specialized submarines decided to produce weapons which would be launched from standard 21in torpedo tubes. These materialized in the form of the Sub-Harpoon anti-ship missile and the Tomahawk anti-ship (T-ASM) and land attack (T-LAM) missiles, but after vast expenditure on the latter programme it has been realised that Tomahawk takes up too much valuable space in the torpedo rooms and it has therefore been decided to fit them in vertical tubes inside the upper casing between the bow sonar and the forward end of the pressure hull. This is a significant capability enhancement at little cost, but it is now irrelevant as to whether the missile can fit a torpedo tube or not.

Harpoon can attack ships out to 60 miles (97km) and the T-ASM to 250 miles (400km),

Above: A French submarine-launched SM.39 Exocet anti-ship missile, showing the separation of the missile from the launch capsule which brought it to the surface. The sequence shows clearly that, unlike many other encapsulated missiles, the SM.39 leaves the surface under full power and that separation takes place while airborne, thus saving valuable seconds in the attack.

Below: The weapons available to a modern submarine now include not only the traditional direct-attack anti-ship and ASW torpedo, but also anti-ship missiles and nuclear-armed crusie missiles.

Los Angeles class weapon systems

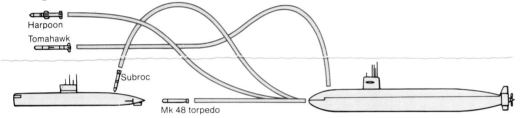

Harpoon
Tomahawk
Subroc
Mk 48 torpedo

while the T-LAM has range of 1,367 miles (2,200km) with either conventional or nuclear warheads. The main problem with T-LAM is that to exploit its capabilities fully it needs external target information and a system known as Outlaw Shark is being deployed to achieve this. The deployment of Tomahawk in this role has, however, increased the need for two-way communications with submarines, a notoriously difficult problem.

The only other submarine-launched anti-ship missile is the French SM39 Exocet, a new version of the very successful missile which achieved such a reputation in the 1982 South Atlantic war. Launched from a standard 21in torpedo tube, the SM39 has a range of over 312 miles (50km).

One of the greatest threats to a submarine on or near the surface comes from aircraft, whose approach is difficult for the submarine to detect under some circumstances. Some years ago three IKL 540 submarines, a version of the Type 206 built under licence by Vickers in the United Kingdom, were fitted with the Submarine-Launched Anti-aircraft Missile (SLAM) system, consisting of a quadruple launcher for the Short Blowpipe short-range SAM mounted in the fin and controlled from below. This remains the only such fitting, but there have been recent reports that the Soviet Navy has a similar system under development, and possible sightings.

MINES

Naval mine warfare is a subject which goes in and out of fashion. Minelaying activity during World War II caused considerable losses and necessitated the deployment of large fleets of minesweepers, and one of the most successful mining campaigns was that waged against Japan in 1945, when some 12,135 mines laid in Japanese and Korean waters resulted in the loss of 65 warships and 605 merchant ships, a total of 1.4 million tons of Japanese shipping.

Following the end of the war mine warfare went through a protracted period of relative ne on-board signal

processing coupled with a two-way fibreoptic link to the parent submarine. A furtglect in most navies. However, the US Navy conducted a mining campaign against North Vietnam, and deliberately mined Haiphong harbour in 1971. Other mining activities have included the alleged Libyan attempt to mine the Red Sea in 1984, when a Libyan merchant ship scattered a number of Soviet-made mines and an international mine clearance operation had to be mounted to restore full

Below: Mines can be laid by submarines, surface ships or aircraft. Here US Captor mines are loaded aboard a B-52 during an exercise; delivery is by means of parachutes.

use of the waterway. One consequence of this return of interest in mine warfare is a marked increase in the types and numbers of minelaying, minesweeping and minehunting ships in many navies, especially those within NATO.

The principle types of mine are ground, moored, floating and active. Ground or seabed mines are in widespread use and a typical weapon is the Italian Misar MR-80, which is designed to be used in depths between 26ft (8m) and 984ft (300m) and is available in various models weighing between 1,323lb (600kg) and 2,511lb (1,139kg). It is made of epoxy resin and fibreglass filled with between 881lb (400kg) and 2,028lb (920kg) of tritolital, HBX-3 or similar explosive, according to the model. The mine is cylindrical in shape and varies in length, but all models are 21in in diameter to enable them to be launched from submarine torpedo tubes. They can also be laid from aircraft or by surface vessel, and they are intended to attack both surface and submarine targets; actuation is by pressure, magnetic or acoustic sensors.

Moored mines are not quite so popular as in World War II but many models still exist. The Torpedini A Rosario (TAR), an interesting variation on an old theme, is designed to provide a defensive screen. The system comprises a cable between the sinker and the mine case, with a number of explosive charges spaced along the cable at regular intervals. The TAR 16 has a maximum practicable mooring depth of 1,640ft (500m) and there are 16 charges along the cable, the lowest being at the 984ft (300m) point. Spacing the charges in this way gives much better coverage than a single charge of the same total weight.

The Soviet Navy has a large armoury of mines designed to form defensive ASW barriers and attack both submarines in hostile waters and general shipping. Possibly the most sophisticated of current mines, however, is the US Navy's Captor, described above under Anti-submarine Weapons.

Sensors

Modern warships are absolutely dependent on their radars, sonars and non-acoustic sensors. The most widely used is radar, which is needed to detect aircraft and surface targets, and is also used for navigation. Air defence radars are invariably mounted as high as possible to give all-round coverage and to maximize their range, which, depending on power output and the height of the antenna and target, may vary between 50 and 200 miles (80-320km).

Surface surveillance radars are also widely used, but are limited currently to the range of the horizon. Research in this field is improving accuracy and definition, with, for example, the detection of submarine periscopes now being feasible with some sets.

At the forefront of air/surface radar technology is the US Navy's Aegis system, based on the SPY-1A electronically scanned fixed-array radar and now at sea on the Ticonderoga (CG 47) class cruisers, whose two pairs of fixed antennas eliminate the need for mechanically rotating antennas. The system also provides target designation data for the missile tracking radars and tracks outgoing missiles. A lighter derivative to be used on the Arleigh Burke class, SPY-1D, has only one transmitter and three illuminators instead of the two and four respectively on the Ticonderogas.

However efficient all these systems may be, they all suffer from the major shortcoming that as active transmitters they are easily detectable by hostile aircraft, ships and satellites. Electronic techniques such as spread-spectrum transmissions and procedural methods such as switching radars on for only very brief periods can make an enemy's task more difficult, but the only real solution seems lies in remote sensors or in passive systems. To this end electro-optical systems are being developed for some applications, but they are currently limited in range and by weather, and are unlikely to provide adequate warning against, say, an incoming supersonic sea-skimmer.

The ASW battle is a curious feature of contemporary peacetime military activities. It is essential that naval powers know as much as possible about any potential adversary's day-by-day submarine deployment, as this will enable them to establish normal deployment patterns and consequently to detect any change in those patterns which might indicate a possible build-up to a war posture. To achieve this, however, ASW detection and identification efforts must be on a virtual war footing themselves in order to provide the breadth of coverage and rapidity of response necessary, especially in the light of the high performance of modern submarines and the ability of nuclear-powered submarines to remain submerged for protracted periods.

Hull-mounted sonars, still the principal ASW sensors for most surface warships, can be used in either active or passive modes, and are supplemented in many ships by variable-depth sonars, which can be kept at a particular depth to detect submarines hiding below a thermal layer, while some are also being fitted with towed arrays. A major problem for surface warships is that hull-mounted sonars cannot be used at high speed, while VDS and towed arrays limit speed and manoeuvrability. This is exacerbated by the ever-increasing speed of some submarines (Soviet Alfa class boats have demonstrated speeds of over 42 kt on NATO exercises), whereas most surface combatants have a maximum speed of some 32 kt in fair conditions and considerably less in a seaway.

The problem can be alleviated by using a shipboard helicopter to detect and attack hostile submarines at extended ranges, and virtually all destroyers and frigates now operate at least one helicopter for this purpose, though the US Navy's Arleigh Burke class destroyers will have helicopter landing decks but no hangars, their LAMPS III aircraft being required to use another ship's hangar facilities whenever necessary. This is an extraordinary reversal of an otherwise universal trend—even the latest Soviet Krivak III frigates have now overcome the one acknowledged weakness of this otherwise excellent design by having the full helicopter facilities missing on Krivak Is and IIs.

RADAR

The term radar is an acronym for radio detection and ranging, and the fundamental principle of radar systems is that they transmit radio frequency (RF) signals which effectively travel in straight lines at the speed of light (300,000km/sec) until their energy is expended or unless they hit an object (target). The target will reflect some of the RF back as an echo which can be received by a suitably sensitive receiver and then displayed to an operator on a cathode-ray tube (CRT). Most naval radars tend to use the higher end of the radio frequency band, and

Right: Radar antennas on this French Tourville class destroyer are, from the front: DRBC-32D gun-control, DRBN-32 navigation, Triton (part of the Vega FCS) and DRBV-26 Jupiter air surveillance.

approximate operating frequencies of typical modern radar sets are 1,200MHz for air search, 5,500MHz for surface search and 8,200MHz for fire control.

Radar systems transmit energy in either pulses or continuous wave (CW). In pulsed radar the transmitter sends out radio waves in a series of short powerful pulses, with pauses in between so that the receiver can detect any echoes, which are time-referenced to determine the distance to the target. A duplexer is used, first to feed the transmit signal to the antenna and secondly to direct any return signals to the receiver, where they are amplified and displayed on a CRT.

CW radars are used to indicate moving targets, for measuring speed and for missile guidance. The transmitter radiates RF energy at a constant frequency from one antenna and

a separate antenna detects any RF energy reflected by a moving target. The echo signal is compared with a reference voltage at the transmit frequency and the difference (beat frequency) is the Doppler shift, which indicates a moving target.

Pulse and CW radars can be combined in pulse-Doppler radars, which use high frequency CW in short bursts. The pulse repetition frequency (prf) is much higher than in conventional pulse radars, and the pulse length is longer. This type of radar measures target velocity as well as distance.

The main function of air surveillance radars is to detect and determine the range and bearing of airborne targets at long ranges. Typical air surveillance radars use lower frequencies than surface search radars to achieve long range and to minimize losses, while wide

pulse widths increase transmit power and help to detect small targets at long range. Wide vertical beam width is used both to broaden the coverage and to compensate for the ship's own pitch and roll.

A typical air surveillance radar is the French TRS 3010 Jupiter system, which is used on the Georges Leygues class destroyers under the designation DBRV-26. This operates in the D-band (23cm) with a peak transmitter output power of 2MW with a 2.5 microsecond pulse at a prf of 450 per second. The antenna, of open wire mesh construction 24.6ft (7.5m) wide and 9.8ft (3m) high, weighs approximately 2,204lb (1,000kg) and rotates at either 7.5rpm or 15rpm. Range is of the order of 124 miles (200km) against a target with a 2m cross-section.

An important air surveillance radar on the Soviet Navy's inventory is Top Pair, carried by Kirov class battle-cruisers and Sovremennyy class destroyers. This system is a back-to-back combination of two radars already seen: Top Sail, a three-dimensional air surveillance radar operating in the 1-2GHZ band which is used on the Moskva class helicopter cruisers and whose scanner, latticed with a rhombic frontal aspect, is 18ft (5.5m) on each side and tilted at 20° and Big Net, a D/E-band long-range system installed on Kresta I class cruisers and some Kashin class destroyers. This

massive combined system must weigh several tons and as it is mounted some 157ft (48m) above the water line, it must cause some complications when planning the stability of the ships.

Surface search radars are used to detect and to determine the range and bearing of surface targets and low-flying aircraft. Maximum range is limited by the radar horizon and high frequencies are needed to give maximum reflection from very small targets such as ships' masts and submarine periscopes. Typically, surface search radars will employ beams which are wide in the vertical plane to detect low-flying aircraft and missiles and to compensate for pitch and roll, and narrow in the horizontal plane to give accurate bearings, coupled with narrow pulse widths to give short minimum ranges and enhanced range accuracy.

A particularly successful example of a surface search radar is the ZW-06/1, widely used in medium-sized warships including the Brazilian Niteroi class and Dutch Kortenaer class frigates and the Argentinian MEKO 360 destroyers. The antenna is a parabolic reflector 8.86ft (2.7m) wide and 3.93ft (1.2m) high rotating at 24rpm and capable of withstanding wind speeds up to 115mph (185km/h). The set operates in the frequency band 8,600-9,500MHz and transmits with a beam width of 19° in the vertical plane and 0.9° in the horizontal plane.

Fire control radars are designed to acquire targets originally detected by search radars, and then to determine accurate ranges, bearings and altitudes of the targets. Very high frequencies are

Above: Antennas on the Soviet carrier Minsk. At the masthead is the Top Knot Tacan, forward of the mast is the Top Sail 3D air surveillance and aft is the Top Steer 3D, possibly for air control.

Below: Kortenaer displaying its Hollandse Signaal apparaten LW-08 long-range air search radar. Before the mast is the round radome of the HSA WM-25 track-while-scan fire control radar.

Below: The island of the carrier USS Enterprise after her 1979-81 refit. The large square antenna in the centre is for the newly fitted SPS-48C long-range air surveillance radar.

used to permit the formation of narrow beam widths with comparatively small antenna arrays for good target definition. Narrow vertical and horizontal beam widths provide accurate bearing and position angles, and a high degree of bearing and elevation resolution.

There are two types of scanning: mechanical and electronic. In the former the radar beam is moved by physically moving the antenna, moving the feeder in relation to a fixed reflector, or moving the reflector relative to a fixed feeder. Most radar antennas rotate to give 360° coverage, but height-finding radars nutate (that is, move back and forth in a rocking or nodding pattern). A variation of this technique is used in fire control radars to produce conical scanning, achieved by nutating the feedhorn while the reflector remains fixed, resulting in a beam which rotates rapidly in a conical shape, the apex of the cone being the centre of the antenna. In electronic scanning the antenna is fixed and the scanning function is performed by electronic means.

A combination of the two is also used in some systems. For example, the US Navy's SPS-52C radar provides three-dimensional coverage from a single antenna by electronic scanning in elevation and mechanical rotation of the antenna in azimuth. The antenna itself is a planar array tilted at 25° to give coverage to high elevation angles and consists of rows of slotted waveguide radiating elements.

Possibly the most advanced surface-to-air weapon system in use today is the US Navy's Aegis system, of which a major element is the SPY-1 multi-function array radar. The phase-scanned arrays, each measuring 12ft (3.65m) by 12ft (3.65m), are mounted in pairs on the forward and after deckhouses to give all-round coverage, and each array has 4,100 discrete elements controlled by UYK-1 digital computers to produce and steer multiple radar beams for target search, detection and tracking. The SPY-1 also tracks its own ship's missiles and provides target designation data for the target illuminating radars, of which there are four on each ship to direct Standard active-homing missiles.

In operation the three-dimensional SPY-1 continually searches with a single horizontal beam out to 45nm for pop-up targets, while covering many times per minute a hemisphere with a radius of 175nm. When a target is detected the radar control computer can allocate within one second more beams to the target, and a smooth target track is obtained in less time than it takes a mechanical scanning radar antenna to complete one revolution.

Once a potential target has been acquired there must be no delay in establishing whether it is friendly or hostile, and an automated system of identification is essential. Although technically not a radar system, IFF (identification friend

or foe) is frequently used in association with radar to enable a friendly ship or aircraft to identify itself automatically. Having spotted a target on radar, the interrogator sends an IFF signal: if the target is equipped with a suitable transponder, and provided that the transponder accepts the coded signal, it will respond automatically with a coded reply.

SONAR

Submarine mission profiles generally follow one of three main patterns, depending on the boats' type and role, but all submarines must set out from a base, which is almost always on the surface and detectable by direct visual means, radio intercepts, satellite observation or seabed sensors on or near the exit routes. They must then, unless they are confined to an area such as the Baltic, transit through the shallow waters of the continental shelf—where they are relatively easy to detect— before reaching the open ocean, and some submarines, particularly those of the USSR, may have to transit passages which are restricted either in depth or breadth (choke points), where detection is particularly easy. Once in the deeper ocean, however, the three main types split.

An SSBN, once clear of the continental shelf, will usually go deep and travel as fast as is compatible with its security to its patrol area; once there it will generally cruise at about three

knots, hiding from detection by varying its depth to match prevailing oceanic conditions. The SSBN cannot help exposing itself to some degree when it needs to communicate with its national command authorities or to update its inertial navigation system. SSNs are faster and more agile, and operate at greater depths, but they may also have to communicate periodically with their base or with the surface task groups with which they are cooperating.

If SSBNs and SSNs only come to the surface infrequently, the problem for diesel-electric submarines is that they must come up to the surface as an absolutely unavoidable routine to obtain air to run the diesels to recharge their batteries. They can achieve this by exposing only the head of the schnorkel tube, but even this is a relatively easy target for modern radars and infra-red sensors, and the exhaust fumes can be detected by sniffers mounted on most types of ASW aircraft unless they are expelled under the surface. As a result, conventional submarines are faced with the paradox that while under normal conditions they are the quietest of all submarines and the most difficult to detect, they are inherently vulnerable due to this inescapable requirement to approach the surface at regular intervals.

A typical ASW engagement, whether by surface ship, aircraft or another submarine, goes through six stages: search,

Aegis cruiser weapon and sensor integration

Below: Schematic drawing of a Ticonderoga class Aegis cruiser showing the major weapon and sensor systems. Not immediately obvious from an external view of the Ticonderoga are the major advances in on-board command and control systems, whose main sensors are the four phased arrays of the three-dimensional SPY-1A radar. Aegis makes it possible to detect, track and engage several missile and aircraft targets both simultaneously and automatically, while the command system also counters surface and subsurface threats.

1 5in DP gun
2 Mk 26 Standard/Asroc launcher
3 SPY-1A phased arrays (forward and starboard)
4 WSC-1(V) satcom antenna
5 Mk 80 directors (2 x 1)
6 Gun fire control radar
7 Datalink antenna
8 LAMPS III helicopter
9 Super RBOC chaff launcher
10 SLQ-32 (V) ECM antennas
11 Mk 15 Phalanx CIWS (2 x 1)
12 Communications antenna

13 Tacan antenna
14 Link 11 datalink antenna
15 IFF antenna
16 SPS-49 air search radar
17 LAMPS III helicopter
18 Mk 80 directors (2 x 1)
19 SPY-1A phased arrays (aft and port)
20 Satcom antenna
21 Torpedo tubes (2 x 3)
22 Mk 26 Standard/Asroc launcher
23 5in DP gun
24 Harpoon launchers (2 x 4)
25 Towed sonar array

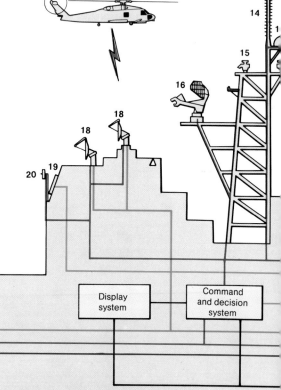

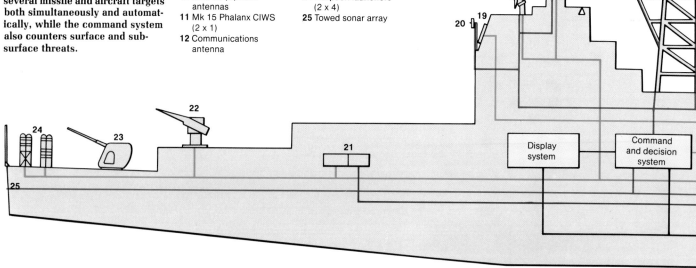

contact, approach, attack, close combat and, in the absence of a decision, disengagement. In the search stage the hunting platform carries out a patrol, either in a general search pattern or, if a component of a task group, in a designated area. In the latter case both surface ships and submarines are faced with the problem that the speed of the group may well be in excess of the optimum ASW search speed. In this stage of the operation the hunter needs to avoid detection and will therefore use passive sensors as far as possible, coupled with inputs from other platforms such as satellites and SOSUS.

A contact should comprise two elements, detection and classification. Detection is an indication that a possible target is actually in the search area and will usually be accompanied by a general bearing, while classification is a refining process, confirming that the contact really is a submarine and not a merchant ship, whale or other harmless object and then seeking to positively identify it. Examination of the contact's acoustic signature and comparison with the hunter's data bank should give at least a broad classification and may well give more definitive information as to type, class and even, under certain circumstances, an individual submarine.

The approach stage begins with tracking, again normally accomplished by passive means to avoid alerting the target,

followed by localization, when the hunter manoeuvres into an attacking position. In the attack stage the hunter should be able to launch its weapons with a fair degree of confidence that the target will be hit, although the primary cause of uncertainty for most navies in recent years lies in weapon (and especially torpedo) performance, rather than sensors. Thus, most submarines will normally close to about half

their torpedoes' theoretical effective range—normally some 10-12nm—before firing in order to raise the probability of hit; this is, in relative terms, very close indeed. Even though most torpedoes now carry their own acoustic sensors, and in many cases have a wire link back to their launchers, there are many limitations which reduce their chances of a successful engagement.

If the initial attack is a failure a

close-combat phase will ensue in which the protagonists seek to eliminate one another. Such a submarine-versus-submarine engagement resembles two fighter aircraft wheeling and manoeuvring in a dogfight, identifying and evading hostile weapons whilst trying all the time to deliver the fatal blow themselves. This is the one phase of ASW in which the mechanical excellence of the submarine is the primary factor. If there is no decisive outcome, the final stage—disengagement—takes place in a return to the previous conditions of quiet, undetected operation.

ASW, the business of finding, hunting and killing submarines, can be divided into four capability areas according to the platform type and mission, submarine ASW, surface ASW, airborne ASW and surveillance ASW, but all must confront a set of similar problems, the greatest of which is the nature of the ocean itself.

Acoustic energy is the one form of radiant energy which can travel any significant distance under water, and sound transmissions, like radar in the atmosphere, will be reflected by solid objects enabling the echoes to be detected by suitable and sensitive receivers. Such detection is, however only the start in a laborious process of identification and classification, a process which is made all the more difficult by the complexity of the ocean environment, whose dynamic nature is equivalent in

Above: The dual antennas of the Mk 91 Fire Control System aboard USS Hewitt (DD 966), a Spruance class destroyer, provide target tracking and illumination for the Sea Sparrow missile system.

Below: The forward superstructure of USS Ticonderoga showing one of four SPY-1A planar arrays, a Mk 80 director and, between funnel and superstructure, an AS-3018A satcom antenna.

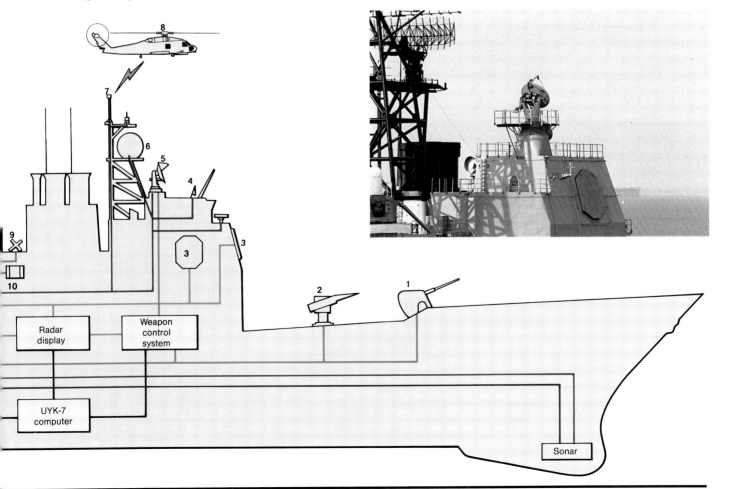

many ways to weather in the atmosphere and is difficult to predict or characterize, a problem exacerbated by the fact that only a few of the oceans' phenomena, such as surface-wave activity, ice, tidal effects and local weather, can be directly observed by the human eye.

Two of the better known characteristics of the oceans are that they contain many dissolved chemicals, including, of course, salt (sodium chloride), and that pressure increases with depth. There are, however, many further factors such as the variation in salinity (haloclines) and temperature (thermoclines), sub-surface currents, counter-currents and waves, the topography and nature of the ocean floor, and the existence of macro- and micro-organisms.

Finally, the situation will be affected by natural noises such as surface agitation (wave noise) and man-made noises produced by ships, oil rigs and harbours, all of which travel surprising distances. All of these characteristics have their effects upon the acoustical and optical properties of the ocean environment.

Active sonar devices transmit acoustic pulses in the audio frequency band (approximately 5-20kHz) with pulses 12.5 to 700 milliseconds apart, and both frequency and pulse repetition must be variable so that adjustments can be made to suit the prevailing oceanic conditions. Active sonars are used in submarines, surface vessels and air-deployed sonobuoys. They are also used in torpedoes, using somewhat higher frequencies (typically 20-35kHz) where the shorter range is offset by the greater spatial resolution.

One characteristic of all moving underwater transducers is that the relative movement between the acoustic transmitter-receiver and the water surrounding it generates noise, and a further complication is that transmission power is limited by the cavitiation effect, which causes gaseous bubbles to form on the emitting surface. The greatest complication, however, remains the complex variations in prevailing conditions and to maximize a platform's sonar capabilities it is frequently necessary to carry various different sonar sets, each optimized for a different regime.

The major problem associated with active sonar has always been that by its very nature it reveals its presence, alerting the target and enabling it to take evasive action. This is especially significant for aircraft, whose presence is very difficult for a submerged submarine to detect until a sonobuoy transmits.

Active sonar systems comprise a large number of transducers mounted in an array. Surface ships use two-dimensional arrays in the form of flat circles or rectangles; a

Sound propagation

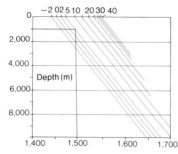

Above: Acoustic energy travels great distances underwater but its velocity depends on a number of variables, including salinity, which ranges from 32 to 37 parts per thousand (ppt). This diagram shows the speed of sound in sea water with salinity level of 35 ppt; for example, at 3,228ft (948m) and at 5° sound velocity is 4,900ft/sec (1,494m/sec).

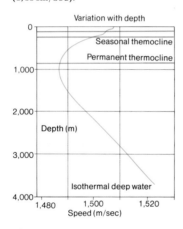

Above: To establish the location of submarines by acoustic means precise knowledge of the speed of sound is essential; this graph shows a typical pattern in a temperate area. Sound has its minimum velocity in the permanent thermocline (also known as the deep sound channel), whose depth varies from 980ft to 1,300ft (300-400m).

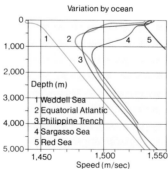

Above: The acoustic characteristics of the world's oceans differ quite markedly, as illustrated in this diagram, which shows the variations in the velocity of sound with depth in different oceanic areas. Such variations would be of particular interest to ASW aircraft on protracted patrol, when sonobuoys might be dropped in widely separated locations.

typical modern system, the US Navy SQS-26, has 576 transducer elements in a cylindrical array, housed in a large bulbous dome at the foot of the stem. Such bow-mounted sonars are usually indicated by a sharply overhanging bow, as on most US Navy ASW ships, whereas a less acute bow angle (for example, on British ships) normally indicates a sonar dome mounted in the keel. Cylindrical arrays are normally used in the bows of submarines.

All these arrays are fixed and beams are formed electronically to give directional resolution, while Doppler shift in the return signal gives moving target indication (MTI), though a very slow moving target with a low Doppler in a noisy or high reverberation environment, such as an SSBN on station, is notoriously difficult to detect.

The most effective current submarine active sonars are the US Navy BQQ-5 installed in the Los Angeles class SSNs and the British Type 2020 now being installed in the Trafalgar class. The BQQ-5 has a bow-mounted spherical array and, by means of the Submarine Active Detection System (SADS) upgrade is integrated with other onboard systems such as the Mine Detection

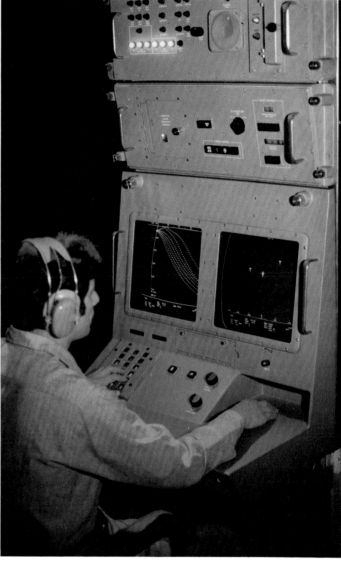

Above: The operator's console (control indicator unit) of the EDO 780 small ship sonar system. The display on the left shows the predicted transmission paths in ambient conditions, taking into account measurements of salinity, temperature and so on, while that on the right shows possible contacts, allowing corrections to be made for propagation distortions.

and Avoidance Sonar (MIDAS), under-ice systems and the forward-mounted conformal array.

Submarines will obviously do everything within their power to avoid detection. One tactic is to go deep to take advantage of oceanic conditions and one possible response by the surface ASW hunter is to place its transducer array below the thermocline using a variable depth sonar (VDS). The French DUBV 43B, a typical VDS system, is deployed on the French Navy's latest ASW ships, the Georges Leygues class destroyers: the stem-mounted VDS fish containing the transducer array is 18ft (5.5m) long, 5.6ft (1.7m) wide and weighs 17,085lb (7,750kg), while the array itself is cylindrical in shape, 3.93ft (1.2m) high and 3.3ft (1m) in diameter, with 192 transducers in 24 vertical staves of eight each. It is deployed on a cable 820ft (250m) long and can be set to run at depths of between 33ft (10m) and 656ft (200m). The system has a power output of 96kW at its maximum operating depth.

Further developments in active sonar are aimed at maximizing its excellent detection capabilities while trying to reduce its characteristic and revealing signature. One method being tried in the USA is spread-spectrum transmission, in which the signal energy is spread over a wide range of frequencies in a pattern known only to the transmitter and receiver, which should, at least in theory, lose the signal in the general oceanic noise. This system has a further benefit in that it enhances the probability of overcoming the fluctuations in the acoustic path inherent in the oceanic environment.

Parametric sonar has also been the subject of much research. This system depends upon the mixing of two high frequencies to produce a difference frequency (higher minus lower) which is then selected for transmission. Careful choice of the two original frequencies can produce a suitable sonar signal, normally in the 100-1,000Hz bracket, which has a narrow band width similar to that of the original higher frequencies, thus giving much better spatial resolution than can be obtained with the wider band widths and low frequencies of normal beams. Although used in minehunting and navigation, parametric sonar has been restricted in its applications by problems with electronic scanning and the difficulty of reducing the transducers to a reasonable size.

Passive sonar is growing rapidly in importance because it makes no transmissions that might give away the hunter's position, but depends solely on the sounds generated by the target. The detector is the hydrophone, a very sensitive listening device which is optimized for submarine noises. Hydrophones can be assembled in a variety of arrays according to the particular task, although the only significant differences lie in the signal processing techniques. Passive hull-borne sonars normally use the same arrays as the active systems, and with a spherical array on a submarine, using digital steering, a coverage of some 270° horizontally and 50° vertically can be obtained.

Two types of processing, narrow-band and wide-band, are used. The former employs very sophisticated techniques which depend on spectrum analyzers and great computer power to produce information, although current advances in microprocessor power are easing this problem. The USA is clearly ahead of the world, and especially of the USSR, in this area, which is of crucial

Sonar operation

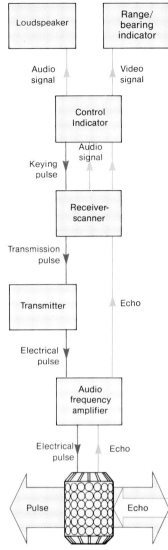

Above: The basic elements of an active sonar system, with the transmission path shown in red, and the receive path in blue. The transducers are shown here mounted in a cylindrical form, but spherical and linear arrays are also used. The electronically formed beam gives directional resolution; return signal Doppler shift gives moving target indication.

importance in detecting and analyzing slow-moving targets.

Broad-band processing, on the other hand, examines the full spectrum of incoming signals and separates constant noises such as submarine flow noise from random noises. It therefore tends to be used for the initial detection of submarine targets and for analyzing the movement of a target relative to the searcher. It is most useful when the noises emitted by the target exceed the ambient noise level, and it provides rapid target detection and relatively accurate target bearings.

Transient acoustic processing is a new technique involving the detection and analysis of sudden noises of brief duration, such as weapon launch or random machine noises, which is adding to the effectiveness of broad-band processing.

Above: The US Navy SQR-18 TACTAS (Tactical Towed Acoustic Sensor) uses eight modular hydrophone sections and is fitted to Knox class frigates. It is streamed from the stern on a cable.

Below: Another method of deploying sonar is from helicopters using dunking sonars such as the US AQS-13B, here being deployed by an Italian Navy AB 212, which has both active and passive modes.

Both submarines and surface ships are now using towed sonar arrays, which consist of large numbers of hydrophones—up to several hundred in some cases—towed behind the vessels on long cables. A typical towed array is part of the BQQ-5 system used aboard the US Navy's Los Angeles class SSNs. The cable is 2,624ft (800m) long and 0.37in (9.5mm) in diameter, while the array, which contains the hydrophones and electronics, is 3.25in (82.5mm) in diameter. A multiplexer is incorporated in the array to stack the information electronically and thus reduce the number of wires running through the towing cable. Not surprisingly, a towed array limits the manoeuvrability of the towing ship as the actual array needs to be straight to obtain a coherent signal. Furthermore, the towing speed is limited,

because the array is liable to oscillate at its natural frequency if it moves through the water above a certain speed, giving rise to false readings and making itself liable to detection. Following a relatively straight course at a constant slow speed makes the towing vessel very vulnerable, a problem heightened for surface ships by the need for separation from the main body of a task group to maximize sonar performance. As the experiences of the British radar picket ships in the 1982 South Atlantic war showed, such isolated ships are highly vulnerable.

For surface ships the stowage of towed arrays is mainly a matter of finding space for the equipment on the quarterdeck. For submarines, however, the problem is more acute and the Los Angeles SSNs, for example, stow their arrays in tubes between the pressure hull and outer casing, with the winch in the forward ballast tank. Earlier classes need to have the cable clipped on as they leave harbour on patrol and removed again when they return, a somewhat awkward arrangement, although it does have the benefit of reducing the total number of arrays needed. One final advantage of towed arrays for submarines is that they are the only means of providing a rearward-looking capability.

One particular application of passive sonar is the Sound Surveillance System (SOSUS), which is a series of separate seabed hydrophone networks in the Pacific and Atlantic oceans. The FFQ-10(V) sensor stations, positioned some 5-15 miles (8-24km) apart and connected by cables to shore stations, are designed to distinguish noises made by submarines from normal oceanic background noises. SOSUS contacts are then followed up by ASW aircraft, usually land-based types such as the P-3 Orion, Nimrod MR.2 or Atlantic, which must make rapid transits to the area of the report.

There is no doubt that over the years the Soviet Navy will have located these US systems, or at least parts of them—for example, the shore-based data-processing stations—and that they will have prepared plans to disrupt them in time of tension or war, probably using specially trained Spetsnaz diving teams. It is also highly probable that the USSR has similar seabed submarine detection systems of its own covering the approaches to the SSBN sanctuaries in the Barents Sea and the Sea of Okhotsk.

Because SOSUS is both inflexible and vulnerable the US Navy is turning to a new concept, the Surveillance Towed Array Sonar System (SURTASS). This comprises a towed array, possibly up to 3.1 miles (5km) in length, towed at a steady three knots by specially built ships designated T-AGOS. There is to

Above: A US Navy diver is dwarfed by this huge sonar array as he checks it out prior to it being lowered to the seabed off Andros Island in the Bahamas. Note the huge, vertically oriented antennas.

be a T-AGOS fleet of 24 or 26 ships, each manned by a civilian crew of 29, carrying out 90-day patrols. The acoustic data will be partially processed on board before transmission over the Defence Satellite Communications System to a shore station at either Norfolk, Virginia or Pearl Harbor, Hawaii, where further processing will take place, including the correlation of the outputs from each ship with those from the other T-AGOS ships and the SOSUS networks.

NON-ACOUSTIC ASW SENSORS

A submerged submarine moving through the water leaves a wake, and this turbulence, conical in shape, eventually reaches the surface well astern of the boat, where it causes minute variations in the wave pattern. Such variations can be detected by active sonar, but the USA, the USSR and a number of other

countries are experimenting with over-the-horizon backscatter (OTH-B) radar in an effort to detect the phenomenon at much greater ranges.

These experiments must have had some success, because it was announced in February 1986 that the USA is building two OTH sites, one at Amchitka Island in the Aleutians and the second at Guam in the Marianas, and that a third will be constructed jointly by the USA and Japan near Okinawa Island. These three OTH sites will then look at long range into the Sea of Japan, the coastal area of Siberia and the Sea of Okhotsk, and are obviously intended mainly for submarine detection.

Depending on the depth of the submarine and the prevailing oceanic conditions, the wake turbulence may also force colder water to rise and mix with warmer water at the surface; this causes a temperature differential detectable by

Below: A topographic relief map of the world's oceans compiled by the US SEASAT system in 1982. The ouput from military satellites will be infinitely more detailed —and very highly classified.

satellite or aircraft sensors.

When a submarine is travelling near the surface it causes a tiny rise in the surface level of the water above the hull and this rise is potentially detectable by satellites. The USSR is known to be interested in this technique, and the US has at least one satellite (SEASAT) carrying a radio altimeter with a vertical resolution of 3.9in (10cm), and it may be assumed that military systems have even higher resolutions which would make them suitable for detecting the phenomenon.

Submarines are also detectable by the electrical and magnetic fields they create. According to a Soviet writer there are electro-chemical processes on a submarine hull which generate varying electrical potentials with currents flowing between them using seawater as the conducting medium. The rate of change of the consequential electrical and electromagnetic fields is detectable by sensitive devices such as very large seabed coils.

A submarine hull is a mainly ferrous body, and as it moves through the lines of force of the Earth's natural magnetic field it creates a magnetic anomaly which is detectable using a magnetic anomaly detector (MAD). MAD equipment is mounted in extensions behind the tails of fixed-wing aircraft or in aerodynamic bodies, known as birds, towed by cable behind helicopters. All advanced ASW aircraft are fitted with such devices, including the US P-3 Orion and S-3 Viking, British Nimrod, French Atlantic and Soviet II-38 (May).

MAD techniques are not suitable for area searches, having a maximum detection range of only some 1,000ft (305m), but they are invaluable for the precise locating of underwater targets detected by other means. However, the use of titanium hulls, as in the Soviet Alfa class, introduces a new factor as titanium is non-magnetic and cannot be detected

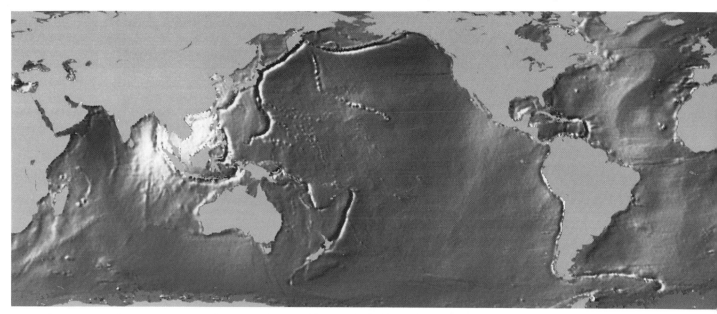

Above: Underwater contacts recorded by surveillance systems must be followed up quickly to achieve positive identification, a task for LRMP aircraft such as this RAF Nimrod.

by MAD sensors. The days of this widely used technique may therefore be limited.

Sea water is an efficient light absorber, but is transparent to light in the blue-green part of the visible spectrum. Efforts are being made to exploit this fact for communications, using blue-green lasers projected by satellites into the target area. The laser could be mounted on the satellite but the power, reliability and life requirements may preclude this for the foreseeable future.

Another possibility is a ground-based laser transmitting a beam which is bounced off an orbiting reflector on to the desired area of the ocean. All the major relevant areas could be covered by three symmetrically placed reflectors in geosynchronous equatorial orbits. This would require great precision in target acquisition, pointing and tracking, but the relevant technology already exists in the form of the NASA space telescope, which can be pointed with an accuracy of 25 nanorads, that is, with an error of not more than 1ft (0.3m) in 7,500 miles (12,069km).

A similar technique could be used to detect submarines, either by detecting minute return reflections from a satellite-borne sensor, or by mounting a blue-green laser and suitable detectors in an ASW aircraft, and the latter could well be a replacement for MAD.

SUBMARINE SENSORS

A submerged submarine is totally dependent upon its sensors, the most important of which is sonar. Most submarines have large sonars mounted in the bows, and US SSNs and SSBNs, among others, are also fitted with conformal arrays.

HSA SIASS-2 submarine integrated attack and surveillance sonar

Above: Sensors incorporated in the SEWACO system include bow-mounted active/passive sonars, conformal hydrophone arrays and towed sonar arrays to detect a wide variety of targets.

Hydrophones are also fitted, usually with arrays near the bow, amidships and near the stern to give all-round coverage.

One important submarine sensor is that for listening to its own noises. Most navies use surface ships to inspect their submarines for noise emissions as they leave harbour, but it is vital to continue such monitoring throughout the patrol to ensure that any new noise is detected and removed, to prevent it acting as a beacon for ASW forces.

Just as important as the sensors themselves is the ability to assimilate and process their outputs, and this is another area where modern technology is making a major contribution, providing processors able to handle vast amounts of information while making them much smaller and easier to use.

Below: Space in a submarine has always been at a premium, and even the large internal volume of the US Navy's latest SSBNs is crammed with equipment: this is the Ohio's sonar suite.

The US Navy's Ohio class SSBNs obviously have comprehensive sensor outfits, most details of which are highly classified, but it is known that the system includes the spherical BQQ-6 bow-mounted passive transducer, the BQR-15 towed array together with its associated BQR-19 signal processor, and a passive sonar consisting of two conformal line arrays on the hull surface, plus an acoustic communications system, a BQR-19 mast-mounted sonar receiver to detect any surface ships near a proposed surfacing point, and a WLR-9A acoustic intercept receiver.

More details are known of the earlier BQQ-2 system, which was fitted to USS *Tullibee* (SSN 597) in the early 1960s. This system comprises the BQS-6 active sonar, BQR-7 passive sonar and BQA-3 computer-indicator group, the spherical BQS-6 bow-mounted sonar array being 15ft (4.57m) in diameter and operating at a frequency of 3.5kHz. This sonar sphere is so large that it could only be installed in the bow of the submarine at the price of displacing the torpedo room and tubes, which had to be relocated amidships. However, its performance benefits are so great that the US Navy was prepared to pay the price, and all subsequent SSNs have a similar arrangement, fitted in the same way, though space considerations are more critical aboard SSBNs, which have accordingly retained the bow torpedo installation.

The BQR-7 passive conformal array comprises 52 groups of three vertically mounted units, and in the early 1960s it was stated that an experimental model was effective at 30-100nm against a snorkelling submarine and 10-50nm against the cavitation noises of a submerged submarine.

Also installed on *Tullibee* is the BQC-2 passive underwater fire control sonar (known as PUFFS from the Passive Underwater Fire Control Feasibility Study), which provides target tracking of up to four targets simultaneously, with continuous, instantaneous range resolution. The system comprises three hydrophone arrays in above-hull sonar domes, though later versions of PUFFS use two conformal arrays on the hull, with the third in the vertical end-plates on the stern hydroplanes.

Another sensor fitted to most US SSNs is an under-ice sonar, which is necessary for detecting and delineating polynyas, iceberg detection, bottom sounding and detecting and depth assessment of overhead ice. A typical set is the BQS-8 fitted to the Sturgeon class SSNs, which operates at 24-32kHz and 200 watts.

Remarkably little is known of Soviet submarine sensor fits, but it is a safe assumption that they are similar to those of the US Navy,

and the only major divergence by other navies seems to involve the position of the main sonar dome in SSNs. As stated above, the US Navy places a large dome in the bow, which displaces the torpedo room, but other navies retain the torpedoes in the bow at the price, presumably, of a smaller array.

AIRBORNE EARLY WARNING

The tactical requirement for early warning of attack by hostile aircraft has long been understood, but it has seldom been so clearly or so dramatically demonstrated as in the 1982 South Atlantic war, when Argentinian Navy Super Etendard aircraft were able to approach ships of the British Task Force at such low levels and high speeds that their first victim was a destroyer deployed as a radar picket to protect the Brititsh fleet from just such a threat.

The main reason for this was that at the Super Etendard's approach speed of around 600mph (965km/h) the rotation rate of the ship's radar antenna (typically 6rpm) becomes a major factor: in the 30-40 seconds necessary to verify a track the aircraft will be some 6.6 miles (10.6km) closer. Ironically, the Royal Navy had appreciated this problem for many years and while it still deployed conventional aircraft carriers had devoted much effort to developing and producing an AEW aircraft, the Fairey Gannet, to guard against this type of attack.

The first specialized AEW aircraft came from the US Navy, which had 36 in service in 1945, carrying surveillance radars which were, for their time, large and powerful and, at least in theory, capable of spotting even low-flying aircraft close to the ground or sea. AEW radars have improved progressively and today giant sets are in use, capable of operating in many

different modes to provide clear and information-packed pictures of the situation out to a distance of some 230 miles (370km).

A few AEW aircraft still use antennas which rotate underneath the fuselage, but most current types mount them above the fuselage. The British have also tried a system with the Nimrod AEW in which there are two antennas, one in the nose and one in the tail, each covering 180°; this arrangement seems, however, to have given rise to virtually insuperable problems of coordination. AEW aircraft also need large digital computers with considerable memory and processing power, together with an IFF system and real-time downlinks to the commanders afloat.

It should not be assumed that height is all that matters for an AEW aircraft and that the higher the aircraft flies the more effective it will be. An attacking aircraft is most vulnerable to detection as it crosses the radar horizon; beforehand it cannot be

Above: A US Navy E-2C Hawkeye carrier-based airborne early warning (AEW) aircraft, with its distinctive 24ft (7.3m) rotodome for the APS-138 radar: antenna; rotation speed is 6rpm.

seen and afterwards it may be obscured by sea clutter. Consequently, an AEW aircraft's optimum height depends on the ambient sea-state and the characteristics of the radar set and may be well below the aircraft's operational ceiling.

Current AEW aircraft include the US Navy's E-2 Hawkeye, the RAF Shackleton and Nimrod and the Royal Navy Sea King AEW Mk 2, which is only helicopter to fill this role. One possible alternative to the helicopter for navies without aircraft carriers is offered by remotely piloted vehicles (RPVs). The technology exists now with RPVs developed to support land operations, and with a secure downlink to pass the sensor data to a ship in the task group for processing and dissemination, there seems to be

no reason why this could not become a viable system.

The Grumman E-2C Hawkeye is one of the most effective AEW systems, and the only carrier-based fixed-wing AEW aircraft. Grumman was the pioneer of sea-going AEW, having produced the AF-2W Guardian and the E-1B Tracer in the 1950s. The first flight of the prototype E-2A took place in 1960 and the E-2C remains in full production today and is unique in that it is the only airframe designed specifically for the AEW role; the others are conversions of civil airliners or, in the case of the Shackleton, of a World War II bomber.

The E-2C's APS-125 radar and Advanced Radar Processing System (ARPS) give good discrimination and detection over both land and water. The antenna is housed in a large rotodome which rotates once every ten seconds and is set at slight positive incidence to give lift at least equal to its own weight, and a new Total Radiation Aperture Control antenna (TRAC-A) will enhance the range coverage, reduce radar sidelobes and give better ECCM performance. E-2C missions last up to six hours, which, at a 200nm operating radius, allows a time on station of up to four hours at a height of 30,000ft (9.1km). The APS-125 is claimed to detect airborne targets anywhere in a three-million cubic mile surveillance envelope and to detect low-flying cruise missiles at ranges of over 115 miles (185km), fighter aircraft at up to 230 miles (370km) and larger aircraft at 289 miles (465km). All friendly and hostile maritime movements are also monitored.

Below: The Royal Navy's quick and successful solution to the lack of carrier-borne AEW in the South Atlantic War was the combination of Sea King helicopter and a Searchwater radar carried on a unique pylon mounting.

The ALR-73 Passive Detection System (PDS) provides four-quadrant 360° coverage using antennas on the nose and tail and on the tips of the tailplane. It can detect electronic emitters in the microwave spectrum at ranges of up to 400 miles (644km), and sends emitter data reports (including such information as pulse width, pulse amplitude and frequency) via its own processor to the E-2C's AYK-14 central processor.

Central to the E-2C's capabilities is its on-board data processing, which is currently provided by the Airborne Tactical Data System (ATDS). This is manned by a crew of three: Combat Information Officer, Air Control Officer and Radar Operator. The high-speed data-processing system enables the E-2C to track automatically more than 250 targets simultaneously and to control up to 30 airborne intercepts.

As mentioned above, the Royal Navy found itself in a fatal dilemma in the 1982 South Atlantic war, because it had no conventional aircraft carriers and was consequently deprived of the AEW facilities which it knew to be essential. Following the loss of HMS *Sheffield* a quick-fix programme was initiated to fit Westland Sea King HAS Mk 2 airframes with a modified version of the Nimrod MR 2's Thorn-EMI Searchwater radar. The radar scanner is mounted on a pylon on the starboard side of the aircraft inside an inflatable protective dome, and the whole installation swivels rearward through 90° when not in use.

The Searchwater radar is a frequency-agile set with a pitch and roll-stabilized antenna, and

Below: The need for an AEW platform, particularly for offshore patrols, that is cheaper than the Boeing E-3 AWACS has brought several proposals, one of which is the P-3 Orion airframe married to the E-2C's APS-138 radar.

Above: The need to police offshore areas has led to a requirement for simple, cheap maritime patrol aircraft, such as this Pilatus Britten-Norman Defender with its Thorn-EMI Skymaster radar.

includes IFF for the interrogation of ships and helicopters as well as aircraft, and a signal processing capability to enhance the detection of surface targets (including submarine periscopes) in high sea states and at long ranges. It is able to detect incoming aircraft at a range of about 115 miles (185km), and also to monitor surface targets, providing an effective, if somewhat expensive, solution to the Royal Navy's dilemma.

OTHER SENSORS

Radar has become a fundamental tool in naval warfare, but it is by definition an active sensor and as such it is open to detection and vulnerable to counter measures such as jamming. In particular, electronic warfare is being used increasingly as a means of degrading radar-based weapon control systems, particularly at the critical moments in an engagement. It is possible to maintain a radar's operational effectiveness by, for example, using frequency-agile or frequency-hopping techniques, but efforts are now being made to find other forms of sensor, ideally passive ones, which could at least support radar, even if they could not supplant it altogether.

Various technologies are being examined. One of the first was infra-red (IR), but this is another active system and easy to detect. Nevertheless, the French Navy has recently put the Pirana IR tracker into service, and is also deploying the Vampir IR surveillance system in C 70 destroyers.

Thermal imaging (TI) seems a much more practicable system. The Galileo NCS2 Shipborne TI is now installed on most major Italian warships as part of the MM-39 electro-optical fire control system. Various navies are also using Image

Intensification (II) in devices such as submarine periscope sights. Finally, Low Light Television (LLTV) is being used as an effective replacement for topside lookouts and spotters, and new systems are appearing which combine some or all of these techniques with computer processing for automatic fire control.

No one technology seems to have any clear advantage at the moment, but this is a rapidly developing field, and what does seem certain is that the days of warships going round the oceans with all their radars and radios transmitting and acting like electromagnetic homing beacons for anyone who cares to look for them are numbered, and some passive alternative to radar must be found.

Below: Video imagery from CCTV and IR sensors on the display of a BAE Sea Archer ship-mounted gun fire control system, here showing centroid automatic tracking of an aircraft target. A laser rangefinder is also incorporated.

Naval Air Power

Because of their expense and complexity, aircraft carriers have been deployed by only a very small number of Western navies in recent decades. The US Navy has maintained a fleet of ever-larger aircraft carriers and by the mid-1980s operated five nuclear powered carriers (CVNs), with a further two building, and ten conventionally powered carriers. The British aircraft carrier force, on the other hand, has dwindled from a strength of 18 fleet and seven escort carriers in service, plus six fleet carriers building, in 1946 to just three, *Invincible, Illustrious* and *Ark Royal*.

The French Navy has two very effective light fleet carriers, *Foch* and *Clemenceau*, and plans to build two nuclear powered carriers to replace them in the 1990s, while Spain and Italy have one brand new light carrier each, though the Italian ship, *Giuseppe Garibaldi*, currently only operates helicopters, despite being capable of operating STOVL aircraft. Elsewhere, there are three very elderly ex-Royal Navy carriers in service with the navies of Argentina (*Veinticinco de Mayo*), Brazil (*Minas Gerais*) and India (*Vikrant*), while other navies which once operated aircraft carriers, such as those of Australia, Canada and the Netherlands, have been forced out by increasing costs. Finally, the Soviet Navy's four Kiev class aircraft carriers will be supplemented by its first nuclear powered aircraft carrier, launched in 1985, and one more under construction.

For many years the Soviet Navy has considered the threat from NATO's nuclear-armed, carrier-borne aircraft to be of great significance to the Russian homeland. For a long time the Soviets did not seem to think they needed carriers of their own, possibly because their maritime ambitions did not run to blue-water operations, but that position has dramatically changed and the Soviet Navy represents ever-increasing power at sea, with some of the most imaginative aircraft carrier designs of the postwar era.

Admiral Gorschkov, the former commander-in-chief, is on record as saying: "The Soviet Navy will no longer be confined to its home waters, but will exploit the freedom of the seas and, through its global presence in peacetime, will spread Communist influence outside the borders of the USSR. Sea power without air power is senseless." Never was the truth of the Soviet admiral's words more clearly demonstrated than in the 1982 South Atlantic war:

Right: The Soviet carrier Kiev in the eastern Atlantic after her 1982 refit. Ka-27 Helix helicopters have replaced the old Ka-25 Hormones and new barriers have been added to reduce flight deck turbulence.

without the air power brought into the theatre by the British aircraft carriers *Hermes* and *Invincible* the operation to retake the Falkland Islands could never have succeeded; indeed, it could scarcely even have started.

AIRCRAFT CARRIERS

There are four current types of aircraft carrier. The biggest operate conventional takeoff and landing (CTOL) aircraft and range in size from the mighty American nuclear powered aircraft carriers (CVNs) of 89,600 tons displacement to the ex-Royal Navy light fleet carriers of about 20,000 tons. These ships operate air wings of sizes proportional to their tonnage, usually including strike, air defence, patrol, AEW and ASW types. The American Nimitz class carriers, each capable of operating up to 85 aircraft, will be countered by the new Soviet CVN of some 75,000 tons full load displacement, which is due for sea trials by the end of the decade, although the Soviet Navy is unlikely to be able to match the US Navy in numbers for perhaps 40 or 50 years, if, indeed, that should ever be its intention. The French Navy is firmly committed to maintaining a force of two aircraft carriers and is currently building one nuclear powered carrier (PAH-1) of some 50,000 tons displacement, with a second (PAH-2) on order, but no other navy was known to have plans for CVNs as of mid-1986.

As in other naval spheres, costs are escalating rapidly: the next two Nimitz class carriers will cost well over $2,000 million each for the

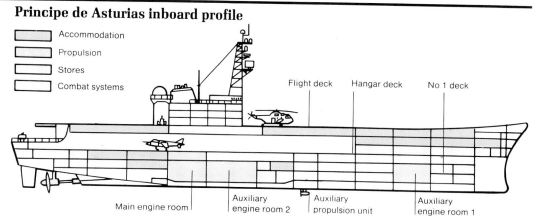

Principe de Asturias inboard profile

Accommodation
Propulsion
Stores
Combat systems

Flight deck   Hangar deck   No 1 deck

Main engine room   Auxiliary engine room 2   Auxiliary propulsion unit   Auxiliary engine room 1

Above: The allocation of space on the new Spanish aircraft carrier Principe de Asturias, whose complement of 20 aircraft will include Harriers and ASW and troop-carrying helicopters. The

ships alone, without counting the air wing. Several nations have, therefore, been looking for a cheaper way to take air power to sea, a search to which STOVL aircraft seem to offer the only realistic answer. The result is the next type, the medium-sized aircraft carrier with a full-length flight deck but operating STOVL aircraft such as the Sea Harrier or Yak-38 Forger together with large numbers of helicopters. Such vessels range in size from the Spanish *Principe de Asturias* (14,700 tons) through the British Invincible class (19,500 tons) to the Soviet Kiev class (42,000 tons).

The problem of escalating costs has, not surprisingly, come up before. In the early 1970s the US Navy found itself faced with the impending block obsolescence of its Essex class ASW aircraft carriers, and the

design, which is based on the US Navy's Sea Control Ship concept of the early 1970s, seems an excellent and relatively inexpensive method of getting air power to sea. Its only major weakness is the light

response proposed in the Chief of Naval Operations' Project 60 involved a new type of aircraft carrier for forward deployment in peace, enabling the high-value CVNs and CVs to be held back in low-risk areas until hostilities started. This new type, known as the Sea Control Ship (SCS), was to be an austere design able to take 14 SH-3 ASW helicopters and three AV-8 Harrier STOVL aircraft.

The SCS would have been relatively cheap — approximately one eighth of the price of a CVN — but soon after Admiral Zumwalt's retirement in 1974 the

Below: An F/A-18 Hornet of the US Navy's Pacific Fleet training squadron VFA-125 Rough Raiders is readied for launch from USS Constellation during carrier trials in July 1983.

on-board weapons fit of four Meroka CIWS. Nevertheless, the ship will add significantly to NATO's capability, and shows great imagination on the part of the Spanish Navy.

project was quietly shelved. There were three contributory factors: first, the SCS was unpopular with naval aviators who saw it as a threat to future funding by Congress of their large, very expensive CVNs; secondly, tests carried out by the USS *Guam*, reroled temporarily from LHA to proto-SCS, suggested it would be unable to defend itself against future Soviet threats; and thirdly, the apparently dramatic increase in the capabilities of current land-based ASW aircraft suggested that they would be better able to deal with the ASW threat, especially in peacetime. The SCS project has had a tangible outcome, however, in the shape of the Spanish Navy's *Principe de Asturias*, which is based closely on the SCS design, but with certain additions, the most noticeable of which is the ski-jump.

The question of aircraft carrier costs was examined again in the US Navy a few years later, when a study group was instructed by the Secretary of Defense to examine the prospects for a medium-sized aircraft carrier of about 50,000 tons displacement as an alternative to building more ships of the Nimitz class. This project, known as the CVNX, suggested three possible designs, but these were quickly shelved. Then, only two years later, the whole issue was reopened, this time with a proposal for a medium-sized conventionally powered carrier under the designation CVV, and a carrier to this design was put into the budget proposals with the support of President Carter. It was, however, strongly opposed by Congress and eventually it was agreed to build a sixth Nimitz class CVN, USS *George Washington* (CVN-73).

The third type of aircraft carrier is a small group of ships with half-length flight decks for operating helicopters. The principal examples are the two ships of the Soviet Moskva class (17,500 tons) and the Italian *Vittorio Veneto* (8,850 tons). Finally, a large number of cruisers,

Representative aircraft carrier flight deck layouts

There are four main types of aircraft-carrying warships, the most common being the numerous frigates, destroyers and cruisers with aft-mounted flight decks for one or two helicopters. Then there are ASW helicopter cruisers with conventional superstructures and forward armament allied to large flight decks aft, such as the Vittorio Veneto (Italy) and the Moskva class (USSR). Dedicated flat-tops are two main types. In the 20,000-ton range are the new light carriers—the Invincible class (UK), Guiseppe Garibaldi (Italy) and (Principe de Asturias (Spain)— which operate a mix of STOVL aircraft (inevitably the BAe Sea Harrier), and ASW helicopters, though the Italian ship does not yet have Sea Harriers for political reasons; each incorporates a ski-jump to enhance the Sea Harrier's payload. At the top end of the scale come the fleet carriers, such as the French Clemenceau class and the US types. In an intermediate category is the Soviet Kiev class, whose offset flight deck leaves enough space for a heavy armament on the foredeck. The flight-deck design of the new Soviet carrier Kremlin will allow for the operation of conventional takeoff and landing fighters and attack aircraft.

Vittorio Veneto

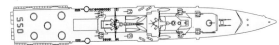

Moskva class

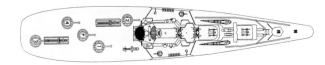

Giuseppe Garibaldi

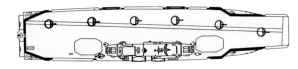

Principe de Asturias

Invincible class

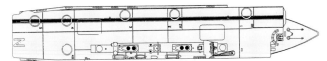

Clemenceau class

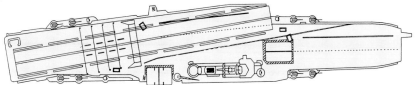

Nimitz class

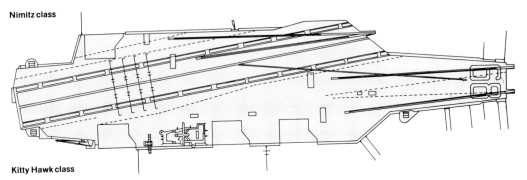

Kitty Hawk class

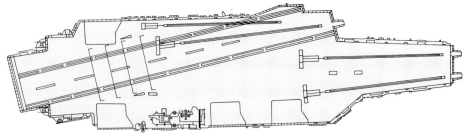

Kiev class

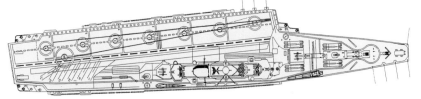

Vittorio Veneto (Italy). Built in the 1960s, the Vittorio Veneto operates nine AB 212 or four SH-3D Sea King ASW helicopters and has two Standard SAM launchers, Otomot anti-ship missiles and the Dardo close-in weapon system.

Moskva (USSR). The two ships of the Moskva class were designed to counter US SSBNs deployed in the Mediterranean. Carrying 15-18 Hormone helicopters, they are similar in concept to the Vittorio Veneto and are able to mount a heavy armament of SAMs, ASW missiles and two 57mm guns.

Giuseppe Garibaldi (Italy). Commissioned in 1985, she carries 12 SH-3D Sea King helicopters, but the Italian Navy hopes she will eventually carry STOVL aircraft as well. Despite the lack of a clear foredeck she carries a heavy armament of Apside SAMs, Otomat SSMs and six 40mm guns for close-in defence.

Principe de Asturias (Spain). After the success of an ex-US light carrier, *Dedalo*, Spain has built its own carrier, based on the US Sea Control Concept. Six to eight Harrier fighters and a similar number of helicopters are carried, but armament is just four Meroka CIWS. The Meroke consists of 12 20mm Oerlikons mounted in two rows of six.

Invincible class (UK). All that remains of the once substantial British carrier fleet is the three Invincible class ships. They carry five Sea Harriers plus nine anti-submarine and two airborne early warning Sea Kings. Armament is Sea Dart SAMs and two Phalanx CIWS.

Clemenceau class (France). Smallest of the fleet carriers, *Clemenceau* and *Foch* (32,780 tons) carry Super Etendard strike fighters, Alizé ASW aircraft and helicopters. With 8° angled decks, steam catapults and 543x97ft (165.5x29.5m) flight decks they have proved a good investment and will be followed by two 50,000-ton nuclear powered carriers in the 1990s.

Nimitz class (USA). The four ships of the 91,400-ton nuclear powered Nimitz class are the mightiest warships afloat. Each carries 24 F-14 Tomcat, 24 F/A-18 Hornet, 10 A-6E and 4 KA-6D Intruder, 4 E-2C Hawkeye, 4 EA-6B Prowler, 10 S-3A Viking and 6 SH-3H Sea King—a more powerful tactical air force than that of many nations. On-board armament comprises Sea Sparrow SAMs and three Phalanx CIWS for point defence: their main protection is provided by patrolling fighters and surface escorts with ASW systems and area defence SAMs.

Kitty Hawk class (USA). Although they are similar in size to the Nimitz class vessels and carry almost identical air wings, the conventionally powered Kitty Hawk class ships displace some 10,000 tons less. The huge area of their flight decks in comparison to those of other carriers is apparent, and at 1,046ft (318.6m) long and 252ft (76.9m) wide they permit operation of all types of aircraft in all weathers. As with the Nimitz class, on-board armament is light and may be strengthened in future.

Kiev class (USSR). Primary mission of the Kiev class ships is ASW, for which 18-21 Ka-25 Hormone helicopters are carried. The angled flight deck also caters for 12 Yak-36 Forger strike aircraft, which have demonstrated that they are capable of rolling takeoffs. the weapons fit includes SAMs, anti-submarine and surface-to-surface missiles, CIWS and torpedoes.

destroyers and frigates have flight decks for one or two helicopters for ASW and over-the-horizon targeting.

FLIGHT DECK DESIGN

The design of the flight deck is crucial to the efficient operation of an aircraft carrier, and there have been a number of innovations since the advent of jet aircraft, including the angled flight deck, automated approach and landing aids and the steam catapult. Further improvements, such as deck-edge lifts, represent sensible, evolutionary steps to increase the deck area. The abortive British CVA-01 design, although conceived in the 1960s, still probably represents the ultimate arrangement for economical and efficient use of deck-space.

The alternative approach is the straight-through flight deck, now only suitable for STOVL aircraft, and the major breakthrough in this area has been the invention of the ski-jump. Like so many great inventions, the ski-jump is cheap and truly simple: not only is it very easy to construct, but no modifications whatsoever are required for the aircraft, while pilots find it safe and simple to use. Ski-jumps have already been fitted to the British carriers *Hermes* (12°), recently sold to the Indian Navy, *Invincible* (7°), *Illustrious* (7°), and *Ark Royal* (12°), the Indian Navy, the Italian *Giuseppe Garibaldi* (6°) and the Spanish *Principe de Asturias* (12°). The US Marine Corps has bought three ramps for training at airfields but so far as is known there had been no proposal to provide a US Navy ship with such a fitting by 1986.

The unique capabilities of the Sea Harrier, combined with the ski-jump, have led to a totally new concept in which a suitable merchant ship would be converted into an aircraft carrier in a matter of days. The Shipborne Containerized Air Defence System (SCADS) involves 230 standard ISO containers mounted on the deck

Above: BAe's two-seat Harrier demonstrator carries out a land-based trial of the Skyhook concept designed to enable Sea Harriers to operate from 500-ton ships. the demonstration of the Harrier's ability to hover in a notional 10ft (3m) cube was a total success.

of a container ship of 30,000 tons or more and topped with a specially prepared flight deck. The containers can be fitted for roles such as missile launcher, fuel storage, aircraft maintenance, personnel accommodation, command post and so on to enable a thoroughly effective aircraft carrier to be produced. This is, in effect, a successor to the MAC-ships used in World War II, and is very

Left: BAe has carried out many demonstrations of the unique capabilities of the Harrier/Sea Harrier: here a group of officers and sailors surround a Harrier on the flight deck of the French Navy's air-capable cruise Jeanne d'Arc. Current users are India, Spain, the UK and USA.

similar to the US Navy's Arapaho system which has been tested by the Royal Navy on the RFA *Reliant* on a protracted deployment to the Falkland Islands with Sea King helicopters embarked.

Another device which does away with the need for a flight deck altogether is the SkyHook proposed by British Aerospace, a ship-mounted crane designed to lift a Sea Harrier outboard and, when the pilot is ready, release it. Recovery would require the aircraft to hover in a 10ft (3m) cube abreast the crane position and moving forward at the same speed as the ship, whereupon the computer-controlled, space-stablized crane would lock on to the aircraft and lift it aboard. The system envisages all on-board aircraft handling being carried out on mechanically operated trestles, which would not only lead to greater efficiency and more economic use of space but also greatly reduce manpower requirements. Mounted in a 5,000-ton hull the system could operate an air squadron of four Sea Harriers and two Sea Kings, giving the ship a capability far beyond that previously considered possible for such a small vessel.

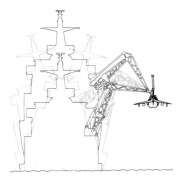

Above: When extended, the ship-mounted Skyhook's pick-up head is space-stabilized by ship motion sensors and hydraulic rams.

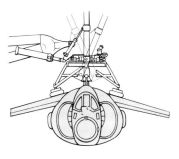

Above: Details of the Skyhook pick-up head, showing the aircraft being held against the resilient docking pads by the lock-on jack.

An intermediate type of flight deck is used on some cruiser-sized ships, mainly to enable large numbers of helicopters to be operated, with conventional superstructures and large flight decks aft. Such ships as the Soviet Moskva class (17,500 tons), the Italian *Vittorio Veneto* (8,850 tons) and the French *Jeanne d'Arc* (12,365 tons) mount a normal gun and missile armament forward, considerably enhancing their ability to defend themselves, but are restricted to operating helicopters or STOVL fixed-wing aircraft, and would not be suitable for CTOL operations.

Finally, virtually every modern cruiser and destroyer and most frigates have flight decks and on-board facilities for one or two helicopters. This adds immeasurably to their ASW capabilities since, as described in more detail elsewhere, the high speeds of modern submarines compared to those of ships and torpedoes mean that a helicopter is essential to provide a timely response at longer ranges. In addition, a number of modern anti-ship missile systems require an airborne relay/control station for over-the-horizon targeting. The smallest hull capable of accommodating a helicopter is that of the British-designed Osprey class, of which the only current examples are the 505-ton fishery protection vessels built in Denmark for the Burmese government.

Surprisingly, the new US Navy Arleigh Burke class destroyers are being built with a flight deck but

no hangar, while the Japanese Hatakaze class destroyers are being built with no aircraft facilities at all; both types will have to depend upon other ships in the group for aircraft support, a most surprising approach which is very unlikely to be repeated.

Most Western air-capable cruisers and destroyers have large and obvious hangars. The Soviet Navy, however, has developed a very neat (although possibly mechanically complicated) hangar, which opens to admit the helicopter and then closes over it. Fitted on ships such as those of the Kara, Kresta and Udaloy classes, this hangar arrangement has many advantages, though working space for the aircraft engineers may be very cramped.

Some navies have developed special devices to capture and control helicopters on such small flight decks. Most widely used of these is the Canadian Bear-Trap, which is mounted in the centre of the flight deck. Having engaged the trap while hovering some 10ft (3m) above the deck, the helicopter is hauled down and held firmly in place. The US Navy is fitting a similar device, the Rapid Hauldown and Traversing System (RAST), to its Oliver Hazard Perry (FFG 7)

Above: The Canadian forces have used the Beartrap system for many years to enable large helicopters to land safely on small ships, especially in the heavy seas found in the North Atlantic.

class frigates. Other navies, although operating in the same waters as the Canadians and Americans, do not seem to think such devices necessary and consider that their helicopters can land on even very small flight decks in almost any sea-state.

WEAPONS

There has been a marked divergence of views on the armament required by aircraft carriers to meet contemporary conditions. In the 1960s the US Navy seemed to go away completely from armament for its aircraft carriers and the Forrestal class ships, for example, which originally had eight 5in guns, had four of these removed in 1967 and the remainder in the early 1970s. Two of the class were then fitted with three Basic Point Defense Missile Systems (BPDMS) each, while the other two now have three. However, following a further reassessment of the

threat, especially from sea-skimming missiles, three Phalanx 20mm CIWS are to be fitted during the Service Life Extension Program (SLEP) refits, although this means that USS Ranger (CV 61) will not have these weapons until May 1994. Each of the two French aircraft carriers is fitted with eight 3.9in (100mm) automatic guns in single mounts on sponsons outboard of the flight deck; four will be replaced by Crotale Navale missile systems at their next refits.

A different approach was taken by the Soviet and Italian navies in the 1960s. In this the flight deck was sited in such a way that the foredeck was left clear for a fairly heavy weapons fit. Thus, Vittorio Veneto carries one twin SAM launcher, four single Teseo SSM launchers, eight 76mm guns, six twin 40mm guns and two triple torpedo tubes, while the Moskva class vessels have two twin SAM launchers, four 57mm twin guns, one twin SUW-N-1 ASW missile launcher and two 12-barrel RBU-6000 ASW rocket launchers.

Both these navies have, however, modified their design concepts for their respective follow-on classes. The Soviet Kiev class has an angled deck, though not, as in the Western aircraft carriers, to leave the forward flight deck clear to launch aircraft, but rather to leave the forecastle clear for a heavy weapons fit. In fact, the Kiev's armament is heavier than the total weaponry of a Krivak II frigate. The Italian Navy, on the other hand, needed to fit a ski-jump for the anticipated STOVL aircraft on the Giuseppe Garibaldi and therefore adopted a straight-through flight deck; even so, it has still managed to include four Teseo launchers for Otomat SSMs, two Albatros SAM launchers, six 40mm guns and six torpedo tubes.

With the Invincible class light aircraft carriers the Royal Navy fitted a straight-through flight deck, but left the forecastle-head clear for a twin Sea Dart launcher (SAM with a limited SSM capability). Following the 1982 South Atlantic war experience, however, Phalanx 20mm CIWS have been fitted, two in Invincible and Illustrious and three in Ark Royal, while all three now have two 20mm GAM-BO1 single guns installed. The Spanish Principe de Asturias, on the other hand, is armed only with four Meroka 20mm CIWS.

There has been much speculation concerning the armament to be fitted to the Soviet Navy's nuclear powered aircraft carrier Kremlin, which was launched in 1985. The various drawings so far released are inevitably highly speculative and disagree on whether the flight deck will continue forward to the bows as in the US Navy's current CVNs and CVs, or will be angled to port, leaving the

foredeck clear for armament as on the current Kiev class. There can be little doubt, however, that the Soviet Navy will take the opportunity to include the heaviest weapons fit possible on such a large hull.

CARRIER-BASED AIRCRAFT

Naval air power has five primary roles—anti-submarine warfare, strike/attack, air defence, electronic warfare and airborne early warning—while airframes divide into three obvious categories: conventional takeoff and landing (CTOL), fixed-wing short takeoff and vertical landing (STOVL) and helicopters.

ASW tasks are performed by a few carrier-based CTOL aircraft such as the S-3 Viking and the Alizé and by many types of helicopters. CTOL ASW aircraft must be able to transit rapidly between the aircraft carrier and the patrol line, and then spend as much time as possible actually on patrol, during which they must be able to detect, locate, identify and finally destroy submarine targets using a variety of on-board sensors, including radar for the detection and classification of surface targets, forward-looking infra-red (FLIR), magnetic anomaly detectors (MAD), sonobuoys and electronic

Below: Images provided to the pilot's cockpit display by the F/A-8 Hornet's AAS-38 forward-looking infra-red (FLIR) targeting pod. The subject is a Tarawa class amphibious assault ship.

countermeasures (ECM) equipment. All these sensors, combined with inputs from the parent carrier and other ships and aircraft, produce so much information that considerable data processing power is needed if timely and effective use is to be made of it. Finally, to attack its targets the aircraft needs a weapon load which ideally includes anti-ship missiles, homing torpedoes, rockets and conventional or nuclear depth bombs.

The only current CTOL aircraft to combine all these facilities is the US Navy's S-3 Viking, although some older and much less capable aircraft such as the S-2 Tracker and Alizé are still in service. The Soviet Navy clearly requires ASW aircraft comparable to the S-3 to equip its new carriers, but no suitable airframe is known to exist.

The alternative to the CTOL ASW aircraft is the helicopter. The earliest ASW helicopters offered little more than a rapid means of delivering torpedoes as a counter to the speeds of nuclear submarines, but as helicopter ranges and payloads have increased the helicopter has become an autonomous weapon system. Further, it has had the exceptional advantage of bringing an air capability to ships as small as frigates.

The most advanced ASW helicopters in service are the US Navy's SH-60B Seahawk LAMPS III (Light Airborne Multipurpose System Mk III), the British Sea King HAS.5 and Lynx HAS.3, and the Soviet Ka-32 Helix. For the future, the most important

Top: US Navy S-3B Viking. Compared with the S-3A, the S-3B has increased sensor processing capability, better ESM and a new sonobuoy receiver; it also carries Harpoon anti-ship missiles.

Above: Sikorsky SH-60B Seahawk. Sensors available include an APS-124 search radar, nose-mounted ALQ-142 ESM system and 25 sonobuoys carried in launch tubes behind the cabin door.

Below: Westland Lynx HAS Mk 2 of the Royal Navy carrying a Mk 46 ASW torpedo and an ASQ-81 (V)-2 magnetic anomaly detector (MAD) 'bird'. Lynx operates autonomously in the ASW role.

aircraft in development is the European Helicopter Industries EH-101, a British/Italian Sea King replacement, which will be equipped with Ferranti Blue Kestrel search radar, Marconi sonar systems, Decca ESM and AQS-81 MAD, all brought together by a Ferranti data-handling system.

Strike/attack missions are normally carried out by fixed-wing aircraft using missiles, bombs or rockets. As was so dramatically demonstrated in the South Atlantic war, fast jets armed with sea-skimming missiles make a lethal combination, and similar capabilities are offered by the US A-6 Intruder and S-3 Viking armed with Harpoon missiles and by the British Sea Harrier with Harpoon or Sea Eagle. The Soviet Navy currently has no equivalent capability, but again it must be presumed that it is developing a suitable aircraft/ missile combination for service on the new carriers. Helicopters can also carry anti-ship missiles, and the French Super Frelon carrying AM39 Exocets has already been used by Iraq in the Gulf war, while the British Lynx used Sea Skuas against a surfaced submarine and surface ships in the South Atlantic War.

Air defence is the exclusive preserve of fixed-wing aircraft, of which the most advanced technically are the F-14 Tomcat and the F/A-18 Hornet. Operating from CVNs and the large CVs, the F-14 also performs the recon-naissance role, while the F/A-18 Hornet doubles as a very effective strike/attack aircraft. The Sea Harrier demonstrated its air defence capabilities in the South Atlantic where it was responsible for shooting down in air-to-air' combat 11 Mirages, eight A-4 Skyhawks, one Canberra, one IA-58 Pucara and one C-130 Hercules. The only Soviet carrier-borne aircraft with any air defence capability is the Yak-38 'Forger', a fixed-wing STOVL machine with strictly limited performance.

The only specialized EW aircraft in service is the EA-6B Prowler, a remarkable design with a comprehensive ECM/ESM capability. No other naval air arm has attempted to produce such a sophisticated aircraft.

In the South Atlantic war it was demonstrated that radar picket ships are an inadequate and very vulnerable substitute for early-warning aircraft. The only effective carrier-based AEW aircraft in service is the E-2C Hawkeye, though the British have produced an AEW version of the ubiquitous Westland Sea King helicopter, equipped with a Searchwater radar mounted in an inflatable radome. Despite being conceived in haste at the height of the war, this has proved an effective solution to the problem, although less economical than a fixed-wing CTOL aircraft.

Above: EH Industries was formed in 1980 by Augusta of Italy and Westland of the UK to design and produce the EH-101 multirole naval helicopter to serve the navies of the two countries in the 1990s.

Right: Soviet Navy Ka-27 Helix on the flight deck of the aircraft carrier Kiev. This Ka-27 has its cockpit, engines and rotor head shrouded in canvas for protection against salt water spray.

Below: A French Navy SA.321G Super Frelon ASW helicopter fires an AM.39 Exocet anti-ship missile. Among the duties of the SA.321G is the 'delousing' of French SSBNs before they leave on patrol.

The Soviet practice of providing land-based AEW cover for its naval task groups will doubtless prove vulnerable and inadequate in war and the Soviets will almost certainly have to develop a carrier-borne AEW aircraft to make their new task groups effective. The same applies to the French Navy, whose new nuclear powered aircraft carriers will inevitably be high-value targets in any naval conflict, and highly vulnerable without an AEW aircraft. This subject is discussed more fully in the chapter on Sensors.

LAND-BASED AIRCRAFT

Land-based aircraft are vital to naval operations. Such aircraft are flown by naval aviators in virtually every country except the United Kingdom where, for historical reasons, they are operated by the

Above: Without equal in any other navy is the USN's Grumman EA-6B Prowler electronic warfare aircraft. A squadron of four Prowlers is one of the supporting elements in each carrier air wing.

RAF. The primary role of land-based aircraft is ASW patrol and maritime strike in support of the naval battle, and they can provide effective support in virtually all weather, but can suffer from range limitations, as in the 1982 South Atlantic war, when the Royal Navy Task Force eventually got beyond the range of support aircraft based on Ascension Island.

Perhaps the most important land-based type is the large ASW aircraft, such as the P-3 Orion, Nimrod, Atlantic, Shin Meiwa PS-1, Kawasaki P-2J, Il-38 May and Tu-20 Bear-F. Only three of these, the Atlantic, PS-1 and P-2J, were designed specifically for the ASW mission, while the Nimrod, P-3 and Il-38 are particularly successful ASW conversions of relatively unsuccessful commercial airliners and the 'Bear-F' is a modified strategic bomber.

The Japanese PS-1 is based on the interesting idea that it can alight on water for the search and localization phase of its ASW patrol and use its powerful on-board sonar, rather than expend masses of sonar buoys. The idea has not caught on, however: not only has no other nation tried it, but the Japanese themselves have returned to the land-based ASW aircraft in the form of a large fleet of P-2Js (licence-built, updated P-2 Neptunes) and P-3 Orions.

Land-based ASW aircraft carry out long-range, long-endurance ocean patrols to detect and track submarines in peacetime, and to destroy them in war. In particular, they are required to follow up and classify submarine contacts made by the US Navy's SOSUS and SURTASS surveillance systems and the Soviet equivalents. Their on-board sensors include radar, forward-looking infra-red (FLIR), low-light television (LLTV), sophisticated ECM suites and MAD, and they also deploy expendable sonobuoys with radio

Above: A Royal Navy Sea Harrier takes off from HMS Invincible's 7° ski-jump. HMS Ark Royal has a 12° ski-jump, which enables even greater payloads to be carried in the short take-off mode.

Below: Pre-flight activity on the deck of a Fench aircraft carrier. In the foreground are two Dassault Etendard IVP recce aircraft; the other aircraft are Super Etendard strike fighters.

uplinks to give them a sonar capability, while their weapons include torpedoes, conventional and nuclear depth bombs and air-to-surface missiles. They are similar in these respects to carrier-based ASW aircraft, but have much greater endurance and payload, and are able to conduct more protracted operations.

Published figures for patrol times are 18 hours for the Atlantic, 12 hours for Nimrod and May, and 16 hours for the P-3 Orion. The endurance of the S-3 Viking is somewhat less at nine hours, but advocates of carrier-based airpower argue that, because it is already at sea, and therefore much nearer the scene of action, the S-3 actually spends much less time in transit and just as much time, or perhaps even more, on patrol. However, only a very few navies have aircraft carriers big enough to be able to operate such an aircraft.

Some navies use shore-based helicopters such as the Sea King for short-range ASW missions, and the USSR has developed a unique type—the Mi-14 Haze—specifically for the shore-based ASW role.

Other shore-based aircraft with naval roles are the specialized maritime strike

Above: The Soviet Il-38 May land-based ASW and maritime patrol aircraft, showing radome and MAD boom during a patrol over the Indian Ocean.

aircraft, such as the Tornado, Buccaneer and Tu-22M Backfire. The British use the Tornado and Buccaneer in the North Atlantic and the GIUK gap, while the Federal Republic of Germany uses its Tornados in the Baltic. The Soviet naval air arm (AV-MF) splits its AS-6-armed Tu-16 Badger-C/Gs among the four main fleets, and they are supported by around 70 Tu-16 Badger-A tankers, but how well these elderly and slow aircraft could survive on long-range anti-shipping strikes in essentially hostile airspace is open to question. The AV-MF also operates Tu-22 Blinders, which are split between the Baltic and Black Sea fleets, and a growing number of Tu-22M Backfires, divided between the Northern and Pacific fleets. The primary targets of the Backfires with the Northern Fleet are believed to be NATO task groups operating in the area of the GIUK gap.

Above: Budy refuelling by Tornadoes of the West German Navy. The receiving aircraft is armed with a pair of Komoran anti-ship missiles.

Another special type developed by the Soviet Union is the over-the-horizon targeting aircraft, necessary to give mid-course guidance to ship and submarine-launched missiles, such as the SS-N-3 ad SS-N-12. The Tu-20 Bear-D certainly has such a role and the Tu-16 Badger-D may fulfil a similar function. The Bear-D has a massive radome in its weapons bay, together with some 40 other antennas, blisters and fairings along the fuselage, wings and tail, and appears to be deployed in pairs in this role, but its chances of survival and of achieving coordinated timings, especially with submarines, seems remote.

Finally, shore-based helicopters are being used with

Below: Dassault-Breguet Atlantic of the French navy. This land-based ASW aircraft is operated by five countries; a new version (Atlantique) is now in production, but only for the French Navy so far.

some success in the minesweeping role. The Sikorsky RH-53D, for example, has a strengthened fuselage and upgraded engines, and is equipped to tow mine countermeasures (MCM) devices for sweeping contact, magnetic and acoustically activated mines. The USSR's Mi-8 Hip is used in the same role, and two were deployed in the ASW cruiser *Leningrad* in 1974 when she took part in the operations to clear the Suez Canal of mines following the Arab-Israeli war.

THE FUTURE

The future of the large, nuclear powered supercarrier seems assured in the US and Soviet navies, with the Americans planning a fleet of 15 and the USSR at least two. These carriers are certainly impressive and carry very significant air power, but they are also expensive and, despite

Below: The Mil Mi-14 Haze has been produced as a land-based ASW helicopter for Warsaw Pact countries. Derived from the Mi-8 Hip, the Mi-14 is somewhat larger than the Sikorsky SH-3 Sea King.

Above: Tuoplev TU-22M Backfire of Soviet Naval Aviation (AV-MF). This swing-wing land-based naval aircraft has been the subject of intense debate as to its true role.

Below: The Tu-20 Bear-D is fitted with numerous sensors for its surveillance role. It also provides mid-course guidance for ship-launched cruise missiles.

their air wing, on-board armament and protective escorts, vulnerable.

There was a time when the huge size, heavy armament, thick armour-plating and imposing aspect of the battleship gave it an aura of invulnerability, and it was air power, primarily in the form of carrier-borne aircraft, that dissipated that aura. Like battle-ships, aircraft carriers represent such concentrations of maritime power that they must inevitably be prime targets for submarine, surface ship, aircraft and tactical missile attacks. They could also be targeted by land-based, long-range missiles: it is reported that the USSR has a proportion of its ICBMs allocated to just such a purpose. There is, therefore, a possibility that the aircraft carrier might one day become as obsolete as the battleship.

The British Royal Navy's experience with the cancellation of CVA-01, and the retirement from the aircraft carrier scene of the Australian, Canadian and

Below: An outstanding strike aircraft, the Buccaneer equips RAF squadrons that have an anti-shipping role. This example is armed with four Sea Eagle anti-ship missiles.

Dutch navies, shows that capabilities can become too expensive. The cost of even medium-sized aircraft carriers, plus the further costs of the specialized aircraft and aircrew in the air wing, can exceed available budgets unless some other capability is deemed to be less important and is sacrificed instead. It would appear, then, that technology must be applied to producing much cheaper, more effective and more survivable carriers for the smaller navies —and perhaps also, with advantage, the large navies. The Italian and Spanish navies are showing what can be achieved if ambitions and operational requirements are kept within reasonable bounds.

For the air component of carrier fleets it appears that there are two major areas for development: more effective and capable STOVL aircraft, and a viable fleet AEW platform that does not need a large CTOL aircraft carrier to accommodate and launch it. The most outstanding area of interest, however, is the forthcoming appearance of the Soviet nuclear propelled aircraft carrier and its air wing. Satellite photographs have already shown the first of the class under construction at Nikolayev, and a 975ft (297m) mock-up flight deck is known to be in use at Saki on the Black Sea.

The aircraft believed to be under development for the *Kremlin*'s air wing are navalized versions of the Su-27 Flanker multi-role fighter/attack aircraft, MiG-29 Fulcrum interceptor, and Su-25 Frogfoot close-support aircraft, together with a STOVL successor to the Yak-38 Forger. There must also be an AEW type under development, although whether this will be of fixed-wing or rotary-wing configuration remains to be seen.

C³ and Electronic Warfare

Communications are among the most complicated of naval systems. Ships need to be able to communicate with both surface and subsurface warships and with merchant ships (ship-to-ship), with aircraft (ship-to-air), and with distant military and civilian agencies (ship-to-shore). This necessitates a mass of communications links: it is difficult enough to fit them all in from a physical point of view, and the electronic aspects are even more complicated, because the profusion of emitters associated with communications, sensor and weapon systems create major problems of electromagnetic compatability and mutual interference, while the proliferation of weapon systems and sensors means that the actual volume of traffic is increasing steadily. The resulting conflicts may be difficult and expensive to resolve, but they are by no means insuperable.

SURFACE COMMUNICATIONS

A good example of the modern approach to surface communications is the British Marconi Integrated Communications System 3 (ICS3), which is now in service on board the Royal Navy's Type 22 frigates, Type 42 destroyers and Invincible class light aircraft carriers, and the Royal Netherlands Navy's Kortenaer class frigates. ICS3 provides for the transmission and reception of communications

in all types of ship-to-ship, ship-to-air and ship-to-shore tactical and strategic communications in the VLF, LF, MF and HF bands as well as interfacing with VHF, UHF and satcom circuits. A telegraph message handling system sorts and stores messages electronically, and there are visual display and editing facilities.

The transmitting and receiving subsystems handle voice, data, teletype and morse signals over a number of circuits, in the 10kHz-30MHz range, using the AM (amplitude modulated) mode, upper sideband and fully suppressed carrier. Transmit power output is variable—100, 250 or 700 watts—according to the range required. The VHF and UHF set is the Type 1203 (Plessey PVS.1730 equipment family), submarine communications are handled by the Type 2008 underwater telephone transmitter/receiver, and satellite communications are by means of the SCOT shipborne terminal, operating in the 7-8GHz frequency band (SHF).

A major requirement of the ICS3 was to improve the ability to switch frequencies and the spacing between receiver and transmitter channels, and also to reduce mutual interference between the communications systems and other electronic systems on the ship.

The distribution and supervisory sub-system has three main functions: the distribution of teletype, voice and morse signals between the ship's radio

equipment and the users; the provision of control facilities at each remote user position; and the provision of central control and monitoring facilities for the management of the ship's communications system. A central switching matrix enables any user position to be connected instantaneously to any UHF, VHF, HF or satcom communications circuit. The telegraph subsystem is an automated message processing and handling package catering for all types of naval telegraph traffic, using minimal manpower in a traditionally manpower-intensive area.

SUBMARINE COMMUNICATIONS

The ability of nuclear submarines ability to hide themselves in the depths of the oceans has a number of obvious advantages, but also incurs two serious problems, the first of which is the difficulty of exercising command and control—that is, the ability of the national command authorities to communicate by reliable, secure and survivable links to their strategic forces. This is especially true of the US SSBNs, whose deterrent mission requires the ability to

Below: The twin Scot satellite communications terminals on HMS Invincible and, to the left of the large dome housing the missile fire control radar, the whip antenna for the ICS3 integrated communications systems.

survive a Soviet first strike and then retaliate.

The orders to start the implementation of the US Government's Single Integrated Operational Plan (SIOP) will originate with the National Command Authority (NCA). Executive instructions are then issued by the National Military Command Center (NMCC) or, if that has been destroyed, by the Alternate NMCC, or, in the last resort, by the National Emergency Airborne Command Post (NEACP).

Primary survivable communications to patrolling SSBNs are provided by the TACAMO (Take Charge And Move Out) system, which comprises four EC-130G and 16 EC-130Q Hercules aircraft, one of which is always airborne over the Atlantic with another over the Pacific. The primary link to submerged submarines is by VLF transmission using a 6.2-mile (10km) trailing wire antenna and a 100kW transmitter: to transmit, the aircraft banks in a continuous tight circle with the antenna hanging vertically below.

The C-130s are due to be replaced by 15 Boeing E-6As, rebuilds of ex-airline Boeing 707s,

Below: The Boeing E-6A will replace the Lockheed EC-130 in the US Navy's TACAMO (Take Charge and Move Out) fleet, which forms the airborne VLF link between the US National Command Authority and SSBNs at sea.

EMP hardened and costing some $100 million each. They will be equipped with special mission-related electronics, ESM systems and the same type of VLF sets and antennas as the C-130s.

TACAMO is essential to the US second-strike capability and is currently regarded as survivable, but the USSR must treat these aircraft as prime targets and is doubtless developing satellites to detect and track them. Their destruction

might be quite a different matter, however.

The communications problems are not confined to SSBNs: because of their roles it is often necessary for SSNs to communicate with their bases, as illustrated during the 1982 South Atlantic war when the British SSN HMS *Conqueror* required clearance to attack the Argentine cruiser *General Belgrano*.

A second major system is ELF (extremely low frequency),

which lies in the 0.3-3kHz band. This will comprise 124 miles (200km) of buried antenna in Michigan. US SSBNs are known to have received ELF at depths of about 330ft (100m), but the drawback of these low frequency systems is their very low data rate.

ELECTRONIC WARFARE

Both surface warships and submarines are almost completely dependent on electronic systems for their internal functioning, for the detection and location of threats, for the launch and control of the appropriate weapon systems, and for communicating both within their group and back to base. If any of these is disrupted for a significant period or at a critical moment during an engagement the ship may well be destroyed.

The electronic systems used by warships range across the entire electromagnetic spectrum, from sonar and ELF radio in the audio frequency band at the extreme lower end to lasers at the higher, making it an arena for campaigns, battles and skirmishes both in war and, increasingly, in peace, which

are deadly even though no bullets are seen to fly. Electronic warfare makes a significant contribution to each zone in the layered defences around a naval task group, and is capable of dealing with air, surface and submarine threats. The tactics of this EW battle are divided up into a number of areas: electronic intelligence (elint), electronic support measures (ESM), electronic countermeasures (ECM) and electronic counter-countermeasures (ECCM).

Elint, which is directly analogous to intelligence in the other areas of military activity, involves the discovery of the uses to which a potential enemy is putting the electromagenetic spectrum. It is achieved by satellites, ground listening stations, special aircraft, ships, balloons and RPVs, as well as by the usual covert and overt intelligence gathering activities. The aim of elint is to discover what active and passive electronic devices exist, where they are, what they do and how they do it, which means detecting and analyzing as many of the relevant electronic parameters as possible—frequencies used, pulse repetition frequencies, pulse widths, scan rates, types of modulation, types of multiplexing, and so on.

There are many means of establishing an elint data base. Both the USA and the USSR fly elint satellite missions, popularly known as ferrets, which are

Submarine laser communications

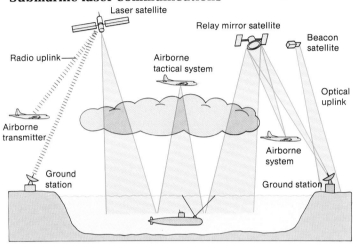

Above: A major strategic problem is that of communicating with submerged submarines, and the use of lasers for this task is now being investigated. There are several possibilities: ground- or air-based radio uplinks could be retransmitted by space-based blue/green laser to submarines, or signals from a land-based laser could be reflected off a space-based mirror using adaptive optics. Direct air-to-submarine laser communications are also feasible.

Below: Modern naval sensor systems use increasingly sophisticated electronic techniques to present user-friendly displays. A good example is this Israeli Elisra NS-9001 ship-borne ELINT system operator's console.

used against electronic targets both on land and at sea. Similarly, both nations, along with many others, use aircraft such as the US U-2R, Soviet Il-18 Coot-A, and the British Nimrod R.2. On the oceans the most immediately obvious elint activity is that of the Soviet Navy, which operates a host of intelligence collectors, ranging from converted trawlers of 700 tons or so up to large, well-equipped ships such as the 4,000-ton Balzam class, which are specially designed for the purpose. It can be assumed, however, that other navies carry out similar activities from normal naval vessels, albeit not as elaborately as the USSR.

From elint stems ESM, which is the interception of enemy electronic emissions and the process of identifying them, usually by reference to a computer-stored memory bank. In a ship, for example, the interception of two different radar signals on a common bearing could lead to a reasonable assessment of the type and nationality of the target without it being detected by any other means. ESM is essentially a passive function and one which an enemy cannot detect.

If ESM is the passive function, ECM is the active, detectable function, the methodology of what to do about the electronic emissions of an actual or potential enemy. One of the principal ECM activities is the jamming of signals, either broadband jamming, which covers a wide frequency bracket, or spot jamming on a specific frequency. The decision to jam is not one to be taken lightly, and there are many situations where jamming may be self-defeating. Alternatively, as in other spheres, it may be feasible to use deception, for example, by transmitting false echoes to mislead an enemy or a missile's seeker as to a ship's actual location.

Finally, ECCM refers to the steps which might be taken to overcome an enemy's ECM. For example, if an enemy uses a jammer a variety of actions can be taken to overcome it, including increasing the transmission power to burn through the jamming, adjusting the frequency to just off the spot jammed frequency, or changing frequency altogether.

A good example of a particularly advanced ESM/ECM system is the US Navy's SLQ-32(V), which comprises three suites of increasing complexity and cost. (V)1, the basic ESM suite, provides warning, identification and bearings of threatening radar-guided anti-ship missiles and their associated threat platforms; intended for installation in Knox class frigates and other small combatants, it comprises port and starboard antenna assemblies giving full

360° coverage and instantaneous frequency measuring (IFM) receivers which cover all major threat frequencies.

(V)2, which adds the antenna and receiver subsystems needed for extended ESM frequency coverage to facilitate the identification and bearing determination of navigation radars and IFF transponders in threat platforms, is being installed in DDGs, FFGs and Spruance class destroyers.

(V)3, the ECM suite, is another hardware add-on comprising the transmitter, transmit antennas, high voltage power supplies, multiple travelling-wave tubes and transponders needed to add a jamming capability. Designed to either prevent or delay the targeting or launch of enemy missiles, or, once the missiles have been launched, to deflect them away from their designated target, it is intended for cruisers and certain other major warship classes. The system uses multiple beam antennas and miniature travelling-wave tubes to develop a very high effective radiated

Right: HSA Sphinx ESM antennas. Two of three frequency antennas can be seen above the ball-shaped M-20, while below it is an eight-sector circular array used to establish bearings.

Above: The Raytheon SLQ-32 is the latest US Navy EW equipment. (V)1 is fitted in small ships, eg, Knox class frigates, (V)2 in DDGs, FFGs and the Spruance class, and (V)3 in cruisers.

Above: The Hughes SLQ-17, shown here mounted on a US Navy aircraft carrier, is a deception jammer for protection against cruise missiles which generates an offset radar image of the target ship.

power, usable against search radars on aircraft such as the Soviet Badger or Bear-D to disrupt their targeting of NATO fleet units.

In defence of its own ship the (V)3 suite counters incoming missiles by diverting or deceiving the missiles' radar seekers, and it also has the ability to deal with submarines trying to achieve pre-launch target acquisition by a quick pop-up radar look by using an automatic, quick-reaction mode which jams the target signal even before it has been properly analyzed.

All three versions of the SLQ-32 use an identical display and control console in the ship's combat information centre (CIC), and they all use the UYK-19 computer, but with memory size increasing from 48K in the (V)1 to 64K in the (V)2 and 80K in the (V)3. All three versions also control the Mk 36 Decoy Launching System, described below.

A British naval system adopted by 18 navies is the Racal RDL series of manual ESM systems. The RDL-1BC, for example, is intended for use on small

warships such as fast patrol boats, and provides instantaneous bearing, automatic pulse analysis, frequency measurement, and an alarm function. The equipment uses solid-state technology and operates in the E to I bands. One valuable facility is that the pulse parameters of up to five sets of known hostile radar transmissions can be set up in the unit using plug-in PCBs, and when a signal received matches any of these parameters a visual or aural warning is given to alert the CIC.

A functionally identical system, the RDL-1BCS, is designed for use in submarines, and add-on units can give the RDL-1BC greater capabilities to match the needs of larger ships. The RDL-2ABC suite, for example, adds frequency measurement, visual pulse analysis and RF amplification in the analysis channel, to give extended range coverage and better analysis facilities.

The Cutlass computer-controlled system, which can be added to tackle signal densities of up to 500,000 pulses per second over the D to J (1-18 GHz) bands

automatically compares signals with the built-in threat library of the parameters of up to 2,000 radars. The operator is then presented with a listing of their identities and the degree of threat: the 25 highest threats are displayed automatically, and the operator can request the next 125 in descending order of priority. Cutlass uses an IFM receiver, which gives a high degree of probability that a short duration signal, such as that of a strike aircraft or a submarine turning on its radar for quick-look tactical updates, will be detected.

Not surprisingly, little is known about the internal details of Soviet warships' EW systems. However, examination of the antenna systems on these ships indicates that this is an area the Soviets take very seriously. For

Kiev and Novorossiysk EW antennas

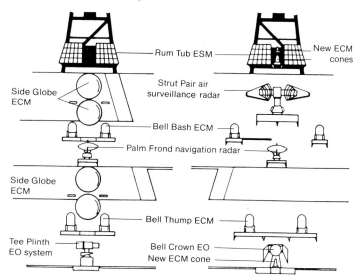

Below: The usual concentration of antennas and sensors to be seen on all Soviet warships, in this case the aircraft carrier Minsk. On the left of the picture are a pair of Rum Tubs with, below them, two pairs of Side Globe antennas. All have an EW/ESM role.

Above: One half of the Soviet carrier Kiev's ESM fit comprises two Rum Tub ESM antennas, two Bell Bash jammer antennas (below the top pair of Side Globes) and two Bell Thump jammers (below the second pair of Side Globes), as on the Minsk.

Above: ESM fit on Novorossiysk comprises Rum Tub, Bell Bash and Bell Thump. Side Globe is not fitted though its function is still performed by a different system. At the foot of the diagram is the Tin Man optronic device replacing Tee Plinth on Kiev (left).

example, the *Kirov* mounts two Round House ECM antennas, eight Side Globe ECM/ESM antennas and four Rum Tub ESM antennas, as well as a variety of DF antennas.

ANTI-MISSILE DECOYS

Another valuable shipboard system to counter the anti-ship missile threat is chaff, which consists of a mass of strips of metal foil. The technique originated during World War II, when it was used during bombing raids: vast clouds of foil strips, code-named Window, cut to specific lengths and released in appropriate patterns, radar displays which caused the operators to become completely confused. Modern naval chaff weapons work on exactly the same principle, but are used to confuse and mislead anti-ship missile radar seeker heads.

There are three primary working modes for naval chaff. In the first, if a radar-guided anti-ship missile is detected before its seeker has selected a target, a number of chaff clouds distributed around the vessel may cause the seeker to lock on to a false return signal. Alternatively, if the ship's ECM equipment succeeds in causing a locked-on missile to break lock, chaff rockets may be used to give the missile a false target on to which it can then lock and home; this is known as the distraction mode. Finally, for last-ditch defence of a ship against a missile detected at short range and in the final stages of flight, the rapid deployment of a chaff cloud within the range cell on which the missile seeker has locked should seduce the missile away from the ship by shifting the centroid of the apparent target.

All navies employ generally similar decoy launchers on

Seduction mode chaff operation

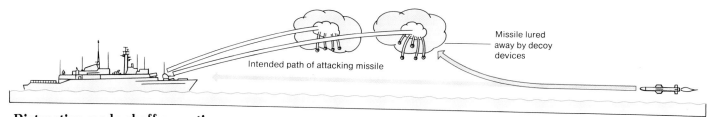

Missile lured away by decoy devices

Intended path of attacking missile

Distraction mode chaff operation

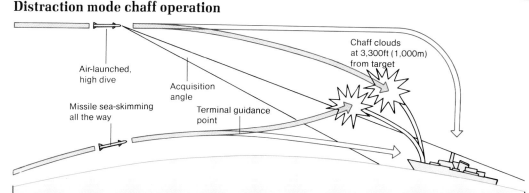

Air-launched, high dive

Missile sea-skimming all the way

Acquisition angle

Terminal guidance point

Chaff clouds at 3,300ft (1,000m) from target

Above: One way of dealing with ASMs is to persuade them to attack decoys. The Plessey Shield system gives distraction and seduction protection for ships of any size; in the distraction mode four chaff clouds are provided at ranges up to 1.25 miles (2km).

Left: Chaff can be shot to heights of 3,000ft (1,000m) or more while the target ship is below the missile's radar horizon, or high-altitude missiles designed for diving attacks (widely used by the USSR) may be lured into premature dive by similar chaff clouds.

board their warships in which chaff and other decoys are launched by mortars sited on the upper decks and controlled from the ship's operations centre as part of the overall defences. The British Vickers Corvus system, for example, consists of two trainable eight-barrel launchers for 3in Plessey Broad-Band Chaff (BBC) rockets; the 16 rockets are sufficient to provide protection against three missile attacks before manual reloading becomes necessary. In the distraction mode this system delays four separate decoy clouds at a range of just over 1,000 yd (1km) from the ship, thus presenting alternative targets to the incoming missiles.

The US Navy uses the Rapid Bloom Off-Board Chaff (RBOC) system, which consists of a series of mortars and cartridges, together with the appropriate command and control measures. The Mk 33 system for destroyers comprises four six-tube launchers arranged in pairs at elevation angles of 55°, 65° and 75°, while the Mk 34 system for smaller combatants has only two launchers. The Mk 171 chaff cartridges burst 3.4 seconds after firing and the payload, a large number of packages of foil, is dispersed radially at high velocity before deploying the chaff. Other cartridges used in this system are the HIRAM (Hycor Infra-Red Anti-Missile) decoy, which deploys an infra-red flare on a parachute and a float to simulate the IR output of a major warship and seduce an IR-homing missile, and the Gemini cartridge, which develops a large radar echo and an IR decoy.

As ASMs become faster and more capable some navies are developing decoy systems with longer ranges in order to deal with the threat at an earlier stage. This leads inevitably to larger and altogether more

Above: The US Navy now uses the Mk 36 Rapid-Bloom Off-Board Countermeasures (RBOC) launcher on many ships. This impressive array of launchers is aboard the battleship USSk Iowa.

elaborate devices. The British Aerospace/Brandt Sibyl, for example, uses rockets of 6.7in (170mm) and 10.4in (263mm) calibre and lengths of 6ft 6in (1.98m) to 8ft (2.44m) to give ranges of up to 5 miles (8km). Six different payloads include an ARM decoy—basically a floating device which simulates a ship's radar emissions—a remotely controlled floating jammer, and a smoke system. The mount for the 12-tube launcher is unusual among decoy systems in that it both trains and elevates.

ANTI-TORPEDO DECOYS

Modern homing torpedoes pose a major threat to both surface warships and submarines, and once locked on they are extremely difficult to evade, but it is possible to mislead them by offering them an apparently more attractive target in the form of a decoy. For surface ships the most usual anser lies in a noise-generating decoy streamed astern, such as the US SLQ-25, which is widely used both in the US Navy and in other NATO countries, and the British Graseby GI 738, a solid-state version of the Type 182 decoy that has been used by the Royal Navy for some years.

In the GI 738 system a towed decoy some 6.6ft (2m) long, 21in (533mm) in diameter and weighing 163lb (74kg) is streamed about 400 yd (366m) astern of the ship, and signals generated within the ship are sent by cable to the towed body for re-transmission. There are two types of signal: simulated propeller noises to decoy passive-

Above: The deployed Replica consists of two linked floating reflectors which give a ship-like signature to attacking missiles. The system can also be used for training by live missiles and guns.

Below: Another way of 'fooling' incoming anti-ship missiles is the Plessey Shield system in which chaff and infra-red decoys are launched by short-range rockets. Operation is fully automatic.

homing torpedoes astern of the target, and continuous-wave signals to simulate the target echo and thus decoy or confuse the torpedo guidance system. In a widely reported incident in the 1982 South Atlantic War, the Royal Navy aircraft carrier HMS Hermes was trailing a Type 182 decoy which was attacked by a torpedo from one of the carrier's own helicopters in prosecuting an ASW attack on a reported submarine contact.

Submarines, which rely on stealth for concealment, do not want to go around streaming noise-making devices, whose

effectiveness depends on being virtually permanently in the transmit mode. However, submarines tend to get much earlier warning than surface vessels of incoming torpedo attacks and they tend therefore to use reactive systems such as bubble generators, first used by German U-boats in World War II, which may mislead acoustic torpedoes. Alternatively, small devices may be fired from the submarine to transmit acoustic signals which will confuse the torpedo seeker head and allow the submarine to take evasive action.

Above: The Combat Information Center aboard USS Spruance. The Plotter Manager (seated) oversees the activities being conducted as part of the Naval Tactical Data System (NTDS).

Below: The Sperry Mk 92 fire control system provides ships with an intergrated radar detection, command and control, and weapon engagement capability. It is used aboard the Perry class FFGs.

Above: A controller mans his station at the gun director of a Mk 56 fire control system for the 3in guns aboard USS Blue Ridge. Such manned directors are increasingly rare on modern warships.

COMMAND AND CONTROL

It will be apparent from this book that naval forces have a major command and control (C) problem. Not only is almost every weapon in itself quite complicated, needing a control system and a tie-in with some sort of sensor, but all the weapon systems operating in a particular environment need to be controlled and coordinated from a central position within every ship. Such ship-wide C must also tie in other elements of the

ship's functions such as propulsion, damage control, seamanship activities, administration, and so on. Finally, offensive and defensive systems on the individual ships must be tied together within a task group.

At the lowest level of C is the control of individual weapons. At its most basic, this can consist of a man or a group of men operating the weapon manually and acquiring the target visually—for example, a machine gun crew—and while there is no doubt that such methods were used to some effect in the South Atlantic war of 1982 there is little place

for them on the modern warship except as a last resort.

Most guns have Gun Fire Control Systems (GFCS). A typical, if somewhat elderly, example is the US Navy's GFCS Mk 56, which is in service on numerous US and foreign warships. Designed to control the fire of dual-purpose guns against subsonic aircraft and surface targets, it is required to track targets and then to compute the necessary instructions to the guns for training, elevation and parallax, and to make fuze settings. The system uses a radar subsystem (Mk 35 I/J band radar) for automatic tracking in range, bearing and elevation for lead angles up to 30° and range rates of 630 knots, up to a maximum range of 15,000 yd (13,716m), while optical tracking of visible targets is performed by a second crew member. There are two electro-mechanical computers, a Mk 42 for primary and secondary ballistics and a Mk 30 for primary gun orders. The complete system weighs 19,417lb (8,685kg).

One of the most recent US Navy GFCS is the Mk 86, whose basic role is the control of Mk 45 5in/54 lightweight automatic gun mounts and Standard missiles. It is being fitted, in a number of versions—Mods 0 to 9—in the Ticonderoga, California and Virginia class cruisers, Spruance and Kidd class destroyers, and amphibious assault ships; it is also being installed as part of the DDG 19 upgrading programme.

The main elements of the system are two radars, an optical system, computers and displays. The radars are the SPQ-9 I-band track-while-scan radar for

surface search and low-level coverage for defence against low-flying threats, and the SPG-60, an automatic scan-to-acquire air target tracking and horizon search radar, while optical components range from a simple CCTV camera to a comprehensive electro-optical sensor system. The computing system, based on the Mk 152 and UYK-7 machines, coordinates the independent radar sensor inputs and provides a two-way interface with other ships' systems. The Mk 86 GFCS has full facilities for radar and visually controlled surface actions, indirect shore bombardment, anti-ship missile defence and air action. The system is managed in the CIC by a control officer and a number of weapons controllers.

The next level is the overall command and control of all ships' sensor and weapon systems. This is achieved by such systems as the US Naval Tactical Data System (NTDS) and Aegis, the Royal Navy's Action Data Automation Weapons System (ADAWS) and the French SENIT (Système d'Exploitation Navale des Informations Tactiques). A major influence on all of these is the application of a systems approach, whereby the sensors, computers and fire control systems are coordinated to optimize the system as a whole, rather than concentrate on the performance of individual sensors and weapons. Thus, the US Navy claims that an Aegis ship has a 60 per cent range advantage with a Standard missile over a virtually identical missile fired by a ship with the Tartar D control system, simply because Aegis can programme the missile to fly a more energy-efficient flight profile. With the extended-range Standard the improvement is more than 100 per cent.

Ships and Weapons

Below: The Ticonderoga class Aegis
cruiser Vincennes (CG 49) fires
an Asroc anti-submarine missile
during sea trials prior to
commissioning on July 6, 1985.

Introduction

The following pages show a selection of modern warships chosen as representative of the latest trends in naval design and technology and to illustrate typical examples of all the major surface and sub-surface naval combatants: aircraft carriers, battleships, cruisers, destroyers, frigates and fast attack craft, plus ballistic missile, cruise missile, nuclear powered hunter-killer and conventional submarines, representing the naval philosophy of Belgium, France, Italy, Japan, the Netherlands, the Soviet Union, the United Kingdom, the United States and West Germany.

Each full-colour perspective view is accompanied by details of some of the weapon systems carried, as well as a line profile indicating the locations of the various weapon and sensor systems with, where appropriate, additional profiles showing variations on the basic design. Full details of dimensions, weights, armament, machinery and sensors are given, and a description of the background to the design of each class outlines its place in the evolution of the modern warship, both in the overall development of modern fighting ships and within the context of individual navies' requirements and traditions. A note on the future gives known details of planned additions to each class, scheduled improvement programmes or the shape of known or anticipated successors.

The information given in the keys to the profile drawings is largely self-explanatory, and the convention has been followed of giving the number of mountings followed by the number of barrels in the case of guns or of cells or launching arms in the case of guided missiles: thus (2 x 8) Sea Sparrow indicates that two mountings are carried in an indicated position, normally port and starboard, each of which has eight cells.

It is customary for naval planners to rely on either their own specialised design staffs for new warship designs, or to draw up specifications on the basis of which commercial or naval shipbuilders are invited to tender. There are, however, also commercial builders who produce their own designs, normally for export. Examples of the latter included here are the British Vosper Thornycroft and West German Blohm and Voss and Howaldtswerke concerns, represented by, respectively, the Niteroi class frigate, the MEKO 360 type frigate and the Type 209 submarine designs, each of which is part of a range of commercial designs produced by each company. Such vessels enable the navies of nations without substantial indigenous naval construction industries to operate modern warships that meet their specific needs, and are often the subject of licence agreements whereby later members of the class are built in the customer's own yards, a practice which facilitates the acquisition of modern construction techniques by a relatively easy and inexpensive route.

At the other end of the scale, only a very few nations can afford to build and operate full-scale aircraft carriers and what has become the ultimate warship—though, we must hope, one destined to achieve the effective redundancy of that ultimate warship of an earlier era, the Dreadnought battleship—the ballistic missile submarine; and none can match the enormous diversity and quantity of naval might fielded by the two superpowers. A single carrier task force of the kind routinely deployed by the US Navy involves more military capability than that mustered by the combined armed forces of most sovereign states, and the dramatic growth of the Soviet Navy over recent decades has resulted in a formidable threat, largely in the form of

US NAVY WARSHIP DESIGNATIONS			
Role	Type	Designation	Classes
Aircraft carrier	Multipurpose	CV	Kitty Hawk, John F. Kennedy, Forrestal, Midway
	Multipurpose, nuclear propelled	CVN	Nimitz, Enterprise
Battleship		BB	Iowa
Cruiser	Gun	CA	Des Moines
	Guided missile	CG	Ticonderoga, Belknap, Leahy Albany
	Guided missile, nuclear propelled	CGN	Virginia, California, Truxtun, Bainbridge, Long Beach
Destroyer	Gun	DD	Spruance, Forrest Sherman, Hull
	Guided missile	DDG	Kidd, Coontz, Charles F. Adams, Forrest Sherman, Converted Hull
Frigate	Gun	FF	Knox, Garcia, Glover, Bronstein
	Guided missile	FFG	Perry, Brooke
Attack submarine	Diesel-electric powered	SS	Barbel
	Nuclear powered	SSN	Los Angeles, Lipscomb, Sturgeon, Ethan Allen, Washington, Thresher, Tullibee, Skipjack, Seawolf, Skate
Ballistic missile submarine	Nuclear powered	SSBN	Ohio, Franklin
Amphibious assault ships	General purpose	LHA	Tarawa
	Multipurpose	LHD	Wasp
	Helicopter	LPH	Iwo Jima
	Transport dock	LPD	Austin, Raleigh
	Command ship	LCC	Blue Ridge
Mine Warfare Ships	Minesweepers	MSO	Acme, Aggressive
	Mine counter-measures vessels	MCM	Avenger
	Minesweeper/ hunter	MSH	Cardinal

For convenience, the US Navy designation system is also used to apply to Soviet ships, and is used as above. There are, however, several types of Soviet ship for which there is no current US type equivalent; for example, the Kirov. Accordingly, the following designations are used:

Battle-cruiser		BC	Kirov
Cruise missile submarine	Diesel-electric powered	SSG	Juliett
	Nuclear powered	SSGN	Papa, Charlie, Oscar

submarine-launched and surface-to-surface missiles, to the US Navy and the navies of the other NATO allies.

At the same time, it is also apparent from the following illustrations that even the more modest frigates operated by Third World nations still embody considerable firepower, as automation has enabled the ratio of manpower to firepower to be significantly reduced and the natural desire of any customer to obtain the most modern and effective systems has been matched by the need of the industrialized nations to subsidise the cost of weapons development and production by the export of new systems. This has given rise to another notable characteristic of many of the warships depicted here: that is, the multi-national nature of the weapon, sensor and equipment fits, so that it would be no surprise to find, say, British engines, Dutch radars and Italian guns firing Swedish ammunition, plus French and American missiles installed in a single hull.

The exception, of course, is in the case of the Soviet Union, which has had to develop its own equipment in all areas, with the result that the Soviet vessels shown here are markedly different both in conception and execution to those of the rest of the world. Partly in response to special strategic and tactical requirements and partly because of its own national approach to the problems, Soviet designers have produced singularly innovative solutions to many of the universal problems of warship design.

Overall, however, the most striking aspect of the illustrations that follow is how much naval technology has progressed in the last 40 years, progress embodied in the plethora of antennas for communications, sensor and electronic warfare equipment, the reduction in the numbers of guns and the dominance of the guided missile.

Left: A Standard surface-to-air missile is fired from the after Mk 10 launcher of the Leahy class cruiser USS England. The Leahys were designed as escorts for fast carrier attack groups, and Standard is the US Navy's area defence AA system.

Above: The development of the torpedo in the late nineteenth century revolutionized naval warfare, providing small boats with a weapon that could sink a battleship and provoking the development of the torpedo-boat destroyer, forerunner of the modern destroyer. Guided missiles have had a similarly fundamental effect on naval warfare, increasing the ranges over which naval engagements can be conducted and superseding torpedoes and guns as the principal surface-to-surface weapon.

SOVIET NAVY WARSHIP DESIGNATIONS

Russian name	Translation	NATO Equivalent	Ship Classes
Atomnaya podvodnaya lodka	Nuclear powered submarine	Attack submarine, nuclear-powered	November, Echo, Hotel, Yankee, Victor-I/II/III, Mike, Sierra, Uniform, Alfa
Atomnaya podlodka raktnaya ballisticheskaya	Nuclear powered ballistic missile submarine	Ballistic missile submarine, nuclear	Hotel-II/III, Yankee I/II, Delta-I/II/III/IV, Typhoon
Atomnaya podloka raketnaya krylataya	Nuclear powered cruise-missile submarine	N/A	Echo-II, Papa, Charlie-I/II/III, Oscar
Atomny raketny kreyser	Nuclear powered missile cruiser	Battle-cruiser	Kirov
Bolshoy desantny korabl	Large landing ship	Landing platform, dock	Rogov, Ropucha, Alligator
Bolshoy protivolodochny korabl	Large anti-submarine ship	Destroyer	Kanin, Kashin, Udaloy, Kresta-II, Kara
Bolshoy raketny korbla	Large missile ship	Destroyer	Kildin, Sovremennyy
Eskadrennyy minonosets		Destroyer	Skoryy, Kotlin
Kreyser	Cruiser	Cruiser	Sverdlov (less A. Senyanin, Zhdanov)
Korabl upravleniy	Command ship	Command ship	Sverdlov-Mod I/II
Korabl vogdushnogo	Radar surveillance ship	Frigate	T58/PGR, T43/PGR
Maly nablyadenya protovolodochny korabl	Small ASW ship	Frigate	Grisha-I/II
Maly raketny korabl	Small missile ship	Missile corvette	Nanuchka, Pauk, Poti, SO 1
Podloka raketnaya krylataya	Cruise missile submarine	Cruise missile submarine, diesel	Juliett
Podvodnaya lodka		submarine, diesel	Quebec, Whiskey, Romeo, Kilo, Zulu-IV, Foxtrot, Tango, Golf
Pogranichny storozhevoy korabl	Border patrol ship	Frigate	Grisha-II, T58, Stenka
Protovolodochnyy kreyser	Anti-submarine cruiser	ASW cruiser/helicopter cruiser	Moskva
Raketny kater	Missile cutter	Fast attack craft — hydrofoil	Matka, Osa, Babochka
Raketny kreyser	Missile cruiser	Missile cruiser	Kynda, Kresta-I, Sverdlov-SAM, Slava
Storozhevoy korabl	Escort ship	Frigate	Krivak, Mirka, Koni, Petya Riga, T58
Stredny desantny korabl	Medium landing ship	Landing ship, medium	Polnochny
Taktichkeskoye avianosnyy kreyser	Tactical aircraft carrying cruiser	Aircraft carrier	Kiev
Torpedny kater	Torpedo cutter	Fast attack craft — torpedo	Sherskhen, Turya

Arleigh Burke (DDG 51) class

Origin: USA
Type: Destroyer (DDG)
Built: 1984-
Class: 1 building; 28 to be ordered
Displacement: 8,400 tons full load
Dimensions: Length 466ft (142.1m) oa; beam 60ft (18.3m); draught 30ft (9.1m) over sonar dome
Propulsion: 2-shaft gas turbine (4 General Electric LM2500), 80,000shp
Performance: Speed 30+ knots; range 5,000nm at 20 knots
Weapons: SSM: 2 x 4 Harpoon launchers; 56 Tomahawk
SAM: Vertically-launched Standard SM-2 (MR)
Guns: 1 5in/54 Mk 45; 2 20mm Phalanx Mk 15 CIWS
ASW weapons: Asroc; 2 x 3 Mk 32 torpedo tubes
Vertical Launch System: 2 Mk 41
Sensors: Radar: SPY-1D (Aegis) multi-purpose phased array; SPS-67(V) surface search; Mk 99 (3 SPG-62 radar) missile fire control system
Sonar: SQS-53C; SQR-19 (TACTAS) towed array
Complement: 303

Background: The Arleigh Burke (DDG 51) class is intended to replace the Adams and Coontz class guided-missile destroyers, which have been in service since the early 1960s. The primary mission of the DDG 51 class will be anti-air warfare, for which they will be fitted with the SPY-1D version of the Aegis system, and they will also have significant anti-surface and anti-submarine capabilities.

The first of class is already under construction at the Bath Iron Works, in Maine, and is due to be commissioned in October 1989. Another two ships will be requested from Congress in FY87, followed by five ships annually in FY88, FY89, and FY90, with a further 11 to follow.

Following the disastrous fire on the USS *Belknap* (CV 26), the only aluminium to be used will be on the funnels, the rest of the ships being constructed of steel. In addition, in consequence of the Royal Navy's experience in the South Atlantic War of 1982, armoured protection is to be reintroduced, with some 70 tons (71,000kg) of Kevlar armour being incorporated in the structure to protect vital spaces.

The early ships of the class will be powered by the proven General Electric LM 2500 gas turbines, but experiments are continuing with the Rankin Closed Cycle Energy Recovery (RACER) system, in which heat from the exhaust gases is used to create steam which drives another turbine. This is estimated to add another 1,000nm to the ship's range. The system is to be tested in a Military Sealift Command vessel (the *Admiral William Callaghan),* and if successful could be installed in the ninth ship of the Arleigh Burke class (DDG 59).

One of the more controversial aspects of the ships' design is that they will not have hangar facilities, though they will have flight decks and be able to refuel and rearm helicopters. This decision was greeted with some incredulity at first. It will certainly impose limitations on single ship deployments, and is obviously now regretted, as it has already been announced that the Improved Arleigh Burke class will have hangar facilities.

There has been much study in various Western naval design bureaux of the possible advantages of a shorter, beamier hull. The US Navy appears to be following this trend with the Arleigh Burkes, which have a beam-to-length ratio of 1:7.9 compared to 1:10.2 for the Spruance class. These shorter, beamier designs are claimed to confer better sea-keeping qualities as well as improved manouvrability and more usable space.

Below: The *Arleigh Burke* as constructed. The greater beam incorporated into this design in comparison with destroyers and frigates constructed in the 1960s and 1970s is obvious from this drawing. Another feature clearly shown is the uncluttered foredeck, which leads uninformed critics to conclude that US ships are poorly armed in comparison with Soviet ships such as those of the Krivak class, whose foredecks bristle with weaponry. In fact, the automatic 5in/54 Mk 45 gun is highly capable and has a large magazine below decks, while the forward Mk 41 Vertical Launch System has no less 29 missiles.

Future: It has already been decided that only 29 ships will be built to the original DDG 51 design. There will then be a follow-on class of 31 ships to be built to an improved design, with better machinery and electronics. In addition, proper helicopter facilities will be installed, indicating that the decision not to fit a hangar is now considered to have been an error.

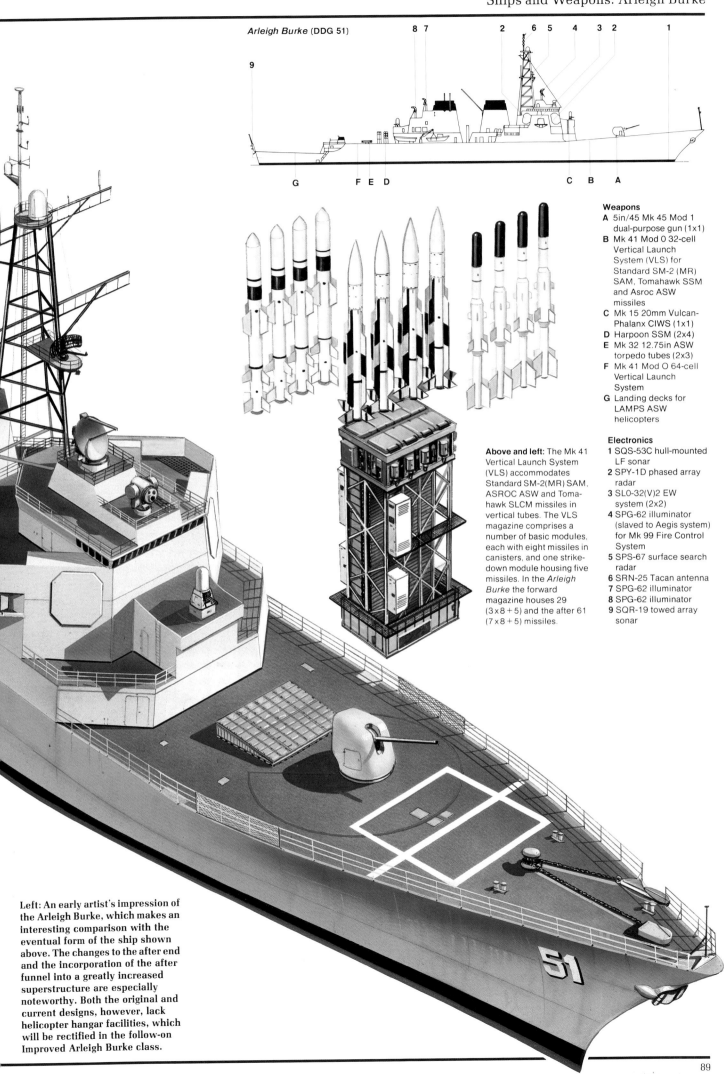

Arleigh Burke (DDG 51)

Weapons

A 5in/45 Mk 45 Mod 1 dual-purpose gun (1x1)
B Mk 41 Mod 0 32-cell Vertical Launch System (VLS) for Standard SM-2 (MR) SAM, Tomahawk SSM and Asroc ASW missiles
C Mk 15 20mm Vulcan-Phalanx CIWS (1x1)
D Harpoon SSM (2x4)
E Mk 32 12.75in ASW torpedo tubes (2x3)
F Mk 41 Mod O 64-cell Vertical Launch System
G Landing decks for LAMPS ASW helicopters

Electronics

1 SQS-53C hull-mounted LF sonar
2 SPY-1D phased array radar
3 SL0-32(V)2 EW system (2x2)
4 SPG-62 illuminator (slaved to Aegis system) for Mk 99 Fire Control System
5 SPS-67 surface search radar
6 SRN-25 Tacan antenna
7 SPG-62 illuminator
8 SPG-62 illuminator
9 SQR-19 towed array sonar

Above and left: The Mk 41 Vertical Launch System (VLS) accommodates Standard SM-2(MR) SAM, ASROC ASW and Tomahawk SLCM missiles in vertical tubes. The VLS magazine comprises a number of basic modules, each with eight missiles in canisters, and one strike-down module housing five missiles. In the *Arleigh Burke* the forward magazine houses 29 (3x8+5) and the after 61 (7x8+5) missiles.

Left: An early artist's impression of the Arleigh Burke, which makes an interesting comparison with the eventual form of the ship shown above. The changes to the after end and the incorporation of the after funnel into a greatly increased superstructure are especially noteworthy. Both the original and current designs, however, lack helicopter hangar facilities, which will be rectified in the follow-on Improved Arleigh Burke class.

Audace class

Origin: Italy
Type: Destroyer (DDG)
Built: 1968-1972
Class: 2 in service
Displacement: 3,600 tons standard; 4,400 tons full load
Dimensions: Length 446.4ft (136.6m) oa; beam 47.1ft (14.5m); draught 15ft (4.6m)
Propulsion: 2-shaft double reduction geared turbines, 73,000shp
Performance: Speed 34 knots; range 3,000nm at 20 knots
Armament: SAM: 1 Mk 13 launcher for Standard (missiles)
Guns: 2 x 1 127mm/54 Compact; 4 x 1 76mm/62 Compact
Torpedo tubes: 2 x 3 Mk 32; 2 x 2 533mm
Aircraft: 2 AB 212 helicopters
Sensors: Radar: SPS-25A air surveillance; 2 SPG-51 tracking and missile guidance; MM/SPS-768v1 air search; SPQ-2D surface search; 3 Orion RTN-10X gun fire control; 3RM-7 navigation
Sonar: CWE 610
Complement: 380

Above: **Ardito (D 550), showing the graceful and balanced lines that have typified Italian warship design for the past 60 years. Well armed and with a comprehensive sensor fit, these are very effective and capable ships, particularly in their intended Mediterranean environment.**

Background: The Impetuoso class, the first postwar destroyers to be designed and built in Italy, were ordered in 1950. Closely tailored to Mediterranean conditions, they were also strongly influenced by American design practice: flush-decked and with twin funnels, they were armed with US guns and fitted with US radars and electronics. In addition to four 5in guns mounted in twin turrets fore and aft they had 16 40mm anti-aircraft guns and an anti-submarine armament comprising a Menon triple-barrel mortar and ASW torpedoes and, like all Italian warships, they were fast.

The two ships of the next class, the Impavidos, commissioned in 1957 and 1959, were an enlarged and improved version of the Impetuoso, with the after 127mm mount replaced by a single Mk 13 SAM launcher capable of launching Tartar or Standard missiles and the American 40mm guns replaced by two Italian Brescia single 76mm weapons, mounted either side of the mainmast. They have no hangar, but operate single Agusta Bell AB 204B ASW helicopters from the stern flight-deck.

The Audace class is a further enlargement and development of the Impavido class. The hull is somewhat larger and the Impavido's American twin 5in mount has been replaced by two single superposed 127mm/54 OTO-Melara Compact guns. The AA armament amidships consists of four 76mm OTO-Melara Compacts in single turrets, one abreast each of the funnels. A large hangar and a very spacious flight-deck have been provided aft for two Agusta Bell AB 204B or AB 212 helicopters, although there has been discussion of replacing these with two SH-3D Sea Kings. The Mk 13 SAM launcher is mounted above the hangar and has a magazine for 36 missiles, and the ships have a comprehensive fit of US radar and Dutch sonar. Two Improved Audace DDGs with either COGOG or CODOG machinery were ordered in 1986.

Future: The Italian Navy has placed an order for a new destroyer class of an Improved Audace design. Once again there is an increase in displacement—to 5,000 tons—and the two on-board helicopters will be the much larger SH-3D Sea Kings. Main armament will be four 76mm OTO Melara Compacts in single mounts, together with four Teseo SSMs, while air defence will be provided by a Mk 13 Standard launcher for long-range engagements and two Albatros systems with Aspide SAMs for close-in protection. Propulsion will be CODOG with two FIAT/General Electric LM 2500 gas turbines and two GMT B230 20 DVM diesels. Names are *Animoso* and *Ardimentoso*.

Although the order was only placed in 1986, the design for the new ships has been in existence since 1975, with funding limitations responsible for the ten-year delay in the start of construction. As a result, some commentators believe that the design of the new destroyers is already out of date: current trends would indicate vertical launchers for the AA missiles and an Aegis-type automatic fire control system. Even with the two new ships the Italian Navy will have only six destroyers, and two of those will be the Impavido class vessels of late-1950s design, so the Italian Navy Staff is planning a new programme to add further to the current force of largely modern, soundly designed equipment.

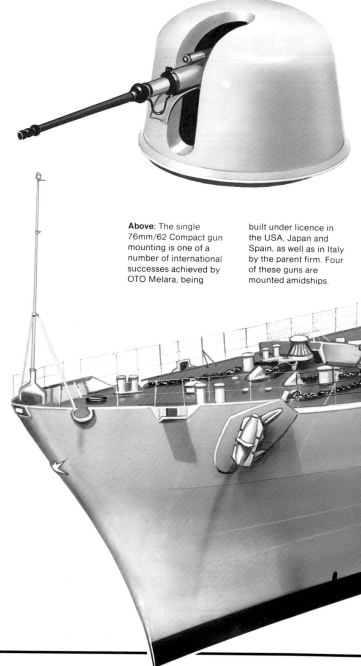

Above: The single 76mm/62 Compact gun mounting is one of a number of international successes achieved by OTO Melara, being built under licence in the USA, Japan and Spain, as well as in Italy by the parent firm. Four of these guns are mounted amidships.

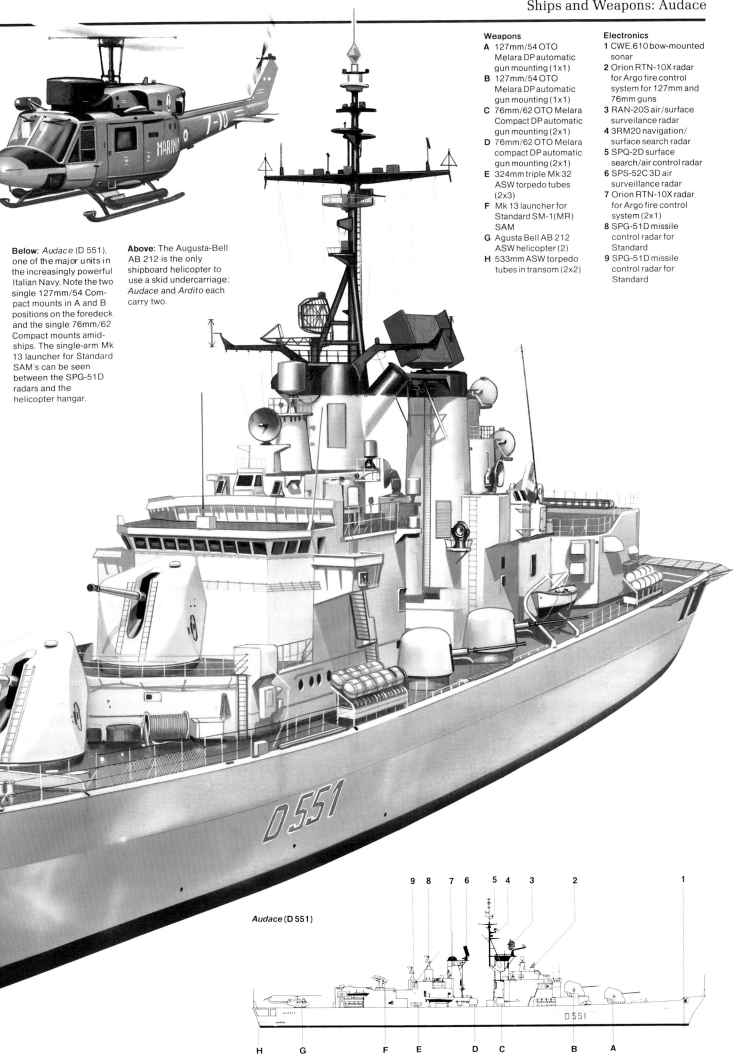

Weapons

- **A** 127mm/54 OTO Melara DP automatic gun mounting (1x1)
- **B** 127mm/54 OTO Melara DP automatic gun mounting (1x1)
- **C** 76mm/62 OTO Melara Compact DP automatic gun mounting (2x1)
- **D** 76mm/62 OTO Melara compact DP automatic gun mounting (2x1)
- **E** 324mm triple Mk 32 ASW torpedo tubes (2x3)
- **F** Mk 13 launcher for Standard SM-1(MR) SAM
- **G** Agusta Bell AB 212 ASW helicopter (2)
- **H** 533mm ASW torpedo tubes in transom (2x2)

Electronics

- **1** CWE.610 bow-mounted sonar
- **2** Orion RTN-10X radar for Argo fire control system for 127mm and 76mm guns
- **3** RAN-20S air/surface surveilance radar
- **4** 3RM20 navigation/ surface search radar
- **5** SPQ-2D surface search/air control radar
- **6** SPS-52C 3D air surveillance radar
- **7** Orion RTN-10X radar for Argo fire control system (2x1)
- **8** SPG-51D missile control radar for Standard
- **9** SPG-51D missile control radar for Standard

Below: *Audace* (D 551), one of the major units in the increasingly powerful Italian Navy. Note the two single 127mm/54 Compact mounts in A and B positions on the foredeck and the single 76mm/62 Compact mounts amidships. The single-arm Mk 13 launcher for Standard SAM's can be seen between the SPG-51D radars and the helicopter hangar.

Above: The Augusta-Bell AB 212 is the only shipboard helicopter to use a skid undercarriage; *Audace* and *Ardito* each carry two.

Audace (D 551)

D 551

Broadsword (Type 22) class

Origin: United Kingdom
Type: Frigate (FF)
Built: 1975-
Class: 7 in service; 5 building; 2 on order
Displacement: (Batch 1) 3,500 tons standard; 4,200 tons full load (Batch 2) 4,100 tons standard; 4,800 tons full load (Batch 3) 4,200 tons standard; 4,900 tons full load
Dimensions: (1) Length 430ft (131.2m) oa; beam 48.5ft (14.8m); draught 19.9ft (6m) (2 and 3) Length 471ft (143.6m) oa; beam 48.5ft (14.8m); draught 21ft (6.4m)
Propulsion: (All Batch 1 and Batch 2 *Boxer, Beaver*) 2-shaft COCOG (2 Rolls-Royce Olympus TM3B/2 Rolls-Royce Tyne RM1C gas turbines), 50,000/9,700shp (Batch 2 *Brave*) 2-shaft COCOG (2 Rolls-Royce Spey SM1A/2 Rolls-Royce Tyne RM1C gas turbines), 37,540/9,700shp (Batch 2 *London, Sheffield, Coventry* and all Batch 3) 2-shaft COCAG (2 Rolls-Royce Spey SM1A/2 Rolls-Royce Tyne RM1C gas turbines), 37,540/9,750shp
Performance: Speed 30-32 knots max; 18 knots on Tynes
Weapons: Missiles: 4 Exocet (Batch 1 and 2); 8 Harpoon (Batch 3); 2 6-cell Seawolf launchers Guns: 1 4.5in/55 Mk 8 (3); 2 single 40mm (1 and 2); 2 single 20mm GAM-BO1 (on deployment); 1 30mm Goalkeeper (3) Torpedo tubes: 2 x 3 STWS for Mk 46 or Stingray torpedoes (except *Broadsword* and *Battleaxe*)
Aircraft: 2 Westland Lynx Mk 2 (only 1 normally carried; *Brave* and subsequent ships can operate Westland Sea King)
Sensors: Radar: Type 967 (967M from *Brave* on) and Type 968 surveillance; 2 Type 910 (Marconi 805 from *Brave* onwards) SAM control; Type 1006 navigation Sonar: Type 2050; Type 2008; Type 2031 towed array (2 and 3)
Complement: Batch 1 224; Batches 2 and 3 273

Background: The United Kingdom had an outstanding success with the Leander class anti-submarine frigates, which have had an excellent record of service in the Royal Navy and have also sold well overseas. After an unsuccessful attempt to agree a standard design with the Netherlands, the Type 22 frigate was designed as the Leanders' successor; the first of the class—HMS *Broadsword*— was laid down on February 7, 1975, and commissioned on May 3, 1979, and another three Batch 1 vessels were commissioned at yearly intervals thereafter.

Changes in the requirement led to the lengthened Batch 2, launched between 1981 and 1985, and Batch 3, which utilize the lengthened hull of Batch 2, but with armament revised to incorporate the lessons of the 1982 South Atlantic war. In the process the Type 22 has changed from a specialized ASW frigate to a multi-role destroyer, and the latest ships of the class are, in fact, virtually equal in dimensions and displacement to the Soviet Kynda class cruisers and larger than the British Type 42 destroyer.

The Batch 1 ships, designed for the ASW mission, carry two triple Mk 32 torpedo tubes for Mk 46 and Stingray torpedoes and two Lynx helicopters. They also have an excellent anti-missile and anti-aircraft capability in their two six-cell Seawolf launchers, and anti-ship weapons in the form of two single MM39 Exocet launchers on the forecastle.

It was then decided to fit so

many additional facilities that the hull had to be lengthened by some 41ft (12.9m), resulting in a 600-ton increase in displacement. This group, designated Batch 2 and sometimes referred to as the Boxer class, differ from the Batch 1 ships principally in having enlarged Action Information Organization (AIO) facilities to handle data from the new Type 2031 towed array sonar.

Two very useful by-products of the stretching are an increase in range from 4,500nm to 7,000nm and an increase in maximum speed of about 2 knots. In addition, water displacement fuel tanks have been fitted to enable virtually all their fuel to be used without compromising stability, although no captain would allow his fuel stocks to run so low if he could avoid it. The first two ships of Batch 2 are otherwise identical to Batch 1, but the third (HMS *Brave*) has Rolls-Royce Speys in place of

the Olympus in a COGOG arrangement, while the fourth and fifth ships have Speys and Tynes in a COGAG arrangement.

Batch 3 ships have the lengthened hull, towed array and larger AIO facilities of the Batch 2 and the Spey/Tyne COGAG arrangement of the later Batch 2s. Following the 1982 South Atlantic war, however, the decision was made to fit a Vickers 4.5in gun, to replace the Exocet SSMs by Harpoons, and to fit the Dutch Goalkeeper CIWS.
Future: It is already planned to update the earlier units of the class by fitting new weapons and sensors wherever possible. This may include the replacement of Exocet by Harpoon, Sea Eagle or Otomat, and the fitting of the Type 2031 towed array in the Batch 1 ships. Vertical launch tubes for Seawolf will also be fitted, as will facilities to operate the much heavier Sea King or EH 101 ASW helicopter.

Below: HMS *Battleaxe* (F 89), second of the Royal Navy's Type 22 frigates, as completed in 1980. All the later Type 22's have the smaller, more streamlined funnel apparent in the main illustration, while all but the first four (Batch 1) ships of the class have the lengthened hull evident in the line profiles opposite.

Above: The Seawolf GWS 25 Mod 3 SAM is fired from a six-cell launcher, two of which are mounted on the Type 22 frigates. This system proved an outstanding success during the 1982 South Atlantic War. A vertical launch system is now under development, although such a system actually reached the prototype stage some years ago, only to be rejected in favour of the six-cell launcher.

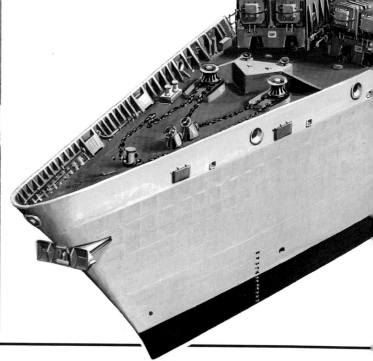

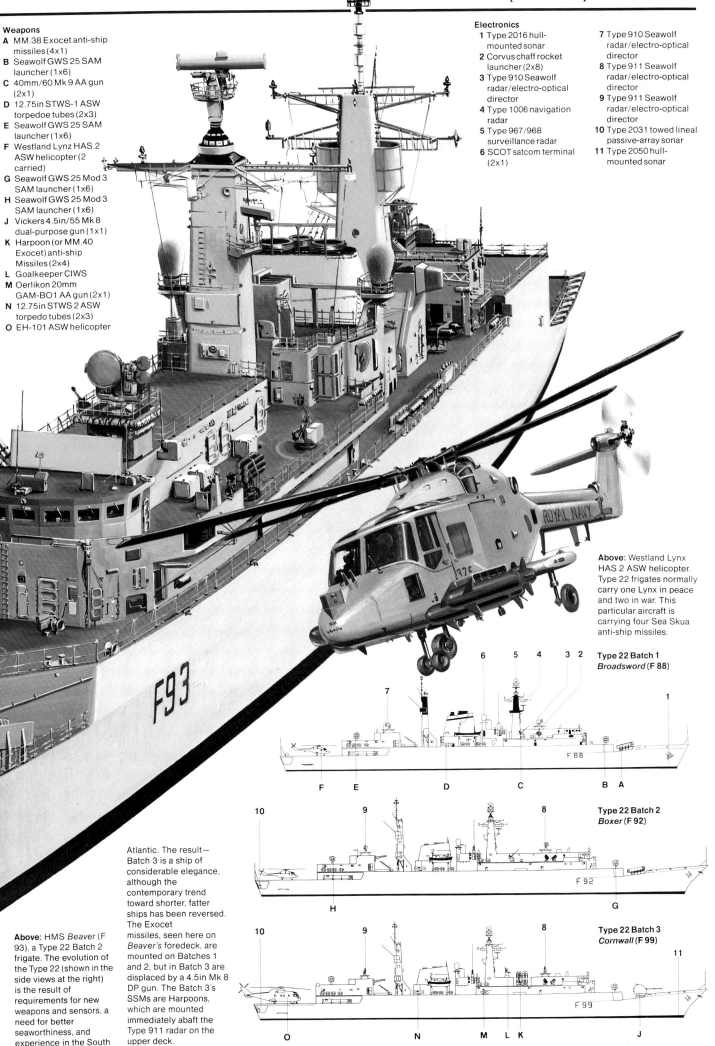

Weapons
A MM.38 Exocet anti-ship missiles (4x1)
B Seawolf GWS 25 SAM launcher (1x6)
C 40mm/60 Mk 9 AA gun (2x1)
D 12.75in STWS-1 ASW torpedoe tubes (2x3)
E Seawolf GWS 25 SAM launcher (1x6)
F Westland Lynx HAS.2 ASW helicopter (2 carried)
G Seawolf GWS 25 Mod 3 SAM launcher (1x6)
H Seawolf GWS 25 Mod 3 SAM launcher (1x6)
J Vickers 4.5in/55 Mk 8 dual-purpose gun (1x1)
K Harpoon (or MM.40 Exocet) anti-ship Missiles (2x4)
L Goalkeeper CIWS
M Oerlikon 20mm GAM-BO1 AA gun (2x1)
N 12.75in STWS 2 ASW torpedo tubes (2x3)
O EH-101 ASW helicopter

Electronics
1 Type 2016 hull-mounted sonar
2 Corvus chaff rocket launcher (2x8)
3 Type 910 Seawolf radar/electro-optical director
4 Type 1006 navigation radar
5 Type 967/968 surveillance radar
6 SCOT satcom terminal (2x1)
7 Type 910 Seawolf radar/electro-optical director
8 Type 911 Seawolf radar/electro-optical director
9 Type 911 Seawolf radar/electro-optical director
10 Type 2031 towed lineal passive-array sonar
11 Type 2050 hull-mounted sonar

Above: Westland Lynx HAS.2 ASW helicopter. Type 22 frigates normally carry one Lynx in peace and two in war. This particular aircraft is carrying four Sea Skua anti-ship missiles.

Type 22 Batch 1
Broadsword (F 88)

Type 22 Batch 2
Boxer (F 92)

Type 22 Batch 3
Cornwall (F 99)

Above: HMS *Beaver* (F 93), a Type 22 Batch 2 frigate. The evolution of the Type 22 (shown in the side views at the right) is the result of requirements for new weapons and sensors, a need for better seaworthiness, and experience in the South Atlantic. The result— Batch 3 is a ship of considerable elegance, although the contemporary trend toward shorter, fatter ships has been reversed. The Exocet missiles, seen here on *Beaver's* foredeck, are mounted on Batches 1 and 2, but in Batch 3 are displaced by a 4.5in Mk 8 DP gun. The Batch 3's SSMs are Harpoons, which are mounted immediately abaft the Type 911 radar on the upper deck.

Clemenceau class

Origin: France
Type: Aircraft carrier (CV)
Built: 1955-1963
Class: 2 in service
Displacement: 27,307 tons standard; 32,780 tons full load
Dimensions: Length 869.4ft (265m) oa; beam 104.1ft (31.7m); draught 28.2ft (8.6m)
Propulsion: 2-shaft (2 sets Parsons geared turbines), 126,000shp
Performance: Speed 32 knots; range 7,500nm at 18 knots, 4,800nm at 24 knots
Weapons: SAM: 4 Naval Crotale at next refit
Guns: 8 100mm in single turrets (4 when Naval Crotale has been fitted)
Sensors: Radar: DRBV 50 surveillance; DRBV 23B air surveillance; DRBV 20C warning; DRBC 31 fire control (2); DRBI 10 heightfinding (2); Decca, NRBA navigation
Sonar: SQS-503 hull-mounted
Complement: 1,338

Background: These two light fleet carriers were laid down in the mid-1950s and incorporated all the advances in carrier design made in the immediate postwar period. They have served the French Navy well, in both European and Pacific waters, operations in the latter being in support of the remaining French colonial territories and of nuclear tests. They are also among the most powerful units in the Mediterranean and at least one carrier was off Lebanon at all times when French military units were ashore as part of the international peacekeeping forces in Beirut. Following the paying-off of the British aircraft carrier *Ark Royal* these are now the largest units in any European navy.

The Clemenceau class aircraft carriers are fairly conventional in design. The flight deck measures 543ft (165.5m) by 97ft (29.5m) and is angled at 8° to the ship's axis. The forward aircraft lift is offset to starboard with one of the two 170ft (52m) catapults to port; the second catapult is located on the angled deck, and the after lift is positioned on the deck edge to increase hangar capacity. The hangar, which is offset to port, has a usable length of 499ft (152m) and a width of 72-79ft (22-24m), with 23ft (7m) clearance overhead.

A new generation of aircraft was designed to operate from these carriers. Two flights, each of ten Etendard IVM ground support fighters (with integral reconnaissance capability), were initially embarked, together with a flight of Alizé turbo-prop ASW aircraft, while F-8E Crusaders were purchased from the USA in 1963 and from 1966 made up the interceptor flight. The Etendard IVM has recently been replaced by the Super Etendard, which can carry Exocet anti-ship missiles and has a nuclear strike capability, but the relatively small size of the ships, together with the limited capacity (20 tonnes) of the lifts and catapults, has made it difficult to find a replacement for the F-8Es. A further limitation on the

effectiveness of these ships is their lack of integral airborne early warning (AEW) aircraft, and they would have the same problems as the British Task Force in the 1982 South Atlantic war if they were to deploy against a reasonably sophisticated enemy. Both carriers normally embark two Super Frelon ASW helicopters and two Alouette IIIs. The French Navy plans to construct two Charles de Gaulle (PAN-1) class nuclear-powered aircraft carriers, the first of which was laid down in 1986 and will join the fleet in 1995. Of 36,000 tons full load displacement, these carriers will have two independent nuclear reactors giving a maximum speed

of 27 knots. The weapons fit will include an air defence missile system (three SADRAL fire units with Matra Mistral missiles) and an unspecified anti-missile defence system, and the PAN-1 class will carry a strike group, probably a mix of Super Etendard and a navalized version of the ACT, and their decks will be capable of operating AEW aircraft.

Under present plans *Clemenceau* is due to pay off in 1995, followed by *Foch* in 1998, but this obviously depends upon satisfactory progress with the new nuclear carriers. Meanwhile, both are to be upgraded at their next refits, which will include replacing four 100mm guns by Naval Crotale SAM launchers.

Right: Clemenceau. The air wing normally comprises 16 Super Etendard strike fighters, 3 Etendard IVP reconnaissance fighters, 7 Alizé ASW aircraft, two Super Frelon ASW helicopters and 2 Alouette liaison helicopters.

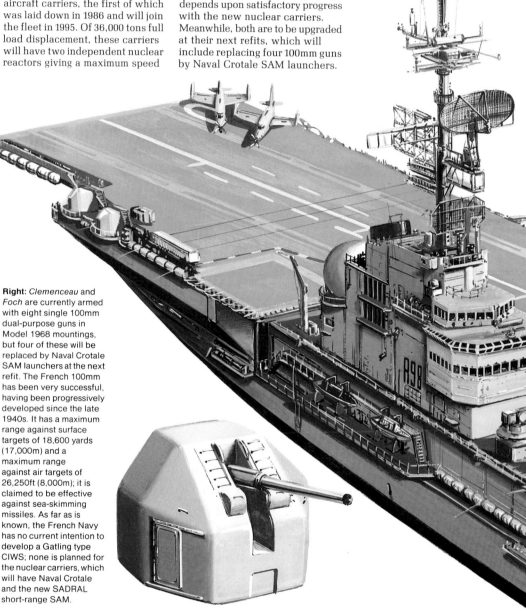

Right: *Clemenceau* and *Foch* are currently armed with eight single 100mm dual-purpose guns in Model 1968 mountings, but four of these will be replaced by Naval Crotale SAM launchers at the next refit. The French 100mm has been very successful, having been progressively developed since the late 1940s. It has a maximum range against surface targets of 18,600 yards (17,000m) and a maximum range against air targets of 26,250ft (8,000m); it is claimed to be effective against sea-skimming missiles. As far as is known, the French Navy has no current intention to develop a Gatling type CIWS; none is planned for the nuclear carriers, which will have Naval Crotale and the new SADRAL short-range SAM.

Clemenceau (R 98)

10 9   8 7 6   5   4   3   2   1

D C   B A

Weapons
A 100mm dual-purpose
   gun Modèle 1953 (2x1)
B 100mm dual-purpose
   gun Modèle 1953 (2x1)
C 100mm dual-purpose
   gun Modèle 1953 (2x1)
D 100mm dual-purpose
   gun Modèle 1953 (2x1)

Electronics
1 SQS-505 hull-mounted
   sonar
2 DRBC-32A gunfire
   control radar
3 DRBN-32 navigation
   radar (Decca 1226)
4 DRBI-10C height-
   finding radar
5 DRBV-23B air surveil-
   lance radar
6 DRBV-50 surface
   search radar
7 SRN-6 Tacan antenna
8 DRBV-20C long-range
   search radar
9 DRBI-10C height-
   finding radar
10 Carrier Control
   Approach (CCA) radar

Left: The carrier
Clemenceau, showing her
typical 1960s flight deck
layout with the 8° angled
deck. There are two
elevators, each 52.5 x 36ft
(16 x 11m) and capable of
lifting a 15-ton aircraft
from the hangar to the
flight deck in nine seconds.
Two Mitchell-Brown steam
catapults are fitted, one
on the forward flight deck,
the second on the angled
deck; both will be replaced
in the mid-1980s. The
ships themselves will be
replaced by 36,000-ton
nuclear powered carriers
in the 1990s.

**Left: The French aircaraft carrier
Clemenceau at sea with 13 Super
Etendard strike fighters, two F-8E
Crusader fighters, one Alizé ASW
aircraft and two Alouette
helicopters on the flight deck.
Clemenceau and her sister-ship,
Foch, are now the largest surface
warships in any European navy.**

Delta class

Origin: USSR
Type: Nuclear-powered ballistic missile submarine (SSBN)
Built: Delta I 1973-77
Delta II 1973-75
Delta III 1976-
Delta IV 1984-
Class: (I) 18 in service
(II) 4 in service
(III) 14 in service, more building
(IV) 2 in service, more building
Displacement: (I) 8,600 tons surfaced; 10,000 tons submerged
(II) 9,600 tons surfaced; 11,400 tons submerged
(III) 11,000 tons surfaced; 13,250 tons submerged
(IV) 12,000 tons surfaced; 14,250 tons submerged
Dimensions: (I) Length 446.1ft (136.1m); beam 38ft (11.6m); draught 32.9ft (10m)
(II) Length 500,9ft (152.7m); beam 38.8ft (11.8m); draught

33.5ft (10.2m)
(III) Length 509ft (155.1m); beam 39.5ft (12m); draught 33.5ft (10.2m)
(IV) Length 525ft (160m); beam 39.5ft (12m); draught 33.5ft (10.2m)
Propulsion: 2-shaft nuclear (pressurized-water nuclear reactors), 60,000shp
Performance: 25 knots dived
Weapons: SLBM: (I) 12 SS-N-8; (II) 16 SS-N-8; (III) 16 SS-N-18; (IV) 16 SS-N-23
Torpedo tubes: 6 x 21in (533mm), 12 reloads
Sensors: Radar: Snoop Tray surface
ECM: Pert Spring
ESM: Brick Pulp
Sonar: 1 LF bow-mounted; towed array in Delta IV only
Complement: Delta I 120; Delta II/III/IV 132

Background: The US Navy had major advantages in the quality and performance of its SLBMs until 1973, when the Soviet Navy introduced is SS-N-8 missile with a range of more than 4,800 miles (7,720km) and a circular error probable (CEP) of only 0.84nm (1.55km). This outranged the US Poseidon, although, unlike its American counterpart, the Soviet missile was not MIRVed and retained the more volatile liquid fuel of earlier Soviet SLBMs. Initial trials of the SS-N-8 were carried out in a converted Hotel III SSBN.

The advanced missile first went to sea as an operational system in the new Delta I SSBN, which had been designed around it, although derived from the basic design of the earlier Yankee class. The Delta I carries only 12 missiles in two rows of six abaft the sail.

These large and impressive boats were built at Komsomolsk

on the Pacific coast and at Severodvinsk in the Arctic, where a second slipway was constructed to expedite their production. Also built at Severodvinsk, the four Delta IIs were lengthened versions carrying 16 missiles, like contemporary Western SSBNs.

The Delta III is somewhat longer than its predecessors and carries 16 of the more advanced SS-N-18 missiles, which have a range of some 5,900 miles (9,500km) and mount MIRVed warheads. Due to the greater length of the SS-N-18 missile the superstructure of the Delta III abaft the sail is even higher than on the Delta I and II and the hydrodynamic matching of the two is very poor. This makes them very noisy, and they would be easy to detect and identify if they were to venture anywhere near a NATO ASW force.

Right: Delta III carries 16 SS-N-18 SLBMs in two rows of eight. There are three versions: Mod 1, with three 200kT MRVs and a 3,530nm (6,541 km) range; Mod 2, with one 450kT RV and a range of 4,350nm (8,616 km); and

Mod 3, with seven MIRVs and a range of 3,530nm (6,541 km). The missile is 44.6ft (13.6m) long, 1.97ft (0.6m) longer than the SS-N-8 carried by the Delta I and II, so that a higher whaleback is needed to accommodate

it. This missile gave the Soviet Navy the ability to launch a nuclear strike against the USA from waters which it could reasonably expect to dominate; the Barents Sea in the west and the Sea of Okhotsk in the east.

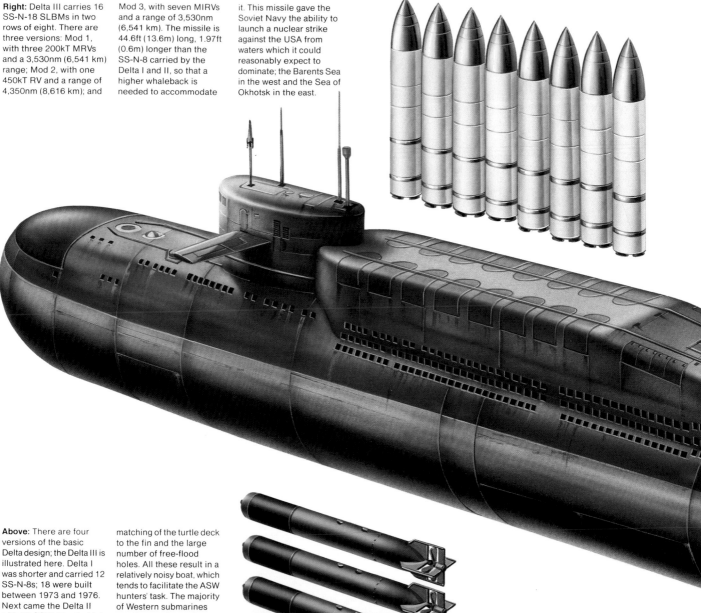

Above: There are four versions of the basic Delta design; the Delta III is illustrated here. Delta I was shorter and carried 12 SS-N-8s; 18 were built between 1973 and 1976. Next came the Delta II with 16 SS-N-8s, of which four were built. Delta III (14 built) was thought in the West to be the final version when the first Typhoon class boat appeared, but the Delta IV is now in service, carrying 16 SS-N-23s. The drawing illustrates the great length of the Delta III, the poor

matching of the turtle deck to the fin and the large number of free-flood holes. All these result in a relatively noisy boat, which tends to facilitate the ASW hunters' task. The majority of Western submarines now have only one large propeller, with five or seven curved blades. Such a propeller turns relatively slowly and cavitation noise is minimized. The Soviets, however, still use twin propellers, which again are a major source of noise.

Left: The Soviet Navy uses a variety of torpedoes, of which the most common is the 21in (533mm) type shown here. The Delta class boats mount six 21in (533mm) torpedo tubes with 12 reloads, although an SSBN, which depends upon secrecy for survival,

would use such weapons only as a final resort. Some Soviet torpedoes have nuclear warheads; the Swedish Navy detected such weapons on board the Whiskey class boat which ran aground off the Karlskrona naval base in October 1981.

Surprisingly, despite the commissioning of the first elements of the Typhoon class in 1983, yet another new version of the Delta class appeared in 1984. The Delta IV carries 16 of another new missile, the SS-N-23, a liquid-fuelled replacement for the SS-N-18, with a range of 4,500 miles (7,240km) and up to seven MIRVs. A fairing on the whaleback casing and a bracket further aft suggest that a towed array is used, while the fin has been modified and is now similar in height and outline to that fitted on the Oscar class SSGN. The 1985 edition of the US DoD's *Soviet Military Power* shows a Delta IV surfaced among Arctic ice firing its missiles.

It is clear from this progressive development that the Delta class has been successful, and all these boats pose a significant threat to the United States, because they can hit North America from launch areas in the Sea of Okhotsk and the Barents Sea — the so-called "SSBN sanctuaries". In those areas the Soviet SSBNs are well out of range of any known countermeasures, and thus probably invulnerable.

Of the 38 Delta class SSBNs in service, 23 are based with the Northern Fleet and 15 with the Pacific Fleet. However, as is normal Soviet Navy practice, only a small proportion are on patrol at any one time.

Future: It would seem that the Delta class is destined to remain in production for some time, although a replacement is almost certainly on the drawing board. The SS-N-23 SLBM may well be retrofitted to Delta III submarines, but it is too large for the Is and IIs.

Left: Delta III SSBN running on the surface, photographed from a NATO ASW aircraft. Such photographs represent virtually the only hard evidence in the West of the appearance of Soviet submarines; the Soviets themselves never publish pictures of their boats until a design has been in service for well over ten years.

Weapons
A 21in (533mm) torpedo tubes (2x3); 12 reloads carried
B SS-N-8 ballistic missile launch tubes (2x6)
C SS-N-8 ballistic missile launch tubes (2x8)
D SS-N-18 ballistic missile launch tubes (2x8)

Electronics
1 LF bow-mounted sonar
2 Pert Spring satellite navigation antenna
3 HF communications mast
4 Periscope
5 Snoop Tray radar
6 Periscope
7 Brick group ESM mast

Delta I class

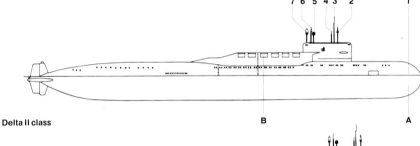

Delta II class

Delta III class

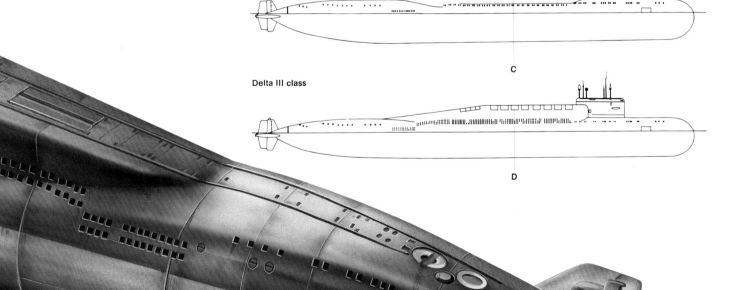

D'Estienne D'Orves (A 69) class

Origin: France
Type: Frigate (FF)
Built: 1972-1984
Class: French Navy: 23 in service
Argentinian Navy: 3 in service
Displacement: 950 tons standard;
1,170 tons full load
Dimensions: Length 249.3ft
(76m) oa; beam 33.8ft (10.3m);
draught 9.8ft (3m)
Propulsion: 2-shaft diesel (2
SEMT-Pielstick 12PC2-V400),
12,000bhp
Performance: Range 4,500nm at
15 knots
Weapons: Missiles: 2 MM.38
Exocet SSM on ships deployed
overseas
Guns: 1 100mm; 2 20mm AA
ASW weapons: 1 375mm Mk 54
rocket launcher
Torpedo tubes: 4 x 533mm for L3
and L5 torpedoes.
Sensors: Radar: DRBV 51A surface/
air search; DRBC 32E fire control;
DRBN 32 navigation
Sonar: DUBA 25 hull-mounted
Complement: 79

Top: The French frigate (Aviso) Détroyat (F 784), which is not fitted with Exocet missiles. The figures on the foredeck give a clear indication of the small size of this compact but nevertheless highly capable class of warship.

Above: Drogou (F 783), with two MM.38 Exocet anti-ship missiles. Shown clearly here are the DRBN-32 navigation radar atop the bridge, the DRBC-32E fire control radar before the funnel and the DRBV-51A search radar at the masthead.

Background: The French Navy built 18 Le Corse (Type E-50) and Le Normand (Type E-52) class seagoing fast escorts between 1951 and 1960. They had a speed of 28 knots, a standard displacement of about 1,290 tons and an armament of three twin 57mm guns plus ASW weapons; steam-turbine powered, they had a reasonable range.

An enlarged class, the Commandant Rivière (Type E-55), was diesel-powered, with a speed of 25 knots and a range of 7,000nm at 15 knots. They were originally armed with three single 100mm guns, but that in X position has since been removed and replaced by four single MM40 Exocets. ASW armament comprises a turret-mounted quadruple mortar and two triple torpedo tubes. Eight ships of this class were built between 1957 and 1965; they can carry two landing craft and an 80-man commando unit for operations in French colonies.

The D'Estienne D'Orves class, designated Avisos in the French Navy, are smaller and more specialized vessels with a very limited anti-aircraft armament. They are intended primarily for anti-submarine operations in coastal waters and are deployed in five three-ship divisions, of which one, the 1st, is based at Cherbourg and two each at Brest and Toulon — the 2nd and 4th and the 3rd and 5th respectively.

The single 100mm gun is mounted forward, immediately ahead of the large bridge, and the 375mm ASW rocket launcher is mounted on the deckhouse aft. France still has considerable overseas interests and the D'Estienne D'Orves class share some of the duties involved. For such distant deployments they mount an MM.38 Exocet SSM on either side of the funnel, which confers some independent offensive capability, although such a small ship is intended to be dependent upon other vessels or aircraft for protection against a serious air or surface threat. However, these relatively cheap and unsophisticated vessels can be built in greater numbers than the missile-armed and helicopter-equipped Georges Leygues (C 70) class.

Two of the class were sold to the Republic of South Africa during construction in 1976, but the sale fell through due to the United Nations embargo on arms sales. They were then sold to Argentina, with the new names Drummond and Guerrico in 1978, and two years later a third ship, Granville, was ordered by the same navy.
Future: These ships will serve the French Navy for many years to come. The first three are due to pay off in 1996 and there will then be a gradual rundown until the last, Commandant Bouan is paid off in 2004. No successor is currently planned. During future refits MM.40 Exocet and a new mast will be fitted, together with more advanced electronics. The last six of the class have been fitted with two Dagaie chaff launchers, and the first nine will be equipped with the new system in place of the original Syllex at their next refits.

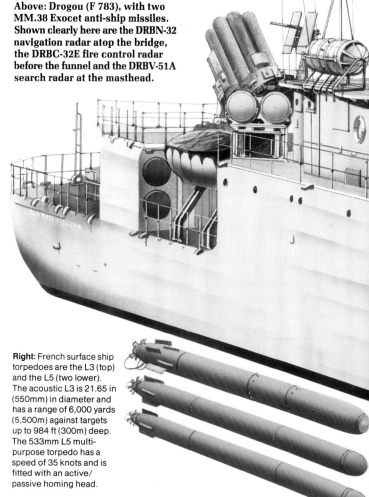

Right: French surface ship torpedoes are the L3 (top) and the L5 (two lower). The acoustic L3 is 21.65 in (550mm) in diameter and has a range of 6,000 yards (5,500m) against targets up to 984 ft (300m) deep. The 533mm L5 multi-purpose torpedo has a speed of 35 knots and is fitted with an active/passive homing head.

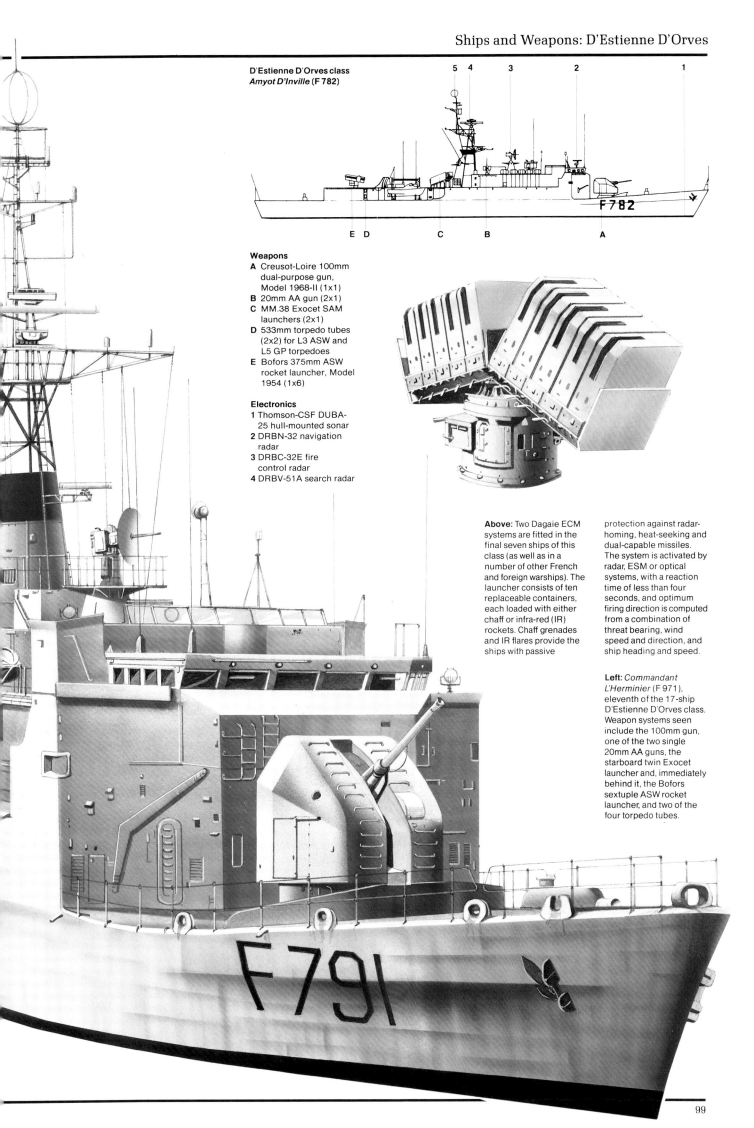

D'Estienne D'Orves class
Amyot D'Inville (F 782)

Weapons
A Creusot-Loire 100mm dual-purpose gun, Model 1968-II (1x1)
B 20mm AA gun (2x1)
C MM.38 Exocet SAM launchers (2x1)
D 533mm torpedo tubes (2x2) for L3 ASW and L5 GP torpedoes
E Bofors 375mm ASW rocket launcher, Model 1954 (1x6)

Electronics
1 Thomson-CSF DUBA-25 hull-mounted sonar
2 DRBN-32 navigation radar
3 DRBC-32E fire control radar
4 DRBV-51A search radar

Above: Two Dagaie ECM systems are fitted in the final seven ships of this class (as well as in a number of other French and foreign warships). The launcher consists of ten replaceable containers, each loaded with either chaff or infra-red (IR) rockets. Chaff grenades and IR flares provide the ships with passive protection against radar-homing, heat-seeking and dual-capable missiles. The system is activated by radar, ESM or optical systems, with a reaction time of less than four seconds, and optimum firing direction is computed from a combination of threat bearing, wind speed and direction, and ship heading and speed.

Left: *Commandant L'Herminier* (F 971), eleventh of the 17-ship D'Estienne D'Orves class. Weapon systems seen include the 100mm gun, one of the two single 20mm AA guns, the starboard twin Exocet launcher and, immediately behind it, the Bofors sextuple ASW rocket launcher, and two of the four torpedo tubes.

Georges Leygues (C 70) class

Origin: France
Type: Destroyer (DD)
Built: 1974-1994
Class: (ASW) 5 in service; 2 building
(AA) 3 building: 1 ordered
Displacement: (ASW) 3,830 tons standard: 4,170 tons full load
(AA) 4,300 tons full load
Dimensions: Length 455.9ft (139m) oa; beam 45.9ft (14m); draught 18.7ft (5.7m)
Propulsion: (ASW) 2-shaft CODOG (2 Rolls-Royce Olympus gas turbines; 2 SEMT-Pielstick 16PA6 CV280 diesels), 53,000/10,400bhp
(AA) 2-shaft diesel (4 SEMT-Pielstick 18PA6 BTC 'diesels rapides'), 42,000hp
Performance: (ASW) Speed 30 knots; range 9,500nm on diesels
(AA) Range 9,200nm at 17 knots, 5,000nm at 24 knots
Weapons: (ASW) SSM: 4 MM38 Exocet (8 from third of class)
SAM: 1 Crotale launcher (26 missiles)
Guns: 1 Model 1968-II 100mm (first four only); 1 Creusot-Loire 100mm Compact (fifth ship); 2 20mm
Torpedo tubes: 2 fixed launchers for L5 torpedoes (10 carried)
(AA) SSM: 8 MM40 Exocet
SAM: 1 Mk 13 launcher for Standard SM1 MR (40 missiles); 2 Sadral PDMS
Guns: One Creusot-Loire 100mm Compact; 2 20mm
Torpedo tubes: 2 fixed launchers for L5 torpedoes (10 carried)
Aircraft: (ASW) 2 Lynx helicopters with Mk 46 torpedoes;
(AA) 1 SA 365 Dauphin
Sensors: (ASW) Radar: DRBV-51C surface/air surveillance; DRBV-26 air search; DRBC-32D fire control; SPG-51C missile control; 2 Decca 1226 navigation
Sonar: DUBV-23D hull-mounted; DUBV-43B variable-depth (first four only); DSBV-61 towed array (fifth ship onwards)
(AA) Radar: DRBJ-11b surface/air surveillance; DRBV-26 air surveillance; DRBC-33 fire control; 2 SPG 551C missile control; Decca 1229 navigation
Sonar: DUBV 25A hull-mounted; DSBV 61 towed array
Complement: ASW — 216; AA — 200

Background: These well designed and very capable ships, the latest in a long and successful line of big French destroyers, represent a notable achievement on the part of the designers, who have achieved a goal that has eluded many others by producing two different types of ship on the same hull.

Developed from the Tourville (F 67) class, the original C 70s are the ASW Georges Leygues class, which the French Navy classifies as 'corvettes' and of which five are currently in service, with another two on order; an eighth was cancelled as an economy measure. The first four are the C 70(1) class, whose details are given above, but the fifth, Primauguet (D 644), and subsequent ships — the C 70(2) class — are being fitted with a DSBV 61 towed array in place of the DUBV 43B variable depth

Above: Jean de Vienne (D 643), fourth ship of the C 70 (ASW) class. This view shows the Naval Crotale SAM launcher, the hangar, the spacious flight deck and the DUBV-43B variable-depth sonar mounted on the stern (replaced by DSBV-61 towed array in the last three ships).

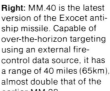

Right: MM.40 is the latest version of the Exocet anti-ship missile. Capable of over-the-horizon targeting using an external fire-control data source, it has a range of 40 miles (65km), almost double that of the earlier MM.38.

sonar, the new Crotale Navale EDIR SAM system, a new 100mm compact gun and the Vampir infra-red surveillance system; they will also have the bridge one deck level higher to overcome the problems the first four have experienced in bad weather. Of these modifications only the Crotale Navale is likely to be retrofitted into the first four.

The AA version is designed to provide the anti-aircraft and anti-missile defences for a carrier task group or a mercantile convoy. Sometimes designated the Cassard class, these ships have a very different armament and propulsion system mounted on an identical hull. Main AA armament, the Mk 13 Standard missile launcher aft, will be taken from the T 47 class destroyers when the latter are removed from service in the late 1980s, but it is intended to fit vertical launch systems for the SAMs in due course. The air defence armament is supplemented by the Sadral short-range self-defence missile system and a single forecastle-mounted Creusot-Loire 100mm/55 dual-purpose gun, plus eight MM.40 Exocet SSMs. Sonar is fitted and there are two hull-mounted quintuple ASW torpedo launchers.

Propulsion for the C 70 (AA) class is provided by four SEMT-Pielstick 18PA6 low compression diesels. These are estimated to be almost as light and easy to

maintain as a gas-turbine system, but do not require such large air intakes and exhaust trunking. A lot of aluminium alloy is already being used in the superstructure to save top weight, a step which the French designers may now be regretting in view of recent naval experiences with aluminium alloys in warships.

Future: These ships will provide the French Navy with a strong force of seven ASW and four AA units serving well into the next century. The ASW ships will reach the currently programmed end of their operational lives in 2004, 2006 (two), 2008, 2011, 2012 and 2014, and the AA ships in 2013, 2015, 2016 and 2017.

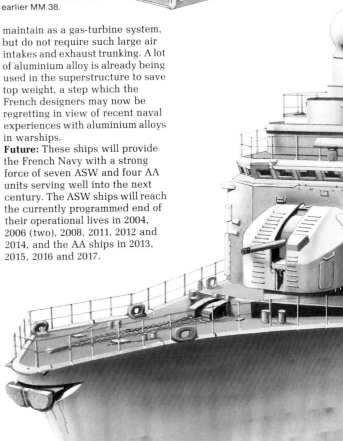

Below: The fine lines of the *Montcalm* (D 642) are dominated by the large funnel. The bridge has proved to be too low in bad weather and is being raised by one deck level in the last three of the class. Note the new Dagaie chaff launcher below the satellite antenna.

Right: Naval Crotale is a navalized version of a French Air Force surface-to-air missile system; the missile is made by Matra and the electronics by Thomson-CSF. Eight missiles are mounted on the launcher and there are 18 reloads in the magazine. The original missile is a beam-rider and has a range of 8,750 yards (8,000m) at altitudes of 150ft (45.7m) to 12,000ft (3,676m). A new version, Crotale EDIR, is capable of dealing with targets flying at speeds of up to Mach 2 at heights of 13ft (4m) and an infra-red tracker is being added to the launcher/director. The C 70 (AA) ships will have the Standard SM-1(MR) missile and Mk 13 launcher instead of Crotale; 40 missiles will be carried. The entire installations are being taken from the four Surcouf class destroyers equipped with Tartar in the early 1960s.

Weapons
A Creusot-Loire 100mm dual-purpose gun mount, Model 1968-II (1x1)
B Catapults for L5 multi-purpose torpedoes (2x1)
C Type A 20mm F2 gun (2x1)
D MM.38 Exocet SSM launchers (2x4) (D 642 onward mount MM.40 version)
E Naval Crotale launcher, System TSE 5500 (1x8)
F Westland Lynx Mk2 ASW helicopter

Electronics
1 DUBV-23D hull-mounted low frequency panoramic sonar
2 Decca 1226 navigation radar
3 CSEE Panda optronic director (back-up system for 100mm gun)
4 DRBC-32D fire control radar (DRBC-32E in D 644)
5 Satcom antenna (2x1)
6 DRBV-26 air search radar
7 ARB-33 jammer
8 Enigme DF antenna arrays
9 ARBR-17 ESM antenna
10 DRBV-51C surface/air surveillance radar (DRBV-15 in D 644-646)
11 Syllex chaff launcher
12 DUBV-43B Variable depth sonar (DSBV-61 towed array in D 644-646)

Below right: C70 (ASW) destroyers carry two Westland Lynx helicopters, one of the types covered by the Anglo-French helicopter agreement of the late 1960s. This aircraft carries a DUAV-4 dipping sonar and is usually armed with Mk 46 or French L4 ASW torpedoes (the latter is shown here). The Lynx has a typical endurance of 1.5 hours, half in forward flight and half hovering. The C70 (AA) carries an SA 365 Dauphin helicopter.

Georges Leygues (D 640)

Giuseppe Garibaldi

Origin: Italy
Type: Light aircraft carrier (CVS)
Built: 1981-1985
Class: 1 in service
Displacement: 10,000 tons standard; 13,600 tons full load
Dimensions: Length 591.1ft (180.2m) oa; beam 76.8ft (23.4m); draught 22ft (6.7m)
Propulsion: 2-shaft COGAG (4 FIAT/General Electric LM2500 gas turbines), 80,000shp
Performance: Speed 30 knots: range 9,000nm at 20 knots
Weapons: SSM: 4 twin Otomat Mk 2 launchers
SAM: 2 octuple Albatros launchers for Aspide missiles
Guns: 3 twin Breda 40mm;
Torpedo tubes: 2 x 3 Mk 32
Aircraft: 16 SH-3D Sea King ASW helicopters (4 on deck, 12 in hangar) or 10 Sea Harrier or AV-8B Harrier II
Sensors: Radar: MM/SPS-768 medium-range air surveillance; MM/SPS-774 long-range surveillance; Selenia RAN-10S short-range air detection; SMA MM/SPS-702 surface detection; NA-30 fire control (for Albatros); SMA MM/SPS-703 navigation
Sonar: Raytheon DE 1160 hull-mounted
Complement: 550, plus 230 air group

Background: *Giuseppe Garibaldi* is the first purpose-built, through-deck carrier to be completed for the Italian Navy. She is designed primarily for anti-submarine warfare, operating the big SH-3D Sea King in place of the AB 204/212 helicopters embarked by the previous generation of Italian ASW cruisers. She is also intended to be able to counter threats from aircraft and surface ships, and can mount amphibious operations as well as taking part in disaster relief operations.

The hangar is located centrally and is 361ft (110m) long and 20ft (6m) high, with a maximum width of 49ft (15m). The centre section, however, is somewhat narrower due to the gas-turbine uptakes to starboard. The hangar is divided into three sections by fire curtains and can accommodate either 12 Sea Kings or a slightly smaller number of the new EH.101 helicopters, or 10 Sea Harriers. Two hexagonal lifts are offset to starboard fore and aft of the massive island, each measuring 59ft (18m) by 33ft (10m) and with a capacity of 15 tons. The flight deck has a 6° ski-jump for V/STOL aircraft and is marked with six helicopter spots.

The principle ASW weapon system is the SH-3 Sea King helicopter, which also has a surface warfare role providing mid-course guidance for the ship-launched Otomat Mk 2 (Teseo) anti-ship missiles. There are four double Teseo launchers fitted on either quarter, plus an octuple launcher on each end of the island superstructure for the Selenia Albatros point defence system, which fires Aspide missiles. Close-in defence is provided by the

Selenia Elsag Dardo system, using three twin Breda 40mm gun mounts, one on either bow and the third amidships aft.

Instead of having reversing controllable-pitch propellers the *Garibaldi* is fited with a Franco-Tosi reversing hydraulic coupling, which enables fixed-pitch propellers to be used, for maximum propulsive efficiency and minimum noise. Each propeller has five blades and a maximum speed of 175 rpm.

Giuseppe Garibaldi has been at the centre of a major political row in Italy as the ship is clearly designed to operate V/STOL aircraft such as the Sea Harrier—the ski-jump forward can have no other purpose. However, under a Law dating back to 1923 the Navy is not permitted to operate fixed-wing aircraft and the Italian Air Force has steadfastly refused to procure and operate such types for the Navy. Nevertheless, *Garibaldi* is now at sea as the flagship of the fleet and senior Italian naval officers are still campaigning for authority to operate fixed-wing aircraft.

There are only two aircraft which could fulfil the requirement: the British Aerospace Sea Harrier

FRS.2 and the McDonnell Douglas AV-B Harrier II. Even if a purchase is finally approved, however, it will take some further time for the Italian Navy to work up a fixed-wing component, a field in which they have no previous experience, and presumably technical assistance would be included in any purchase deal.

Even without its fixed-wing aircraft this is a formidable ship, which considerably enhances the NATO fleet capability in the

Mediterranean. Somewhat smaller and cheaper than the British Invincible class, it makes an interesting comparison with the Spanish *Principe de Asturias*.
Future: This ship is intended to replace the ageing *Andrea Doria* and *Caio Duilio*. It was very expensive and its fixed wing component (Harrier II/Sea Harrier), if bought, will add considerably to the cost. It is unlikely, therefore, that any more units of this class will be built.

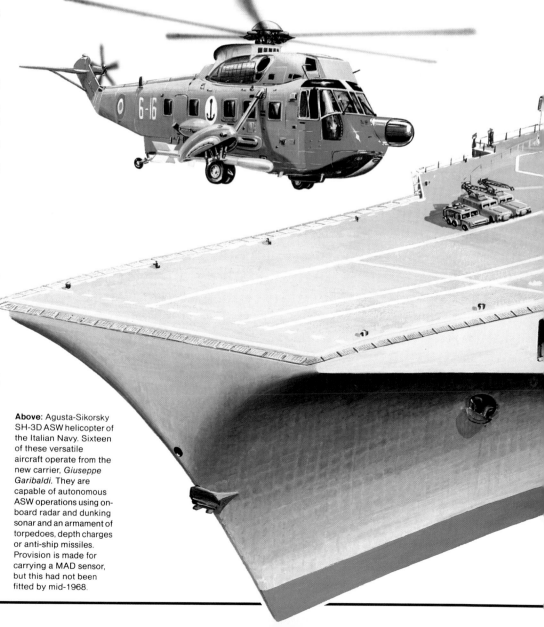

Above: Agusta-Sikorsky SH-3D ASW helicopter of the Italian Navy. Sixteen of these versatile aircraft operate from the new carrier, *Giuseppe Garibaldi*. They are capable of autonomous ASW operations using on-board radar and dunking sonar and an armament of torpedoes, depth charges or anti-ship missiles. Provision is made for carrying a MAD sensor, but this had not been fitted by mid-1968.

Left: The launching of the Giuseppe Garibaldi on June 10, 1983, was the realization of a dream for the Italian Navy. Unfortunately, due to an inter-Service dispute with the Air Force, the Navy still cannot purchase the STOVL aircraft for which this carrier is designed, as shown by the lines of the ski-jump so clearly evident in this picture. Note also the large size of the superstructure.

Right: Rather than put weapon systems on the foredeck, as in the Kiev (USSR) and Invincible (UK) classes, the Italians have installed SAM launchers immediately forward and aft of the bridge, leaving the flight deck clear. The Albatros Aspide SAM system uses an Italian version of the Sea Sparrow SAM on an octuple launcher.

Below: This illustration shows to advantage the neat and workmanlike design of the first Italian aircraft carrier to attain operational status. All weapon systems are concentrated on the bridge superstructure, except for the Breda Dardo CIWS on sponsons below the flight deck level. This leaves a totally clear and uncluttered flight deck, permitting efficient and economical aircraft handling. Aircraft complement is either 16 SH-3D/H ASW helicopters or 10 fixed-wing STOVL aircraft, which could only be Sea Harriers or AV-8B Harrier IIs. This ship, together with the French Foch and Clemenceau and the Spanish Principe de Asturias, considerably enhances non-US shipborne air power available to NATO in the Mediterranean.

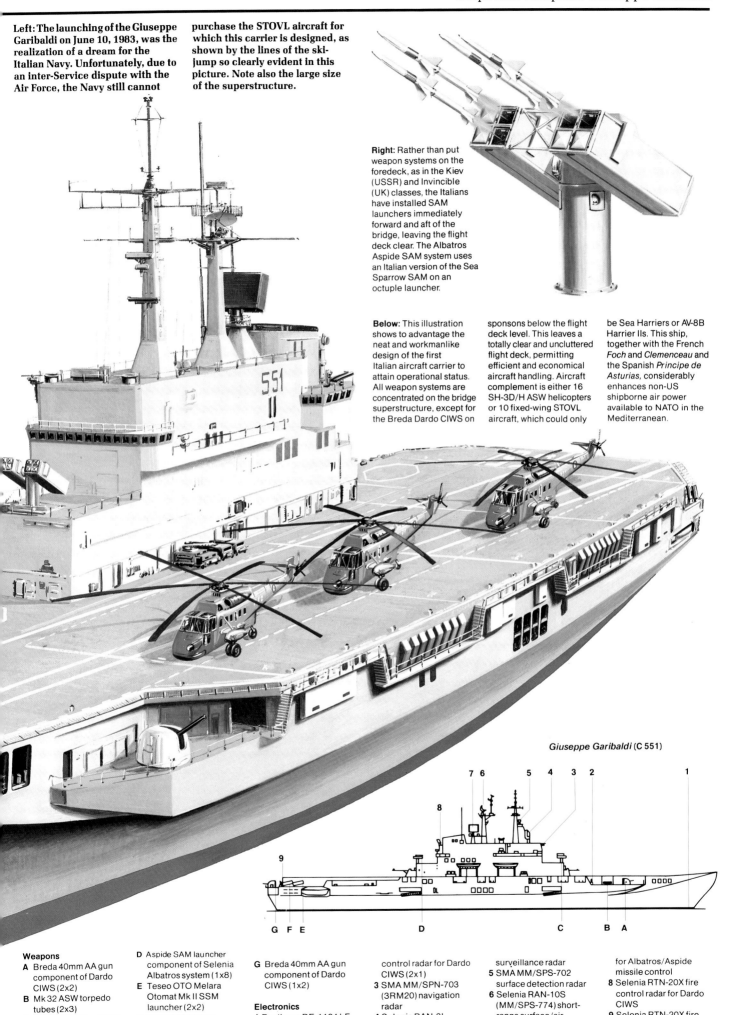

Giuseppe Garibaldi (C 551)

Weapons
A Breda 40mm AA gun component of Dardo CIWS (2x2)
B Mk 32 ASW torpedo tubes (2x3)
C Aspide SAM launcher component of Selenia Albatros system (1x8)
D Aspide SAM launcher component of Selenia Albatros system (1x8)
E Teseo OTO Melara Otomat Mk II SSM launcher (2x2)
F Teseo OTO Melara Otomat Mk II SSM launcher (2x2)
G Breda 40mm AA gun component of Dardo CIWS (1x2)

Electronics
1 Raytheon DE-1164 LF hull-mounted sonar
2 Selenia RTN-30X fire control radar for Dardo CIWS (2x1)
3 SMA MM/SPN-703 (3RM20) navigation radar
4 Selenia RAN-3L (MM/SPS-768) medium-range air surveillance radar
5 SMA MM/SPS-702 surface detection radar
6 Selenia RAN-10S (MM/SPS-774) short-range surface/air search radar
7 Hughes RTN-30X radar for Albatros/Aspide missile control
8 Selenia RTN-20X fire control radar for Dardo CIWS
9 Selenia RTN-20X fire control radar for Dardo CIWS

Hatsuyuki class

Origin: Japan
Type: Destroyer (DD)
Built: 1983-1987
Class: 9 in service; 3 building
Displacement: 3,050 tons standard; 3,800 tons full load
Dimensions: Length 426.4 (130m) oa; beam 44.6ft (13.6m); draught 13.4ft (4.1m)
Propulsion: 2-shaft COGOG (2 Rolls-Royce Olympus TM3B/2 Rolls-Royce Spey RM1C gas turbines, 45,000/13,600shp
Performance: Speed 30 knots
Weapons: Missiles: 2 quad Harpoon launchers; 1 NATO Sea Sparrow Mk 29 octuple launcher
Guns: 1 76mm/62 OTO-Melara Compact; 2 20mm Phalanx CIWS (third and susequent ships) ASW weapons: 1 US Mk 16 octuple Asroc launcher; 2 x 3 Type 68 torpedo tubes
Aircraft: 1 Mitsubishi HSS-2B ASW helicopter
Sensors: Radar: OPS-14B air search; OPS-18 surface search; GFCS-2-21/21A gun fire control; MFCS-2-12A missile control Sonar: OQS-4(II) hull-mounted
Complement: 190

Above: Hatsuyuki (DD 122), lead ship of the Japanese Maritime Self-Defence Force's latest class of ASW destoyers, at sea.

Background: Japan's strategic position as an offshore Asian power, on the western edge of the Pacific Ocean and on the southern edge of the USSR's SSBN haven in the Sea of Okhotsk, demands a strong navy. Japan's constitution forbids the maintenance of armed forces for aggressive purposes and the Japanese Maritime Self-Defence Force (JMSDF) is, therefore, tasked with purely defensive missions. Foremost among these is the protection of the sea lanes around Japan, which, in view of her lack of natural resources, especially oil, are essential to her economy. Consequently, the force built up since the naval reconstruction began in the late 1950s has been orientated primarily toward anti-submarine warfare, although a recent reappraisal of the air threat has led to the development of a class of anti-air warfare destroyers.

A series of destroyer designs built since the late 1950s, despite showing some indications of US influence in the early designs and weapon fits, has become increasingly independent and impressive, as befits a nation with such a long naval history and advanced techno-logical capability. There are cur-rently no fewer than 33 destroyers in service of ten classes, with another nine ships under con-struction, as well as 18 frigates in service and another three under construction.

Japanese destroyer design is currently following two develop-ment streams. In the first are the Shirane, Haruna and Hatakaze classes of approximately 6,000 tons full load displacement, with two in each class. The Shiranes and Harunas all have very large hangars accommodating no fewer than three Mitsubishi SH-3B ASW (Sikorsky SH-3B Sea King) heli-copters, and large flight-decks. The latest (Hatakaze) class, however, has a helicopter flight-deck but no hangar, a most surprising development, especially as the ship is by no means small, but an interesting parallel to the US Navy's Arleigh Burke. A further development of the Hatakaze class will be two specialized anti-aircraft ships authorized as part of the defence build-up plan 59-*Chyu Gyo*, which will include major elements of the US Navy's Aegis system to deal with the simul-taneous multiple target threat.

The second stream of develop-ment is a series of slightly smaller ships, of which the latest (and numerically the largest class of destroyers to be built for the JMSDF) is the Hatsuyuki class. Nine are currently in service, with another three due to join the fleet in 1987, while an improved design is already under construction.

The Hatsuyuki class ships have ASW as their primary mission and therefore carry a single Mitsubishi HSS-2B helicopter, backed up by the Asroc system and two triple Mk 68 trainable torpedo tubes. Air defence is provided by the NATO Sea Sparrow system, whose Mk 29 launcher is mounted near the stern, and a forward-mounted OTO-Melara dual-purpose gun. Close-in defence is provided by two 20mm Phalanx, although the first ship of the class, *Hatsuyuki* (DD-122), needs modification to take this system, while the second, *Shirayuki* (DD-123), has the modi-fications but has not yet had the weapons fitted. Anti-ship armament is provided by two quadruple Harpoon launchers, one on either side of the massive funnel.

These are impressive ships, which, although optimized for the ASW mission, nevertheless have respectable anti-aircraft and anti-ship capabilities as well. They make an interesting comparison with the French Georges Leygues class, being very similar in appearance and armament. Indeed, the only major external difference is that the Japanese ships have the helicopter flight-deck at the 01 level, whereas the French ships have theirs at the upper deck level.
Future: Seven ships of the Improved Hatsuyuki class are on order, with the first due to join the fleet in May 1988. These will be 21.3ft (6.5m) longer, 3.4ft (1m) wider in the beam and 1.2ft (0.4m) greater in draught than the Hatsuyukis. A major difference is that four Rolls-Royce Spey SM1A gas-turbines will be fitted in a COGAG arrange-ment, in place of the earlier ships' COGOG. Much improved sensors are also fitted, and SQR-19 TACTAS and a variable-depth sonar will greatly improve ASW capabilities. The TACTAS towed array will also be retrofitted to all the earlier ships of the class.

The development of the JMSDF has to a large extent been ignored in the West, but they have produced a constant series of well designed and well balanced ships in the destroyer category. For political and historical reasons the Japanese use foreign weapons systems such as the US Harpoon, Asroc and Vulcan/Phalanx and Italian guns. Sensors, on the other hand, are now virtually all of Japanese design and manufacture, although it has been announced that the air defence command and control system for the new 6,500 ton air defence destroyers, which would be very expensive to develop in a purely national programme, will be the SPY-1D Aegis system.

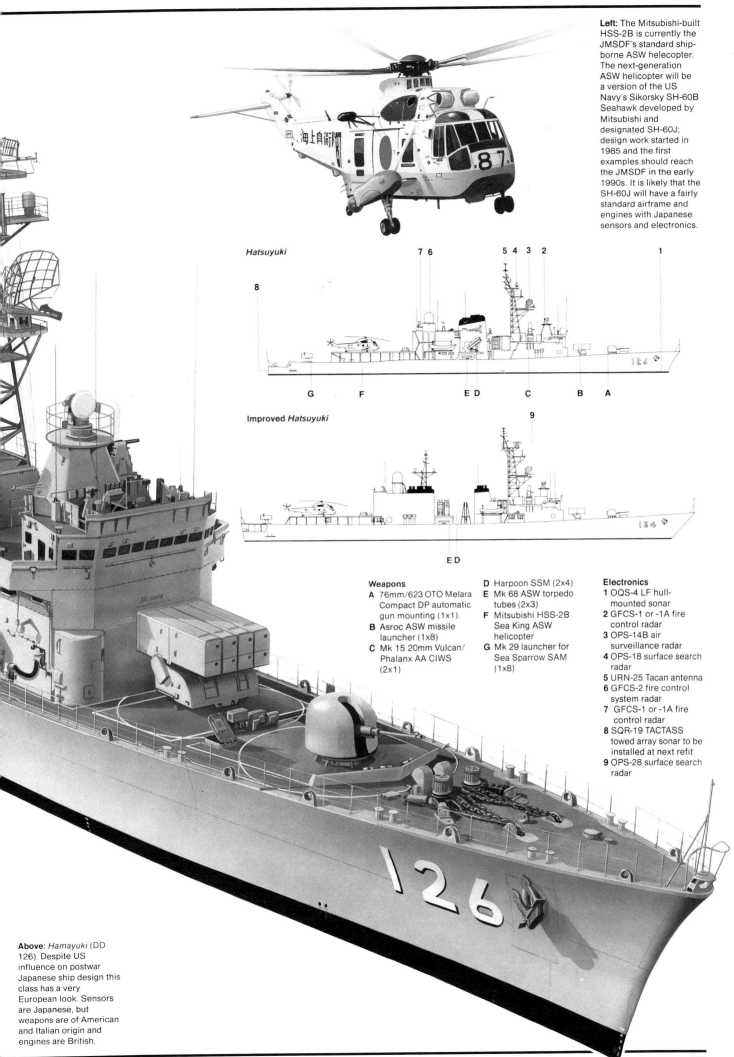

Left: The Mitsubishi-built HSS-2B is currently the JMSDF's standard ship-borne ASW helecopter. The next-generation ASW helicopter will be a version of the US Navy's Sikorsky SH-60B Seahawk developed by Mitsubishi and designated SH-60J; design work started in 1985 and the first examples should reach the JMSDF in the early 1990s. It is likely that the SH-60J will have a fairly standard airframe and engines with Japanese sensors and electronics.

Hatsuyuki

Improved *Hatsuyuki*

Weapons

A 76mm/623 OTO Melara Compact DP automatic gun mounting (1x1).

B Asroc ASW missile launcher (1x8)

C Mk 15 20mm Vulcan/ Phalanx AA CIWS (2x1)

D Harpoon SSM (2x4)

E Mk 68 ASW torpedo tubes (2x3)

F Mitsubishi HSS-2B Sea King ASW helicopter

G Mk 29 launcher for Sea Sparrow SAM (1x8)

Electronics

1 OQS-4 LF hull-mounted sonar

2 GFCS-1 or -1A fire control radar

3 OPS-14B air surveillance radar

4 OPS-18 surface search radar

5 URN-25 Tacan antenna

6 GFCS-2 fire control system radar

7 GFCS-1 or -1A fire control radar

8 SQR-19 TACTASS towed array sonar to be installed at next refit

9 OPS-28 surface search radar

Above: *Hamayuki* (DD 126). Despite US influence on postwar Japanese ship design this class has a very European look. Sensors are Japanese, but weapons are of American and Italian origin and engines are British.

Invincible class

Origin: United Kingdom
Type: Light aircraft carrier (CVS)
Built: 1973-1985
Class: 3 in service
Displacement: 16,000 tons standard; 19,500 tons full load
Dimensions: Length 677ft (206.6m) oa; beam 90ft (27.5m); draught 26ft (8m)
Propulsion: 2-shaft gas turbine (4 Rolls-Royce Olympus TM3B)
Performance: Speed 28 knots; range 5,000nm at 18 knots
Weapons: SAM: 1 twin Sea Dart launcher (with secondary SSM capability)
Guns: 2 20mm Phalanx CIWS (*Invincible, Illustrious*); 3 20mm Phalanx CIWS (*Ark Royal*)
Aircraft: 7 Sea King HAS.5; 2 Sea King AEW; 5 Sea Harrier FRS.1 (8 from 1988)
Sensors: Surveillance radar: Type 1022
Search radar: Type 992 R
Fire control radar: 2 Type 909 for Sea Dart
Navigation radar: 2 Type 1006
Complement: 670, plus 284 air group

Background: Following the mid-1960s political decision not to proceed with a new generation of attack carriers for the Royal Navy, design work started on a large, air-capable anti-submarine cruiser for deployment within the NATO EASTLANT area of operations. The design went through a series of changes in response to both political and naval manoeuvring in the British Ministry of Defence.

Originally intended to operate only large helicopters, the vessel was subject to late design changes to enable it to operate the Sea Harrier STOVL aircraft needed to intercept hostile reconnaissance and ASW aircraft, while a final change in 1976-77 established a requirement for the type to be capable of operating as commando cruisers. The original designation of 'through-deck cruiser' (adopted primarily for political reasons) was dropped in 1980 and the type was given the more accurate designation of ASW aircraft carrier.

Unlike previous Royal Navy carriers, but following the lead given, for example, by the Italian *Vittorio Veneto* and the Soviet *Moskva*, the Invincible class has an open forecastle-head deck which is utilized for weapons systems. The current fit comprises a twin Sea Dart GWS.30 SAM launcher with a 22-round magazine, supplemented as a result of the lessons of the 1982 South Atlantic war by Phalanx 20mm CIWS. In *Invincible* and *Illustrious* the first Phalanx is mounted on the forecastle alongside the Sea Dart launcher and the second is mounted at the after end of the flight-deck on the starboard side. *Ark Royal*, the last of the three to be completed, has three Phalanx: the first is mounted in the eyes of the ship, the second at the forward end of the flight-deck on the starboard side and the third on a sponson on the port quarter just below flight-deck level. *Ark Royal*

also has two twin BMARC 30mm mountings: one on a flight-deck level sponson on the starboard side abreast the mainmast, and the second on a larger sponson on the port side at hangar deck level. The Sea Dart, apart from being a highly effective SAM, also has a very reasonable anti-ship capability.

The flight-deck, which measures 550ft (167.8m) in length and 44ft (13.4m) in width, is very slightly angled and is offset to port to clear the Sea Dart launcher. The ski-jump at the forward end of the flight-deck is angled at 7° on *Invincible* and *Illustrious* and 12° on *Ark Royal*. Underneath this flight-deck is the aircraft hangar, which narrows somewhat at the centre due to the exhaust uptakes for the gas turbines on the starboard side. This is not too serious for helicopter handling but does impose some constraints for the Sea Harriers.

The usual peacetime aircraft complement is 14, normally divided into nine Sea Kings and five Sea Harriers (eight from 1988). As a result of experience in the South Atlantic two of the Sea Kings will almost invariably be of the AEW version. Furthermore, in wartime the number of aircraft can be increased by using deck parks, allowing up to 10 Sea Harriers to be embarked.

As these ships wil obviously be used to command ASW task groups they are fitted with a very comprehensive command centre, which has proved its worth on many NATO exercises. That on *Invincible* also proved invaluable during Operation Corporate, the British undertaking to repossess the Falkland Islands. Prior to that operation the British Government planned to offer *Invincible* for sale to the Royal Australian Navy, but the value of this class was made so clear that the plan was quickly shelved at the war's end.

Ark Royal, in addition to the armament differences noted above, has other changes from the first two of the class. The ship's interior has been redesigned with better workshop space, more storerooms and better living accommodation. The hangar is fitted out to take the Anglo-Italian EH.101 helicopter when that machine enters service in the 1990s, and greatly improved electronic systems are also fitted.

The design, size and capabilities of the Invincible class makes a very interesting comparison with the Italian *Giuseppe Garibaldi* and the Spanish *Principe de Asturias*.
Future: These ships have already served the Royal Navy well, and, in view of what happened in the 1982 South Atlantic war, it is as well that the *Invincible* was available for the Task Force. The additional features in *Ark Royal* amount to those destined for her two pre-decessors at their first refit. There has been no discussion on the next generation of aircraft carrier for the Royal Navy, which may well cause a crisis as severe as that over CVA-01, since the cost of such large ships is escalating.

Left: Sea Dart (GWS 30) is a medium-range SAM system fitted to the British Invincible class carriers, and to the Types 42 and 82 destroyers. Maximum range is 35 miles (56.3km) in an interception envelope of 100-60,000 ft (30-18,300m). The fire control radar is the Type 909.

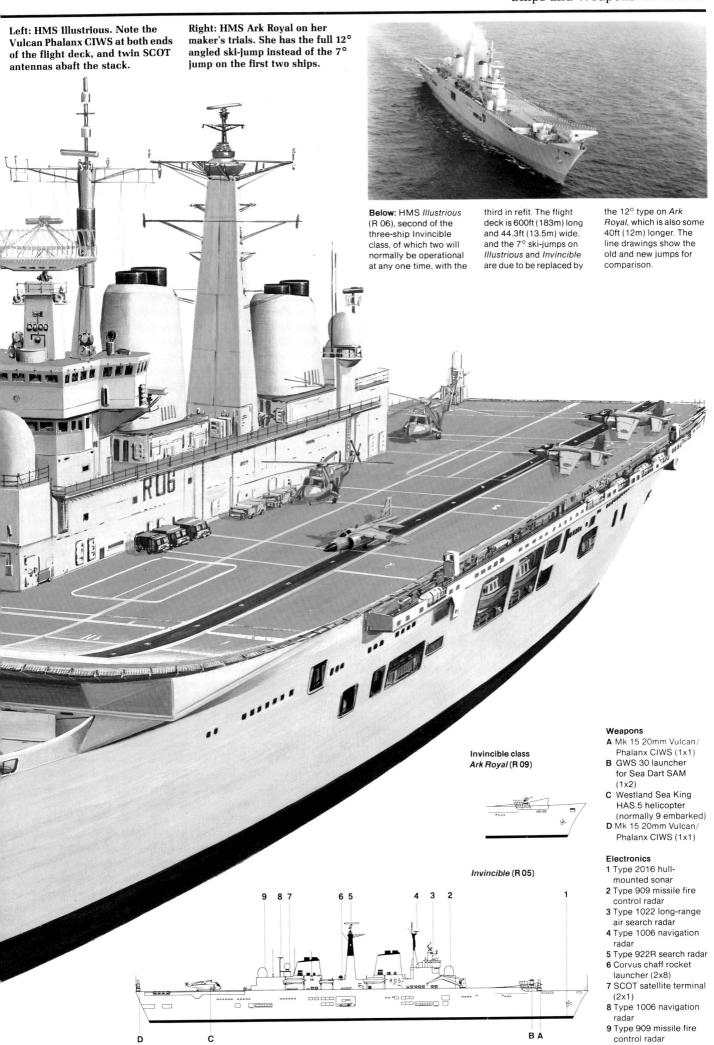

Left: HMS Illustrious. Note the Vulcan Phalanx CIWS at both ends of the flight deck, and twin SCOT antennas abaft the stack.

Right: HMS Ark Royal on her maker's trials. She has the full 12° angled ski-jump instead of the 7° jump on the first two ships.

Below: HMS *Illustrious* (R 06), second of the three-ship Invincible class, of which two will normally be operational at any one time, with the third in refit. The flight deck is 600ft (183m) long and 44.3ft (13.5m) wide, and the 7° ski-jumps on *Illustrious* and *Invincible* are due to be replaced by the 12° type on *Ark Royal*, which is also some 40ft (12m) longer. The line drawings show the old and new jumps for comparison.

Invincible class
Ark Royal (R 09)

Invincible (R 05)

Weapons
A Mk 15 20mm Vulcan/ Phalanx CIWS (1x1)
B GWS 30 launcher for Sea Dart SAM (1x2)
C Westland Sea King HAS.5 helicopter (normally 9 embarked)
D Mk 15 20mm Vulcan/ Phalanx CIWS (1x1)

Electronics
1 Type 2016 hull-mounted sonar
2 Type 909 missile fire control radar
3 Type 1022 long-range air search radar
4 Type 1006 navigation radar
5 Type 922R search radar
6 Corvus chaff rocket launcher (2x8)
7 SCOT satellite terminal (2x1)
8 Type 1006 navigation radar
9 Type 909 missile fire control radar

Iowa (BB 61) class

Origin: USA
Type: Battleship (BB)
Built: 1940-1944
Class: 3 in service; 1 reactivating
Displacement: 45,000 tons standard; 58,000 tons full load
Dimensions: Length 887.2ft (270.4m) oa; beam 108.2ft (33m); draught 38ft (11.6m)
Propulsion: 4-shaft geared turbines, 212,000shp
Performance: Speed 30 knots; range 5,000nm at 30 knots, 15,000nm at 17 knots
Weapons: SSM: 4 twin Mk 43 launchers for Tomahawk; 4 quad launchers for Harpoon
Guns: 9 16in/50 (3 x 3); 12 5in/38 (*Iowa* and *New Jersey*); 20 5in/38 (*Missouri, Wisconsin*); 4 20mm Mk 15 Phalanx CIWS (*New Jersey, Iowa, Missouri*)
Aircraft: 4 LAMPS II or III helicopters
Sensors: Surface search radar: SPS-67(V)
Air search radar: SPS-49(V)
Navigation radar: LN-66
Complement: 1,606

Background: In 1938 the US Navy started design work on a new class of fast battleship to success the South Dakota class then building. Armed with nine 16in/50 guns in three triple turrets and 20 5in/38 DP guns, these ships had very powerful engines giving them a maximum speed of 33 knots and making them the fastest battleships ever built. They were also exceptionally well armoured, with a 12.1in (30.7cm) main belt designed to survive direct engagement by the 18in guns of the rumoured Japanese battleships.

Commissioned in 1943-44, all four ships fought in the Pacific campaign; they were then placed in reserve in the late 1940s, when the era of the battleship was almost universally considered to be over. Reactivated during the Korean War (1950-53) for use in the shore bombardment role, they were then mothballed again, only for *New Jersey* to be reactivated once more in 1967 for use in the Vietnam War before decom-

missioning for the third time in 1969.

The appearance of the Soviet Navy's Kirov class battlecruisers resulted in yet another reappraisal of these elderly ships, and it was decided to reactivate them with the task of providing "a valuable supplement to the carrier force in performing presence and strike missions, while substantially increasing our ability to provide naval gunfire support for power projection and amphibious assault missions" (Caspar Weinberger, US DoD Annual Report to the Congress, FY1985).

On December 28, 1982, USS *New Jersey* joined the Pacific Fleet: starting her first operational deployment on June 9, 1983, she served first off Central America and later off Lebanon, before returning to the USA on May 5, 1984 after one of the US Navy's longest peacetime deployments. In 322 days at sea she covered a distance of some 76,000 miles (122,307km). *Iowa* was recommissioned in April 1984, to be followed by *Missouri* in July 1986 and *Wisconsin* in January 1988.

The reactivation programme involves the modernization of all electronic and communications equipment, renovation of all accommodation and domestic utilities to meet contemporary standards, converion to US Navy distillate fuel, the reshaping of the afterdeck to accommodate four LAMPS helicopters and the removal of extraneous equipment such as the aircraft crane. It was planned at one time to remove the rear turret and to install a proper aircraft hangar and a flight-deck, but this idea was dropped.

The main armament remains the massive 16in guns firing armour-piercing projectiles weighing up to 2,700lb (1,225kg) to a maximum range of 23 miles (39km) at a theoretical rate of two rounds per gun per minute. Both barrels and ammunition are long out of production, but no fewer than 34 spare barrels remain in storage, together with over 20,000 shells

and charges. The secondary armament comprises 5in guns, but four of the original ten turrets have been removed to make way for two quadruple Mk 143 Tomahawk SLCM launchers. Two quadruple Harpoon SSM launchers have been fitted either side of the after funnel, while four Phalanx CIWS mounts are also fitted, two just forward of the foremast and two forward of the after funnel.

Future: The reactivation of these ships is a triumph, achieved at a cost per ship less than that of a new Oliver Hazard Perry class frigate, and the US Navy owes a large debt of gratitude to the man who decided to preserve these fine ships instead of scrapping them, the fate of battleships in every other navy. Indeed, the Royal Navy could well regret the passing of HMS *Vanguard*, the finest of all British battleships, completed in 1946 and scrapped in 1960: had she remained in existence, she could have been given an equally cost- and combat-effective rejuvenation.

Left: USS New Jersey (BB 62) following her refurbishment and return to active duty. A far-sighted naval administrator ensured years ago that, instead of being scrapped like the battleships of other nations, these ships were preserved against some possible future requirement. His perspicacity served the US Navy well and, refitted and partially modernized at a cost less than that of one new Oliver Hazard Perry class frigate, these four ships are an important addition to the US Navy's global capability. Prominent in this view are the four Vulcan/Phalanx CIWS and the port Tomahawk SSM launchers between the funnels.

Below: Secondary gun armament of the Iowa class is the 5in/38 twin Mk 12 Mod 1; a dual-purpose, semi-automatic weapon in the Mk 32 mount. This gun has a maximum effective range of 14,217 yards (13,000m) against surface targets and 26,250ft (8,000m) against aircraft. Rate of fire is about 18rds/min per barrel with a well-trained crew.

Iowa class
New Jersey (BB 62)

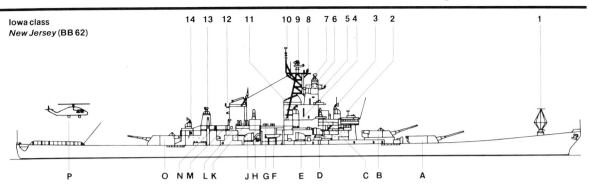

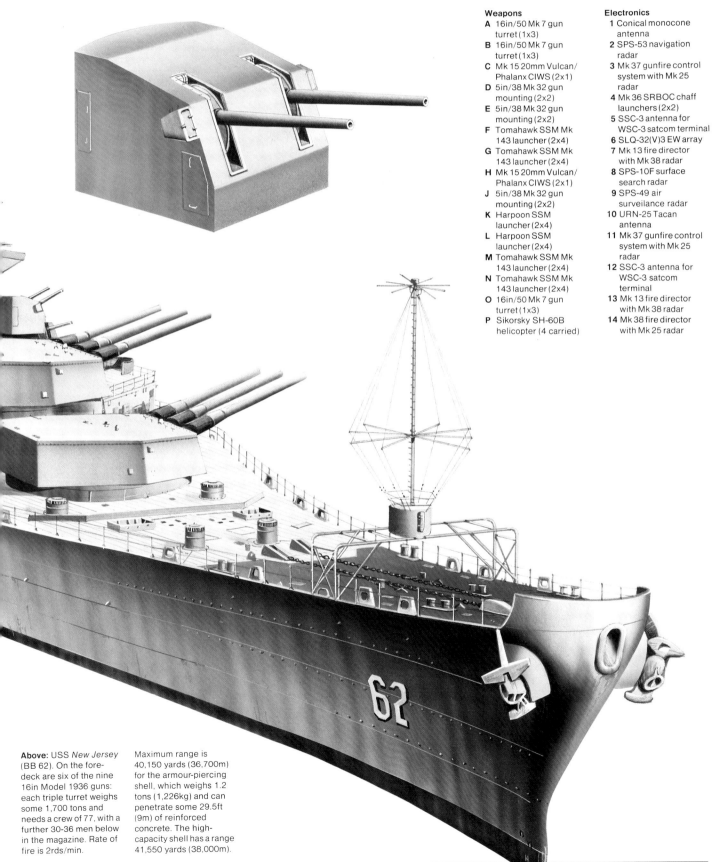

Weapons
A 16in/50 Mk 7 gun turret (1x3)
B 16in/50 Mk 7 gun turret (1x3)
C Mk 15 20mm Vulcan/Phalanx CIWS (2x1)
D 5in/38 Mk 32 gun mounting (2x2)
E 5in/38 Mk 32 gun mounting (2x2)
F Tomahawk SSM Mk 143 launcher (2x4)
G Tomahawk SSM Mk 143 launcher (2x4)
H Mk 15 20mm Vulcan/Phalanx CIWS (2x1)
J 5in/38 Mk 32 gun mounting (2x2)
K Harpoon SSM launcher (2x4)
L Harpoon SSM launcher (2x4)
M Tomahawk SSM Mk 143 launcher (2x4)
N Tomahawk SSM Mk 143 launcher (2x4)
O 16in/50 Mk 7 gun turret (1x3)
P Sikorsky SH-60B helicopter (4 carried)

Electronics
1 Conical monocone antenna
2 SPS-53 navigation radar
3 Mk 37 gunfire control system with Mk 25 radar
4 Mk 36 SRBOC chaff launchers (2x2)
5 SSC-3 antenna for WSC-3 satcom terminal
6 SLQ-32(V)3 EW array
7 Mk 13 fire director with Mk 38 radar
8 SPS-10F surface search radar
9 SPS-49 air surveilance radar
10 URN-25 Tacan antenna
11 Mk 37 gunfire control system with Mk 25 radar
12 SSC-3 antenna for WSC-3 satcom terminal
13 Mk 13 fire director with Mk 38 radar
14 Mk 38 fire director with Mk 25 radar

Above: USS *New Jersey* (BB 62). On the fore-deck are six of the nine 16in Model 1936 guns: each triple turret weighs some 1,700 tons and needs a crew of 77, with a further 30-36 men below in the magazine. Rate of fire is 2rds/min.

Maximum range is 40,150 yards (36,700m) for the armour-piercing shell, which weighs 1.2 tons (1,226kg) and can penetrate some 29.5ft (9m) of reinforced concrete. The high-capacity shell has a range 41,550 yards (38,000m).

Kiev class

Origin: USSR
Type: Aircraft carrier (CVSG)
Built: 1975-1985
Class: 4 in service
Displacement: 30,000 tons standard; 38,000 tons full load
Dimensions: Length 895.7ft (273m) oa; beam 107.3ft (32.7m); draught 32.8ft (10m)
Propulsion: 4-shaft steam (4 turbines), 200,000shp
Performance: Speed 32 knots; range 13,500nm at 18 knots, 4,000nm at 30 knots
Weapons: SSM: 4 twin SS-N-12 (16 reloads)
SAM: 2 twin SA-N-3 (72 missiles); 2 twin SA-N-4 (40 missiles)
Guns: 4 twin 76mm; 8 30mm Gatling
Torpedo tubes: 10 x 21in (533mm)
ASW: 1 twin SUW-N-1 launcher for FRAS 1; 2 12-barrel RBU-6000
Aircraft: 12 Yak-38 Forger A; 1 Yak-38 Forger B; 16 Ka-25 Hormone-A or Ka-27 Helix; Hormone-B
Sensors: Search 3D radar: Top Sail
Air/surface search radar: Top Steer
Fire control radar: Trap Door (SS-N-12); 2 Head Light-C (SA-N-3); 2 Pop Group (SA-N-4); 2 Owl Screech (76mm); 4 Bass Tilt (Gatlings)
Aircraft control radar: Top Knot
Navigation radar: Don Kay (not *Novorossiysk*; 2 Don 2 *Novorossiysk*; Palm Frond; Two Strut Pair
Sonar: 1 LF bow-mounted; 1 MF hull-mounted; 1 MF variable-depth
Complement: 1,200, plus air group

Background: Classified by the Soviet Navy as *takticheskye avianostny kreysera* (tactical aircraft-carrying cruisers), the four ships of the Kiev class incorporate the lessons learned from the Moskva class but are equipped with an angled flight-deck to enable them to operate V/STOL aircraft as well as helicopters. As with the Moskvas, however, the forward part of the ship has been devoted to gun and missile systems, giving the Kievs a unique carrier/cruiser configuration. These are very impressive ships which, in addition to their wartime tasks, have obvious applications in projecting Soviet sea-power on a global scale during peacetime deployments.

The basic concept of the Kiev class design originated in the 1960s when the main threat to the Soviet Union was assessed to be the US Navy's Polaris submarines (SSBNs). The Kievs' primary mission is, therefore, ASW and the ships carry an outfit of weapon systems almost identical to that of the Moskva class: a squadron of some 16 Ka-25 Hormone-A helicopters, an SUW-N-1 launcher for FRAS-1 missiles, two anti-submarine rocket launchers and two quintuple banks of torpedo tubes. Target data is provided by a large low-frequency bow sonar and a stern-mounted variable-depth sonar, supplemented, of course, by data from the ships' ASW helicopters

and other ships in the task unit.

The air defence missile systems are more extensive than in the Moskvas and are split between the forecastle and the after end of the island superstructure to give a good all-round coverage. A particularly heavy CIWS armament is fitted, consisting of eight of the Soviet Navy's standard 30mm Gatlings, and an impressive anti-ship capability is provided by the four pairs of SS-N-13 launchers located on the forecastle, with a reload magazine between them.

The flight-deck is angled at 4.5° and is marked with seven helicopter spots and a large circle aft for Yakolev Yak-38 Forger landings. The angled portion of the flight deck and the after deck aircraft park are covered with heat-resistant tiles to absorb the heat from the Forger's two vertical lift engines. A long hangar runs beneath the flight-deck; the forward section is probably some 49ft (15m) wide increasing to about 69ft (21m) aft and up to 35 aircraft can be accommodated. There are two aircraft lifts; the larger is amidships, between the angled deck and the island superstructure, while the other is immediately aft of the island. There are several smaller lifts for deck tractors, personnel and munitions.

All four ships of this class (*Kiev*, *Minsk*, *Novorossiysk* and *Baku*) are now in service, giving the Soviet Navy an unprecedented blue ocean capability. In April 1985, for example, a carrier battle group consisting of *Novorossiysk*, three Kara I and one Kresta II cruisers, and one Krivak I and one Krivak II frigates deployed from Vladivostok into the Pacific Ocean. Leaving the frigates, the larger ships moved initially at a speed of 14-18 knots, but the return to the Tsushima Straits was carried out at a speed of 20 knots, a very high cruising speed. This was a very successful and impressive operation, although the carrier group far outstripped its replenishment tankers, which would lead to severe logistic problems in wartime.
Future: The first of the class, *Kiev*, has recently finished her first major refit; this lasted two years, but full details of the changes have not yet been published. She has been seen, however, operating her Forger-A aircraft in rolling take-offs, a capability previously demonstrated only by *Novorossiysk*; these takeoffs are being performed on the standard deck and not, as at one time predicted, from a ski-jump.

It would appear that the Soviet Navy will keep these four ships in service for many years, updating them as necessary in their periodic refits. Construction appears to have ended with the fourth ship, *Baku*, and all efforts are now being concentrated on the new Kremlin class nuclear powered carriers, the first of which was laid down in 1983 and launched in December 1985 at the Nikolayev yard on the Black Sea; she is due to start sea trials in 1988.

Above: Novorossiysk, third of the four-ship Kiev class, the Soviet Navy's biggest air-capable ships, showing a formidable array of weapons on the foredeck. This class will be succeeded by the even larger aircraft carriers now being built, the so-called Kremlin class.

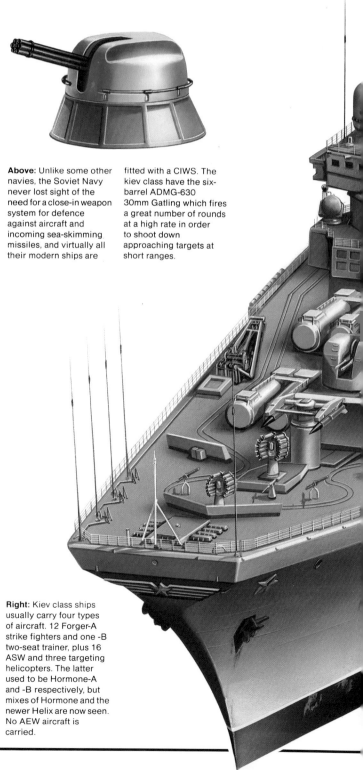

Above: Unlike some other navies, the Soviet Navy never lost sight of the need for a close-in weapon system for defence against aircraft and incoming sea-skimming missiles, and virtually all their modern ships are fitted with a CIWS. The kiev class have the six-barrel ADMG-630 30mm Gatling which fires a great number of rounds at a high rate in order to shoot down approaching targets at short ranges.

Right: Kiev class ships usually carry four types of aircraft. 12 Forger-A strike fighters and one -B two-seat trainer, plus 16 ASW and three targeting helicopters. The latter used to be Hormone-A and -B respectively, but mixes of Hormone and the newer Helix are now seen. No AEW aircraft is carried.

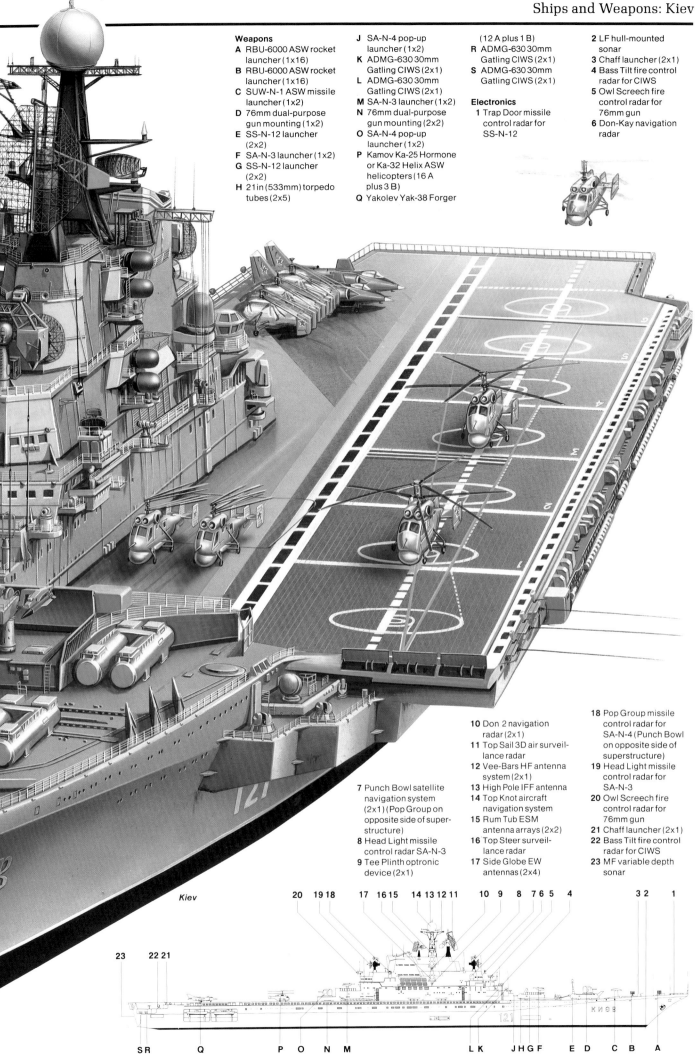

Weapons

A RBU-6000 ASW rocket launcher (1x16)
B RBU-6000 ASW rocket launcher (1x16)
C SUW-N-1 ASW missile launcher (1x2)
D 76mm dual-purpose gun mounting (1x2)
E SS-N-12 launcher (2x2)
F SA-N-3 launcher (1x2)
G SS-N-12 launcher (2x2)
H 21in (533mm) torpedo tubes (2x5)

J SA-N-4 pop-up launcher (1x2)
K ADMG-630 30mm Gatling CIWS (2x1)
L ADMG-630 30mm Gatling CIWS (2x1)
M SA-N-3 launcher (1x2)
N 76mm dual-purpose gun mounting (2x2)
O SA-N-4 pop-up launcher (1x2)
P Kamov Ka-25 Hormone or Ka-32 Helix ASW helicopters (16 A plus 3 B)
Q Yakovlev Yak-38 Forger

(12 A plus 1 B)
R ADMG-630 30mm Gatling CIWS (2x1)
S ADMG-630 30mm Gatling CIWS (2x1)

Electronics

1 Trap Door missile control radar for SS-N-12

2 LF hull-mounted sonar
3 Chaff launcher (2x1)
4 Bass Tilt fire control radar for CIWS
5 Owl Screech fire control radar for 76mm gun
6 Don-Kay navigation radar

7 Punch Bowl satellite navigation system (2x1) (Pop Group on opposite side of super-structure)
8 Head Light missile control radar SA-N-3
9 Tee Plinth optronic device (2x1)

10 Don 2 navigation radar (2x1)
11 Top Sail 3D air surveillance radar
12 Vee-Bars HF antenna system (2x1)
13 High Pole IFF antenna
14 Top Knot aircraft navigation system
15 Rum Tub ESM antenna arrays (2x2)
16 Top Steer surveillance radar
17 Side Globe EW antennas (2x4)

18 Pop Group missile control radar for SA-N-4 (Punch Bowl on opposite side of superstructure)
19 Head Light missile control radar for SA-N-3
20 Owl Screech fire control radar for 76mm gun
21 Chaff launcher (2x1)
22 Bass Tilt fire control radar for CIWS
23 MF variable depth sonar

Kiev

Kilo class

Origin: USSR
Type: Patrol submarine (SS)
Built: 1976-
Class: 5 in service; 2 building
Displacement: 2,500 tons surfaced; 3,200 tons submerged
Dimensions: Length 229.6ft (70m) oa; beam 29.5ft (9m); draught 23ft (7m)
Propulsion: 1-shaft diesel-electric (2 diesel engines; 1 electric motor)
Performance: Speed 12 knots surfaced, 16 knots submerged
Weapons: Torpedo tubes: 6 x 21in (533mm) for torpedoes and mines
Sensors: Sonar: 1 LF bow-mounted Radar: 1 fin-mounted
Complement: 55-60

Background: The Soviet Navy has long been a firm believer in the value of submarines and it is frequently forgotten in the West that the USSR entered World War II with the largest undersea fleet of any navy. After the war captured German designs, designers and actual U-boats were used to rebuild and modernize this fleet; the initial plan being to build the astonishing total of 1,200 sub-marines between 1950 and 1965 at a starting rate of 78 per year. This proved to be much too ambitious and far beyond the technical and industrial resources of even the USSR; as a result, the numbers built were far smaller, but still impressive enough to give the West a dreadful shock in the late 1950s and early 1960s as the scope of the Soviet Union's building programme gradually became apparent. The long-range boats were of the Zulu class (28 built), followed later by the Foxtrot class (62), while the medium-range fleet comprised 20 Romeos and no fewer than 240 Whiskeys.

Despite the advent of the nuclear vessels the Soviet Navy, unlike its US counterpart, has persisted in the construction of long—and medium—range con-ventional boats. The Tango class (3,700 tons submerged displace-ment) appeared in 1972 and was built at a rate of two per year until the eighteenth boat joined the fleet in 1982. One of the uses to which the Soviet Navy puts its conventional submarines was revealed when a Whiskey class submarine ran aground and was exposed to the world's Press off the Swedish Karlskrona naval base in October 1981.

Construction of the Kilo class started in 1979 at an initial rate of one per year, but this has now doubled. Unlike all previous Soviet conventionally powered boats, those of the Kilo class have teardrop hulls for higher under-water speeds, much quieter running and greater manoeuvrability; the hull itself is coated with Cluster Guard anechoic tiles.

The only armament so far identified is six conventional torpedo tubes, for which a mix of free-running, wire-guided and homing torpedoes will be carried. It seems possible, however, that missiles such as SS-N-15 or SS-N-16 may also be carried, as in the Tango class. As is the case with virtually all Soviet submarines, mines can be carried and laid from the torpedo tubes.

All Kilos built to date have been constructed at the Amur Yard at Komsomolsk in the Far East, and are serving with the Soviet Pacific fleet.

Future: The Kilo has replaced the Tango in production and it would appear that, like its predecessor, it will remain in production at a rate of two per year until replaced by a new design in the 1990s. It is notable that neither the Tango nor the Kilo class has been exported, despite the fact that there are good markets for their type and size of conventional submarine.

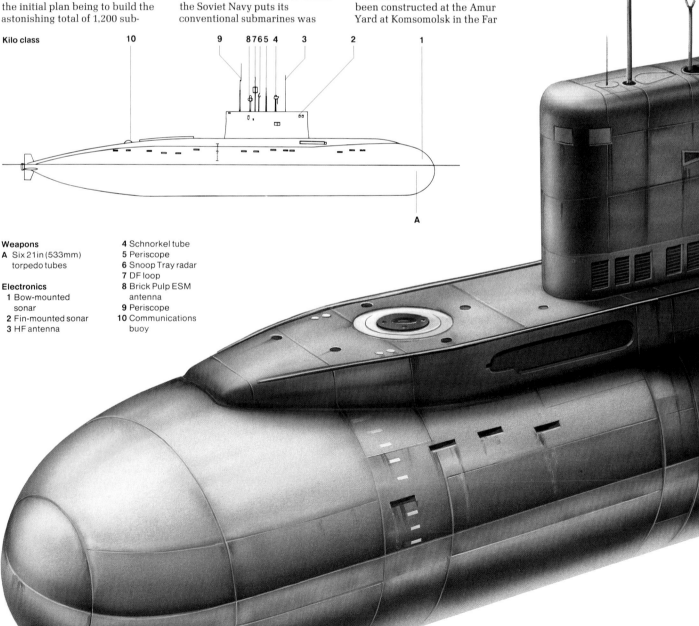

Kilo class

Weapons
A Six 21in (533mm) torpedo tubes

Electronics
1 Bow-mounted sonar
2 Fin-mounted sonar
3 HF antenna
4 Schnorkel tube
5 Periscope
6 Snoop Tray radar
7 DF loop
8 Brick Pulp ESM antenna
9 Periscope
10 Communications buoy

Above: Kilo class diesel-electric submarine in the Pacific showing her totally new hull shape, more akin to Western types than to any previous Soviet conventional submarine; bow wave and wake patterns resemble those associated with US submarines, suggesting a similar bow shape. The Kilo is also the first conventionally powered Soviet combat submarine to have a single shaft and propeller.

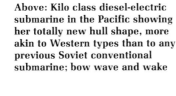

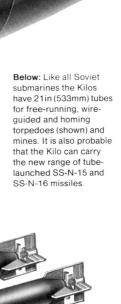

Below: Like all Soviet submarines the Kilos have 21in (533mm) tubes for free-running, wire-guided and homing torpedoes (shown) and mines. It is also probable that the Kilo can carry the new range of tube-launched SS-N-15 and SS-N-16 missiles.

Above: The advances in Soviet submarine hull technology are shown clearly in this drawing of a Kilo class submarine. The traditional long, thin hull form was continued in the Soviet Navy right up to the Tango class (the Kilos' immediate predecessor), but now appears to have been abandoned. The fully rounded bow and much greater beam-to-length ratio, single propeller and much cleaner hull coated with anechoic tiles result in a much more effective submarine. Although all these developments are almost certainly the result of the very extensive Soviet submarine research programme, the general characteristics of the Kilo class are very similar to those of the Dutch Walrus, British Upholder and Japanese Yuushio classes, which suggests that the various national research programmes are coming to the same conclusions. What is not known is whether the Soviets are making any progress in the most important area of all—the development of life-support and propulsion systems which would enable non-nuclear submarines to operate below the surface for much more protracted periods and thus avoid the risks involved in forays to the surface.

Kirov class

Origin: USSR
Type: Nuclear-powered missile cruisers (CBN)
Built: 1977-
Class: 2 in service; 1 building
Displacement: 24,000 tons standard; 28,000 tons full load
Dimensions: Length 814ft (248m) oa; beam 92ft (28m); draught 29ft (8.8m)
Propulsion: 2-shaft CONAS (2 nuclear reactors, 2 steam turbines), 150,000shp
Performance: Speed 33 knots; range 3,000nm at 33 knots (CONAS), 150,000nm at 25 knots (nuclear only)
Weapons: Missile launchers: 20 SS-N-19 (20 missiles); 12 SA-N-6 (96); 2 twin SA-N-4 (40); (Frunze only) 16 SA-N-8 (128)
Guns: 2 single 100mm (Kirov); 1 twin 130mm (Frunze); 8 30mm CIWS
ASW weapons: 1 twin SS-N-14 (Kirov only); 1 RBU-6000; 2 RBU-1000
Torpedo tubes: 2 x 5 21in (533mm)
Sensors: Radar: Top Pair 3D air surveillance; Palm Frond navigation. Sonar: LF bow-mounted; LF variable depth.
Aircraft: 3 Ka-25 Hormone or Ka-27 Helix
Complement: 900

Background: Since the mid-1960s Soviet naval construction has shown a consistent trend toward bigger ships with greater firepower, endurance and sustainability for distant operations. The latest example is the Kirov class, the largest surface combatants other than aircraft carriers built since the end of World War II. Their size, heavy armament and general sophistication have impressed Western navies, and the US Navy has felt compelled to refurbish and recommission four Iowa class battleships. The Kirov class ships appear to have two major roles, acting either as lynch-pins of aircraft carrier escorts in high-threat areas or as flagships for an independent task force.

Classified by the Soviet Navy as *Atomny raketny kreyser*, or nuclear-powered missile cruisers, the Kirov class is a descendent of the battle-cruiser, a controversial concept for large, heavily armed and fast but very lightly armoured warships promoted in the early years of this century. The two ships now at sea, *Kirov* and *Frunze*, show several important differences in armament: both are exceptionally well-armed, but the *Frunze* appears to emphasize the air defence role, whereas *Kirov* is better equipped for anti-submarine warfare, though the differences may simply be intended to test the operational capabilities of various armament fits.

In place of the big guns of earlier capital ships the Kirovs have a powerful battery of 20 long-range SS-N-19 vertical launchers (probably armoured) located in the forecastle. Over-the-horizon (OTH) targeting data for these 300nm (555km) range missiles is supplied by a command post ashore via a communications satellite; direct by surveillance satellites using electronic intelligence, active radar, infra-red detection techniques; or by the vessels' own on-board helicopters.

The Kirovs also have sophisticated air defence systems. The SA-N-6 is a new high-performance model whose track-via-missile (TVM) guidance system enables the ship to control several rounds simultaneously and engage multiple targets. The missile itself has a range in excess of 46.5nm (80km) and a speed of Mach 5-6. Each of the 12 launchers is supplied by a rotating eight-round magazine.

Kirov's short-range air defence missile system is the SA-N-4, a pop-up launcher housed in a magazine bin containing 20 missiles, but *Frunze* also has the SA-N-6. All *Kirov's* SAM launchers are on the forecastle, leaving the after quadrant somewhat naked; this has been rectified in the *Frunze* by siting two four-tube SA-N-8 launchers on the quarter-deck, displacing the 30mm Gatling CIWS which have been moved to the after superstructure.

Kirov mounts two dual-purpose 100mm guns aft. In *Frunze* these have been replaced by one twin 130mm turret, identical to those fitted to the Sovremennyy and Slava classes. Close-range anti-missile defence in both ships comprises four pairs of 30mm Gatling guns, sited port and starboard fore and aft to give all-round coverage.

These ships have to play a major part in their own anti-submarine defence, although there would, of course, be an escort of destroyers or frigates. *Kirov* has a reloadable launcher for SS-N-14 ASW missiles on the forecastle, and both ships have rocket launchers, torpedo tubes and three Kamov Ka-25 Hormone-A/B (or Ka-32 Helix) helicopters for ASW and missile guidance.

There is a large low-frequency sonar in the bow and an LF variable-depth sonar in the stern. The extensive electronics suite includes two major 3D air surveillance radars, Top Pair and Top Steer, plus individual gun and missile fire control radars. *Kirov* is fitted with the standard 1970s ECM/ESM outfit, with eight Side Globe broad-band jammers and four Rum Tub ESM antennas around the top of the tower mast, but neither system is fitted in *Frunze*, each being replaced by a different type of bell-shaped radome.

The communications fit is also changed in the newer ship, the main visible change being the replacement of *Kirov's* Vee-Tube C by large bell-covered satellite antennas. This appears to represent a logical change in emphasis from long distance HF communications, notoriously liable to interception and jamming, to satellite links which are both more secure and able to handle much greater traffic volumes.
Future: It is known that at least one more Kirov class ship is under construction, and this will certainly include yet further refinement of the weapon and sensor fits. No further information is available on the Soviet Navy's plans, though given its discovery of the value of such large ships in peacetime power projection (to say nothing of their value in war), it can safely be assumed that further and perhaps even larger examples of big warships will be built.

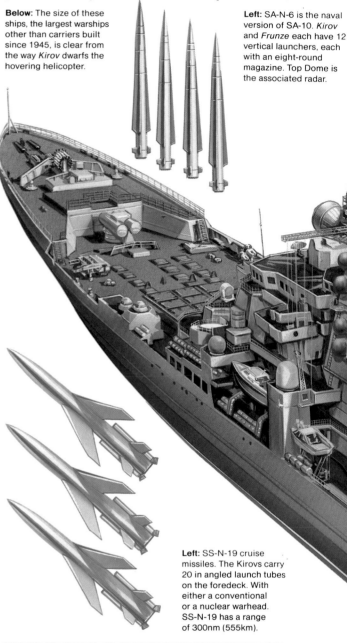

Below: The size of these ships, the largest warships other than carriers built since 1945, is clear from the way *Kirov* dwarfs the hovering helicopter.

Left: SA-N-6 is the naval version of SA-10. *Kirov* and *Frunze* each have 12 vertical launchers, each with an eight-round magazine. Top Dome is the associated radar.

Left: SS-N-19 cruise missiles. The Kirovs carry 20 in angled launch tubes on the foredeck. With either a conventional or a nuclear warhead. SS-N-19 has a range of 300nm (555km).

Kirov class
Frunze

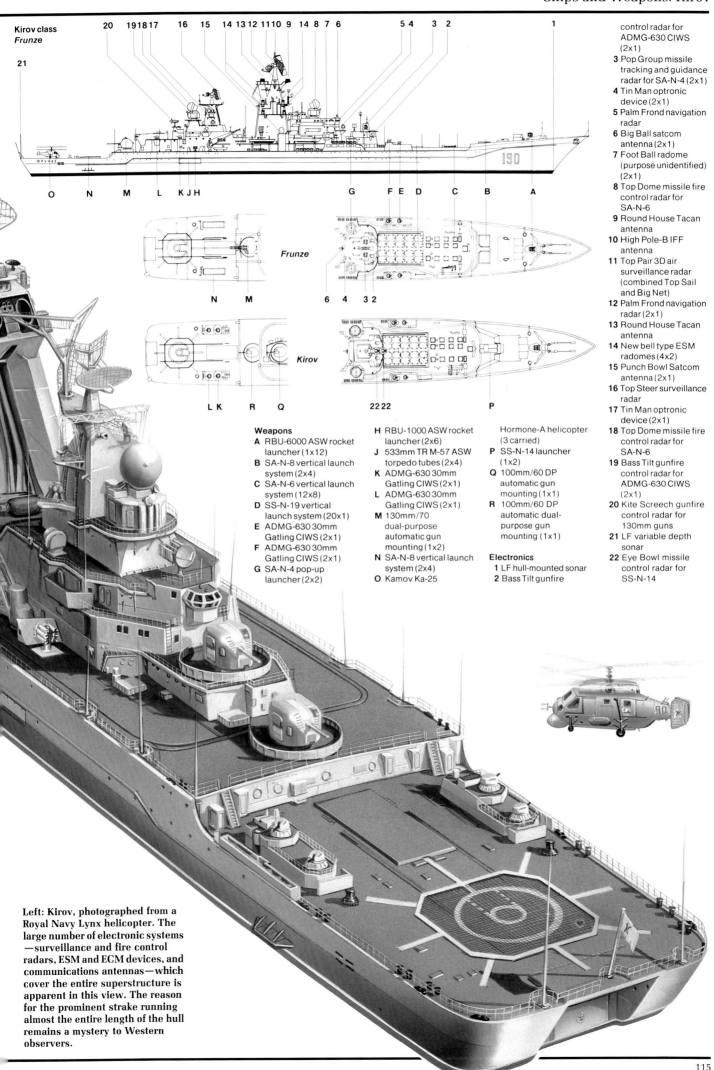

Frunze

Kirov

control radar for
ADMG-630 CIWS
(2x1)
3 Pop Group missile
tracking and guidance
radar for SA-N-4 (2x1)
4 Tin Man optronic
device (2x1)
5 Palm Frond navigation
radar
6 Big Ball satcom
antenna (2x1)
7 Foot Ball radome
(purpose unidentified)
(2x1)
8 Top Dome missile fire
control radar for
SA-N-6
9 Round House Tacan
antenna
10 High Pole-B IFF
antenna
11 Top Pair 3D air
surveillance radar
(combined Top Sail
and Big Net)
12 Palm Frond navigation
radar (2x1)
13 Round House Tacan
antenna
14 New bell type ESM
radomes (4x2)
15 Punch Bowl Satcom
antenna (2x1)
16 Top Steer surveillance
radar
17 Tin Man optronic
device (2x1)
18 Top Dome missile fire
control radar for
SA-N-6
19 Bass Tilt gunfire
control radar for
ADMG-630 CIWS
(2x1)
20 Kite Screech gunfire
control radar for
130mm guns
21 LF variable depth
sonar
22 Eye Bowl missile
control radar for
SS-N-14

Weapons
A RBU-6000 ASW rocket
launcher (1x12)
B SA-N-8 vertical launch
system (2x4)
C SA-N-6 vertical launch
system (12x8)
D SS-N-19 vertical
launch system (20x1)
E ADMG-630 30mm
Gatling CIWS (2x1)
F ADMG-630 30mm
Gatling CIWS (2x1)
G SA-N-4 pop-up
launcher (2x2)

H RBU-1000 ASW rocket
launcher (2x6)
J 533mm TR M-57 ASW
torpedo tubes (2x4)
K ADMG-630 30mm
Gatling CIWS (2x1)
L ADMG-630 30mm
Gatling CIWS (2x1)
M 130mm/70
dual-purpose
automatic gun
mounting (1x2)
N SA-N-8 vertical launch
system (2x4)
O Kamov Ka-25

Hormone-A helicopter
(3 carried)
P SS-N-14 launcher
(1x2)
Q 100mm/60 DP
automatic gun
mounting (1x1)
R 100mm/60 DP
automatic dual-
purpose gun
mounting (1x1)

Electronics
1 LF hull-mounted sonar
2 Bass Tilt gunfire

**Left: Kirov, photographed from a
Royal Navy Lynx helicopter. The
large number of electronic systems
—surveillance and fire control
radars, ESM and ECM devices, and
communications antennas—which
cover the entire superstructure is
apparent in this view. The reason
for the prominent strake running
almost the entire length of the hull
remains a mystery to Western
observers.**

Kitty Hawk (CV 63) class

Origin: USA
Type: Multi-purpose aircraft carriers (CV)
Built: 1956-1968
Class: 4 in service
Displacement: 60,100-61,000 tons standard; 79,724-81,773 tons full load
Dimensions: Length 1,046-1,052ft (318.8-320.7m) oa; beam 130ft (39.6m); draught 37ft (11.3m)
Propulsion: 4-shaft (4 Westinghouse geared turbines), 280,000shp
Performance: 30 knots
Weapons: SAM: 3 Mk 29 launchers for NATO Sea Sparrow Guns: 3 20mm Phalanx Mk 15 CIWS.
Aircraft: 24 F-4 Phantom or F-14 Tomcat; 24 A-7 Corsair II or F/A-18

Hornet; 10 A-6 Intruder; 10 S-3 Viking; 6 SH-3 Sea King; 4 EA-6B Prowler; 4 KA-6 Intruder; 4 E-2 Hawkeye; 1 C-2A Greyhound
Sensors: Air search radar: (CV 63, 66) SPS-49(V) and SPS-48 (3D); (CV 64) SPS-37A, SPS-48C (3D); (CV 67) SPS-65(V), SPS-48C (3D).
Surface search radar: SPS-10 series
Fire control: Mk 91 MFCS for Sea Sparrow
Complement: 2,000, plus 2,150 air wing

Background: There are major differences between the first pair of aircraft carriers completed, *Kitty Hawk* (CV 63) and *Constel-*

lation (CV 64), and the second two, *America* (CV 66) and *John F Kennedy* (CV 67). These four ships are, however, generally grouped together because of their common propulsion systems and flight-deck layout.

Kitty Hawk and *Constellation* were ordered as improved versions of the Forrestal class, incorporating a number of important modifications. The flight-deck was increased slightly in area, and the layout of the lifts revised to enhance aircraft-handling arrangements. On the Forrestals the port side lift is located at the forward end of the angled deck, making it unusable during landing operations,

so the lift was repositioned at the after end of the overhang on the Kitty Hawks, where it no longer interferes with flying operations. In addition, the centre lift on the starboard side has been repositioned to be ahead of the island structure, enabling two lifts to be used to serve the forward catapults.

A further improved feature of the lifts themselves is that an angled section at the forward end enables longer aircraft to be accommodated. This arrangement is so successful that it has been copied in all subsequent US carriers.

The third ship of the class, *America* (CV 66), was laid down

Below: USS *Constellation* (CV 64), second of this class to be completed. The huge extent of the flight deck makes an interesting comparison with that of the French *Clemenceau*. The three lifts are sited well clear of flying operations: the port side lift is at the after end of the overhang, while the two starboard lifts, serving the forward catapults, are sited ahead of the island. The relatively small landing area leaves a lot of deck space clear for launching and aircraft marshalling.

Above: USS America (CV 66) under way in the Indian Ocean, with F-14 Tomcats, A-6 Intruders, S-3 Vikings, E-2 Hawkeyes and other aircraft on the flight deck—the air wing is some 90 aircraft strong. One of three Mk 29 launchers for

the Mk 57 NATO Sea Sparrow surface-to-air missile system can be seen on the forward starboard sponson and the unique white radome of a Mk 15 Vucan Phalanx CIWS is just visible on the forward port sponson.

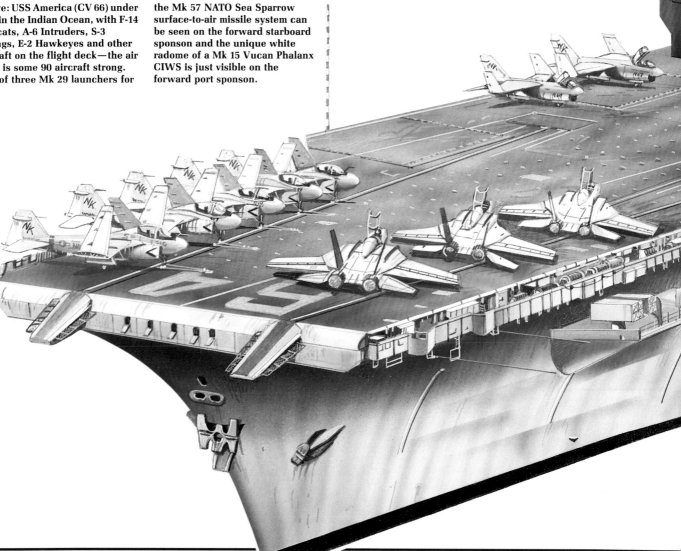

four years after *Constellation* and incorporates a number of further modifications. She has a narrower smokestack and is fitted with a bow anchor, in anticipation of the fitting of an SQS-23 sonar. It was decided in 1963 that the fourth carrier due to be laid down in FY1984 should be nuclear powered, but Congress flatly refused to fund it and the ship was finally built to a modified Kitty Hawk design as a conventionally-powered carrier.

The major visible differences are that the *John F Kennedy* has a canted stack — designed to keep the flight-deck clear of corrosive exhaust gases — and a flight deck of differently shaped forward end. The Terrier missile system, which consumed valuable space on the flight-deck and, in any case, duplicated similar area defence systems aboard the carrier escorts, was dropped in favour of the Mk 57 NATO Sea Sparrow Missile System and has subsequently been deleted from the previous three ships.

These four ships are very powerful fighting units, second only to the US Navy's nuclear powered aircraft carriers in combat capability. However, all recent US Congresses have set their faces against anything but nuclear power for ships of this size, rejecting proposals for a CVV in 1979 and for a modified *John F Kennedy* in 1980, finally forcing the President to order a fourth Nimitz class CVN in the FY80 programme. It would, therefore, seem that these four ships could be the last conventionally powered aircraft carriers to be build for the USA Navy.

Future: All four of these carriers are to be modernized under the US Navy's Service Life Extension Programme (SLEP). *Kitty Hawk* will be the first (July 21, 1987 to November 29, 1989) at a cost of $717 million, followed by *Constellation* (October 1989 to February 1992), *America* (April 1994 to August 1996) and finally *Kennedy* (July 1996 to November 1998). These 28-month refits will extend each ship's life by some 10-15 years. The work programme includes fitting new and more powerful catapults, updating the aircraft facilities, modernizing all electronics and extensive refurbishment of the hull, propulsion systems and electrics. The *Kitty Hawk's* condition is so good that a less extensive and much cheaper SLEP than anticipated will be required.

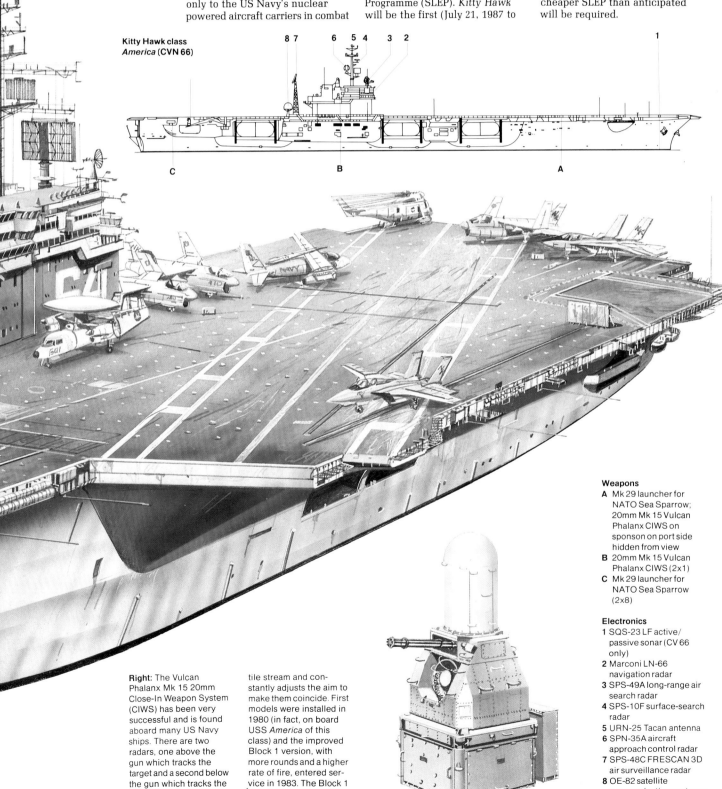

Kitty Hawk class
America (CVN 66)

Right: The Vulcan Phalanx Mk 15 20mm Close-In Weapon System (CIWS) has been very successful and is found aboard many US Navy ships. There are two radars, one above the gun which tracks the target and a second below the gun which tracks the projectiles: an on-board computer correlates the target track and projec-tile stream and constantly adjusts the aim to make them coincide. First models were installed in 1980 (in fact, on board USS *America* of this class) and the improved Block 1 version, with more rounds and a higher rate of fire, entered ser-vice in 1983. The Block 1 also introduced the Mk 149 depleted uranium round.

Weapons
A Mk 29 launcher for NATO Sea Sparrow; 20mm Mk 15 Vulcan Phalanx CIWS on sponson on port side hidden from view
B 20mm Mk 15 Vulcan Phalanx CIWS (2x1)
C Mk 29 launcher for NATO Sea Sparrow (2x8)

Electronics
1 SQS-23 LF active/ passive sonar (CV 66 only)
2 Marconi LN-66 navigation radar
3 SPS-49A long-range air search radar
4 SPS-10F surface-search radar
5 URN-25 Tacan antenna
6 SPN-35A aircraft approach control radar
7 SPS-48C FRESCAN 3D air surveillance radar
8 OE-82 satellite communications antenna
9 Mk 91 Mod 1 director for NATO Sea Sparrow

Kortenaer class

Origin: Netherlands
Type: Frigate (FF)
Built: 1975-1983
Class: Netherlands Navy 12 in service; Greek Navy 2 in service; West German Navy 6 in service
Displacement: 3,050 tons standard; 3,630 tons full load
Dimensions: Length 428ft (130.5m) oa; beam 47.9ft (14.6m); draught 20.3ft (6.2m)
Propulsion: 2-shaft COGOG (2 Rolls-Royce Olympus TM3B gas turbines), 50,000/8,000shp
Performance: Speed 30 knots; endurance 4,700nm at 30 knots
Weapons: Missiles: 1 NATO Sea Sparrow SAM laucher; 8 Harpoon SSM
Guns: 1 x 76mm/62 OTO Melara Compact; 1 x 40mm
ASW: Two twin Mk 32 torpedo tubes for Mk 46 torpedoes.
Aircraft: 2 Lynx helicopters
Sensors: Radar: LW-08 air search; DA-05 surface search; STIR fire control; ZW-06 navigation
Sonar: SQS-505 bow-mounted
Complement: 176

Background: The Royal Netherlands Navy undertook a fundamental reappraisal of its role and organization between 1975 and 1983 with the aim of creating an integrated, efficient and balanced force. At the heart of the resulting plan is the creation of three task groups, each with a flagship, six ASW frigates and a logistic support vessel two of which will be allocated to the NATO commands CINCEASTLANT and the third to CINCHAN. The original plan was that the 18 ASW frigates would comprise the six Van Speijik (modified Leander) class and 12 new Kortenaer class vessels. Two of the flagships would be existing Tromp class destroyers and the third a modified Kortenaer, bringing the planned total Dutch order for these ships to thirteen.

This plan was disrupted by the placing of an order for one Kortenaer class frigate by the Greek Navy. The Greeks signed the contract on September 15, 1980 and, not surprisingly, wanted their ship quickly. The Dutch, showing commendable flexibility, allocated the sixth unit to this order, delivering the ship to the Greek Navy on November 16, 1981. An order for a second ship was placed on June 7, 1981; the seventh Dutch unit was allocated and delivered in October 1982. The Greek ships — the Elli class — are substantially the same as the Dutch ships, except that a second 76mm gun is situated on the hangar roof and the hangar is 6.6ft (2m) longer to accommodate Agusta Bell AB.212 helicopters. An order for a further three to be built in Greece has been discussed, but not yet placed.

The West German Navy is in the process of replacing its ex-US Fletcher class destroyers and the first three of its six Köln class frigates by building a modified version of the Kortenaer for service in the Baltic. Six were ordered in 1976 and deliveries took place between 1982 and 1984. These ships—the Bremen or Type 122 class—have been built in West German yards and include many modifications, one of the most important being that the propulsion system comprises two General Electric LM 2500 51,600hp gas turbines and two MTU 20V 956 TB92 10,400hp diesels in a CODAG arrangement. The sensor fit is also different due to the West German Navy's need to operate in the restricted conditions of the Baltic, whereas the Dutch designed the Kortenaer for blue-water operations in the North Atlantic.

Having allowed two of their order to the Greek Navy, the Dutch ordered a further two ships for themselves, designated the Jacob van Heemskerck class and modified as flagships with an air defence armament. The primary weapon system is the Standard SM1 (MR) SAM on a Mk 13 launcher replacing the 76mm gun on the forecastle. Surprisingly, there are no helicopter facilities.

A potential order from the Portuguese Navy for three Kortenaer frigates was discussed at considerable length, but was finally and formally cancelled on August 29, 1984.

With 20 built and more in prospect the Kortenaer is clearly a most important type in the NATO inventory, and the design represents a fine balance between heavy armament and economy in manpower. Armament includes one 76mm gun forward, a Sea Sparrow launcher, two Harpoon launchers amidships and four torpedo tubes, while a point defence system is mounted on the hangar roof, the original 40mm gun (two on *Pieter Florisz*) being scheduled for replacement by the Signaal Goalkeeper. The hangar can accommodate two Lynx helicopters, but only one is carried in peacetime. And all this is achieved with a complement of only 176.

Future: Production of these excellent frigates appears to have come to an end with the NATO standard frigate remaining a most elusive goal.

Right: Goalkeeper stand-alone CIWS uses the General Electric GAU-8/A 30mm 7-barrelled Gatling in combination with an HSA track-while-scan radar fire control system. Rate of fire is 4,200 rds/min, and 1,190 rounds are carried on the mount in a linkless system. Operation is fully automatic throughout.

Below: Van Kinsbergen (F 908), third ship of the class, at sea off the Danish coast in 1982. These well designed ships with their balanced armament have proved to be a great success and are also used by the Greek and West German navies (Elli class and Type 122).

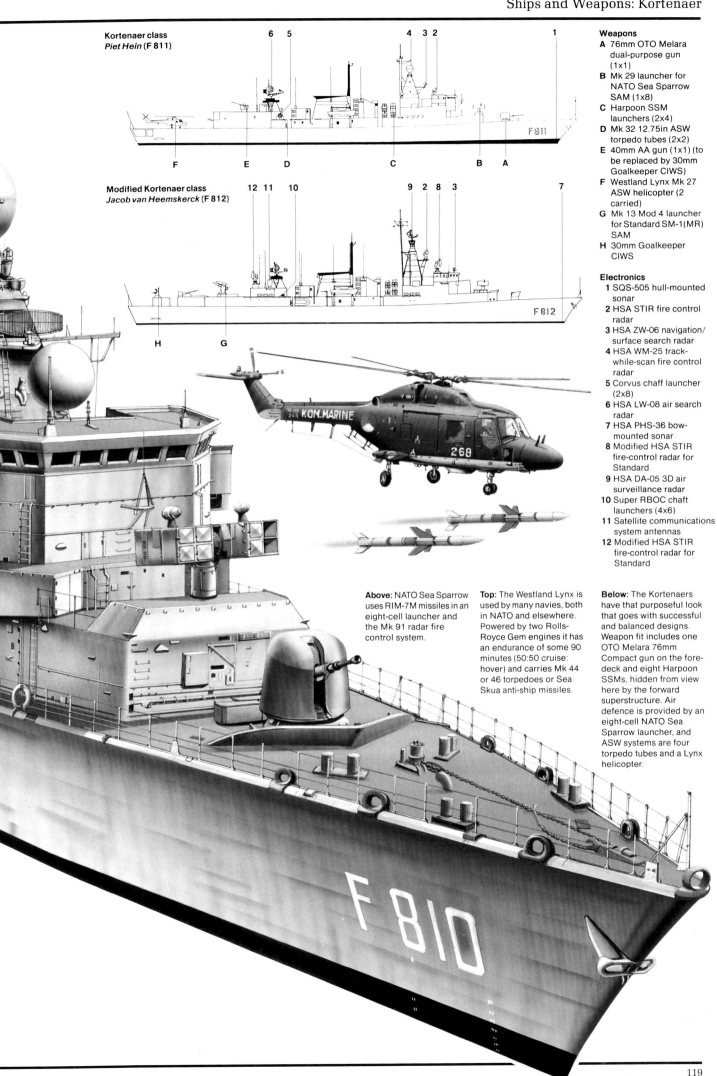

Kortenaer class
Piet Hein (F 811)

6 5   4 3 2   1

F 811

F   E   D   C   B   A

Modified Kortenaer class
Jacob van Heemskerck (F 812)

12 11   10   9 2 8 3   7

F 812

H   G

Weapons

A 76mm OTO Melara dual-purpose gun (1x1)
B Mk 29 launcher for NATO Sea Sparrow SAM (1x8)
C Harpoon SSM launchers (2x4)
D Mk 32 12.75in ASW torpedo tubes (2x2)
E 40mm AA gun (1x1) (to be replaced by 30mm Goalkeeper CIWS)
F Westland Lynx Mk 27 ASW helicopter (2 carried)
G Mk 13 Mod 4 launcher for Standard SM-1(MR) SAM
H 30mm Goalkeeper CIWS

Electronics

1 SQS-505 hull-mounted sonar
2 HSA STIR fire control radar
3 HSA ZW-06 navigation/ surface search radar
4 HSA WM-25 track-while-scan fire control radar
5 Corvus chaff launcher (2x8)
6 HSA LW-08 air search radar
7 HSA PHS-36 bow-mounted sonar
8 Modified HSA STIR fire-control radar for Standard
9 HSA DA-05 3D air surveillance radar
10 Super RBOC chaff launchers (4x6)
11 Satellite communications system antennas
12 Modified HSA STIR fire-control radar for Standard

KON.MARINE 268

Above: NATO Sea Sparrow uses RIM-7M missiles in an eight-cell launcher and the Mk 91 radar fire control system.

Top: The Westland Lynx is used by many navies, both in NATO and elsewhere. Powered by two Rolls-Royce Gem engines it has an endurance of some 90 minutes (50:50 cruise: hover) and carries Mk 44 or 46 torpedoes or Sea Skua anti-ship missiles.

Below: The Kortenaers have that purposeful look that goes with successful and balanced designs. Weapon fit includes one OTO Melara 76mm Compact gun on the foredeck and eight Harpoon SSMs, hidden from view here by the forward superstructure. Air defence is provided by an eight-cell NATO Sea Sparrow launcher, and ASW systems are four torpedo tubes and a Lynx helicopter.

F 810

Krivak class

Origin: USSR
Type: Frigate (FFG)
Built: Krivak I 1968-1983; Krivak II 1973-1982; Krivak III 1981-
Class: (I) 22 in service; (II) 11 in service; (III) 1 in service, 2 building
Displacement: 3,100 tons standard; 3,800 tons full load
Dimensions: Length 405.2ft (123.5m) oa; beam 45.9ft (14m); draught 16.4ft (5m)
Propulsion: 2-shaft COGAG (2 cruise gas turbines/2 boost gas turbines), 14,000/55,000shp
Performance: Speed 32 knots; range 4,500nm at 16 knots, 700nm at 30 knots
Complement: 220
Weapons: Missiles: 1 quad SS-N-14 SSM launcher (I and II); 4 SA-N-4 twin SAM launchers (I and II); 1 twin SA-N-4 (III)
Guns: 2 twin 3in aft (I); 2 single 4in aft (II); 1 4in forward (III); 2 30mm Gating (III)
Torpedo tubes: 2 x 4 21in (533mm) TR M-57 (I,II and III)
ASW weapons: 2 12-barrel RBU-6000 (I, II and III)
Mines: 20 (I); 50 (II)
Aircraft: 1 Kamor Ka-25 Hormone or Ka-27 Helix helicopter (III)
Sensors: Radar: Head Net C (search); 2 Eye Bowl SS-N-14 control (I and II); Pop Group SA-N-4 control (I and II); 1 Pop Group (III); 1 Owl Screech gun control (I); 1 Kite Screech gun control (II and III); Don Kay, Palm Frond A/B or Don 2 navigation
Sonar: 1 MF in bow; 1 MF variable depth

Weapons

A SS-N-14 (1x4)
B SA-N-4 pop-up twin launcher housing
C RBU-6000 (2x12)
D 21in (533mm) torpedo tubes TR M-57 (2x4)
E SA-N-4 (1x2)
F Twin 3in/59 gun
G Twin 3in/59 gun
H Mine rails (maximum 50 mines)
J 100mm/L60A gun (1x1)
K 100mm/L60A gun (1x1)
L 30mm ADMG-630 Gatling CIWS (2x1)
M Kamov Ka-32 Helix

Electronics

1 Medium frequency hull-mounted sonar
2 Bell Shroud ESM antenna
3 Don 2 navigation radar
4 Pop Group missile control radar for SA-N-4
5 VHF rod antenna
6 Eye Bowl missile control radar for SS-N-14
7 Eye Bowl missile control radar for SS-N-14

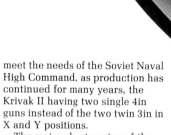

Background: The Krivak was first seen by Western observers in 1970, and its long, sleek lines and combination of powerful armament and effective propulsion system have frequently given rise to admiring comment. Although it followed the Kashin class in chronological terms this is a completely new design, being smaller, easier to build and possessing an altogether more sophisticated ASW system. Its ease of construction has enabled the smaller shipyards on the Baltic and Black Seas to be utilized for its construction, leaving the larger yards to concentrate on major warships (the US Navy's Oliver Hazard Perry class was ordered for similar reasons).

The task of the Krivaks is anti-submarine warfare, and their most important weapon system is the SS-N-14, mounted in a rather inelegant quadruple launcher on the forecastle. This is backed up by two RBU-6000 launchers forward of the bridge and two quadruple torpedo tubes amidships. A bow sonar is fitted and there is a VDS at the stern.

The complement of ASW missiles is small by Western standards, but perhaps the most critical deficiency of the Krivak I and II is their lack of an on-board helicopter to provide target data and engage submarines at long ranges; nor do air defence and ECM capability seem adequate for open-ocean operations, at least by the standards of Western navies. The ships, however, clearly

meet the needs of the Soviet Naval High Command, as production has continued for many years, the Krivak II having two single 4in guns instead of the two twin 3in in X and Y positions.

The major shortcoming of the Krivak I and II has been remedied in the helicopter-equipped Krivak III, which appeared in 1984 and appears to be intended for use by the KGB Naval Border Units in the Pacific. The hangar and flight-deck are located aft, displacing the gun turrets, and a single 100mm gun is mounted on the forecastle, replacing the quadruple SS-N-14 launcher.
Future: One third of the Krivak Is and IIs are in the Baltic, where

they are the major ASW type. The remaining ships serve with the other three fleets, complementing the ASW force formed by their larger sisters. It appears that production of the Krivak I and II has now ceased, but at least three Krivak IIIs are being constructed. A new class is probably about to appear.

8 Don Kay/Palm
Frond navigation
radar
9 Head Net C air
surveillance radar
10 High Pole IFF
antenna
11 Pop Group missile
control radar for
SA-N-4
12 Owl Screech fire
control radar for
76mm gun

13 VHF rod antenna
14 VHF rod antenna
15 Chaff launcher
16 Medium frequency
variable depth sonar
17 Spin Trough
navigation radar
18 Kite Screech fire
control radar for
100mm gun
19 High Pole B IFF
20 Bass Tilt fire control
radar for 30mm CIWS

Krivak I class

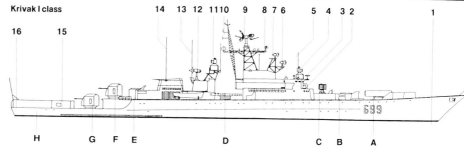

Krivak II class

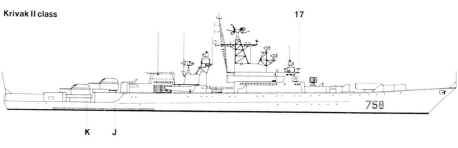

Krivak III class
Menzhinsky

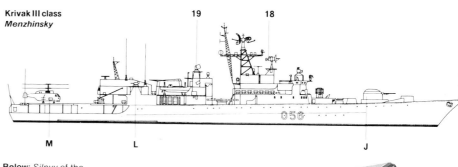

Below: *Silnyy* of the
Krivak I class, with the twin
3in/59 gun mounts
characteristic of this
sub-type clearly shown.
Note also the quarterdeck
VDS housing, and the
cylindrical housing for
the SA-N-4 missile system
between the stack and 'X'
turret.

Left: The widely used
SA-N-4 surface-to-air
missile system is mounted
on a retractable twin-arm
launcher. A naval version
of the Soviet Army's SA-8
Gecko system, SA-N-4 is
controlled by the Pop
Group radar director (see
key), and has a range of
9,850 yards (9,000m). It
has a limited secondary
capability against surface
targets.

**Left: Krivak II destroyer of the
Soviet Navy, photographed in the
Indian Ocean by the US Navy in
September 1981. The neat,
workmanlike design and elegant
lines of this class are widely
admired in Western naval circles.**

Le Redoutable class

Origin: France
Type: Nuclear-powered ballistic missile submarine (SSBN)
Built: 1967-1985
Class: 6 in commission
Displacement: 8,045 tons surfaced; 8,940 tons submerged
Dimensions: Length 422.5ft (128.7m) oa; beam 34.9ft (10.6m); draught 32.9ft (10m)
Propulsion: 1-shaft nuclear (1 pressurized-water-cooled nuclear reactor; geared steam turbines; 2 turbo-alternators; 1 electric motor), 16,000shp
Performance: 20 knots surfaced, 25 knots submerged
Weapons: Missiles: 16 MSBS M-20 (first five boats); 16 M-4 TN-70 (*L'Inflexible* on building and all except *Le Foudroyant* during refit) Torpedo tubes: 4 x 21in (533mm), 18 L5 and L7 torpedoes; SM39 missiles to be added
Sensors: Sonar: DUUV 23 panoramic (first five boats); DUUX 21 ranging (first five boats); DSUX 21 multipurpose (*L'Inflexible* on building and all others during refit)
Complement: 135

Background: Like the British across the English Channel, the French decided that it was necessary to build nuclear-powered ballistic missile submarines to ensure a viable national nuclear deterrent policy. Unlike the British, however, with their Polaris and Trident submarines, the French *Force de Dissuasion* has been developed virtually independently of the USA, although some covert assistance may have been given. This has entailed a much greater effort spread over a much longer timescale, and resulted, initially at least, in heavier missiles carrying smaller warheads over a shorter range.

Le Redoutable-class SSBNs follow US design philosophy in that they have two rows of eight missiles abaft the sail. However, unlike the Americans and the British, the French did not already have SSN designs which could be

Above: Le Redoutable, first of the French Navy's SSBN's, running on the surface with crew members posing for the camera on the fin. The forward bow wave shows that the French designers have used a quite different hull shape from those of SSBNs in other navies. Also clearly shown are the American style fin-mounted hydroplanes.

Le Redoutable (S 611)

Weapons
A 533mm torpedo tubes (2x2) for L3 and L5 torpedoes and SM.39 Exocet missiles (total of 18 carried)
B MSBS M-20 ballistic missile launch tubes (2x8); M-20 to be replaced by M-4

Electronics
1 DUUV-23 passive sonar array
2 ESM mast
3 Periscope
4 DRUA-30 Calypso radar
5 Periscope
6 ESM mast
7 HF antenna

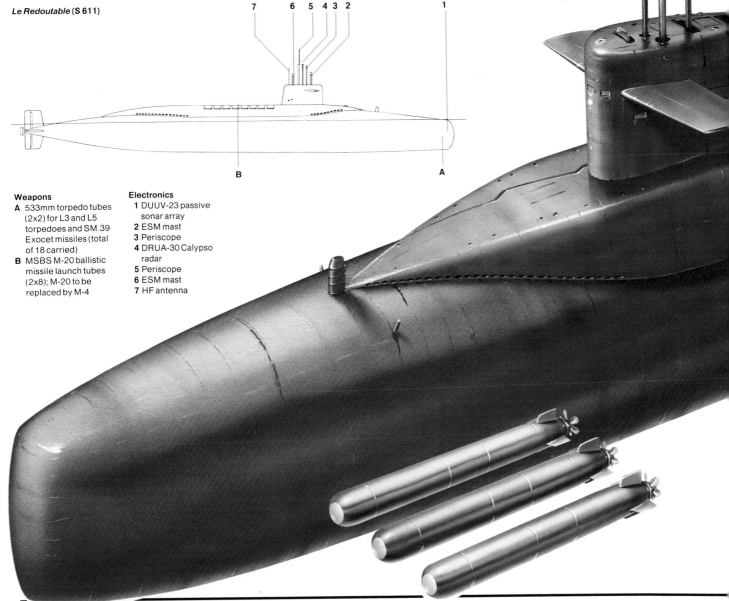

lengthened to accommodate the missile section.

The French SSBNs have pressurized-water-cooled nuclear reactors and turbo-electric propulsion. They also have two auxiliary diesels that can be cut in to provide power should the primary system fail; sufficient fuel is carried for 5,000 miles (8,046km). The forward hydroplanes are mounted on the fin as in US Navy SSBNs.

French policy is to have three SSBN hulls available at any one time, of which two must be on patrol. To achieve this the sixth boat, L'Inflexible, was ordered in 1979 and entered service in 1985. This is of an interim design, essentially an improved Le

Redoutable but incorporating a number of modifications based on experience with the earlier boats and on recent technological developments. L'Inflexible, for example, can dive some 328ft (100m) deeper than her predecessors.

The French Navy has had tactical problems as a result of the short range of the earlier types of missile. The Mer-Sol Balistique Stratégique (MSBS) M-1 SLBM, for example, which was fitted in the first two boats had a range of only 1,500 miles (2,400km), but this has been progressively increased in successive missile systems. The first four boats were all modified to take the MSBS M-2, but have subsequently been modified again

to take the M-20. The fifth boat was constructed from the outset to take the latter missile.

An even better missile — the M-4 — with a MIRVed warhead entered service in 1985 on L'Inflexible. This has a range in excess of 2,485 miles (4,000km) and is armed with six of the new 150kT TN70 warheads. Le Tonnant will be modified for the M-4 during her next long refit, as will all other of the earlier boats with the exception of the first, Le Redoutable, which is considered too old.

All boats are also armed with four 21in (533mm) bow-mounted torpedo tubes, and 18 torpedoes are carried. The Le Redoutable class is equipped with Calypso

I-band navigation and attack radar, and has a bow-mounted DSUX 21 sonar.

The French SSBN/SLBM programme is a major national success, though one achieved only at a high price.

Future: On November 13, 1981, after visiting Le Tonnant on patrol, President Mitterrand announced an order for a seventh SSBN, also of the interim class, for delivery in the mid-1980s, a clear endorsement by the government of France's independent nuclear deterrent policy. It is planned to replace all five first-generation boats with a totally new class in 1990-2000, starting with Le Redoutable in 1995 and with the interim design boats being replaced later.

Left: These MSBS M-20 missiles first reached operational status in Le Tonnant (below); 16 are carried in two rows of eight. M-20 is 35ft (10.7m) long and its two-stage solid fuel motor gives it a range of 1,860nm (3,500km); payload is one thermonuclear warhead with a 1MT yield. M-20 will be succeeded by the longer range M-4, with seven 150kT RVs.

Below: Le Tonnant (S 614) was the fifth SSBN (SNLE) to be built for the French Navy as part of its Force Oceanique Stratégique (FOST). FOST has its headquarters at Houilles, near Paris, and its operational base is at Ile Longue in the naval base at Brest. The drawing shows the differences in hull shape compared to other nations' SSBNs, especially in the bow,

where the French boats have a much less rounded form. Otherwise, although design and construction are, entirely French, the overall design philosophy is very similar to that of

the US Navy's early SSBNs, with 16 missiles in two rows of eight carried behind the fin. A sixth boat, L'Inflexible, has now joined FOST, armed with the new M-4 missile.

Below: Le Redoutable at sea. The French Sous-marin Nucléaire Lanceur d'Engins (SNLE) has been the subject of a very successful, if expensive, national programme. Unlike the UK, which relies on a fleet of four, France plans on six hulls guaranteeing two at sea at all times.

Left: All French SSBNs are fitted with four bow-mounted 533mm torpedo tubes. These are currently used to fire French L5 torpedoes (shown here), but in due course will be used to launch SM.39 Exocet SSMs as well; a total of 18 rounds can be carried. The L5 is an electric powered torpedo, of which the Mod 3 version is used by submarines. The L5 weighs some 2,865lb (1,300kg) and has a speed of 35 knots and a range of

5.75 miles (9.25km). It is fitted with a Thomson-CSF active/passive guidance system, which is capable of several mission profiles, including direct attack and programmed search. SM.39 is the submarine-launched version of the successful and widely used Aérospatiale AM.39 Exocet air-launched anti-ship missile and has a range of some 39nm (72km); its payload is a 363lb (165kg) high-explosive warhead.

Los Angeles (SSN 688) class

Origin: USA
Type: Nuclear-powered attack submarine (SSN)
Built: 1972-
Class: 35 in service; 6 building; 7 on order
Displacement: 6,000 tons standard; 6,900 tons submerged
Dimensions: Length 360ft (109.7m) oa; beam 33ft (10.1m); draught 32.3ft (9.9m)
Propulsion: 1-shaft nuclear (1 S6G pressurized-water-cooled nuclear reactor; 2 geared turbines), 35,000shp
Performance: 30+ knots dived
Weapons: Torpedo tubes: 4x 21in (533mm) for conventional torpedoes, Subroc and Mk 48 A/S torpedoes; tube-launched Tomahawk SLCM in SSN 688-720 Vertical launch tubes: 15 for Tomahawk SLCM from SSN 721 onwards
Sensors: Sonar: BQQ-5 long-range; BQS-15 short-range; BQR-15 towed array Radar: BPS 15
Complement: 127

Background: In the late 1960s the US Navy was considering two separate classes of SSN: a high-speed attack and ASW submarine, and a very quiet type intended for barrier operations. The latter requirement led to the USS *Glenard P Lipscomb* (SSN 685), the outcome of a development programme for a quiet submarine stretching back to USS *Tullibee* (SSN 597) of the early 1960s. The *Lipscomb*, which was launched in 1973, has many interesting features aimed at achieving silent running, a number of which have been incorporated into the Los Angeles class.

Like *Tullibee*, *Lipscomb* is powered by a pressurized-water-cooled reactor driving a turbo-electric plant. This removes the requirement for gearing, which is one of the prime sources of noise in nuclear submarines. It was decided, however, that rather than go in for the considerable extra expense of two separate classes, the Los Angeles could perform both roles, and, although *Lipscomb* remains in front-line service, the turbo-electric drive system was not repeated in the Los Angeles class.

The USS *Los Angeles* (SSN 688) entered service in 1976, and by the end of 1985 there were 35 in service, with 13 more authorized by Congress and building; the Pentagon was also seeking funds from Congress for a further 20 to be built between 1986 and 1989. They are much larger than any previous US SSN and the hull is optimised for high submerged speed, with a very small sail. One unfortunate consequence is that the sail-mounted planes cannot be rotated to the vertical, so the Los Angeles class boats cannot break through ice. It has been reported that later boats will have their planes moved back to the more traditional bow position to restore the under-ice capability.

The comprehensive sensor fit includes the BQQ-5 sonar system in the bows and a passive tactical towed sonar array. The cable and winch for the latter are mounted in the ballast tanks, but the array itself is housed in a prominent fairing running almost the entire length of the hull.

The most remarkable feature of the class, however, is its armament. These powerful submarines are armed with Subroc and Sub-Harpoon, as well as conventional and wire-guided torpedoes. SSN 703, 704, 712 and 713 are already fitted to fire tube-launched Tomahawk and eventually all boats from SSN 688-720 will be able to carry up to 12 Tomahawk as part of their torpedo loads. From SSN 721 onward, however, 15 vertical launch tubes for Tomahawk will be fitted in the space in the bow between the inner and outer hulls, thus restoring the torpedo capacity. So, although their primary mission is still to hunt other submarines and to protect SSBNs, they can also be used without modification to sink surface ships at long range with Sub-Harpoon while Tomahawk enables them to operate against strategic targets well inland. It has also been announced that from

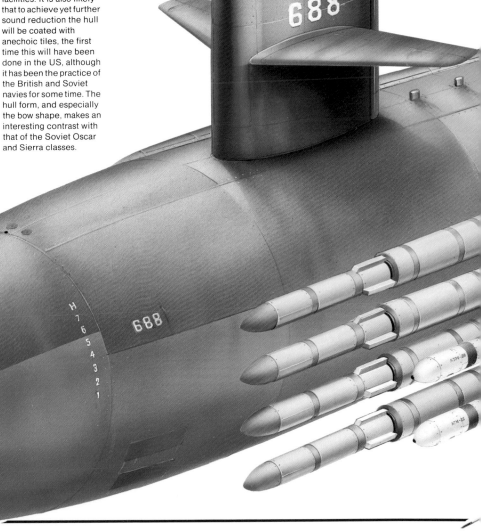

Right: The Los Angeles (SSN 688) class has proved to be one of the US Navy's great successes, with 35 in service, six building and a further seven on order. At a cost in 1981 dollars of some 495.8 million each, they represent one of the most costly military programmes in history. These are the most sophisticated attack submarines in any navy: their ASW armament comprises torpedoes (including the Mk 48) and Subroc, while Tomahawk cruise missiles provide a tactical and strategic capability against surface targets. SSN 688-720 use the tube-launched version of Tomahawk, but SSN 721 onward have 15 Tomahawks in vertical launch tubes, thus restoring the full torpedo load. The hull design is exceptionally clean, with very few protuberances, though the mounting of the forward hydroplanes on the fin has led to criticism, especially of their inability to surface through ice, and it has recently been announced that in future designs the planes will be mounted in the traditional bow position. An improvement programme for the Los Angeles class includes relocating the torpedo tubes in the bow, an increase in the number of tubes from six to eight, and enhancements to the command and control facilities. It is also likely that to achieve yet further sound reduction the hull will be coated with anechoic tiles, the first time this will have been done in the US, although it has been the practice of the British and Soviet navies for some time. The hull form, and especially the bow shape, makes an interesting contrast with that of the Soviet Oscar and Sierra classes.

FY1985 the Los Angeles class will be given a mine-laying capability.

The Los Angeles class is very sophisticated: each boat is an extremely potent fighting machine, and with a production run of at least 48 it must be considered a very successful design. However, these boats are becoming very expensive: the first cost $221.25 million, while the boat bought in 1979 cost $325.6 million, and the two in 1981 $495.8 million each. It would seem that not even the USA can afford to go on spending

money at that rate indefinitely.
Future: The Reagan Administration has ordered a speeding-up of the Los Angeles building programme: two were built in 1982 and by 1986 the rate was three per year. The Tomahawk missile programme has also been accelerated, with these new missiles being fitted in SSN 719 onward.

The new SSN 21 class of submarine, currently under development, in which the key design objective will be sound-quieting, will carry even more

weapons, have improved sensors and be able to operate under the ice more effectively. The new class is scheduled to enter production in FY1989.

There has been much criticism of the complexity and cost of the Los Angeles design, and it is alleged that too many sacrifices were made to achieve the very high speed. A design for a cheaper and smaller SSN, under consideration in 1980 as a result of Congressional pressure, was later shelved, but may well reappear,

especially if the proposed new class should turn out to be even more expensive than the Los Angeles, which is entirely possible.

Meanwhile, there are plans to improve the Los Angeles boats, especially their sensors, weapon systems and control equipment. Such improvements will include moving the torpedo tubes back to the bow and increasing their number to eight. The Los Angeles boats will also probably be the first US submarines to be given anechoic coatings.

Left: USS Salt Lake City (SSN 716) on trials prior to commissioning. The long fairing running down the starboard side of the boat houses the BQR-15 towed array. SSN 716 is one of the earlier units of the class with tube-launched Tomahawk; the vertical-launch version is fitted in SSN 721 onward.

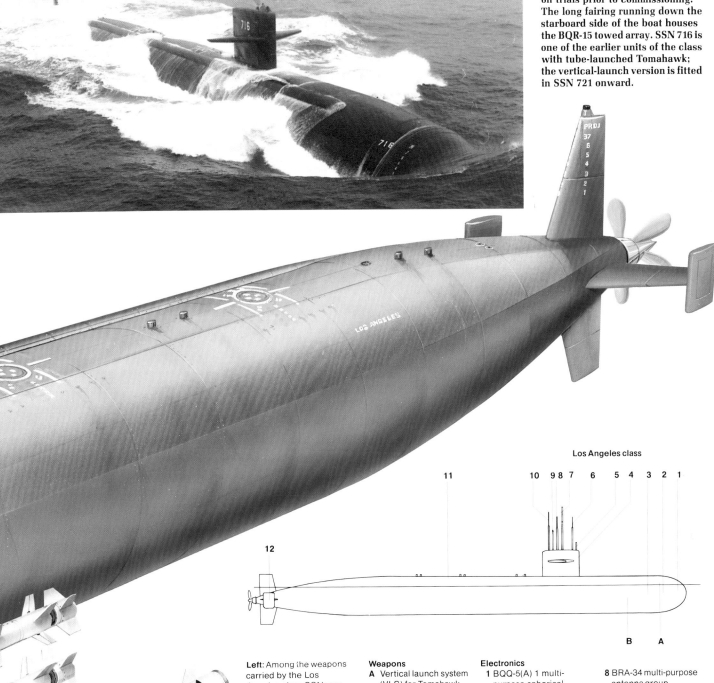

Los Angeles class

Left: Among the weapons carried by the Los Angeles class SSNs are UUM-44A-2 SUBROC (far left), UGM-84 Sub-Harpoon (centre) and BGM-109 submarine-launched Tomahawk (right). In addition, any of the current range of US Navy torpedoes can be carried. These are the most heavily armed submarines ever deployed.

Weapons
A Vertical launch system (VLS) for Tomahawk anti-ship missiles (from SSN 721)
B 21 in torpedo tubes (2x2) for Harpoon SSM (4 carried); Tomahawk SSM (8 carried SSN 703/704/712/713); Subrock ASW missiles (to be superseded by Sea Lance ASW/SOW) Mk 48 ASW torpedoes; total 25 weapons

Electronics
1 BQQ-5(A) 1 multi-purpose spherical sonar array
2 Hydrophone array
3 BQR-21 DIMUS (DIgital MUltibeam Steering) sonar conformal array
4 BQS-15 short-range sonar array
5 BPS-15 surface detection radar
6 BRA-34 multi-purpose antenna group
8 BRA-34 multi-purpose antenna group
9 General-purpose periscope Type 15B Mod 1
10 BRD-7 radio direction-finding antenna
11 BRQ-15 towed array fairing
12 Hydrophone array

MEKO 360 type

Origin: Federal Republic of Germany
Type: Destroyer (DDG)
Built: 1980-1982
Class: (H1) 1 in service (Nigeria) (H2) 4 in service (Argentina)
Displacement: (H1) 3,630 tons full load
(H2) 2,900 tons standard; 3,360 tons full load
Dimensions: (H1) Length 412ft (125.6m) oa; beam 49.2ft (15m); draught 14.1ft (4.3m)
(H2) Length 413.1ft (125.9m) oa; beam 46ft (14m); draught 19ft (5.8m)
Propulsion: (H1) 2-shaft CODAG (2 Rolls-Royce Olympus TM3B gas turbines; 2 MTU Type 20 V 956 Tb92 diesels) 56,000/10,000shp
(H2) 2-shaft COGAG (2 Rolls-Royce Olympus TM3B and 2 Rolls-Royce Tyne gas turbines), 56,000/10,680shp
Performance: (H1) Speed 30.5 knots; range 6,500nm at 18 knots
(H2) Speed 30.5 knots; range 4,500nm at 18 knots
Weapons: (H1) SSM: 8 x 1 Otomat launchers
SAM: 1 octuple Aspide launcher (24 missiles)
Guns: 1 127mm OTO-Melara; 4 x 2 40mm/70 Breda Bofors
Torpedo tubes: 2 x 3 Plessey STWS-1B
(H2) SSM: 2 x 4 MM40 Exocet launchers
SAM: 1 octuple Aspide launcher (24 missiles)
Guns: 1 127mm OTO-Melara; 4 x 2 40mm/70 Breda Bofors
Torpedo tubes: 2 x 3 ILAS-3
Rocket launchers: 2 ELSAG 105mm SCLAR
Aircraft: (H1) 2 Lynx ASW helicopters
(H2) 2 AB 212 ASW helicopters
Sensors: (H1) Radar: Plessey AWS-5 surface/air surveillance; WM 25 and STIR search/fire control; Decca 1226 navigation
Sonar: KAE80 hull-mounted
(H2) Radar: HSA DA-08A surface/air surveillance; 2 HSA LIROD radio/optronic fire control systems; HSA ZW-06 and Decca 1226 navigation
Sonar: KAE80 hull-mounted
Complement: 200

Background: Two major themes in modern naval construction are the ever-increasing complexity and cost of warships, and the growing size and ambitions of the smaller navies. Numerous designers have, therefore, sought to produce warships of destroyer or frigate size which would accommodate a variety of weapons and electronic fits to suit different customers' needs on a standard hull, thus facilitating longer production runs and keeping down costs.

The basis of the MEKO concept, a range of standard hulls, is complemented by the MEKO/FES range of standard-size, functionally self-contained modules with standard interfaces to the ship platform. These ingenious systems have enabled Blohm und Voss to offer destroyer- and frigate-sized warships to navies which might otherwise have been unable to afford such large ships. Current types on

offer are the MEKO 100, MEKO 140, MEKO 200 and MEKO 360.

Weapon functional units are used for the installation of guns, SAM and SSM launchers and anti-submarine rocket launchers. These units are bedded into a unit foundation using a plastic resin compound, which transfers the static and dynamic loads to the ship's structure. Units on offer inclue Otomat SAMs, Aspide SSMs, 127mm guns and twin 40mm Breda dual-purpose guns.

Electronic functional units, used for the installation of surveillance radars, fire control radars, ESM and ECM systems, sonar and communications facilities, come in light alloy containers of inter-national standard size and are shock-mounted to avoid the need for individual shock-mounting of units inside. Pallets are used for the installation of operator consoles, tactical displays and auxiliary equipment. There is also a variety of engine fits.

Largest in the current range is the MEKO 360, a general-purpose destroyer design for world-wide operation under all climatic con-ditions. It can be fitted with a variety of propulsion options, including CODOG and COGOG, driving two shafts fitted with variable-pitch propellers. Current operators of MEKO 360s are Argentina (*Almirante Brown*, com-missioned in 1982, *La Argentina* 1983, *Heroina* 1983, *Sarandi* 1984) and Nigeria (*Aradu* 1982). Most significant are the Argentine ships, which constitute a major

new naval force in the South Atlantic of considerable concern to both Chile and the United Kingdom.

The Turkish Navy has ordered four of the somewhat smaller MEKO 200 frigates of 2,400 tons full load displacement. These will be armed with eight Harpoon SSM, Aspide SAM, one 127mm gun, three Oerlikon Zenith 4-barrel 25mm CIWS and two triple Mk 32 torpedo tubes and will carry an AB 212 ASW helicopter. Two are being built in West Germany and the remaining two in the Turkish yard at Golcuk.

Argentina has also built four MEKO 140 frigates, with another two still under construction. This design is virtually a scaled-down MEKO 360 with a 1,700 tons full load displacement. Known as the Espora class, the ships are armed with four Exocet SSMs, a 76mm gun, four 40mm guns, and six torpedo tubes, and each carries a

helicopter. The last three are fitted with telescopic hangars for the helicopter and a similar facility will be retrofitted to the first three.
Future: With the Nigerian and Argentinian ships in service, no more orders have been received for MEKO 360s; indeed, there have been rumours that the Argentinian Navy may be trying to sell two of its four ships as a result of the drastic squeeze being imposed on defence spending.

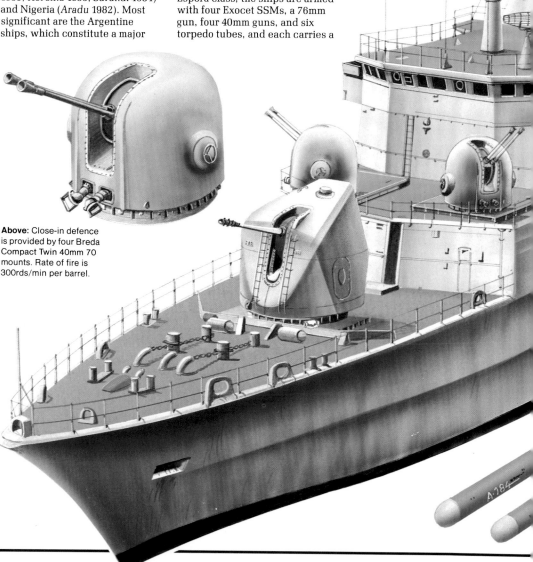

Above: Close-in defence is provided by four Breda Compact Twin 40mm 70 mounts. Rate of fire is 300rds/min per barrel.

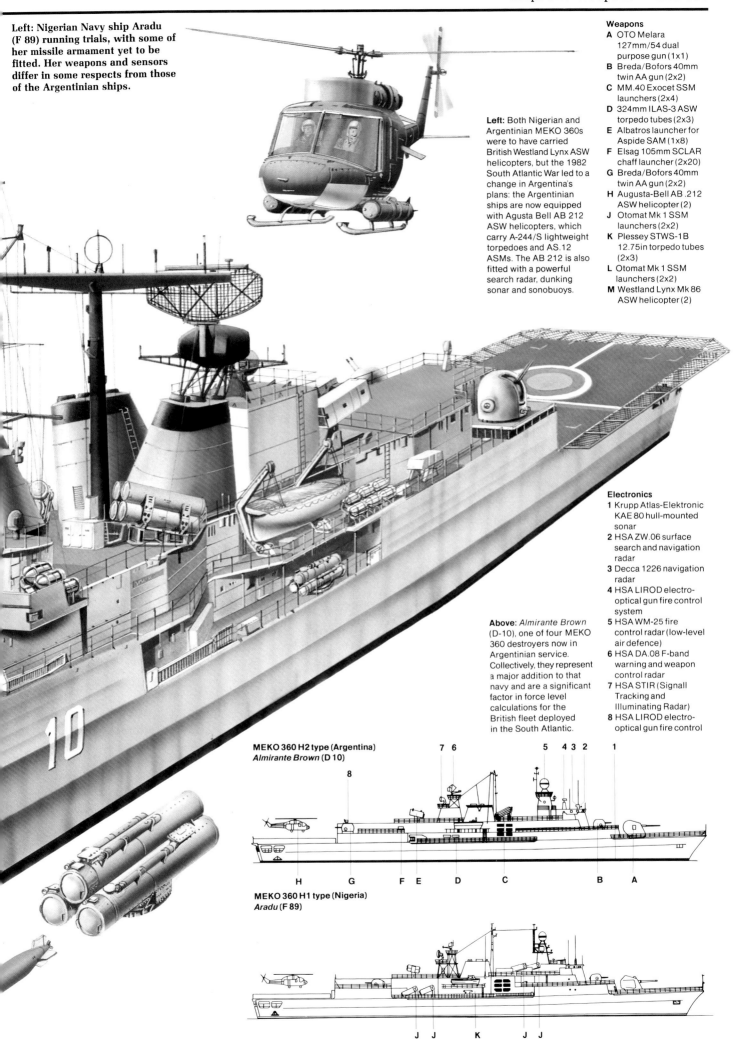

Left: Nigerian Navy ship Aradu (F 89) running trials, with some of her missile armament yet to be fitted. Her weapons and sensors differ in some respects from those of the Argentinian ships.

Left: Both Nigerian and Argentinian MEKO 360s were to have carried British Westland Lynx ASW helicopters, but the 1982 South Atlantic War led to a change in Argentina's plans: the Argentinian ships are now equipped with Agusta Bell AB 212 ASW helicopters, which carry A-244/S lightweight torpedoes and AS.12 ASMs. The AB 212 is also fitted with a powerful search radar, dunking sonar and sonobuoys.

Weapons
A OTO Melara 127mm/54 dual purpose gun (1x1)
B Breda/Bofors 40mm twin AA gun (2x2)
C MM.40 Exocet SSM launchers (2x4)
D 324mm ILAS-3 ASW torpedo tubes (2x3)
E Albatros launcher for Aspide SAM (1x8)
F Elsag 105mm SCLAR chaff launcher (2x20)
G Breda/Bofors 40mm twin AA gun (2x2)
H Augusta-Bell AB .212 ASW helicopter (2)
J Otomat Mk 1 SSM launchers (2x2)
K Plessey STWS-1B 12.75in torpedo tubes (2x3)
L Otomat Mk 1 SSM launchers (2x2)
M Westland Lynx Mk 86 ASW helicopter (2)

Electronics
1 Krupp Atlas-Elektronic KAE 80 hull-mounted sonar
2 HSA ZW.06 surface search and navigation radar
3 Decca 1226 navigation radar
4 HSA LIROD electro-optical gun fire control system
5 HSA WM-25 fire control radar (low-level air defence)
6 HSA DA.08 F-band warning and weapon control radar
7 HSA STIR (Signall Tracking and Illuminating Radar)
8 HSA LIROD electro-optical gun fire control

Above: *Almirante Brown* (D-10), one of four MEKO 360 destroyers now in Argentinian service. Collectively, they represent a major addition to that navy and are a significant factor in force level calculations for the British fleet deployed in the South Atlantic.

MEKO 360 H2 type (Argentina)
Almirante Brown (D 10)

7 6 5 4 3 2 1

8

H G F E D C B A

MEKO 360 H1 type (Nigeria)
Aradu (F 89)

J J K J J

Moskva class

Origin: USSR
Type: Helicopter cruiser (CVS)
Built: 1963-1968
Class: 2 in service
Displacement: 15,500 tons standard; 19,200 tons full load
Dimensions: Length 620ft (189m) oa; beam 111.5ft (34m); draught 27.89ft (8.5m)
Propulsion: 2-shaft geared steam turbines, 100,000shp
Performance: Speed 31 knots; range 9,000nm at 18 knots, 4,500nm at 29 knots
Weapons: SAM: 2 twin SA-N-3 launchers (48 missiles)
Guns: 4 twin 57mm/L70A
ASW: 1 twin SUW-N-1 launcher (24 SS-N-16 missiles); 2 12-barrel RBU-6000
Aircraft: 16 Ka-25 Hormone-A; 2 Hormone-B
Sensors: Search radar: Top Sail 3D; Head Net C 3D
Fire control radar: 2 Head Light C (SA-N-3); 2 Muff Cob (57mm guns)
Navigation radar: 3 Don 2
Sonar: 1 LF hull-mounted; 1 MF variable-depth
Complement: 840, plus air wing

Background: Designated *proto-volodchny kreyser* (anti-submarine cruiser) by the Soviet Navy, *Moskva* first appeared in 1967, followed by *Leningrad* in 1968, both having been built in the Nosenko Yard in Nikolayev. The design of these two impressive-looking ships may have been influenced to a certain extent by the helicopter cruisers built by the French and Italian navies during the early 1960s, such as the *Jeanne d'Arc* and *Vittorio Veneto*, but the Soviet ships are much larger and able to operate an air group of up to 18 aircraft. They also helped to serve notice on the West that the Soviet Navy was starting to move into the ship-borne aviation business in a big way.

There is no doubt that the principal mission for which these two ships were designed was to hunt and destroy US Navy Polaris SSBNs in the eastern Mediterranean. However, they have played a major role in introducing large-scale air operations to the Soviet Navy and in training ships' officers, crews and aviators in the techniques of operating large numbers of aircraft from shipborne platforms. They have thus served as stepping-stones to the *Kiev*, and ultimately to the Kremlin class aircraft carriers.

The air group comprises 15-18 Ka-25 Hormones housed in a spacious hangar beneath the half-length flight deck. This is

served by two aircraft lifts, which are somewhat narrow and limit operational deployments to Hormones. This was demonstrated clearly when *Leningrad* deployed to the Suez Canal area in the summer of 1974 with Mi-8s Hips: these were too large for the lifts and could not be struck down into the hangar.

The primary ASW weapons system of the Moskvas is the Ka-25 helicopter, which is normally of the Hormone-A ASW type, although some of the -B version are also carried. Unlike Western aircraft carriers at the time they were designed, the forward part of these Soviet ships is occupied by a comprehensive weapons outfit of ASW and air defence systems. There is a twin SUW-N-1 anti-submarine missile launcher on the forecastle, and two RBU-6000 rocket launchers in the bow. There is also an SA-N-3 area air defence system, and two twin 57mm dual-purpose gun-mountings seem to have been fitted almost as an afterthought.

ASW sensors include a hull-mounted LF sonar and a stern-mounted VDS. As built, the two ships had torpedo tubes mounted in line with the bridge and just above the water-line. These have since been removed, almost certainly because they must have been inoperable in any sort of seaway. The tall, pyramid-shaped superstructure includes the bridge, funnel and numerous radio, radar and ESM antennas.

Moskva was used in 1973 for the carrier trials of the Yak-36 Forger. No operational deployment has ever taken place with this V/STOL aircraft, possibly because of the limitations imposed by the lifts.

Future: The two units of the class built, *Moskva* and *Leningrad*, have served the Soviet Navy well. However, Soviet interest in medium-sized air-capable ships seems to have waned in favour of the much larger ships of the Kiev class.

Above: An excellent view of Moskva (taken before the torpedo tubes were deleted and the embrasure plated over) showing the unique pyramid superstructure and the numerous sensors, notably the Headlight A missile control radars.

Below: Moskva with five Kamov Ka-25 Hormone helicopters on the flight deck. Note the helicopter control bridge on the stack, the open door to the small hangar below it and the narrow lift, which prevents embarkation of larger aircraft.

Right: SA-N-3 Goblet missiles and twin-arm launcher. This missile has a range of 32,800 yards (30,000m) and an interception altitude of 300ft (91m) to 80,000ft (24,400m). Missile control is by the Headlight A director.

Right: Soviet aircraft designers receive credit and publicity for their work, but their naval designer compatriots are anonymous, hidden men who receive no publicity. Yet they must be remarkable people, as many of their ship designs are so daring and full of original ideas. An early example of their skills is the Moskva class air-capable ASW cruiser, which combines a large, uncluttered flight deck aft with a heavy and effective armament forward and a varied and apparently comprehensive sensor fit. Also clear from this drawing is the unusual shape of the hull —virtually ovoid or teardrop in plan view— which may give a large flight deck, but which probably also makes for unusual motion.

Above: Moskva class ASW cruisers carry an air wing of 16 Kamov Ka-25 Hormone-As (shown here) and two Hormone-Bs. The ASW version, Hormone-A, is fitted with a chin radome, dipping sonar and sonobuoys and carries depth charges or torpedoes. Hormone-B has a video data link system for over-the-horizon targeting.

Weapons
A RBU-6000 ASW rocket launcher
B RBU-6000 ASW rocket launcher
C SUW-N-1 launcher for FRAS-1 missiles (1x2)
D SA-N-3 launcher (1x2)
E SA-N-3 launcher (1x2)
F Former location for torpedo tubes, now removed
G Twin 57mm/70 AA gun mounting (2x2)
H Kamov Ka-25 Hormone-A ASW helicopter (14 carried)

Electronics
1 LF hull-mounted sonar
2 Twin DF loops
3 Don 2 navigation radar
4 Headlight A missile control radar for SA-N-3
5 Side Globe EW antennas (2x4)
6 Don 2 navigation radar
7 Head Light A missile control radar for SA-N-3
8 Bell Top EW antenna (2x1)
9 Bell Clout EW antenna (2x1)
10 Head Net C air surveillance radar
11 Top Sail 3D air surveillance radar
12 Bell Slam EW antenna (2x1)
13 Muff Cob fire control radar for 57mm AA gun (2x1)
14 Don 2 navigation radar
15 MF variable-depth sonar

Moskva class *Leningrad*

Nimitz (CVN 68) class

Origin: USA
Type: Nuclear-powered aircraft carrier (CVN)
Built: 1968-1991
Class: 4 in service; 1 building; 1 ordered
Displacement: *(Nimitz)* 72,798 tons light; 90,944 tons full load; *(Others)* 72,916 tons light; 91,487 tons full load
Dimensions: Length 1,092ft (332.9m) oa; beam 134ft (40.8m); draught 37ft (11.3m)
Propulsion: 4-shaft nuclear (2 A4W/A1G pressurized-water-cooled nuclear reactors; 4 geared teamn turbines), 260,000shp
Performance: 30+ knots
Weapons: Guns: 3 20mm Phalanx CIWS (*Nimitz, Eisenhower*); 4 20mm Phalanx CIWS (remainder) SAM: 3 Basic Point Defence Missile System (BPDMS) launchers for Sea Sparrow
Aircraft: 24 F-14A Tomcat; 24 A-7E Corsair or F/A-18 Hornet; 10 A-6E Intruder; 4 KA-6D Intruder; 4 E-2C Hawkeye; 4 EA-6B Prowler; 10 S-3A Viking; 6 SH-3H Sea King
Sensors: Radar: SPS-48 3D air search; SPS-43A air search (*Nimitz, Eisenhower*) SPS-49(V) air search (others); SPS-10F surface search (*Nimitz, Eisenhower, Vinson*); SPS-67(V), SPS-64 surface search (others); LN-66 navigation
Complement: 3,300, plus 3,000 air wing

Background: The Nimitz class aircraft carriers are the mightiest and most powerful warships in history. Each ship normally carries some 90 aircraft whose capabilities range from nuclear strike, through interception and ground-attack to close-in anti-submarine protection —a more powerful and better balanced tactical air force than many national air forces. Each carrier is manned by a crew of 3,300 with an air wing of a further 3,000. And their nuclear reactors have cores which enable them to operate for thirteen years at a stretch, equivalent to steaming up to one million miles.

Such extraordinary statistics will only be challenged when the Soviet Navy's nuclear-powered supercarriers enter service in the 1990s, and it is, in fact, the perceived threat from the Nimitz class that has caused such massive development in the Soviet Navy over the past 15 years.

The original nuclear-powered carrier, USS Enterprise (CVN 65), commissioned in 1961, was built in the remarkably short time of 45 months and was so successful that, when the time came to plan a replacement for the Midway class, nuclear power was the preferred means of propulsion. The advances that had been made meant that the eight A2W reactors used in *Enterprise* (each producing 35,000shp) could be replaced by just two A4W reactors, each producing approximately 130,000shp. In addition, the uranium cores need to be replaced much less frequently than those originally used in *Enterprise*.

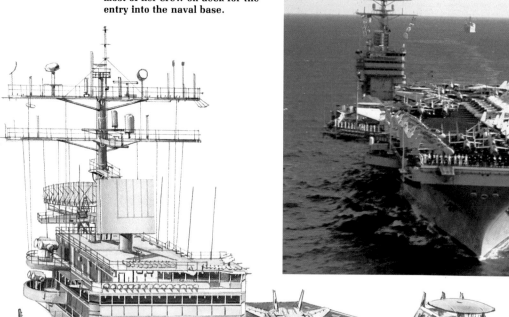

Right: USS Carl Vinson (CVN 70) approaching Pearl Harbor, with virtually her entire air wing and most of her crew on deck for the entry into the naval base.

This reduction in the number of reactors also permitted major improvements in the internal arrangements below hangar deck level. In *Enterprise* the entire centre section of the ship is occupied by machinery rooms, with the aviation fuel compartments and the missile magazines pushed out towards the end of the ship, but in *Nimitz* the propulsion machinery is divided into two separate units with the magazines between and forward of them. The improved layout has resulted in an increase of 20 per cent in aviation fuel capacity and a similar increase in the volume available for munitions and stores. The flight-deck layout for the Nimitz class is almost identical to that of the *John F Kennedy* (CV 67) of the Kitty Hawk class.

The provision of defensive weapons and sensors on the first two — Nimitz (CVN 68) and Eisenhower (CVN 69) — was initially on a par with that on the *John F Kennedy* (CV 67), although the third ship, Carl Vinson (CVN 70), has NATO Sea Sparrow and Phalanx in place of the BPDMS launchers on earlier ships, which will be similarly fitted in the near future. This parallels the increase in defensive armament taking place on the carriers of other

navies. *Vinson* is also fitted with an ASW control centre and specialized maintenance facilities for the S-3 Viking; these will also be installed in *Nimitz* and *Eisenhower* at future refits.

Delays in construction caused by shipyard problems resulted in rocketing costs and in the late 1970s the Carter Administration attempted unsuccessfully to block authorization funds for the construction of a fourth carrier in favour of a smaller (50,000 ton), conventionally-powered design, known as the CVV. However, the CVV was never popular with the US Navy, and the Reagan Administration has now committed itself to the continuation of the CVN programme.

Current deployment has *Nimitz* and *Eisenhower* in the Atlantic and *Vinson* in the Pacific, but when the *Roosevelt* is commissioned late in 1986 she will join the Atlantic

Fleet, releasing *Nimitz* for a move to the Pacific Fleet, balancing the CVN force.

Future: The three carriers of this class under construction— *Theodore Roosevelt* (CVN 71), *Abraham Lincoln* (CVN 72) and *George Washington* (CVN 73) — will be commissioned in late 1986, 1990 and 1991 respectively, and when the last is commissioned the USS *Coral Sea* (CV 43), a Midway class carrier commissioned in 1947, will be retired from the front-line force to become a training carrier.

Nimitz (CVN 68)

6 5   4 3 2 1

D   C   B A

Right: Raytheon RIM-7H Sea Sparrow missile being launched from a Mk 29 lightweight launcher; Mk 25 launchers are installed on *Eisenhower* (CVN 69). The Basic Point Defence Missile System (BPDMS) Sea Sparrow system used Asroc launchers and RIM-7E versions of the AIM-7E Sparrow missile.

Below: The sheer size of these nuclear carriers can be gauged from the way the aircraft are dwarfed by the flight deck. The Carrier Air Wing carried by each of the CVNs is larger and better balanced than most national air forces. The CAW usually comprises 24 F-14 Tomcats, 24 F/A-18 Hornets, 10 A-6E Intruders, four KA-6D Intruder tankers, four E-2C Hawkeye AEW aircraft, 10 S-3A Viking ASW aircraft, and six SH-3H Sea King ASW helicopters plus transports.

Weapons
A Mk 29 launcher for NATO Sea Sparrow SAM (1x8)
B Mk 15 20mm Vulcan Phalanx CIWS (2x1)
C Mk 29 launcher for NATO Sea Sparrow SAM (2x8)
D Mk 15 20mm Vulcan Phalanx CIWS (2x1)

Electronics
1 LN-66 navigation radar
2 SPS-48B 3D long-range air surveillance radar
3 SPS-10F surface search radar
4 URN-20 Tacan antenna
5 SPS-49 2D air search radar
6 SPS-43A long-range air search radar

Niteroi class

Origin: United Kingdom
Type: Frigate (FF)
Built: 1972-1980
Class: 6 in Brazilian service
Displacement: 3,200 tons standard; 3,800 tons full load
Dimensions: Length 425.1ft (129.2m) oa; beam 44.2ft (13.5m); draught 18.2ft (5.5m)
Propulsion: 2-shaft CODOG (2 Rolls-Royce Olympus TM3B gas turbines/4 MTU diesels), 56,000bhp/15,670shp
Performance: Speed 30 knots (gas turbines); endurance 5,300nm at 17 knots (2 diesels)
Weapons: Missiles: 2 twin Exocet SSM launchers (GP version); 2 triple Seacat launchers (GP and ASW)
Guns: 2 4.5in/55 Vickers Mk 8 (GP); 1 4.5in/55 Vickers Mk 8 (ASW); 2 40mm/70 Bofors (ASW)
ASW weapons: 1 Ikara launcher (10 missiles) (ASW); 1 Bofors 375mm rocket launcher; 1 depth-charge rail
Torpedo tubes: 2 triple Plessey STWS-1.
Aircraft: 1 Westland Lynx.
Sensors: Radar: Plessey AWS-2 air warning; Signal ZW-06 surface warning; 2 Selenia RTN-10X weapon control; 1 Ikara tracker (ASW) Sonar: EDO 610E hull-mounted; EDO 700E variable-depth
Complement: 209

Background: A number of European and American shipyards have tried to design a warship which would be attractive to the smaller naval powers through a combination of combat-effectiveness and economy, both in capital cost and in use of expensive manpower. French, Italian, West German and British yards have been particularly active in this field and many designs have appeared over the past 25 years, one of the most successful being Vosper Thornycroft series of inter-related corvette and frigate designs, of which the Mk 10 is currently the largest and most impressive.

The Vosper Thornycroft concept was made feasible by a number of technological developments, especially the advent of the marine gas turbine with its very high power-to-weight ratio and a generation of weapons and fire control systems which combined substantially greater power than their predecessors with reduced size and weight allied to greater reliability. In the weapons area the promise of a surface-to-surface missile which could seriously damage any normal warship without an elaborate and expensive control system offered a solution enabling a small surface combatant to carry the firepower which in the past had required a large hull.

These factors not only enabled firepower and speed to be built into the design, but also made possible the reduction in crew without which the concept could not have become a practical proposition. Each man in a ship requires some 180ft² (5m²) of space, so a drastic reduction in complement enables the designer to produce a smaller, more cost-effective warship.

The Mk 1 design was a 500-ton corvette armed with a 4in gun and a Squid mortar: two were delivered to the Ghanaian Navy in 1964-65 and one to the Libyan Navy in 1966. The Mk 3 was a little larger at 660 tons displacement and was armed with two 4in guns, two Bofors 40mm and two 20mm cannon; two were delivered to the Nigerian Navy in 1972.

The Mks 1 and 3 were too small for gas turbines, but CODOG propulsion became practicable with the Mk 5 frigate, considerably heavier at 1,540 tons and armed with Sea Killer SSMs, Seacat SAMs, a 4.5in main gun and two 35mm Oerlikon cannon; four were bought for the Imperial Iranian Navy as the Saam class and commissioned in 1971-72. A single Mk 7 frigate (1,780 tons), armed with one 4.5in, two 40mm and one twin 35mm guns, one Seacat launcher and a Mk 10 ASW mortar, was the subject of an order from Libya.

Next to appear was the Mk 9 corvette, two of which were ordered for the Nigerian Navy and commissioned in 1980-81. This class is of only 780 tons displacement, but is armed with Seacat, one 76mm main gun, one 40mm Bofors, two 20mm cannon and a Bofors ASW rocket launcher.

Perhaps the greatest success, however, was an order from the Royal Navy for eight Type 21 frigates—the Amazon class—which have a displacement of 3,250 tons and armament that includes a 4.5in gun and four MM38 Exocet but is still a recognizable member of the family. No fewer than seven were deployed to the scene of operations during the 1982 South Atlantic war, and two—*Ardent* and *Antelope*—were sunk in action.

The Mk 10 frigate, as bought by the Brazilian Navy, is somewhat bigger than the Royal Navy's Type 21, and by far the largest in the series. Designated the Niteroi class in Brazilian service, they are heavily armed and relatively large ships, but the complement of only 209 represents a remarkable reduction on that of previous designs of comparable size and complexity. The seven ships include two of a General Purpose design, the *Constituição* and *Liberal*, four of a dedicated ASW version, the *Niteroi, Defensora, Independencia* and *União*, and a single specialized training ship, the *Brasil*.

Future: The Vosper Thornycroft Mk 10 frigate is a well-balanced and efficient design, though no further orders had been announced by the beginning of 1986. The last two ASW frigates as well as the training ship were built in Rio de Janeiro, where two new Brazilian frigates of the V 28 class, the *Jaceguary* and *Inhouma*, were launched in 1985 and 1986 respectively. Another two of the V 28 class were expected to be ordered.

Right: The Short Seacat surface-to-air missile system in the Brazilian frigates uses a lightweight launcher mounting three missiles. The missile has a maximum effective range of some 6,000 yards (5,500m).

Below: The Australian Branik ASW system involves an Ikara missile carrying a torpedo (usually Mk 44 or 46) to a computer-assessed dropping point.

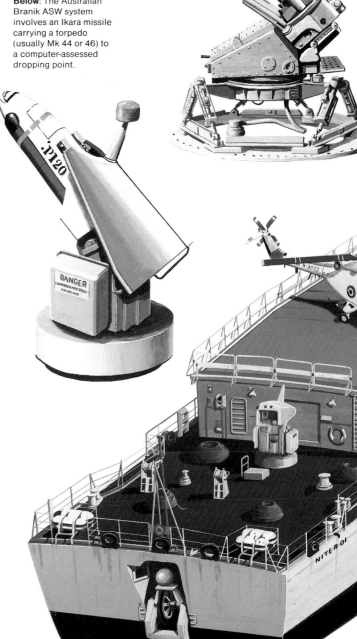

Left: Liberal (F 43) is one of two Vosper Thornycroft Mark 10 general-purpose frigates built for the Brazilian Navy. These differ from the four ASW ships by having a second 4.5in gun aft in place of the Branik ASW missile launcher and four MM.38 Exocet launchers forward of the mainmast. These are powerful units, well armed and with a comprehensive sensor fit, and are similar in general appearance to The Royal Navy's Type 21 frigates, also designed by Vosper Thornycroft.

Below: The Brazilian ASW frigate Niteroi (F 40), name ship of the class. Note, in particular, the Seacat launchers above the hangar, the Westland Lynx ASW helicopter on the flight deck, the Branik ASW missile launcher on the quarter-deck, and the EDO 700E VDS in the stern. The ASW weapon fit is particularly strong, comprising a Bofors rocket launcher, a helicopter, the Branik system, ASW torpedoes, and depth charges; most Western ASW frigates have only a helicopter and torpedoes. These ships represent the of a long line of development by Vosper Thornycroft: they are among the most powerful and modern ASW units of their size and would be able to give a good account of themselves in any South American conflict.

Weapons

A Vickers 4.5in/55 Mk 8 automatic dual-purpose gun (1x1)
B Bofors 375mm ASW rocket launcher (1x2)
C Bofors 40mm AA gun (2x1)
D 12.75in STWS-1 ASW torpedo tubes (2x3)
E Shorts Seacat SAM launcher (2x3)
F Westland Lynx Mk 21 ASW helicopter
G Ikara ASW missile launcher
H Depth-charge rack (5 DCs)
J MM.38 Exocet SSM (2x2)
K Vickers 4.5in/54 Mk 8 automatic dual-purpose gun (1x1)

Electronics

1 EDO Model 610E hull-mounted sonar
2 Branik tracking/guidance radar for ASW system
3 Selenia Orion RTN-10X fire control radar
4 HSA ZW-06 surface search radar
5 Plessey AWS-2 air search radar
6 Selenia orion RTN-10X fire control radar
7 EDO 700E variable-depth sonar

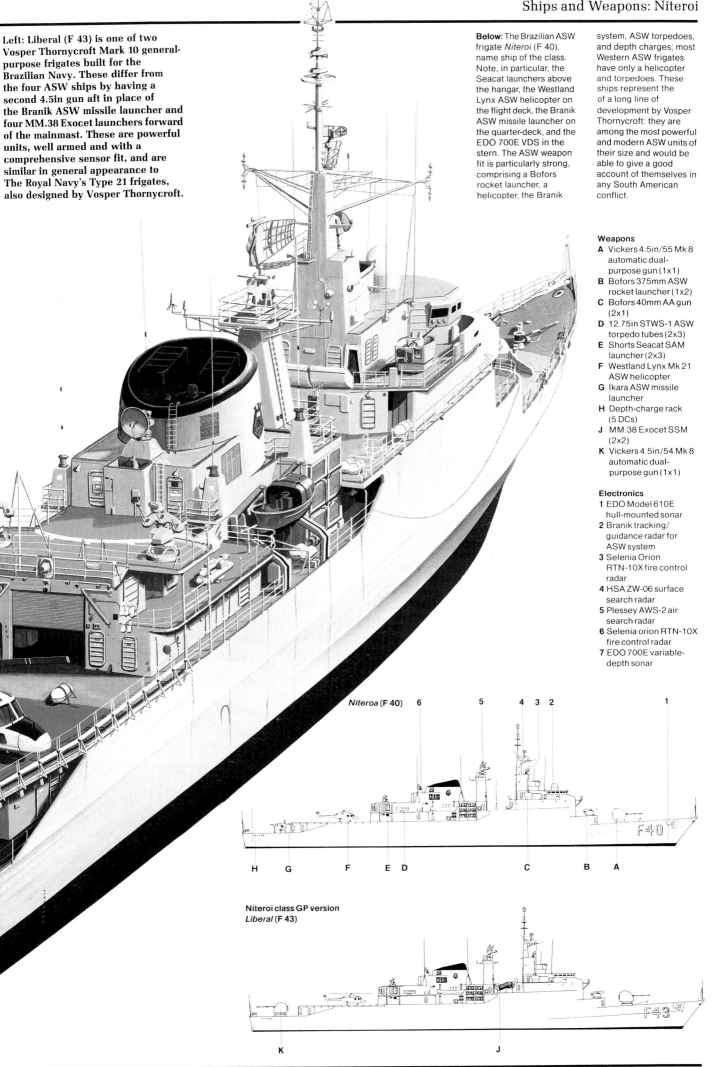

Niteroa (F 40)

Niteroi class GP version
Liberal (F 43)

Ohio class

Origin: USA
Type: Nuclear-powered ballistic missile submarine (SSBN)
Built: 1976-
Class: 7 in service; 7 building; 10 ordered
Displacement: 16,600 tons surfaced; 18,700 tons submerged
Dimensions: Length 560ft (170.7m) oa; beam 42ft (12.8m); draught 35.5ft (10.8m)
Propulsion: 1-shaft nuclear (1 S8G pressurized-water-cooled nuclear reactor; 2 geared turbines)
Performance: 30+ knots submerged
Weapons: SLBMs: 24 Trident I or II Torpedo tubes: 4 x 21in (533mm)
Sensors: Sonar: BQQ-5 passive bow-mounted; towed array?
Complement: 133

Background: With the upgrading of the US Navy's later Polaris ballistic missile submarines to carry Poseidon under way in the early 1970s, development of an entirely new SLBM was started. The resulting Trident I C-4 has a range of 4,400 miles (7,100km) and is now in service aboard 12 converted Lafayette-class SSBNs. However, it was decided that, to take full advantage of this missile, and to accept the slightly bigger Trident II D-5, a new class of larger SSBNs should be built. It was also decided to design the new boats to take 24 missiles rather than 16, and to incorporate all the latest techniques, especially of quietening.

Congress baulked initially at the enormous cost of the new system, but when the Soviet Navy introduced its own long-range SLBM, the 4,200-mile (6,760km) SS-N-8, in the Delta class, US reaction was to hastily authorize and accelerate the Trident programme; the first of the Ohio-class boats was laid down on April 10, 1976, and by 1986 the first three of these purpose-built Trident submarines had joined the fleet and 12 more had been authorized.

The eventual number of Trident-carrying submarines depends on two principal factors: the outcome of the US-Soviet Strategic Arms Reduction Talks (START) and the expense of the programme. However, current US Navy plans are for a force of 24 Ohios, of which ten would be allocated to the Pacific Fleet and ten to the Atlantic Fleet. With an anticipated availability of 65 per cent, that would give an average of 15 submarines at sea at any one time, with a total of 360 missiles.

The great advantage of the current generation of US and Soviet SLBMs is that they can be launched from their respective home waters, making detection of the launch platform and destruction of the submarine or the missiles very difficult, if not impossible, and enhancing their deterrent value.

The Ohio-class SSBNs have 24 vertical launch tubes abaft the sail; the first eight have Trident I SLBMs, but subsequent boats will have Trident II. Ohio-class SSBNs also have four bow-mounted torpedo tubes firing conventional torpedoes.

Sensors include the BQQ-5 sonar system in the bows and a passive tactical towed sonar array, for which the cable and winch are mounted in the ballast tanks. The array itself is housed in a prominent fairing which runs along almost the entire length of the hull.

Future: The Trident II D-5, to be deployed on the ninth and subsequent boats of the class and retrofitted to the first eight, carries a larger payload and is more accurate than Trident I, thus enabling the SSBN force to put

Right: The Trident I C-4 SLBM became operational in 1978. Twelve converted Lafayette/Franklin class SSBNs carry 16 each; the early Ohios carry 24, but will convert to the Trident II D-5. Trident I C-4 has a range of 4,350nm (7,900km) and carries up to eight MIRVs, each with a 100kT nominal yield.

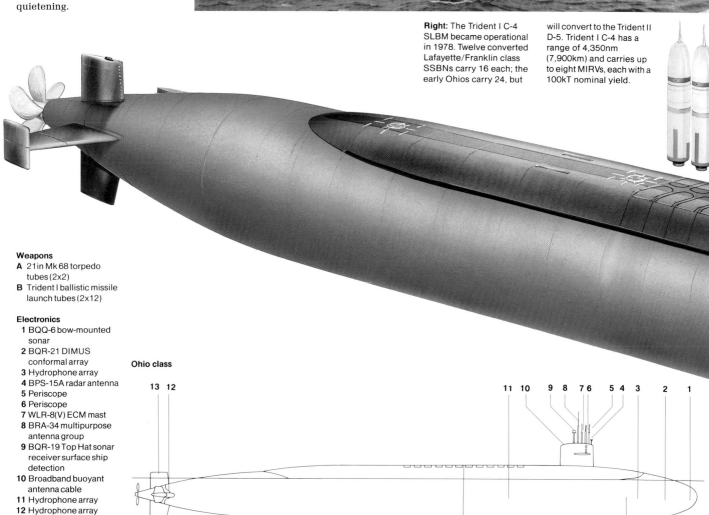

Weapons
A 21in Mk 68 torpedo tubes (2x2)
B Trident I ballistic missile launch tubes (2x12)

Electronics
1 BQQ-6 bow-mounted sonar
2 BQR-21 DIMUS conformal array
3 Hydrophone array
4 BPS-15A radar antenna
5 Periscope
6 Periscope
7 WLR-8(V) ECM mast
8 BRA-34 multipurpose antenna group
9 BQR-19 Top Hat sonar receiver surface ship detection
10 Broadband buoyant antenna cable
11 Hydrophone array
12 Hydrophone array
13 BQR-15 towed sonar array

Ohio class

hardened targets at risk—a significant expansion of the SSBN/SLBM role, which up to now has been that of a survivable, second-strike, counter-value deterrent system.

The position from the late 1990s, when the last of the modified Lafayettes will be retired, is the subject of current debate in the US. As always, there is pressure to find a less expensive alternative, which is not surprising in vew of the Ohios' cost—$1.8 billion per submarine in the FY1985 budget—and a further factor must be the possibility of a breakthrough in submarine detection (for example, by space-based sensors) which would deprive SSBNs of their current relative immunity.

Left: USS Ohio (SSBN 726) showing most of her periscope and sensor masts. This view shows how well the missile compartment is blended into the hull, which improves both speed and quietness. With 24 Trident-I C-4 SLBMs, the Ohios carry 192 100kT RVs with a total raw yield of 19.2MT.

Right: USS Michigan (SSBN 727) showing her rescue hatch markings and typical US Navy fin-mounted hydroplanes. High-speed surface shots make dramatic pictures; in reality, any SSBN will avoid the surface except when absolutely essential (eg, to enter or leave port), seeking shelter and survival in the ocean depths.

Left: USS *Ohio* (SSBN 726) is 560ft (170.7m) long and exceptionally clean in shape; note, in particular, the absence of free-flood holes which are still a feature of most Soviet submarines. Note also the large, slow-turning seven-bladed propeller, again is in marked contrast to the twin propellers still used by most Soviet submarines. The missiles are mounted vertically in two rows of 12 and are launched sequentially from an undisclosed depth. The after hydroplanes have vertical end-plates which not only aid control but also house part of the hydrophone array. These SSBNs have a planned schedule of 70 days on patrol followed by 25 days refitting, with a 12-month major overhaul every nine years, an average availability of 66 per cent and a considerable improvement over the Franklin/Lafayette figure of 55 per cent. Two crews per vessel are required to optimize the use of such expensive boats.

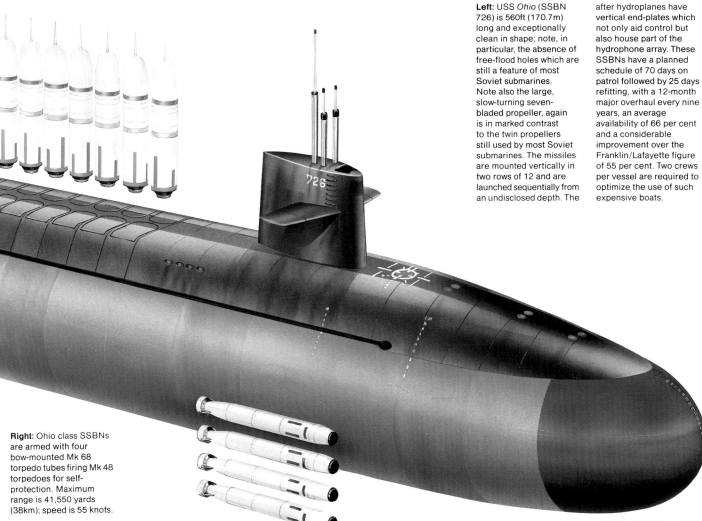

Right: Ohio class SSBNs are armed with four bow-mounted Mk 68 torpedo tubes firing Mk 48 torpedoes for self-protection. Maximum range is 41,550 yards (38km); speed is 55 knots.

Oliver Hazard Perry (FFG 7) class

Origin: USA
Type: Frigate (FFG)
Built: 1975-
Class: (US Navy) 42 in service; 9 building; 1 on order
(Royal Australian Navy) 4 in service; 2 building
(Royal Spanish Navy) 1 in service; 4 building
Displacement: 2,750 tons light; 3,605 tons full load
Dimensions: Length 445ft (135.6m) oa; beam 45ft (13.7m); draught 14.8ft (4.5m) keel, 24.5ft (7.5m) sonar
Propulsion: 1-shaft gas turbine (2 General Electric LM2500), 40,000shp
Performance: Speed 29 knots; range 4,500nm at 20 knots
Weapons: Missiles: 1 Mk 13 launcher for Harpoon SSM (4 carried) and Standard SAM (36 carried)
Guns: 1 3in Mk 75; 1 20mm Phalanx CIWS
Torpedo tubes: 2 x 3 Mk 32
Aircraft: 2 LAMPS helicopters
Sensors: Radar: SPS-49 long-range search; SPS-55 search and navigation; STIR (modified SPG-60) weapon control
Sonar: SQS-56 hull mounted; SQR-19 TACTAS towed array (US Navy FFG 36-43, 45-60).
Complement: 185

Background: The Oliver Hazard Perry (FFG 7) class originated in the Patrol Frigate programme, which was to constitute the cheaper component of a high/low technology mix, providing large numbers of escorts with reduced capabilities and correspondingly reduced price. These were intended to balance the very expensive specialized ASW and AAW ships, whose primary mission was to protect carriers, and strict limitations were placed on cost, displacement and manpower.

The FFG 7s have been built in small yards utilizing simple construction techniques, making maximum use of flat panels and bulkheads and ensuring that internal passageways are kept as straight as possible. In addition, the hull structure is prefabricated in modules of varying size (35, 100, 200 or 400 tons), to permit shipyards to select the most convenient size for their capabilities.

As with the US Navy's previous frigate classes, the Perrys have only one screw, but the use of gas turbines means that engine-room layout is much more compact. The gas turbines are of the same model used in the Spruance class, and are located side by side in a single engine room. An unusual feature is that two small retractable propulsion pods are fitted just aft of the sonar dome to provide emergency power and to give assistance in docking; each has a 325hp engine, and the two in combination can propel the ship at a speed of some 10 knots.

The armament is air-defence orientated, including a Mk 13 launcher forward for Standard (MR) SAMs and Harpoon ASMs, and an OTO-Melara 76mm (US Navy Mk 75) gun on top of the superstructure. Asroc is not fitted, but there is a large hangar aft for the two LAMPS helicopters.

Starting with USS *Underwood* (FFG 36), the Rapid Haul Down and Traversing System (RAST) is being installed, necessitating an 8ft (2.4m) increase in overall length. This is being achieved by angling out the ship's transom to approximately 45°, and without increasing the waterline length. RAST, TACTAS and LAMPS III support facilities are being installed in all new-build ships from FFG 36 onward. RAST and LAMPS III support facilities will not, at least for the time being, be retrofitted into the earlier ships (FFG 7, 9-16 and 19-34), which will continue to operate LAMPS I (FFG 8 was used as the prototype for the LAMPS III conversion).

The SQS-56 sonar, hull-mounted inside a rubber dome, is a new type, much less sophisticated than the SQS-26. It was planned, however, that the FFG 7 class frigates would operate in company with other frigates equipped with the SQS-26 and would receive target information from sensors on board those ships via data links.

The success of the design can be gauged from the large numbers being built for the US Navy and the fact that it has also been ordered by the Royal Australian and Royal Spanish Navies. The former has already taken delivery of four built in the USA, with another two ordered for construction in Australia, while the latter took delivery of its first two FFG 7 frigates in 1986, when it had a further three on order.

Future: The FFG 7 has been tailored to accommodate only those systems envisaged in the near future, including the SH-60 LAMPS III, SQR-19 towed tactical array, fin stablizers, Link 11 data transfer system and Phalanx CIWS. Once these have been installed, however, there remains only a further 50-ton margin for additional equipment.

Forty-two of the class are currently in service with the US Navy, with a further nine building and another one on order, to complete the authorized total of 52.

The Royal Australian Navy has ordered two to be built to a slightly modified design in Australia (in addition to four built in the US); these will be completed in 1991 and 1993. Five are being built at Ferrol by Bazan for the Royal Spanish Navy. The first was commissioned in 1986 and the remainder will join the fleet between late 1986 and 1990.

Below: USS Robert E Bradley (FFG 49) showing her flight deck, large hangars, Vulcan/Phalanx CIWS and SPG-60 STIR search and tracking radar. These ships have good protection against fragmentation and splinter damage, including ¾in (1.9cm) Kevlar over vital compartments.

Right: The RIM-66B Standard SM-1 (MR) missile has a range of 25nm (46.3km) and uses semi-active homing. The FFG 7 frigates now carry SM-1 (MR) Block 6 missiles with a digital computer and monpulse radar, and 36 are stored in a below-deck magazine. The SM-1 (MR) is fired from a single-arm Mk 13 launcher, which is also capable of firing Harpoon anti-ship missiles four are carried in the same magazine). The Mk 92 Mod 4 system controls the fire of both the SAMs and the 76mm Mk 75 dual-purpose gun, using a STIR antenna and a US-built HSA WM-28 radar.

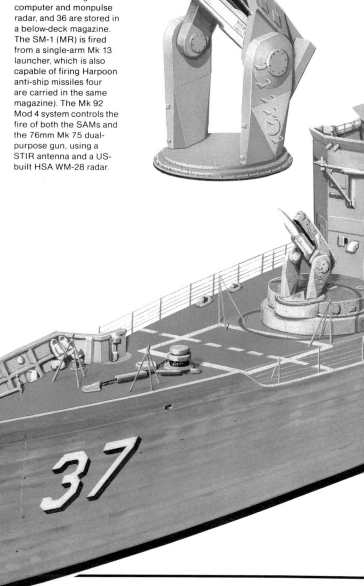

Below: USS *Crommelin* (FFG 37). The large box-like nature of the superstructure is clear from the drawing; this was, at least in part, intended to reduce construction costs, but also gives considerable internal volume.

Below: Sikorsky SH-60B Seahawk LAMPS III ASW helicopter, of which two can be carried by the later FFG 7 class frigates. FFG 7 to FFG 35 (less FFG 8) do not have the facilities for LAMPS III and thus retain the Kaman SH-2F Sea Sprite LAMPS I

helicopter. FFG 8 (the trials ship) and FFG 36 onwards have the longer stern, fin stabilizers and other systems required for LAMPS III, while the Recovery, Assistance, Securing and Traversing (RAST) system wil also be fitted to FFG 50 and later

ships. The SH-60B carries 25 sonobuoys and two Mark 46 ASW torpedoes, and is equipped with ASQ-81 (V) 2 MAD and the ALQ-42 ESM system. All sensor displays are repeated back to the controlling ship via a real-time downlink.

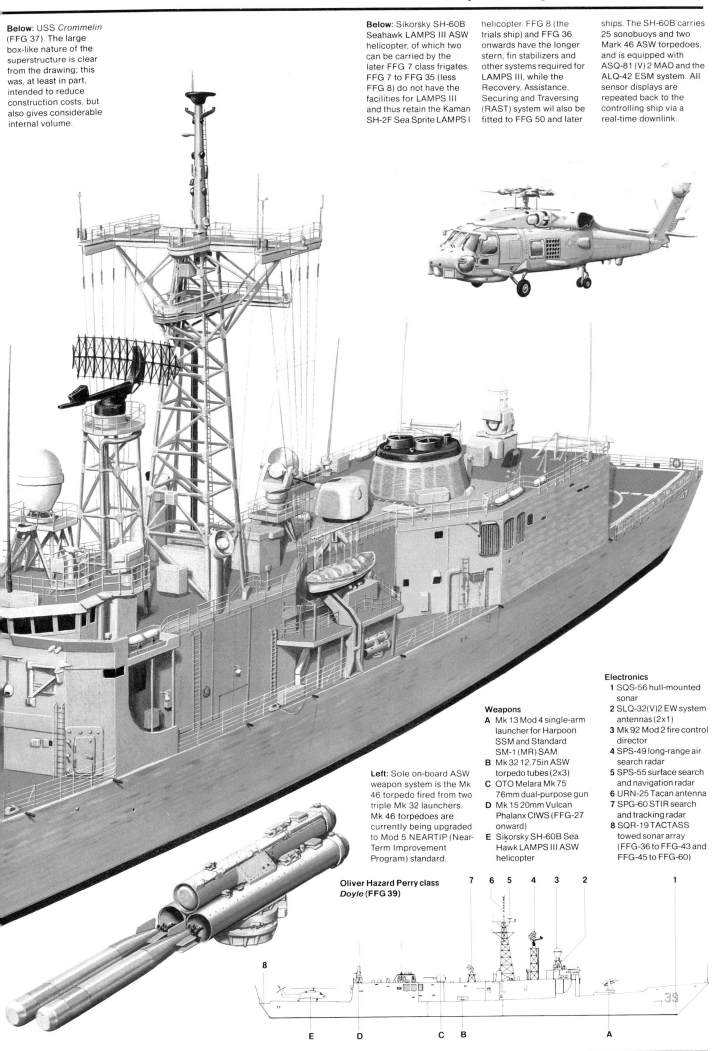

Left: Sole on-board ASW weapon system is the Mk 46 torpedo fired from two triple Mk 32 launchers. Mk 46 torpedoes are currently being upgraded to Mod 5 NEARTIP (Near-Term Improvement Program) standard.

Weapons
A Mk 13 Mod 4 single-arm launcher for Harpoon SSM and Standard SM-1 (MR) SAM
B Mk 32 12.75in ASW torpedo tubes (2x3)
C OTO Melara Mk 75 76mm dual-purpose gun
D Mk 15 20mm Vulcan Phalanx CIWS (FFG-27 onward)
E Sikorsky SH-60B Sea Hawk LAMPS III ASW helicopter

Electronics
1 SQS-56 hull-mounted sonar
2 SLQ-32(V)2 EW system antennas (2x1)
3 Mk 92 Mod 2 fire control director
4 SPS-49 long-range air search radar
5 SPS-55 surface search and navigation radar
6 URN-25 Tacan antenna
7 SPG-60 STIR search and tracking radar
8 SQR-19 TACTASS towed sonar array (FFG-36 to FFG-43 and FFG-45 to FFG-60)

Oliver Hazard Perry class *Doyle* (FFG 39)

Oscar class

Origin: USSR
Type: Nuclear powered cruise missile submarine (SSGN)
Built: 1978
Class: 2 in service; 1 building; production continuing
Displacement: 11,500 tons surfaced; 14,500 tons submerged
Dimensions: Length 492ft (150m) oa; beam 60ft (18.3m); draught 36ft (11m)
Propulsion: 2-shaft nuclear (2 nuclear reactors; 2 steam turbines), 60,000shp
Performance: Speed 35 knots submerged
Weapons: Missiles: 24 SS-N-19 SLCM.
Torpedo tubes: 6 x 21in (533mm)/25.6in (650mm), 18 torpedoes; mines can also be laid
Sensors: Sonar: LF active/passive; MF active.
Radar: Snoop Tray.
Complement: 130.

Background: The Soviet Navy's cruise missile submarines were conceived in the 1950s as an answer to the threat posed by the US Navy's aircraft carrier task groups. Some crude conversions of Whiskey-class boats were followed by the purpose-designed nuclear-powered Echo and conventionally powered Juliett classes, the former adapted from the November class SSNs and the first models carrying six SS-N-3C missiles. These Echo Is were soon superseded by the larger Echo II design, with eight SS-N-3A missiles, 29 are still in service, around ten having had their SS-N-3A missiles replaced by SS-N-12s.

The second-generation Charlie class, which first appeared in 1968, represents a significant improvement, being smaller, quieter and faster and carrying eight SS-N-7 cruise missiles in hatch-covered launch tubes set into the bow casing, where they can be launched while the submarine is submerged. The earlier SSGNs had to surface before firing their missiles.

The first Papa class SSGN was observed by the West in 1973 and, so far as is known, this was the only example ever built. It appears to be a development of the Charlie class, but slightly larger and with a more angular fin, a flatter top profile and square covers on the missile tubes. It may have been built as a general trials and development boat or, more specifically, as part of the development programme for the Oscar class.

The year 1980 saw the launching of two Soviet Navy giants in the shape of the first Typhoon class SSBN and Oscar class SSGN. The 14,000-ton Oscar is armed with no fewer than 24 SS-N-19 anti-ship missiles, which are capable of being fired from underwater. With a submerged speed well in excess of 30 knots an Oscar class SSGN could operate as the advance guard of a Soviet task group, capable of attacking major surface combatants out the 200-250nm range of which the missile is estimated to be capable.

It is assumed that the primary target of Soviet SSGNs continues to be NATO carrier task groups, and that the Oscar class is probably intended to counter the increased protection afforded to US Navy carrier groups in the 1970s by Los Angeles class SSNs and S-3 Viking carrier-borne ASW aircraft. The increased capability required by the SS-N-19, which has an estimated range of 200-250nm. The missile is estimated to be some 32ft (10m) long and is launched from vertical tubes on surface warships such as *Kirov* or submerged submarines. The large number of missiles carried by the Oscar class SSGNs

Weapons
A 21in (533mm) torpedo tubes for ASW torpedoes and SS-N-15/16 missiles (2x3)
B SS-N-19 cruise missile launch tubes (2x12)

Electronics
1 Sonar
2 Periscope
3 Unidentified sensor housing
4 Periscope
5 HF antenna
6 Towed sonar array

Oscar class

Below: This view of an Oscar gives an excellent impression of its shape, but cannot convey its size—with a length of 492ft (150m), 60ft (18.3M) beam and 11,500 ton displacement it is a huge vessel. The hump at the rear of the 105ft (32m) fin (probably the biggest on any submarine) is still a mystery, as is the concave cover on the top of the fin. The hatches abeam the fin cover twin SS-N-19 launchers.

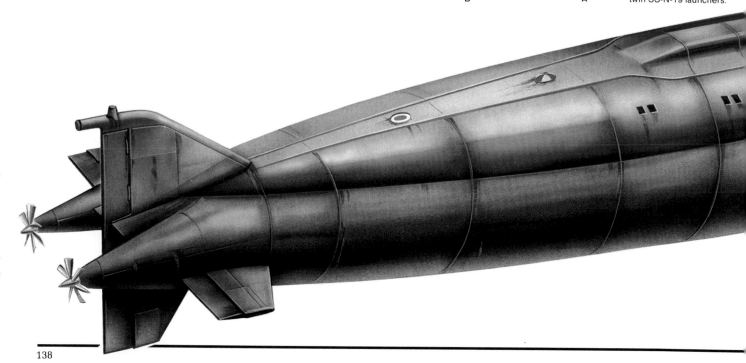

suggests that such an attack might be launched with several missiles, with the intention of overwhelming the task group defences by sheer weight of numbers.

The Oscar class submarines are double-hulled, with 12 missile launch tubes mounted between the inner and outer hulls on each side. The hull, of the usual Soviet shape, is consequently much broader in profile. A prominent tube-shaped device on the tip of the vertical rudder is probably the mooring for a towed sonar array.

Future: Two Oscars are known to have been completed, the first making its trial voyage in June 1981 before deployment with the Northern Fleet. Another Oscar was reportedly seen in a 1984 satellite picture moored alongside a jetty in Vladivostock naval base. Production is therefore assumed to be continuing, although the development of long-range cruise missiles which can be launched from the torpedo tubes, such as SS-NX-21 and an even larger counterpart now under development, may be causing the Soviet Navy to reconsider the need for specialized SSGNs.

Left: A surfaced Oscar shows its rectangular missile hatches, low, squat fin, and the tube on the vertical rudder which is thought to be the mooring point for a towed array. At least two Oscars are now in service and more are building in a major construction programme.

Above: The Oscar's anechoic tiles are fitted in a manner similar to that used for the ablative tiles on the US Space Shuttle—the adhesion problems seem to be similar, too. The hump at the rear of the fin, with two hatch covers, can be seen; its purpose is still unknown.

Left: SS-N-19s are carried by Kirov class battle-cruisers and Oscar class SSGNs. An improved SS-N-12, SS-N-19 is around 30ft (9.1m) long and weighs about 10,000lb (4,536kg); powered by a turbojet, it has a cruise speed of Mach 1.6 and carries either a 350kT nuclear or a conventional high-explosive warhead. Target aquisition requires external inputs.

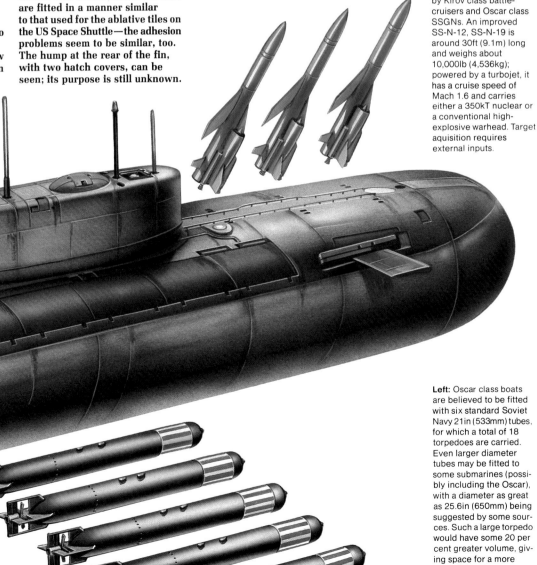

Left: Oscar class boats are believed to be fitted with six standard Soviet Navy 21in (533mm) tubes, for which a total of 18 torpedoes are carried. Even larger diameter tubes may be fitted to some submarines (possibly including the Oscar), with a diameter as great as 25.6in (650mm) being suggested by some sources. Such a large torpedo would have some 20 per cent greater volume, giving space for a more powerful motor, and longer range and larger warheads than is possible with the 21in weapon.

Pauk class

Origin: USSR
Type: Fast attack craft (PG)
Built: 1977-
Class: 14 in service; more building
Displacement: 480 tons standard; 580 tons full load
Dimensions: Length 187.7ft (57.2m) oa; beam 34.4ft (10.5m); draught 8.2ft (2.5m)
Propulsion: 2-shaft diesel, 20,000shp
Performance: Speed 28-32 knots
Weapons: Missiles: 1 SA-N-5 SAM launcher (18 missiles);
Guns: 1 3in 160; 1 30mm ADMG-630 Gatling
ASW Weapons: 4 x 1 16in (406mm) UTR torpedo tubes; 2 RBU-1200; 2 depth-charge racks (12 DCs)
Sensors: Radar: Peel Cone combined search; Bass Tilt fire control; Spin Trough navigation
Sonar: 1 MF hull-mounted; 1 MF dipping on transom
Complement: 40

Background: The Soviet Navy, with considerable experience in protecting the very long coastline of the USSR, has developed a series of small warships for close-in protection, ranging from 200-ton fast attack craft such as the Stenka class to 1,000-ton corvettes such as the Petya and Grisha classes. The latest type, falling between the two extremes, is the Pauk class (Pauk, the Russian word for spider, has been allocated by NATO; the Soviet name is not known).

Designated *maly protivolodochny korabl* (small anti-submarine ship) by the Soviet Navy, the Pauk design is especially interesting as one of the smallest specialized anti-submarine ships in any contemporary navy. First seen by Western observers in 1980, it is intended to replace the ageing Poti class.

The ASW sensor and weapon fit is probably as comprehensive as possible in a hull of this size. There is a prominent housing for a dipping sonar on the transom, making the Pauk the smallest ship to carry such a device, as well as a hull-mounted sonar in the bow position. Main ASW weapons are four 16in (406mm) electric-powered acoustic homing torpedoes, mounted amidships; there are also two RBU-1200 250mm ASW mortars for close-in attack and, for good measure, two six-round depth-charge racks mounted at the stern on either side of the VDS housing.

In an unusual step for the Soviet Navy, the hull is identical with that of the Tarantul class, a neat, workmanlike design. The dipping sonar is housed in a box 10.5ft (3.2m) long, 10.5ft (3.2m) wide and 13.8ft (4.2m) high and inset into the transom with a 4.26ft (1.3m) overhang. There is a curious side-deck on the starboard side abreast the mast, which serves no readily apparent purpose apart from giving roof cover for one of the four torpedo tubes; it may be for a future weapons system.

The Soviet predilection for ever larger guns is followed on the Pauk, which has a single 3in

dual-purpose mounting on the forecastle. For close-in air defence there is an ADMG-630 six-barrel Gatling on the after superstructure, together with an SA-N-5 Grail SAM launcher below it on the quarter-back. These air-defence systems are controlled by a single Bass Tilt director, mounted on a pedestal at the after end of the bridge structure. The propulsion system is all-diesel, exhaust outlets being located in the hull sides.

The Pauk class has only been encountered so far in the Baltic Sea and the Pacific Ocean. Some are believed to be operated by the KGB as patrol boats.

As in so many other classes, the Soviet naval architects have managed to pack a great deal in a small hull and this class represents a substantial addition to the Soviet short-range ASW forces. Western ship designers could well take note of this class, which will undoubtedly be built in large numbers.

Future: The Pauk class is in full production at three yards: Yaroslavl, Khabarovsk and one other. It seems probable that the type, having proved itself, will continue in production for some years to come: the Poti class, which it replaces, numbered 59.

Above: Pauk class fast attack craft of the Soviet Navy, photographed in the Baltic. This picture shows clearly the neat lines of this type, and how good design has enabled heavy weapon and sensor outfits to be fitted into a comparatively small hull. The Pauk is typical of the large numbers of small (ie, under 1,000 tons) but nevertheless very effective surface combatants serving with the Soviet Navy and KGB border guard units for offshore duties.

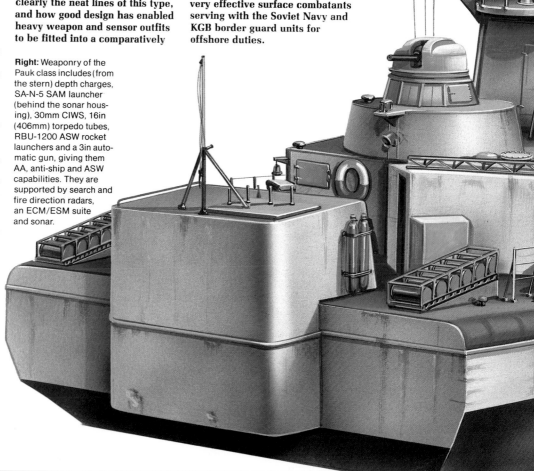

Right: Weaponry of the Pauk class includes (from the stern) depth charges, SA-N-5 SAM launcher (behind the sonar housing), 30mm CIWS, 16in (406mm) torpedo tubes, RBU-1200 ASW rocket launchers and a 3in automatic gun, giving them AA, anti-ship and ASW capabilities. They are supported by search and fire direction radars, an ECM/ESM suite and sonar.

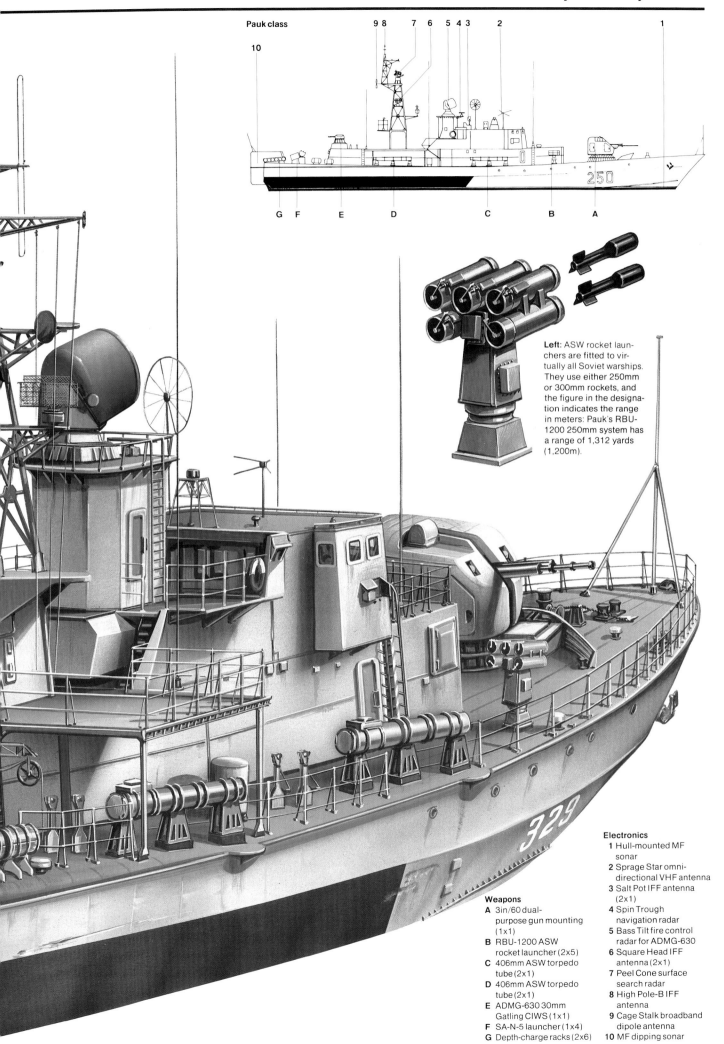

Pauk class

Left: ASW rocket launchers are fitted to virtually all Soviet warships. They use either 250mm or 300mm rockets, and the figure in the designation indicates the range in meters: Pauk's RBU-1200 250mm system has a range of 1,312 yards (1,200m).

Weapons
A 3in/60 dual-purpose gun mounting (1x1)
B RBU-1200 ASW rocket launcher (2x5)
C 406mm ASW torpedo tube (2x1)
D 406mm ASW torpedo tube (2x1)
E ADMG-630 30mm Gatling CIWS (1x1)
F SA-N-5 launcher (1x4)
G Depth-charge racks (2x6)

Electronics
1 Hull-mounted MF sonar
2 Sprage Star omni-directional VHF antenna
3 Salt Pot IFF antenna (2x1)
4 Spin Trough navigation radar
5 Bass Tilt fire control radar for ADMG-630
6 Square Head IFF antenna (2x1)
7 Peel Cone surface search radar
8 High Pole-B IFF antenna
9 Cage Stalk broadband dipole antenna
10 MF dipping sonar

Resolution class

Origin: United Kingdom
Type: Nuclear-powered ballistic missile submarine (SSBN)
Built: 1966-1969
Class: 4 in service
Displacement: 7,600 tons surfaced; 8,500 tons submerged
Dimensions: Length 425ft (129.5m) oa; beam 33ft (10.1m); draught 30ft (9.1m)
Propulsion: 1-shaft nuclear (1 pressurized-water-cooled nuclear reactor; geared steam turbines), 15,000shp
Performance: 20 knots surfaced, 25 knots submerged

Weapons: Missiles: 16 Polaris A-3 SLBM
Torpedo tubes: 6 x 21in (533m)
Sensors: Sonar: Type 2001; Type 2007
Radar: I-band search
Complement: 143

Background: In the late 1950s the British government planned that the Royal Air Force would continue to provide the national strategic nuclear deterrent through the 1960s and 1970s, using V-bombers armed with the US Skybolt missile. However, following the unilateral (and very unexpected) US decision to abandon Skybolt, President Kennedy agreed at the hastily convened 1962 Nassau conference to provide Polaris A-3 missiles for installation in British-built nuclear submarines. An important feature of the agreement was that the British would provide the nuclear warheads and reentry vehicles, enabling them to retain control over the use and targeting of the missiles.

Four submarines were built of a planned total of five, the last boat being cancelled in the 1965 Defence Review. Much technical assistance was obtained from the US and the Resolution class is generally similar to the US Lafayette-class SSBNs, although the Resolutions' actual design was developed from that of the British Valiant-class SSNs, with the addition of a missile compartment between the control centre and the reactor room.

The first boat was commissioned on October 2, 1967, and the fourth and last on December 4, 1969. Because of the need always to have at least one boat in refit, the

Right: Resolution class SSBNs are armed with 16 Polaris SLBMs mounted in two rows of eight abaft the fin. The Royal Navy is now the only user of the Polaris, although all its missiles have been updated with Chevaline MRV warheads. Chevaline is based on the fascinating idea that, instead of using decoys that resemble RVs, the RVs are made to resemble decoys.

Below: Royal Navy Resolution class SSBN running at speed on the surface. Its bow wave and wake pattern, similar to those of US SSBNs offer an interesting contrast with those of the French Le Redoutable class boats. The four British SSBNs completed in 1966-69 need replacing in the 1990s; the first of the new Trident boats was ordered in 1986.

Above: The British Resolution class SSBN design was developed from that of the Valiant class SSN, with a missile compartment being added between the control centre and the reactor section. The result has been a most successful class, which celebrates the twentieth anniversary of its first operational patrol on June 22, 1987. Each boat has two crews ('Gold' and 'Silver'). One of the class is always in long refit, one in short refit, and one always at sea. The fourth is usually, but not always, also at sea, and it has been a matter of regret for many that the fifth hull was never built. The new Trident class SSBNs will have a displacement of some 14,800 tons; they will be about 492ft (150m) long with a beam of 42ft (12.8m). The first, *Vanguard*, has been laid down at the Vickers yard in Barrow-in-Furness and the boat will enter operational service in the early 1990s, armed with Trident II D-5 SLBMs. The whole programme has caused considerable controversy in the UK, both on the political desirability of such a plan and also whether it is militarily the best option for the British in the 1990s. Certainly it will be very expensive, but unless the UK decides to opt out of the strategic nuclear business altogether, there seems to be no practicable and affordable alternative.

Royal Navy can only guarantee to have one boat on patrol at any one time, with a second some of the time. Many problems would have been avoided had the fifth boat been built, and it is noteworthy that the French, in a similar strategic position, planned to have five boats but have gone on to build a sixth.

The Resolution-class SSBNs have 16 vertical missile launch tubes abaft the sail. The actual missiles are Polaris A-3s purchased from the USA, but age-related deterioration has recently necessitated the

fitting of new rocket motors, a very expensive undertaking involving reopening the production lines and the use of 1960s technology.

The three reentry vehicles (RVs) have also been replaced to overcome updated Soviet defences. Because of the national requirement for targeting autonomy the British undertook this as a national programme, codenamed Chevaline, at a cost of some £1,000 million. The total number of the new manoeuvrable reentry vehicles (MRVs) is believed to be in the region of three per missile; the yield of individual

MRVs has also not been announced but is probably about 40kT.

Future: Following prolonged debate, which has included detailed consideration of a variety of alternative options, the British government has announced its intention to purchase Trident II D-5 missiles from the USA. As with the Polaris missiles, an entirely British front-end will be fitted, thus ensuring national control of the system. Apart from replacing the elderly Polaris missiles, the Royal Navy also needs to replace the Resolution-class SSBNs, which,

although very reliable and successful, will be obsolete by the beginning of the 1990s, so the new missiles will be deployed in this new class of British-designed and-built SSBN. Four are currently planned, but, as with the Resolution class, the decision on the fifth will be taken later (in view of the escalating costs of the programme, this almost inevitably means that history will be repeated and the fifth boat will not be built). Construction of the SSBNs started in 1986; the first should be operational.

Right: HMS Resolution (S 22) passes under the Forth road bridge on her way to another patrol, part of the ceaseless vigil which is essential to maintain the peace in the current balance of power.

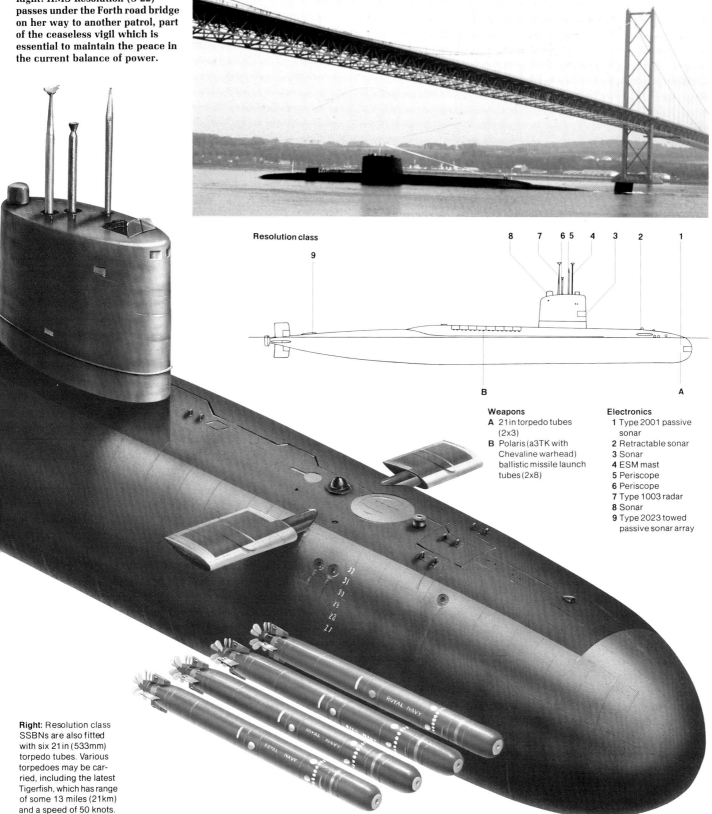

Resolution class

Weapons
A 21in torpedo tubes (2x3)
B Polaris (a3TK with Chevaline warhead) ballistic missile launch tubes (2x8)

Electronics
1 Type 2001 passive sonar
2 Retractable sonar
3 Sonar
4 ESM mast
5 Periscope
6 Periscope
7 Type 1003 radar
8 Sonar
9 Type 2023 towed passive sonar array

Right: Resolution class SSBNs are also fitted with six 21in (533mm) torpedo tubes. Various torpedoes may be carried, including the latest Tigerfish, which has range of some 13 miles (21km) and a speed of 50 knots.

Rubis (SNA 72) class

Origin: France
Type: Nuclear-powered attack submarine (SSN)
Built: 1976-1991
Class: 2 in service; 3 building
Displacement: 2,385 tons surfaced; 2,670 tons submerged
Dimensions: Length 236.5ft (72.1m) oa; beam 24.9ft (7.6m); draught 21ft (6.4m)
Propulsion: 1-shaft nuclear (1 48MW nuclear reactor; 2 turbo-alternators; one main motor)
Performance: Speed 25 knots submerged; diving depth 980ft (300m)
Weapons: Torpedo tubes: 4 x 21in (533mm); 14 L17 and L5 Mod 4 torpedoes and SM.39 missiles
Sensors: Sonar: DSUV 22 passive; DUUA 2B active; DUUX 2 or DUUX 5 ranging
Radar: Calypso IV surface navigation
Complement: 66.

Background: The US, Soviet and British navies started their nuclear-powered submarine fleets with SSNs and then graduated to SSBNs, because missile technology lagged behind that of propulsion systems. France, however, was late on the scene, and under strong pressure from President de Gaulle the French Navy went straight to SSBNs. Not surprisingly, such a massive programme, which for political reasons had to be entirely French in character, took up all available resources for many years, and it was not until the 1974 programme that the French Navy was able to turn its attention to SSNs. The first of class, *Rubis* (S 601)—originally named *Provence*—was laid down in December 1976 and launched on July 7, 1979. She joined the fleet on February 28, 1983, after extensive trials.

The Rubis class boats are the smallest SSNs in any navy. Their hull design is based fairly closely on that of the Agosta class conventional submarines, but they are characterized by a bigger sail with the horizontal hydroplanes set about two-thirds of the way up it. To be able to construct such a small nuclear-powered submarine suggests that the French Navy has made significant progress in nuclear reactor design since producing the rather large devices in the Le Redoubtable class SSBNs, and it is generally accepted that this involves the use of liquid metal cooling in the reactor.

Armament, sonar and fire-control systems are based on those currently in service in the Agosta class, including torpedo tubes of the international standard 21in (533mm) diameter, indicating a final abandonment of the 21.7in (550mm) torpedo. From 1985 onward the Rubis class has been equipped to launch the SM.39 derivative of the very successful MM.38 Exocet anti-ship missile. Like the US Navy's Sub-Harpoon, the SM.39 is designed to be tube-launched from a submerged submarine.

There are two crews for each submarine, each of nine officers

Rubis class

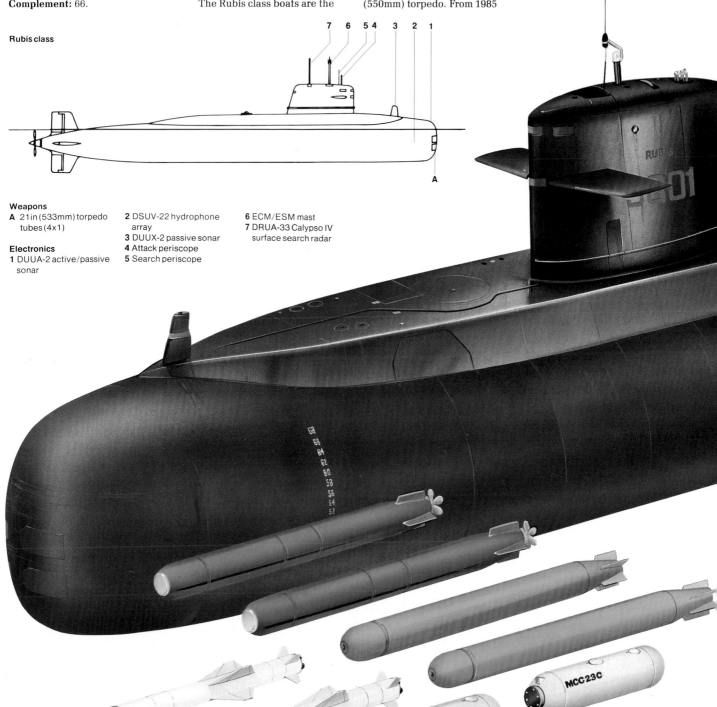

Weapons
A 21in (533mm) torpedo tubes (4x1)

Electronics
1 DUUA-2 active/passive sonar
2 DSUV-22 hydrophone array
3 DUUX-2 passive sonar
4 Attack periscope
5 Search periscope
6 ECM/ESM mast
7 DRUA-33 Calypso IV surface search radar

and 57 ratings, ensuring maximum utilization of the hull. The average patrol is estimated to last 45 days.

The *Rubis* and her two crews were subject to an exacting test of their capabilities in 1985, when she carried out a round-the-world voyage. Leaving Toulon on March 25, she steamed to Noumea, South Caledonia, arriving on May 10, and after three weeks of routine maintenance and a change of crew she participated in joint exercises in the Pacific, before leaving Tahiti on July 28. When she returned to Toulon on September 4 she had travelled 33,000nm submerged.

Future: The French Navy intends to construct five of these submarines, to be based at Toulon and Lorient. The third of the class, *Casablanca*, will join the fleet in mid-1987, and the remaining two, S 604 and S605, in 1989 and 1991.

Above: The French Navy's first SSN, Rubis (S 601), at sea. She is by far the smallest of the current SSNs, a fact which is generally attributed to a major advance by the French in maritime nuclear propulsion technology. The hull is similar in size and design to that of the conventional Agosta class, which helped shorten the development cycle for the new class. A total of five are currently planned.

Below: Sapphir (S 602), second of the five-boat Rubis class, is launched from her construction hall at Cherbourg on September 1, 1981. The large space required for the bow-mounted Thomson-CSF DUUA-2 sonar is clearly visible. At this stage of construction the fin has not been completed and the fin-mounted hydroplanes have yet to be installed. This class has been designed to give the 66-man crew optimum living conditions for their long, totally submerged patrols.

Left: Rubis class SSNs are armed with four torpedo tubes, for which 14 torpedoes and missiles can be carried. The F17 (top left pair), designed for use against surface ships, is either wire-guided or automatic homing and can switch rapidly between the two. The L5 Mod 4 (not illustrated) is an anti-submarine torpedo. The SM.39 Exocet missile is tube-launched inside a container (centre) and operates in a similar manner to the US Navy's Sub-Harpoon. Finally, a variety of mines can be laid, including the Thomson-CSF TSM 35 10 (MCC-23C) seabed weapon shown here, a multi-sensor device.

Above: The *Rubis* is typical of modern French practice, with a blunt, straight-stemmed bow, a cylindrical hull with angular top deck, fin-mounted forward and cruciform stern hydroplanes, and a single slow-turning large-diameter propeller. The bow shape makes an interesting comparison with the much more rounded bows of other modern submarines such as the Trafalgar and Walrus, and is in total contrast to the bulbous bow shape now used by the Soviets, for example in the Oscar class. Compared with the Agosta class, the fin is much larger and the forward hydroplanes are fin-mounted.

Sheffield (Type 42) class

Origin: United Kingdom
Type: Destroyer (DDG)
Built: 1972-1985
Class: (Batch 1) 4 in service (Batch 2) 4 in service (Batch 3) 4 in service
Displacement: (1 and 2) 3,500 tons standard; 4,100 tons full load (3) 4,775 tons full load
Dimensions: (1 and 2) Length 412ft (125m) oa; beam 47ft (14.3m); draught 19ft (5.8m) (3) Length 462ft (141.1m) oa; beam 49ft (14.9m); draught 19ft (5.8m)
Propulsion: 2-shaft COGOG (2 Rolls-Royce Olympus TM3B and 2 Rolls-Royce Tyne RMIC gas turbines), 50,000/9,700shp
Performance: Speed 29 knots (30 knots 3); range 4,000nm at 18 knots
Armament: SAM: 1 x 2 Sea Dart launcher (22 missiles) Guns: 1 x 4.5in/55 Mk 8; 2 20mm Oerlikon (GAM-B01)
Aircraft: 1 Lynx Mk 2 helicopter
Sensors: Radar: Type 1022 search; Type 992Q/R surveillance and target indication; 2 Type 909 Sea Dart fire control; Type 1006 navigation Sonar: Type 184M (Type 2016 in later ships) hull-mounted
Complement: (1 and 2) 253; (3) 301

Background: Area air defence for Royal Navy carrier-based task forces was provided in the 1960s and 1970s by the County class destroyers armed with the Sea Slug SAM and these were to have been followed by the Bristol class (Type 82) guided-missile destroyers. These three-funnel warships of 7,100 tons full load displacement were designed around the smaller, more capable Sea Dart SAM with a single 4.5in Mk 8 mount and an Ikara ASM launcher forward. Their great cost (over £30 million at 1970 prices), coupled with the cancellation of the aircraft carrier CVA-01, led to the cancellation of the class as a whole, although one Type 82 — HMS *Bristol* (D 23) — was actually completed.

The Type 42 class was designed as a cheaper, smaller and less sophisticated version of Bristol, although the vessels are still complex and highly automated vessels, and the latest of the class cost some £78.5-85 million each at 1979 prices. They have the Rolls-Royce Olympus/Type COGOG machinery combination, which is virtually standard for this genera-tion of surface warships in the Royal Navy, and a hangar and flight deck aft for a Lynx ASW helicopter. The Sea Dart SAM has a limited SSM capability and the single launcher is fitted forward between the gun mount and the bridge. The unsightly and extremely unpopular exhausts fitted to *Sheffield's* funnel to overcome efflux problems were removed and have not featured on any other ships of the class.

Two ships of this class were lost during the 1982 South Atlantic war. On May 4 HMS *Sheffield* sank after being hit by an air-launched Exocet several days earlier, while on May 25 HMS *Coventry* was hit by several bombs

which exploded in or near her machinery spaces, and she capsized shortly afterwards with the loss of 19 lives.

The third batch of ships of this class has been completed to a rather different design, with beam and length increased, in an operation similar to that performed on the Type 22 frigates, to improve speed and sea-keeping qualities and to provide more space for weapon systems, although it goes against the modern concept of shorter, beamier ships. These later ships also incorporate a number of improvements based on experiences with their sisters in the South Atlantic war.

Future: A number of ships of this class took part in the 1982 South Atlantic war and two—*Sheffield* and *Coventry*—were lost in combat. This led to a reappraisal of the weapons fit and extra mountings can be embarked on all ships when required. These will normally comprise two BMARC twin 30mm and two extra single 20mm (GAM-B01) at either side of the forward end of the hangar. Consideration is also being given

to fitting the vertical launch version of Sea Wolf. If this goes ahead *Birmingham* (Batch 1) will probably be the first to be so fitted.

Perhaps the major area of controversy in future British surface warship design is that of the hull shape of destroyer/frigate sized ships. So involved and heated have the arguments between the traditional 'long thin' and the innovatory 'short fat' schools become that an unofficial committee, chaired by former Chief of the Defence Staff Admiral of the Fleet Lord Hill-Norton, has examined the whole issue. It reported in June 1986 that an official enquiry, chaired by an independent expert, was needed to resolve the issues, having concluded that the shorter, beamier S90 frigate (designed by naval architects Thornycroft Giles and Associates) could be built for £73.8 million compared with £100 million for the new offically designed Type 23.

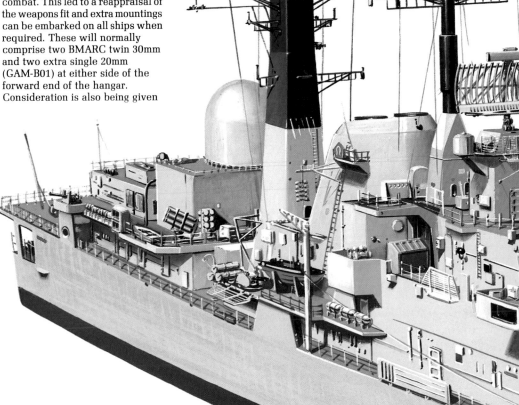

Right: The Westland Lynx HAS.2 has proved itself to be an excellent ASW weapons system. It carries two Mk 44 or Mk 46 ASW torpedoes or up to four Sea Skua air-to-surface missiles.

Right: Having followed the common trend and progressively reduced close-in anti-aircraft gun armament during the 1960s and 1970s, the Royal Navy found itself woefully short of such systems in the 1982 South Atlantic War. Various weapons were hastily procured, inclu-ding the Vulcan/Phalanx CIWS (which were fitted to the carriers), Oerlikon single 20mm AA Type GAM-B01 and Oerlikon 30mm twin GCM-A02 (shown here). Eight GCM-A02 mounts were acquired, all of which were fitted to Type 42 destroyers. In the long term, however, a radar-controlled, multi-barrelled system is needed, such as the Dutch Goalkeeper.

Left: Type 42 Batch 1 guided-missile destroyer, HMS Glasgow (D 88), which suffered a fire during fitting-out; her completion was much delayed as a result. The 4.5in Mk 8 DP gun shares the foredeck with the Sea Dart GWS 30 Mod 2 guided missile system. Note the huge twin-stack Type 965M radar and the two radomes for the Type 909 fire control radar, which controls both the Sea Dart missiles and the 4.5in gun. Two of the class, Sheffield (D 80) and Coventry (D 118), were lost in the South Atlantic War, the first to an Exocet, the second to bombs.

Weapons

A Vickers 4.5in/55 Mk 8 dual-purpose automatic gun (1x1)
B GWS 30 Mod 2 Sea Dart SAM launcher (1x2)
C 20mm AA gun (2x1)
D 12.75in STWS-1 ASW torpedo tubes (2x3)
E Westland Lynx HAS.2 ASW helicopter
F 30mm Oerlikon GCM-AO2 AA gun (2x1)
G 20mm Oerlikon GAM-BO1 AA gun (2x1)

Electronics

1 Type 162M sonar
2 Type 184M sonar
3 Type 909 fire control radar for GWS 30 Sea Dart system and gunlaying
4 Type 965M long-range air search radar
5 SCOT satellite communications antenna
6 Type 1006 naviagation radar
7 Type 992Q surface/air target information radar
8 Corvus chaff rocket launcher (2x8)
9 Type 909 fire control radar for GWS 30 Sea Dart system/gunlaying
10 Mk 36 Super RBOC chaff rocket launcher (2x6)
11 Type 2016 sonar
12 Type 1002 air search radar

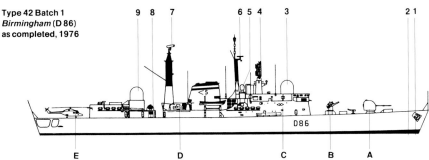

Type 42 Batch 1
Birmingham (D 86)
as completed, 1976

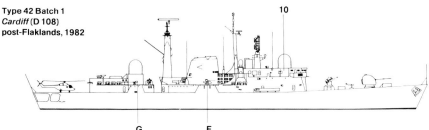

Type 42 Batch 1
Cardiff (D 108)
post-Flaklands, 1982

Type 42 Batch 3
Manchester

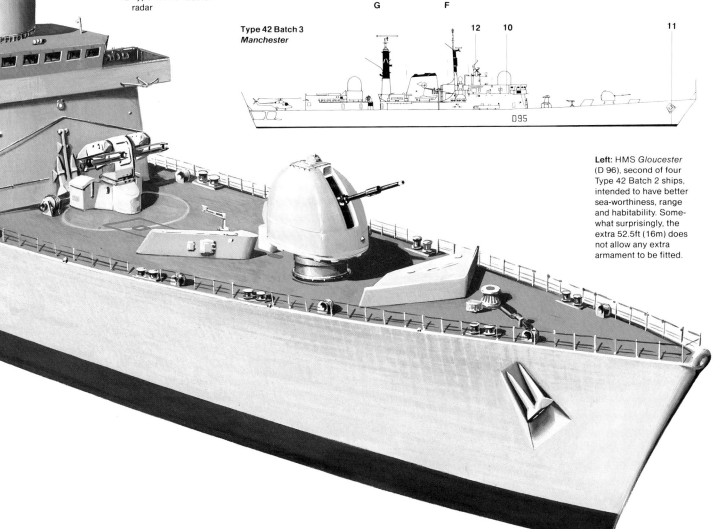

Left: HMS *Gloucester* (D 96), second of four Type 42 Batch 2 ships, intended to have better sea-worthiness, range and habitability. Somewhat surprisingly, the extra 52.5ft (16m) does not allow any extra armament to be fitted.

Sierra class

Origin: USSR
Type: Nuclear-powered attack submarine (SSN)
Built: 1982-
Class: 2 in service; more building
Displacement: 8,000 tons submerged
Dimensions: Length 360.8ft (110m) oa; beam 36ft (11m); draught 24ft (7.4m)
Propulsion: 1-shaft nuclear (2 nuclear reactors; 1 steam turbine), 40,000shp approx
Performance: Speed 32 knots
Weapons: Missiles: SS-N-15, SS-N-16 and SS-N-21
Torpedo tubes: 6 x 21in
Sensors: Sonar: 1 LF bow-mounted
Complement: 85 approx

Background: The Soviet Union's submarine building rate and the multiplicity of classes in simultaneous production continues to astonish and dismay observers in the West. By 1986 there were three classes of SSN (Mike, Sierra, and Akula) and two of SSBN (Delta IV and Typhoon) as well as Oscar class SSGNs and Kilo class SSKs under construction, indicating an allocation of financial, industrial and manpower resources that the whole of the West in combination can scarcely equal.

The first Soviet SSNs, the November class, entered service between 1958 and 1963. They had a long, inefficient hull with a multiplicity of free-flood holes, making them very noisy and relatively easy to detect, and several were involved in accidents, including one which sank in the Western Approaches to the English Channel in April 1970. The Victor class that followed was a substantial step forward, with teardrop hulls and a new nuclear reactor system. The 16 Victor Is built between 1965 and 1974 were followed by seven Victor IIs (1970-78), whose hulls were lengthened by 29ft (9m) to house the SS-N-15 anti-submarine missile system. The design was further improved to produce the Victor III class (1978-84), the first of 20 being built at Leningrad and the remainder at Komsomolsk. This version incorporated a variety of improvements, the most noticeable being the bullet-shaped housing for the towed sonar array mounted on top of the vertical rudder.

Next to appear was the impressive Alfa class. These titanium-hulled boats have a diving depth of 2,500ft (700m) and their submerged speed of more than 42 knots has been demonstrated to spectacular effect on at least one NATO exercise. It appears that the Alfa class boats may have been used as operational test-beds for various features; production has been slow and at least one of the class was scrapped after only a few years' service. This line of development has led to the new Mike class.

The first boat of the Sierra class was launched in July 1983 and went to sea in 1984. It is bigger and faster than the Victor III and has a similar 'bullet' atop the vertical rudder. At first thought to be for a towed sonar array, this may, in

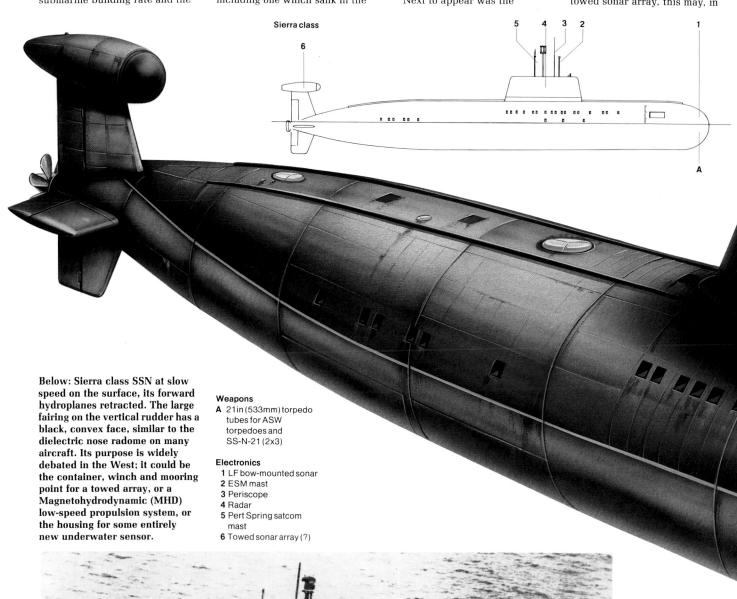

Sierra class

Below: Sierra class SSN at slow speed on the surface, its forward hydroplanes retracted. The large fairing on the vertical rudder has a black, convex face, similar to the dielectric nose radome on many aircraft. Its purpose is widely debated in the West; it could be the container, winch and mooring point for a towed array, or a Magnetohydrodynamic (MHD) low-speed propulsion system, or the housing for some entirely new underwater sensor.

Weapons
A 21in (533mm) torpedo tubes for ASW torpedoes and SS-N-21 (2x3)

Electronics
1 LF bow-mounted sonar
2 ESM mast
3 Periscope
4 Radar
5 Pert Spring satcom mast
6 Towed sonar array (?)

Above: The Sierra class SSN shows the result of many years of underwater research by Soviet designers (helped by espionage against the West), which results in a hull form closely resembling that of a large whale. The forward hydroplanes are shown retracted for surface running; they may also be progressively retracted underwater as speed increases.

fact, be for some form of propulsion, possibly associated with a magnetohydrodynamic (MHD) generator. Compared with the Victor III, the forward hydroplanes are further down on the bow and the fin is somewhat more angular, although markedly lower than in Western SSNs.

These are clearly very capable boats, and are built specifically for use against other submarines. No Western expert is certain (at least in public) why the Soviet Navy is producing three types of nuclear powered attack submarine simultaneously, though it is possible that the Mike class represents the high end of the technology spectrum while the Sierra is the low end, using tried and trusted techniques in a modest advance on the Victor III class. A similar approach has seen the advanced Kirov class battle-cruisers and the more conventional Slava class produced concurrently, the latter providing a safeguard against failure. On the other hand, it could be that at least one of the three submarines is an experimental type, as was the case with the single Papa class SSGN produced in the early 1970s.

Future: The precise way in which the Mike, Sierra and Akula classes fit into the Soviet Navy's plans is not yet clear. However, it seems improbable that even Soviet resources can support the continuing construction of three quite different types of SSN, all of much the same size and apparently similar capabilities.

Right: 1984 photograph of a Sierra class SSN lying motionless on the surface, with a group of seagulls enjoying the unexpected resting place. The purpose of the twin track lines running along the top of the hull is still not clear. The low height of the fin means that when running at periscope depth the top of the hull, and, probably more significantly, the stern bullet fairing, will be very close to the surface, making detection relatively easy for any surface or airborne sub-hunter. The bullet is some 29.5ft (9m) long and around 8.2ft (2.5m) in diameter.

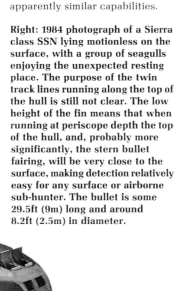

Above: The SS-N-21 cruise missile is fired from standard 21in (533mm) torpedo tubes. Conceptually similar to the US Tomahawk, it flies low at high subsonic speed.

Slava class

Origin: USSR
Type: Guided-missile cruiser (CG)
Built: 1976-
Class: 3 in service
Displacement: 7,375 tons standard; 10,200 tons full load
Dimensions: Length 607.9ft (185.3m) oa; beam 65.6ft (20m); draught 21ft (6.4m)
Propulsion: 2-shaft COGOG (4 gas turbines), 121,000shp
Performance: Speed 33 knots; range 10,000nm at 16 knots
Weapons: Missiles: 16 SS-N-12; 8 SA-N-6 vertical launchers (64 missiles); 2 twin SA-N-4 launchers (40 missiles)
Guns: 1 twin 130mm L/70; 6 ADMG-630 30mm CIWS
ASW: 2 RBU-6000; 2 x 5 533mm M/57 torpedo tubes
Aircraft: 1 Ka-25 Hormone-B or Ka-27 Helix helicopter
Sensors: 3D surveillance radar: Top Pair; Top Steer
Fire Control radar: Front Door/Front Piece (SS-N-12); Top Dome (SA-N-6); 2 Pop Group (SA-N-4); 3 Bass Tilt (30mm Gatlings); Kite Screech (130mm)
Navigation radar: Three Palm Frond
Sonar: 1 MF bow-mounted; 1 MF variable-depth
Complement: 480

Background: There was some surprise in Western naval circles in the 1960s when the Soviet Navy's Kresta-II class cruisers appeared with their fixed battery of eight launchers mounted alongside the bridge—it was remarked that the Soviet designers were "putting all the ship's armament in the shop window". There was even greater surprise when the *Slava* revealed her unique battery of 16 SS-N-12s in fixed launch tubes sited en echelon either side of the bridge superstructure.

The Slava class was initially known in the West as BLACKCOM

1 (BLACK Sea COMbatant), as it was being built at the Nikolayev North shipyard on the Black Sea. Then, for a short period it was designated the Krasina class, before the first ship was finally observed at sea and the Soviet class name Slava discovered.

The object of this design is presumably to provide the ship with the largest possible number of missiles without the complexity of automatic reloading devices. The SS-N-12 launchers are mounted at a fixed elevation of about 8°, and there are no reloads. Two rows of four SA-N-6 silos are installed between the funnels and the aircraft hangar, and there is a twin SA-N-4 silo at each side of the after end of the hangar. A twin 130mm automatic gun is mounted on the foredeck, and the close-in system comprises six 30mm Gatlings, two on the forward superstructure and another two on each side just forward of the funnel. ASW weapons include quintuple fixed 533mm torpedo tubes either side of the aircraft hangar and two RBU-6000 rocket launchers forward

of the bridge.

The sensor fit is to the usual comprehensive Soviet standards, including a stern-mounted variable-depth sonar of the same type as fitted to the Kirov and Udaloy classes.

These large ships have nothing revolutionary in their design and it is generally agreed that they were constructed against the possible failure of the far more adventurous Kirov class battle-cruisers—indeed, the whole design smacks of playing safe. Nevertheless, they are still very powerful units, clearly intended for major actions against surface and air attack, and capable of distant-water deployments.

Future: The Slava class appears to be an interim type, produced against the possible failure of the Kirov class battle-cruisers. Only three are known to have been constructed and it may well be that the class will not be expanded.

Above: Slava in the Mediterranean, January 26, 1986. The pennant number differs from that in the main illustration because the Soviet Navy allocates such numbers for a tactical purpose; when the mission changes so does the number.

Below: Slava, name ship of the class. Note the large launch bins for the SS-N-12 anti-ship missiles, with the Punch Bowl satellite communications antenna above

the after pair. Also clearly shown is the ECM/ESM fit (on the left of the picture), with the vertical row of four Side Globe EW antennas flanked by two Rum Tubs.

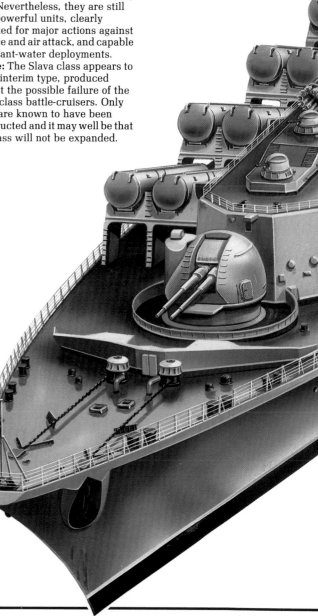

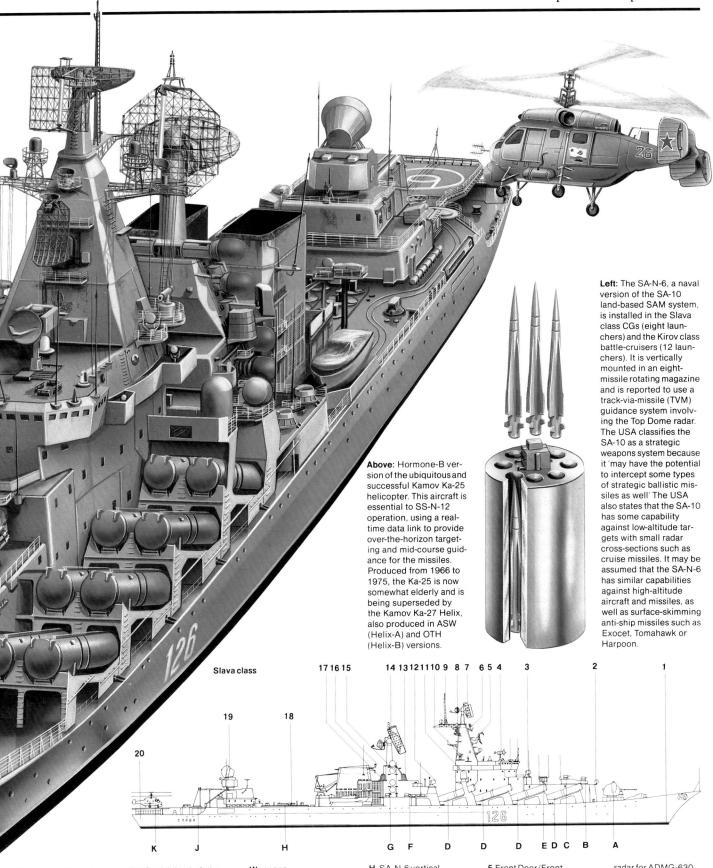

Above: Hormone-B version of the ubiquitous and successful Kamov Ka-25 helicopter. This aircraft is essential to SS-N-12 operation, using a real-time data link to provide over-the-horizon targeting and mid-course guidance for the missiles. Produced from 1966 to 1975, the Ka-25 is now somewhat elderly and is being superseded by the Kamov Ka-27 Helix, also produced in ASW (Helix-A) and OTH (Helix-B) versions.

Left: The SA-N-6, a naval version of the SA-10 land-based SAM system, is installed in the Slava class CGs (eight launchers) and the Kirov class battle-cruisers (12 launchers). It is vertically mounted in an eight-missile rotating magazine and is reported to use a track-via-missile (TVM) guidance system involving the Top Dome radar. The USA classifies the SA-10 as a strategic weapons system because it 'may have the potential to intercept some types of strategic ballistic missiles as well.' The USA also states that the SA-10 has some capability against low-altitude targets with small radar cross-sections such as cruise missiles. It may be assumed that the SA-N-6 has similar capabilities against high-altitude aircraft and missiles, as well as surface-skimming anti-ship missiles such as Exocet, Tomahawk or Harpoon.

Slava class

Above: The Slava class has been overshadowed by the Kirov class battle-cruisers, and it tends to be forgotten that these are among the biggest modern surface warships (apart from carriers) with an extremely potent weapons fit. Clearly shown here is the unique layout of the 16 SS-N-12 launchers, together with the twin 130mm DP gun mount, twin RBU-6000 ASW rocket launchers and numerous 30mm

CIWS. Visible abaft the twin stacks are some of the SA-N-6 launchers, and the circular cover of the port SA-N-4 launcher is at the forward end of the flight deck. Also apparent are the numerous sensors, identified in the key to the right. Note the very large bridge and spacious superstructure, which provide plenty of room for C² facilities, though they would probably be very vulnerable in combat.

Weapons

A Twin 130mm/70 dual-purpose gun mounting (1x2)
B ADMG-630 30mm Gatling CIWS (1x1)
C ADMG-630 30mm Gatling CIWS (1x1)
D Twin SS-N-12 Sandbox launchers (8x2)
E RBU-6000 ASW rocket launcher (2x12)
F ADMG-630 30mm Gatling CIWS (2x1)
G ADMG-630 30mm Gatling CIWS (2x1)

H SA-N-6 vertical launchers (8x1)
J SA-N-4 'pop-up' launchers (2x2)
K Kamov Ka-25 Hormone-B targeting helicopter

Electronics

1 Hull-mounted LF sonar
2 DF loop
3 Bass Tilt fire control radar for ADMG-630
4 Kit Screech fire control radar for 130mm guns
5 Front Door/Front Piece missile control radar for SS-N-12
6 Palm Frond navigation radar
7 Top Steer surveillance radar
8 Palm Frond navigation radar (2x1)
9 High Pole-B IFF antenna
10 Tee Plinth electro-optical fire control system
11 Punch Bowl satellite navigation antenna
12 Bass Tilt fire control

radar for ADMG-630 (2x1)
13 Rum Tub EW antenna (2x1)
14 Top Pair (combined Top Sail and Big Net) radar antennas
15 Side Globe EW antennas (2x4)
16 Rumb Tub EW antennas (2x1)
17 Disc Cone-2 antenna
18 Chaff launchers (2x1)
19 Top Dome control radar for SA-N-6
20 MF variable depth sonar

Sovremennyy class

Origin: USSR
Type: Destroyer (DDG)
Built: 1976-
Class: 6 in service; 2 building
Displacement: 6,000 tons standard; 7,900 tons full load
Dimensions: Length 511.8ft (156m) oa; beam 56.8ft (17.3m); draught 21.3ft (6.5m)
Propulsion: 2-shaft steam turbines, 110,000shp, 2,400nm at 32 knots, 6,500nm at 20 knots
Performance: Speed 32 knots; range 2,400nm at 32 knots, 6,500 nm at 20 knots
Armament: SSM: 2 x 4 SS-N-22 SAM: 2 SA-N-7 (44 missiles)
Guns: 4 x 130mm L70A (2 x 2); four 30mm Gatlings
ASW weapons: 2 6-barrelled RBU-1000 (120 rockets)
Torpedo tubes: 2 x 2 21in (533mm) TR M-57 torpedo tubes.
Mines: Maximum 100
Aircraft: 1 KA-27 Helix helicopter
Sensors: Radar: Top Steer surveillance; 1 Band Stand (SS-N-22) and 6 Front Dome (SA-N-7) missile control; 1 Kite Screech (130mm) and 2 Bass Tilt (30mm Gatling) gun control; 3 Palm Frond navigation Sonar: 2 active MF hull-mounted
Complement: 320

Background: These impressive ships were built at the same yard (Zhdanov, Leningrad) as the Kresta-II class, and were originally designated BAL-COM 2 by NATO (BALtic COMbatant). The first of class, *Sovremennyy*, was launched in November 1978 and was first seen at sea by Western observers in August 1980, when she appeared in the Baltic on her engine trials, but still without a weapon fit. The following winter her guns and missile systems were mounted and she joined the Baltic Fleet in January 1982.

Constructed in parallel with the Udaloy class, the *Sovremennyy* is optimized for surface warfare. Her large internal volume, which is considerably greater than that of earlier Soviet Navy types, although less than Western equivalents such as the Spruance, indicates

that she is designed for distant-water deployments. She has a heavy armament of eight SS-N-22, mounted in bins in two groups of four either side of the bridge.

The SS-N-22 is an upgraded version of the SS-N-9, with a range of approximately 70nm, while the 130mm guns are fully automatic, are fitted with water cooling, indicating a high rate of fire, and are mounted in a new design of turret. Air defence missile armament consists of two SA-N-7 launchers (44 missiles) and four 30mm Gatlings. One Kamov Ka-27 Helix helicopter is carried, and the hangar is of an entirely new telescopic type not seen previously on Soviet warships.

It is somewhat surprising that this class is powered by conventional steam turbines rather than the gas turbines which have been fitted in many other major classes of Soviet warship since the early 1970s. Available evidence suggests that this class is powered by a pressure-fired automated steam propulsion plant similar to that fitted in the Kresta class, which gives very rapid acceleration (10-32 knots in less than two

minutes). These are modern, state-of-the-art ships, capable of protracted ocean deployments, with very good anti-air and anti-surface capabilities, but they would need to operate in company with ASW ships to survive against a major submarine threat.
Future: There are six of these destroyers at sea (*Sovremennyy*,

Otchyannyy, *Otlichnyy* and *Osmotritelnyy*, plus two whose names are not yet known), with a further two building. Those currently in service are all with the Northern Fleet and seem likely to remain there. Judging by previous Soviet Navy practice the known eight units will be followed by a new class.

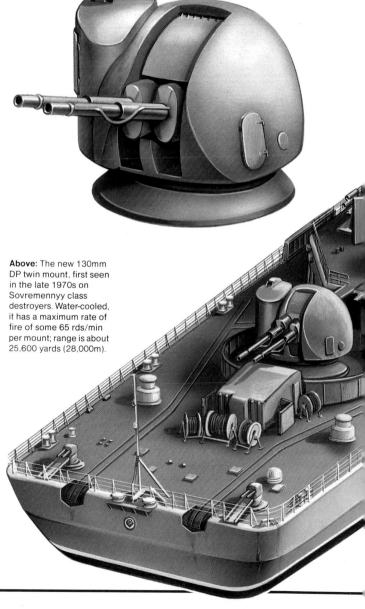

Above: The new 130mm DP twin mount, first seen in the late 1970s on Sovremennyy class destroyers. Water-cooled, it has a maximum rate of fire of some 65 rds/min per mount; range is about 25,600 yards (28,000m).

Below: Sovremennyy class destroyers are optimized for surface warfare, with two twin 130mm L70A turrets, eight SS-N-22 anti-ship missiles and a Hormone-B targeting helicopter. AA fit is two SA-N-7 launchers, four Gatling CIWS and the 130mm guns. ASW weapons are torpedo tubes, RBU-1000 and mines.

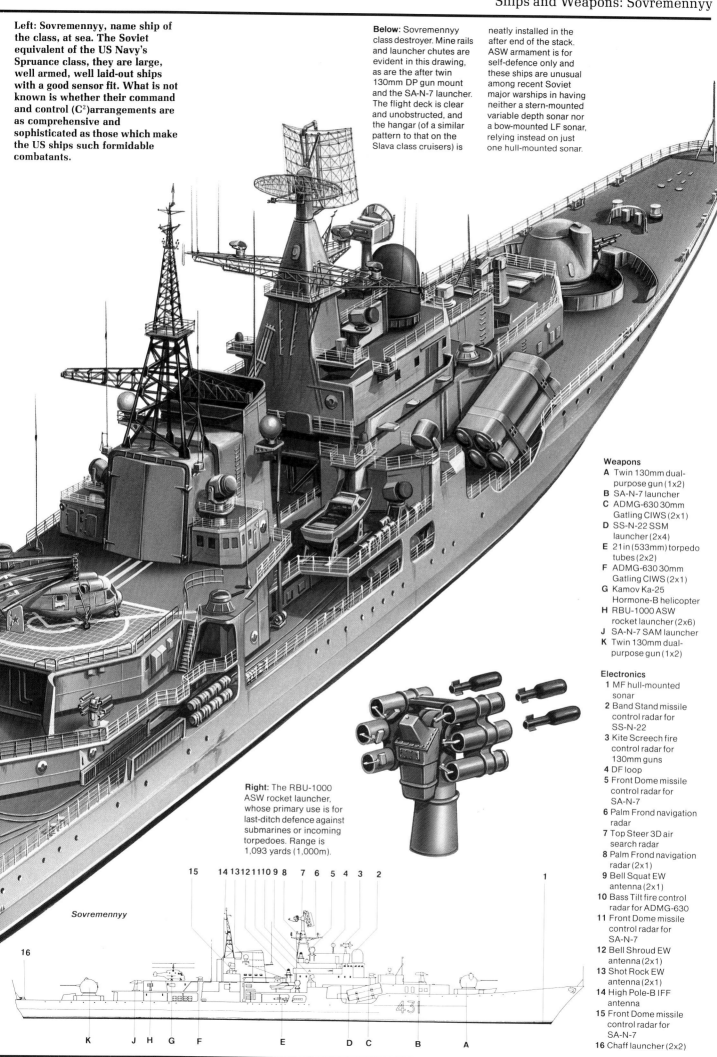

Left: Sovremennyy, name ship of the class, at sea. The Soviet equivalent of the US Navy's Spruance class, they are large, well armed, well laid-out ships with a good sensor fit. What is not known is whether their command and control (C²)arrangements are as comprehensive and sophisticated as those which make the US ships such formidable combatants.

Below: Sovremennyy class destroyer. Mine rails and launcher chutes are evident in this drawing, as are the after twin 130mm DP gun mount and the SA-N-7 launcher. The flight deck is clear and unobstructed, and the hangar (of a similar pattern to that on the Slava class cruisers) is neatly installed in the after end of the stack. ASW armament is for self-defence only and these ships are unusual among recent Soviet major warships in having neither a stern-mounted variable depth sonar nor a bow-mounted LF sonar, relying instead on just one hull-mounted sonar.

Right: The RBU-1000 ASW rocket launcher, whose primary use is for last-ditch defence against submarines or incoming torpedoes. Range is 1,093 yards (1,000m).

Weapons
A Twin 130mm dual-purpose gun (1x2)
B SA-N-7 launcher
C ADMG-630 30mm Gatling CIWS (2x1)
D SS-N-22 SSM launcher (2x4)
E 21in (533mm) torpedo tubes (2x2)
F ADMG-630 30mm Gatling CIWS (2x1)
G Kamov Ka-25 Hormone-B helicopter
H RBU-1000 ASW rocket launcher (2x6)
J SA-N-7 SAM launcher
K Twin 130mm dual-purpose gun (1x2)

Electronics
1 MF hull-mounted sonar
2 Band Stand missile control radar for SS-N-22
3 Kite Screech fire control radar for 130mm guns
4 DF loop
5 Front Dome missile control radar for SA-N-7
6 Palm Frond navigation radar
7 Top Steer 3D air search radar
8 Palm Frond navigation radar (2x1)
9 Bell Squat EW antenna (2x1)
10 Bass Tilt fire control radar for ADMG-630
11 Front Dome missile control radar for SA-N-7
12 Bell Shroud EW antenna (2x1)
13 Shot Rock EW antenna (2x1)
14 High Pole-B IFF antenna
15 Front Dome missile control radar for SA-N-7
16 Chaff launcher (2x2)

Sovremennyy

Spruance (DD 963) class

Origin: USA
Type: Destroyer (DDG)
Built: 1972-1983
Class: 31 Spruance plus 4 Kidd class in service
Displacement: 5,770 tons light; 7,810 tons full load
Dimensions: Length 563.2ft (171.7m) oa; beam 55.1ft (16.8m); draught 29ft (8.8m) sonar, 19ft (5.8m) keel
Propulsion: 2-shaft gas turbine (4 General Electric LM2500), 80,000shp
Performance: Speed 33 knots; range 6,000nm at 20 knots
Weapons: SSM: 2 x 4 Harpoon launchers
SAM: 1 NATO Sea Sparrow Mk 29 launcher
Guns: 2 x 1 5in/54 Mk 45; 2 20mm Phalanx Mk 15 CIWS
ASW weapons: 1 8-tube Asroc launcher (24 rounds); 2 x 3 Mk 32 torpedo tubes (14 torpedoes)
Aircraft: 1 SH-3 Sea King or two SH-2D LAMPS II helicopters
Sensors: Radar: SPS-55 and SPS-40 search (SPS-49(V) in DD 997); SPG-60 and SPQ-9A fire control
Sonar: SQS-53 or SQS 53C hull-mounted; SQR-19 TACTAS towed array
Complement: 296

Background: One of several post-war classes to arouse considerable controversy, especially in the US Congress, the Spruance class was designed to replace the war-built destroyers of the Gearing and Sumner classes, which, despite modernization programmes, were nearing the end of their useful lives by the early 1970s. The Spruances epitomize the US Navy's design philosophy of the 1970s, with their large hulls and block superstructures maximizing internal volume. They would be fitted with machinery that was easy to maintain or replace and equipped with high-technology weapon systems that could be added to or updated by modular replacement at a later date.

The object was to minimize platform costs in favour of greater expenditure on the weapon systems payload in order to ensure that the ships would remain in the front-line throughout their 30-year life expectancy. In a further attempt to minimize platform costs the entire class was ordered from a single builder (Litton/Ingalls), which invested heavily in a major production facility at Pascagoula, using advanced modular construction techniques.

The only visible weapon systems aboard the Spruances are two single 5in Mk 45 lightweight gun mountings and an Asroc box launcher forward of the bridge. In view of the size and cost of the ships this caused an immediate public outcry. The advanced ASW capabilities of the ships are, however, largely hidden within the hull and the bulky superstructure. The Asroc launcher, for example, has a magazine beneath it containing no fewer than 24 reloads, while the large hangar to port of the after funnel uptakes can accommodate

two LAMPS II helicopters and two sliding doors on either side of the superstructure conceal triple Mk 32 torpedo tubes and torpedo handling rooms.

Of even greater significance are the advanced submarine detection features of the class. The SQS-53C bow sonar can operate in a variety of active and passive modes, including direct path, bottom-bounce and convergence zone. This system has proved so successful that the SQS-35 VDS initially scheduled will not now be fitted.

The all-gas turbine propulsion system, with paired General Electric LM2500 gas turbines en echelon, was selected primarily for its ease of maintenance and low manning requirements. Gas turbines also have significant advantages in reducing underwater noise emission and the Spruances are therefore capable of near-silent ASW operations.

The Spruances are fitted with the latest computerized data systems in well designed Combat Information Centres. They also have the most up-to-date digital fire control systems in the Mk 86 Gun Fire Control System and the Mk 116 underwater system.

Besides the weapon systems fitted on completion, the ships of the Spruance class were designed to accept a variety of other systems then at the design stage. All ships have now received the Sea Sparrow Improved Point Defence System (IPDMS) and Harpoon anti-ship missiles (aft of the forward funnel), and three Whiskey-3 (WSC-3) satellite communications transceivers and SLQ-32(V)2 ECM systems have also been fitted.

The inherent flexibility of the Spruance design is such that it has formed the basis for the new Ticonderoga class Aegis cruisers. The Kidd class also stemmed from the Spruance design: originally destined for the Imperial Iranian Navy, and optimized for the general warfare role rather than ASW, the four-ship order was cancelled following the Iranian revolution, and the ships were purchased by the US Navy and completed as designed, making them the most powerful destroyers in the fleet. The major difference from the Spruances is that the Kidds have two twin Mk 26 Standard/Asroc launchers.

Future: Starting from the FY85 overhauls, major improvements being made to the Spruances will enable them to remain effective ASW units well into the next century. Improvements include the installation of the LAMPS III shipboard electronics and the Recovery Assist Secure and Traverse system (RAST) for helicopter handling.

An improved version of the 5in/54 Mk 65 gun is under consideration, and the Tomahawk system wil be fitted in all ships of the class, as will the Mk 41 Vertical Launch System with a 61-round magazine in place of the Asroc.

Below: USS Deyo (DD 989). Like many US ships, the Spruance class was subject to ill-informed criticism in their early days, but their merits are now appreciated.

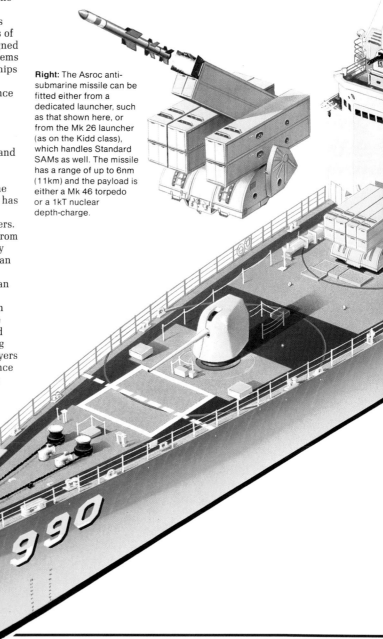

Right: The Asroc anti-submarine missile can be fitted either from a dedicated launcher, such as that shown here, or from the Mk 26 launcher (as on the Kidd class), which handles Standard SAMs as well. The missile has a range of up to 6nm (11km) and the payload is either a Mk 46 torpedo or a 1kT nuclear depth-charge.

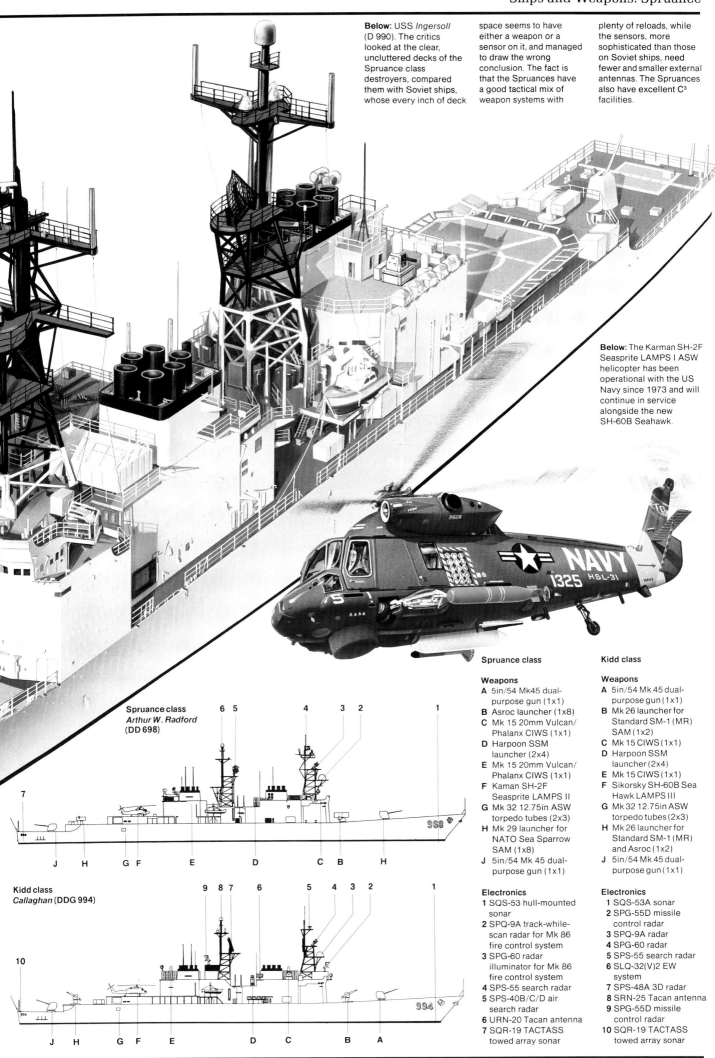

Below: USS *Ingersoll* (D 990). The critics looked at the clear, uncluttered decks of the Spruance class destroyers, compared them with Soviet ships, whose every inch of deck space seems to have either a weapon or a sensor on it, and managed to draw the wrong conclusion. The fact is that the Spruances have a good tactical mix of weapon systems with plenty of reloads, while the sensors, more sophisticated than those on Soviet ships, need fewer and smaller external antennas. The Spruances also have excellent C³ facilities.

Below: The Karman SH-2F Seasprite LAMPS I ASW helicopter has been operational with the US Navy since 1973 and will continue in service alongside the new SH-60B Seahawk.

Spruance class
Arthur W. Radford
(DD 698)

Kidd class
Callaghan (DDG 994)

Spruance class

Weapons
A 5in/54 Mk45 dual-purpose gun (1x1)
B Asroc launcher (1x8)
C Mk 15 20mm Vulcan/Phalanx CIWS (1x1)
D Harpoon SSM launcher (2x4)
E Mk 15 20mm Vulcan/Phalanx CIWS (1x1)
F Kaman SH-2F Seasprite LAMPS II
G Mk 32 12.75in ASW torpedo tubes (2x3)
H Mk 29 launcher for NATO Sea Sparrow SAM (1x8)
J 5in/54 Mk 45 dual-purpose gun (1x1)

Electronics
1 SQS-53 hull-mounted sonar
2 SPQ-9A track-while-scan radar for Mk 86 fire control system
3 SPG-60 radar illuminator for Mk 86 fire control system
4 SPS-55 search radar
5 SPS-40B/C/D air search radar
6 URN-20 Tacan antenna
7 SQR-19 TACTASS towed array sonar

Kidd class

Weapons
A 5in/54 Mk 45 dual-purpose gun (1x1)
B Mk 26 launcher for Standard SM-1 (MR) SAM (1x2)
C Mk 15 CIWS (1x1)
D Harpoon SSM launcher (2x4)
E Mk 15 CIWS (1x1)
F Sikorsky SH-60B Sea Hawk LAMPS III
G Mk 32 12.75in ASW torpedo tubes (2x3)
H Mk 26 launcher for Standard SM-1 (MR) and Asroc (1x2)
J 5in/54 Mk 45 dual-purpose gun (1x1)

Electronics
1 SQS-53A sonar
2 SPG-55D missile control radar
3 SPQ-9A radar
4 SPG-60 radar
5 SPS-55 search radar
6 SLQ-32(V)2 EW system
7 SPS-48A 3D radar
8 SRN-25 Tacan antenna
9 SPG-55D missile control radar
10 SQR-19 TACTASS towed array sonar

Ticonderoga (CG 47) class

Origin: USA
Type: Guided-missile cruiser (CG)
Built: 1980-
Class: 4 in service; 6 building; 6 ordered; 12 projected
Displacement: 9,600 tons full load
Dimensions: Length 566.8ft (172.8m) oa; beam 55ft (16.8m); draught 31ft (9.5m)
Propulsion: 2-shaft gas turbine (4 General Electric LM2500), 80,000shp
Performance: Speed 30 knots
Weapons: SSM: 8 Harpoon; 30 Tomahawk (CG 52 onward)
SAM: 2 twin Mk 26 launchers with 88 Standard SM-2(MR)/Asroc (CG 47-51); 2 Mk 41 Vertical Launch Systems for 122 Standard SM-2(MR)/Asroc/Tomahawk (CG 52 onward)
Guns: 2 single 5in/54 Mk 45; 2 Phalanx 20mm/76 Mk 16 CIWS; 2 40mm (saluting)
Torpedo tubes: 2 x 3 Mk 32 21in
Aircraft: 2 LAMPS I or III helicopters
Sensors: Radar: SPY-1A 3D phased arrays (CG 47-58); 2 SPY-1B (CG 59 onward); SPS-49(V) air search; SPS-55 surface search; SPQ-9 fire control; LN-66 navigation (CG 47-53); SPS-64 navigation (CG 54 onward)
Sonar: SQS-53A (CG 47-CG 53) bow-mounted; SQS-53B (CG 54 onward); SQR-19 (TACTAS) towed array (CG 54 onwards)
Complement: 375

Background: The US Navy is well used to public criticism of its new ships, especially from Congress, and the Spruance, Oliver Hazard Perry and Virginia classes have all had their fair share. Seldom, however, has so much ill-informed and hostile comment been directed at any one class as that provoked by the Ticonderogas. The ship and her electronics systems have recently vindicated themselves in a series of rigorous tests, backed up by some very successful operational deployments, and they are now among the most potent warships afloat.

The Aegis Combat System, one of the most important break-throughs in naval technology of recent years, was developed in response to the threat of saturation missile attacks that form the basis of Soviet anti-carrier tactics during the 1980s and beyond. To cope with such tactics, sensors must be able to react virtually instantaneously and have a virtually unlimited tracking capability, but con-ventional rotating radars are limited both in data-processing capacity and in the number of target tracks they can handle; therefore a new system had to be found.

The solution adopted with the Aegis system is to mount four fixed planar arrays on the super-structure of the ship, two on each of the forward and after deck-houses. Each array has 4,100 radiating elements and is controlled by a UYK-1 digital computer to produce and steer multiple beams for target search, detection and tracking. Targets are evaluated,

Below: The McDonnell Douglas Harpoon has proved an outstanding success, with well over 2,000 on order for the US and numerous foreign navies. The missile can be fired from aircraft (AGM-84), submarines (UGM-84) and surfcae ships (RGM-84A), and is propelled by a turbojet, through the surface and submarine versions both have an additional rocket booster; cruise speed is Mach 0.85. Maximum range is 60nm (111km) in the original version and 85nm (157km) in the improved Block 1 missiles, but external targeting sys-tems such as helicopters are required to achieve over-the-horizon ranges.

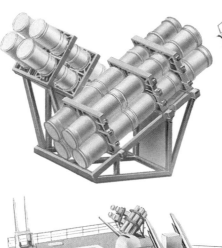

arranged in priority of threat and then engaged, either automatically or with manual override, by a variety of defensive systems. The system also produces target designation data for the Raytheon target illuminating radars which direct the semi-active radar homing Standard SM-2 (ER) missile.

At longer ranges air targets are engaged by the SM-2 missile, fired from one of two Mk 26 launchers. Up to 18 missiles can be kept in the air in addition to four in the terminal phase, and the Mk 99 illuminators switch rapidly from one target to the next under computer control. Close-range defence is provided by two 5in/54 guns, while the final line of defence is provided by two Phalanx CIWS.

It was originally envisaged that this very sophisticated system would be installed in nuclear-powered escorts such as the planned Strike Cruiser (CSGN) or the Modified Virginia (CGN-42) class, but the enormous cost of the system, coupled with that of nuclear propulsion, proved to be prohibitively expensive, especially in the budgetary climate of the later years of the Carter Adminis-tration. Since it was considered that two Aegis escorts would be required for each of the 12 carrier battle groups and because not all of the carriers concerned would

The shipborne version is usually launched from a simple canister. Despite its ruggedness, the mounting on the Ticonderogas is in an exposed position and must suffer in a seaway.

be nuclear powered, it was decided to utilize the growth potential of the gas turbine powered Spruance design to incorporate the necessary electronics.

Ticonderoga and her sisters are designed to serve as flagships and are, therefore, equipped with an elaborate Combat Information Centre, which has an integral flag function and is able to accept and coordinate data from other ships and aircraft in the group. This was found to be invaluable during USS *Ticonderoga*'s deployment off Beirut, and the admiral in command routinely exercised command from this ship because of the excellent facilities. In addition, because the Aegis system worked so well, he was able to reduce the Combat Air Patrol (CAP) cover, a significant contribution to the combat effectiveness of the task group.
Future: Twenty-eight units are currently projected and it is envisaged that they will operate in conjunction with specialized ASW and AAW DDGs of the Spruance and Arleigh Burke.

Right: USS Vincennes (CG 49), her massive superstructure and its two SPY-1A arrays clearly visible. Note also the two Mk 80 illuminator-directors above the bridge with the ball-shaped cover for the SPQ-9 fire control radar antenna above them. The hull of the Ticonderoga class cruisers is identical with that of the Spruance class destroyers, a fact which has produced considerable savings.

Weapons

A 5in/54 Mk 45 dual-purpose gun (1x1)
B Mk 26 Mod 1 missile launcher (1x2) for Standard SM-2(MR) SAM and Asroc ASW missiles
C 20mm/76 Mk 15 Vulcan/Phalanx CIWS (2x1)
D Sikorsky SH-60B Sea hawk LAMPS III ASW helicopter (2 carried)
E Mk 32 12.75in ASW torpedo tubes (2x3) for Mk 46 torpedoes
F Mk 26 Mod 1 missile launcher (1x2) for Standard SM-2(MR) SAM and Asroc ASW missiles
G 5in/54 Mk 45 dual-purpose gun (1x1)
H Mk 141 launchers for RGM-84A Harpoon SSM (2x4)

Electronics

1 SQS-53 bow-mounted sonar
2 SPY-1A phased array radar forward and starboard arrays (SPY-B from CG 59)
3 WSC-1V satellite communications antenna
4 Mk 80 illuminator-director (SPG-62 radar) (2x1)
5 SPQ-9 gun fire control radar
6 SPS-55 surface search radar
7 URD-1 direction-finding antenna
8 SLQ(V)3 jammer (2x1)
9 Communications antenna
10 UPX-29 IFF interrogator (circular array)
11 SPS-49(V)6 air search radar
12 Mk 80 illuminator-director (SPG-62 radar)
13 Mk 80 illuminator-director (SPG-62 radar)
14 SPY-1A phased array radar aft and port arrays (SPY-1B from CG 59 onward)
15 SQR-19 variable depth sonar (to be installed in Cg 54 onward)

Ticonderoga (CG 47)

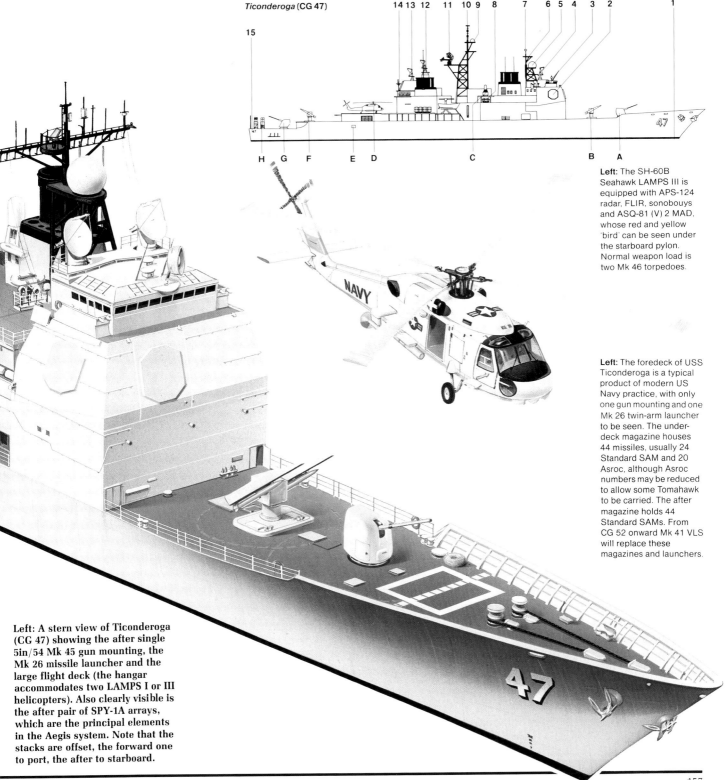

Left: The SH-60B Seahawk LAMPS III is equipped with APS-124 radar, FLIR, sonobouys and ASQ-81 (V) 2 MAD, whose red and yellow 'bird' can be seen under the starboard pylon. Normal weapon load is two Mk 46 torpedoes.

Left: The foredeck of USS Ticonderoga is a typical product of modern US Navy practice, with only one gun mounting and one Mk 26 twin-arm launcher to be seen. The under-deck magazine houses 44 missiles, usually 24 Standard SAM and 20 Asroc, although Asroc numbers may be reduced to allow some Tomahawk to be carried. The after magazine holds 44 Standard SAMs. From CG 52 onward Mk 41 VLS will replace these magazines and launchers.

Left: A stern view of Ticonderoga (CG 47) showing the after single 5in/54 Mk 45 gun mounting, the Mk 26 missile launcher and the large flight deck (the hangar accommodates two LAMPS I or III helicopters). Also clearly visible is the after pair of SPY-1A arrays, which are the principal elements in the Aegis system. Note that the stacks are offset, the forward one to port, the after to starboard.

Trafalgar class

Origin: United Kingdom
Type: Nuclear powered attack submarine (SSN)
Built: 1978-
Class: 3 in service; 3 building; 1 ordered
Displacement: 4,200 tons light; 5,208 tons submerged
Dimensions: Length 280.1ft (85.4m) oa; beam 32.1ft (9.8m); draught 26.9ft (8.2m)
Propulsion: 1-shaft nuclear (1 pressurized-water-cooled nuclear reactor; General Electric geared steam turbines), 15,000shp; 2 Paxman auxiliary diesels, 4,000shp
Performance: Speed 32 knots submerged
Weapons: Missiles: Sub-Harpoon (tube-launched)
Torpedo tubes: 5 x 21in (533mm), 20 reloads; Spearfish or Tigerfish torpedoes mines, Sea Urchin or of Shellfish
Sensors: Sonar: Type 2007; Type 2020; Type 183; Type 2024 towed array
Complement: 130.

Background: The British Royal Navy now has its fourth class of SSN in production and will soon have 17 boats in service, including two of the Valiant and three of the very similar Churchill classes, and one of the latter, HMS *Conqueror*, has the distinction of being the only nuclear-powered submarine to have sunk a surface warship in anger—the Argentinian cruiser *Belgrano*, on May 2, 1982. The next class—the Swiftsures — entered production in 1969 and have a shorter, fuller hull form, together with a somewhat shorter sail, which reduces the periscope depth. The Swiftsures are coated with anechoic tiles which, together with other noise-reducing measures, makes them much quieter than any other contemporary class of SSN.

The first of the Trafalgar class was launched on July 1, 1981, and commissioned on May 27, 1983. By 1986 four of these boats were in service with two building and an order placed for a seventh. Details of the class are sparse, but it is clear that they are a logical development of the Swiftsure design with a very similar hull, except that the parallel section has been stretched by the inclusion of one more 6ft (2.5m) section; the diameter of the pressure hull remains unchanged, but there is an increase in submerged displacement over the Swiftsures' 4,500 tons to 4,920 tons. A new type of reactor core is used, and the machinery is mounted on rafts to insulate it from the hull and cut down radiated noise. HMS *Trafalgar* has a seven-bladed propeller, but later boats have a shrouded pump-jet.

The cost of these boats is a good indicator of the problem facing the major navies. At 1976 prices the building costs of the Swiftsure class were: *Swiftsure* £37.1 million, *Superb* £41.3 million, *Sceptre* £58.9 million and *Spartan* £68.9 million, while the cost of the fourth Trafalgar, including weapon systems and equipment, will be £175 million. The cost of the seventh, HMS *Triumph*, is over £200 million, which is reported to be considerably less than that of the sixth.

The Trafalgar class boats are claimed by the Royal Navy to be the quietest submarines in service, quieter even than the diesel-electric Oberon class. It is interesting to note, however, that despite its large and very successful SSN fleet the Royal Navy continues to commission conventional diesel-electric submarines, and the first of the new Vickers Type 2400 Upholder class has recently been ordered. In this respect the Royal Navy's attitude is similar to that of its Soviet equivalent, but contrary to that of the US Navy.

Future: If past patterns are repeated a new class, again a logical development of the Trafalgar class, can be expected to appear in the 1990s.

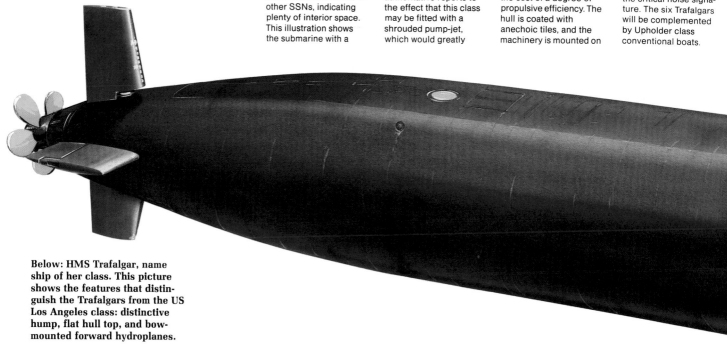

Below: A Trafalgar class submarine. The hull is rather fatter than those of other SSNs, indicating plenty of interior space. This illustration shows the submarine with a conventional propeller, but there are a number of authoritative reports to the effect that this class may be fitted with a shrouded pump-jet, which would greatly reduce the noise signature, though possibly at the cost of a degree of propulsive efficiency. The hull is coated with anechoic tiles, and the machinery is mounted on rafts to insulate the hull from vibration to reduce the critical noise signature. The six Trafalgars will be complemented by Upholder class conventional boats.

Below: HMS Trafalgar, name ship of her class. This picture shows the features that distinguish the Trafalgars from the US Los Angeles class: distinctive hump, flat hull top, and bow-mounted forward hydroplanes.

Right: Some of Trafalgar's weaponry. In the left-hand row, nearest the submarine hull, are three Tigerfish torpedoes, with outboard of them two Sub-Harpoon capsules and a Stonefish mine. In the right-hand row are a Sea Urchin mine and two Sub-Harpoon missiles. The Tigerfish wire-guided/acoustic homing submarine-launched ASW torpedo has an electric motor and twin contra-rotating propellers, giving it a speed of some 50 knots and a range of about 21km. Sub-Harpoon is a submarine-launched version of the successful US anti-ship missile. Sea Urchin and Stonefish are British-designed ground mines.

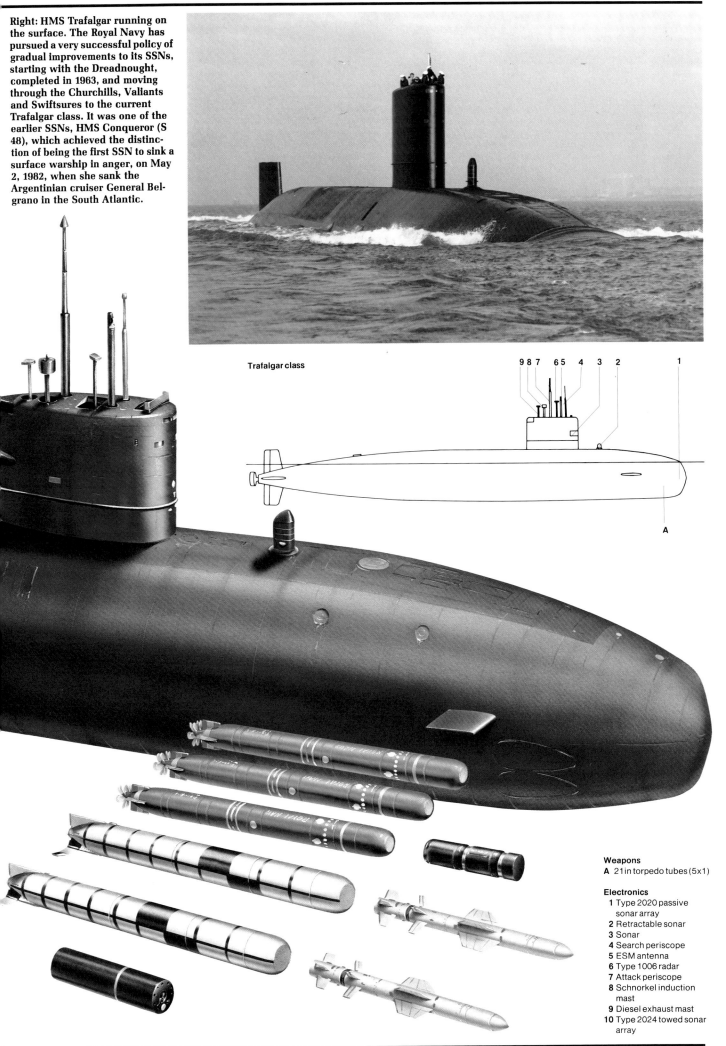

Right: HMS Trafalgar running on the surface. The Royal Navy has pursued a very successful policy of gradual improvements to its SSNs, starting with the Dreadnought, completed in 1963, and moving through the Churchills, Valiants and Swiftsures to the current Trafalgar class. It was one of the earlier SSNs, HMS Conqueror (S 48), which achieved the distinction of being the first SSN to sink a surface warship in anger, on May 2, 1982, when she sank the Argentinian cruiser General Belgrano in the South Atlantic.

Trafalgar class

Weapons
A 21in torpedo tubes (5x1)

Electronics
1 Type 2020 passive sonar array
2 Retractable sonar
3 Sonar
4 Search periscope
5 ESM antenna
6 Type 1006 radar
7 Attack periscope
8 Schnorkel induction mast
9 Diesel exhaust mast
10 Type 2024 towed sonar array

Type 209

Origin: Federal Republic of Germany
Type: Patrol submarine (SS)
Built: 1970-
Class: 32 in service; 2 building; 16 on order
Displacement: 1,185 tons surfaced; 1,285 tons submerged
Dimensions: Length 183.4ft (55.9m) oa; beam 20.5ft (6.3m); draught 17.9ft (5.5m)
Propulsion: 1-shaft diesel (4 MTU diesel generators), 5,000shp
Performance: Speed 10 knots surfaced, 23 knots submerged
Weapons: Torpedo tubes: 8 x 21in (533mm), 6 reloads
Sensors: Various active and passive sonar fits.
Complement: 32
(Details for Argentinian Type 1200)

Background: Germany has a special place in the history of the submarine, having ended World War II with some outstanding designs which, fortunately for the Allies, failed to attain operational status in significant numbers, but it was 1954 before the postwar Federal Republic was allowed to construct the Type 205, a small coastal submarine, 12 of which were built for use in the Baltic. Two improved Type 205s were built in Denmark (Narvhalen class) and a further 15 improved Type 205s, optimized for deep-sea operations, and designated Type 207, were built in West Germany for Norway.

Design work then began on a follow-on class of 450 tons, the main concern being with greater battery power to meet the demands of the ever-increasing number of electrical and electronic devices, but without reducing submerged speed or endurance. Construction of the first boat began in November 1969 and the eighteenth and last joined the Bundesmarine in September 1971. Constructed of special non-magnetic steel, these

submarines have served the West German Navy well and, so far as is known, have avoided the notorious corrosion problems that effected the Type 205s. The opportunity was taken in this class to upgrade the sonars and fire-control system, and wire-guided torpedoes were fitted for the first time in a German submarine design.

Agreement by the Western Allies to raise the displacement limit on German submarine con-

struction to 1,000 tons led to the design of the very successful Type 209, which has met the need of many navies for a new submarine, conventionally powered but with up-to-date sensors, armament and electronics, and with minimal demands on highly skilled manpower. Current operators include Greece (four Type 1100, four Type 1200), Argentina (two Type 1200), Peru (six Type 1200), Colombia (two Type 1200 with 34-man crews), Chile (two Type 1300 with fin and masts lengthened by 19.7in (50cm) to cope with Pacific waves), Ecuador (two Type 1300), Indonesia (two Type 1300), Venezuela (two Type 1300) and Turkey (six Type 1200 with 33-man crews). Improved versions, longer and with better sensors, have been ordered by India, Brazil and Indonesia, and Turkey, having received three from Howaldtswerke, is now producing the type, with two completed by 1986 and another eight planned.

The Type 209 is similar in shape and layout to the Type 205 but has increased dimensions, greater battery capacity and more powerful propulsion. The hull is completely smooth, with retractable hydroplanes mounted low on the bows, cruciform after control surfaces and a single screw, and careful hull design and powerful motors result in an underwater burst speed of 23 knots. Designed for patrols of up to 50 days, these boats are armed

Above: A fine bow view of a Type 209 submarine, showing its exceptionally clean hull form. The Type 209 was developed from a long line of postwar West German submarines, which in turn incorpor- **ated many features of the final classes of the World War II German Navy. The Type 209 has been sold to many navies, and one Argentinian example took part in the South Atlantic War in 1982.**

Above: The Type 209 submarines *San Luis* (S 32) of the Argentinian Navy, built by Howaldtswerke, Kiel, 1970-1973. Designed in the mid-1960s by Ingenieurkontor Lubeck (IKL), the Type 209 is designed as an ocean-going submarine with a maximum endurance of 50 days, but its relatively short overall length also makes it suitable for coastal work. As can be seen from the drawing, the hull

is completely smooth and scoop-shaped fins are used in place of conventional forward hydroplanes. These boats have the very high underwater burst speed of 22 knots, although this could not be sustained for any length of time. The design has proved to be remarkably adaptable and IKL have made numerous changes to suit individual customers: the Chilean boats, for example, have had the fin and the

associated masts raised by some 20in (50cm) to cope with the greater wave heights encountered in the South Atlantic. The sensor fit is also changed to suit individual customers' requirements, but most use French radars, and French or West German sonars. The drawing also shows the arrangement of the eight torpedo tubes, with six in a semicircle and two in the centre. Six reloads are carried. This par-

ticular boat, *San Luis*, operated against the Royal Navy in the South Atlantic War, and gave the Task Force some anxious moments. There is still some controversy as to exactly how successful she was, with the efficacy of the torpedoes being a matter of particular dispute, but in the final analysis she did not actually sink anything; her sister, *Salta*, was undergoing a refit during the conflict.

Right: Type 209s can carry a variety of 21in (533mm) torpedoes. One model carried by many is the West German AEG-Telefunken SST-4, which is an internationalized version of the Seal/Seeschlange series of torpedoes used by the Federal German Navy.

SST-4 is wire-guided with an on-board computer, enabling it to be guided to its target either by signals from the launch ship or by self-homing using the torpedo's own active/passive homing head. Impact and magnetic proximity fuzing is used.

with eight 21in (533mm) torpedo tubes and have a full range of sensors. They are one of the most successful contemporary submarine designs and during the 1982 South Atlantic war the Royal Navy treated the Argentinian Type 209 San Luis with the greatest respect, although it is still not clear just how successful she was. IKL has obviously assessed potential customers, requirements with re-markable accuracy.

Future: Building of the Type 209 continues apace. India has ordered six of the slightly larger Type 1400 (Ingenieurkontor Lübeck with a standard displacement of 1,450 tons and a crew of 40; two will be built in Germany and the remainder in India. Brazil has two Type 1400s on order, of which the first will be built at HDW, Kiel, and the second in Brazil. Turkey is continuing to build at a rate of one per year until she has a total of 12 in service. Indonesia plans two more Type 1300s plus a further two slightly larger boats, for a total submarine fleet of six.

Above: Type 209 submarine run-ning on the surface. Construction of these boats will continue well into the 1990s both in the HDW yard in West Gemany, and in loacl yards in Turkey and India. With 32 in service and at least 18 under construction or on firm order, this is one of the most successful postwar submarine designs, a status further confirmed by the recent order from the Indian Navy.

Weapons
A 8x21in (533mm) torpedo tubes (6 reloads)

Electronics
1 Krupp-Atlas AN-526 passive sonar
2 Thomson-CSF DUUX-2 passive sonar
3 Krupp-Atlas CSU AN 407 A9 active sonar
4 Search periscope
5 Schnorkel induction mast
6 Communications mast
7 Attack periscope
8 Thomson-CSF Calypso surface search radar

Type 209 1100

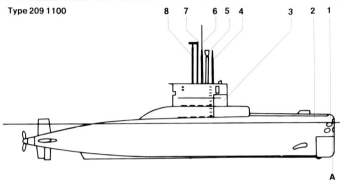

Type 209 1200

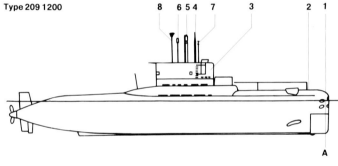

Type 209 1300

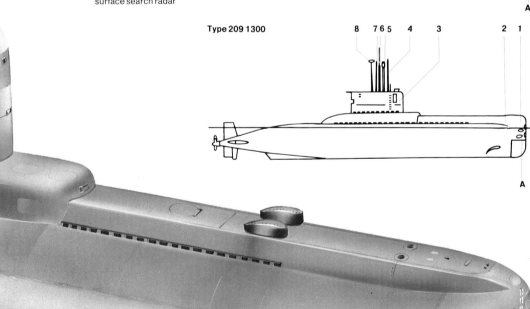

Typhoon class

Origin: USSR
Type: Nuclear-powered ballistic missile submarine (SSBN)
Built: 1978-
Class: 3 in service: 4 building
Displacement: 29,000 tons submerged
Dimensions: Length 561ft (171m); beam 75.45ft (23m); draught not known
Propulsion: 2-shaft nuclear (2 nuclear reactors, steam turbines), 80,000shp
Performance: 24 knot dived (see Background)
Weapons: Missiles: 20 SS-N-20 SLBM; possibly tube-launched SS-N-15, SS-N-16 or SS-N-21 Torpedo tubes: 6 x 21in (533mm)
Sensors: No details available
Complement: 150

Background: Persistent rumours in Western military circles were confirmed in November 1980 by the NATO announcement that the USSR had launched the first Typhoon-class SSBN. This event created much interest because unlike the Delta-class—a progressive development of the Yankee-class—the Typhoon was the first Soviet SSBN of completely new design for some 20 years. Particularly interesting was the sheer size of this enormous craft, whose submerged displacement and overall length made it by far the biggest submarine ever built.

Among the design's many unusual features is the extraordinarily wide beam; the normal length-to-beam ratio for SSBNs is in the region of 13:1, but the Typhoon almost halves that to 7:1. This may indicate a considerable degree of separation — up to 15ft (4.6m) — between concentric outer and inner hulls, or simply a huge inner hull, but most authorities agree that there are probably two separate side-by-side pressure hulls surrounded by a single outer hull, a concept similar to that behind the triple-hull Dutch Dolfijn class of the 1950s.

Another significant departure from previous practice is that 20 missile tubes are located forward of the fin. The reason for this is not yet clear, although it is possible that the propulsion machinery is so large and heavy that the missile compartment had to be moved forward to compensate. It has also been suggested that there may be some connection with the Typhoon's under-ice capability, although the Delta IV is also known to operate under the ice-cap with the conventional layout of missiles abaft the fin.

Principal armament of the Typhoon is 20 SS-N-20 ballistic missiles carried in two rows of ten launch canisters. The SS-N-20 has between six and nine MIRVed warheads and a range of 5,157 miles (8,300km). A battery of torpedo tubes is located forward of the missile compartment, and as well as conventional torpedoes these may well be able to launch cruise missiles such as the SS-NX-21 and lay mines — classes of weapons which would be very useful if the Typhoons were deployed in distant waters. One advantage of the unique layout is that all weapons are concentrated in one integrated area forward of the combat control centre.

In the open oceans this submarine would seem to be relatively easy for opposing ASW forces to detect—its very size facilitates detection by some methods. On the other hand, the large hull volume makes quietening, a major problem in SSBN design, rather easier. One possibility would seem to be that the Typhoon is simply intended to be an invulnerable missile launching platform, required only to move out a short distance across the Barents Sea and loiter under the Arctic ice-cap. Time on station would be limited only by the endurance of the crew, whose accommodation can be assumed to be more spacious and comfortable than that in any previous SSBN.

There is, however, another possibility: that the Typhoon is designed to operate for protracted periods a long way from its bases. The 4,500-mile (7,240km) range of its SS-N-20s would certainly enable the Typhoon to operate in the southern oceans, thus posing a threat to the United States from completely new directions and necessitating an expensive realignment of US warning and detection radar systems.

The speed of the Typhoon is the subject of much debate in the West. Conventional wisdom

Right: The Soviet Navy's Typhoon class SSBN is, by a very wide margin, the world's biggest submarine; 561ft (171m) long and with a beam of 75.45ft (23m) it is virtually the same length as the US Navy's Ohio class SSBN but twice as broad. This picture shows the extraordinary beam, and also the interesting and very large fairing which blends the fin into the hull. It is also sufficiently detailed to show the anechoic tiles which completely cover the hull.

Below: The overall design of the Typhoon can be seen from this drawing. Unlike any previous class of SSBN, the Typhoons have their missiles forward of the fin, mounted in two rows of ten. The Typhoons also have torpedo tubes, which are probably 21in (533mm) calibre, although it is possible that the new 25.6in (650mm) tubes may be fitted, either in addition to or even in place of the 21in tubes. Nor is the total number of tubes yet clear; it may be eight, as shown here, or six. The relatively conventional control surfaces and their small size in relation to the hull suggest that the Typhoon would not be very manoueverable.

Right: The Typhoons are designed to carry the SS-N-20 ballistic missile, one of the latest Soviet missile systems. SS-N-20 is 49ft (14.9m) long and its three-stage solid fuel propulsion system gives it a range of some 4,478nm (8,300km) with up to nine 2-300kT MIRV warheads, each with a CEP of 700 yards (640m). The missile was reported to have suffered some problems in early flight trials, but these have apparently been overcome and SS-N-20 is now in full service, though only, as far as is known, with this class. The Typhoons have shown the ability to fire more than one missile simultaneously, a totally new capability for an SSBN.

Right: Soviet Navy standard 21in (533mm) torpedoes. Little is known of Soviet torpedo development, but like many Western navies, the Soviets incorporated German ideas into their early postwar designs.

suggests twin nuclear reactors, twin screws and an underwater speed of about 25-30 knots. However, it is possible that the well-documented Soviet experiments in boundary-layer control may have reached fruition, in which case very powerful engines could produce a much higher speed, and it is interesting that some US authorities have credited the Typhoon with an underwater speed in the region of 64 knots, an achievement only possible if some major breakthrough in hull design or propulsion technology has been achieved.

The sheer size of the Typhoon causes much comment in the West. However, the Soviets have frequently exhibited a fascination with size and have built extremely large aircraft and ships for many years. Their latest ships—the Kirov (battle-cruiser), Kiev (aircraft carrier), Oscar (SSGN) and the Typhoon classes—seem to fit in with this general pattern.

Future: Three Typhoons are currently in service and a further four are believed to be under construction. It is forecast that at least eight will be in service by 1990. An even more accurate version of the SS-N-20 is in the flight test stage.

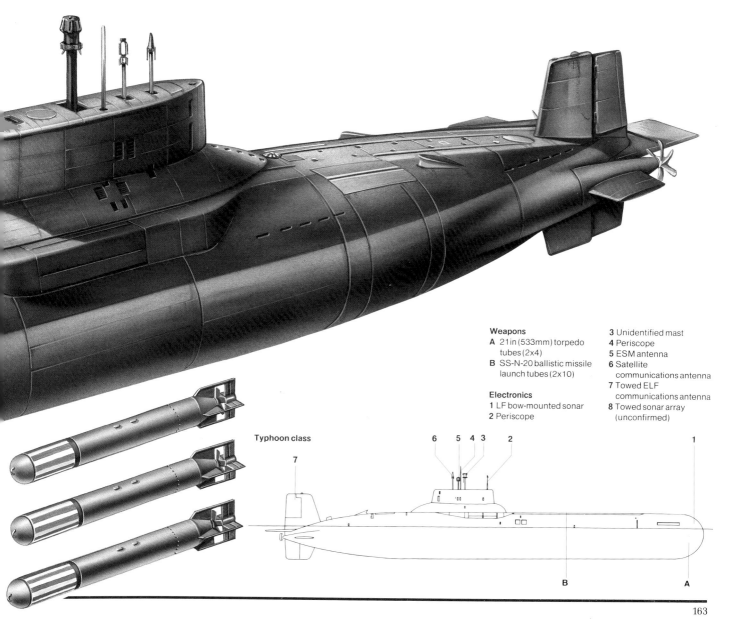

Weapons
A 21in (533mm) torpedo tubes (2x4)
B SS-N-20 ballistic missile launch tubes (2x10)

Electronics
1 LF bow-mounted sonar
2 Periscope

3 Unidentified mast
4 Periscope
5 ESM antenna
6 Satellite communications antenna
7 Towed ELF communications antenna
8 Towed sonar array (unconfirmed)

Typhoon class

Udaloy class

Origin: USSR
Type: Destroyer (DDG)
Built: 1978-1986
Class: 8 in service; 1 building
Displacement: 6,500 tons standard; 7,900 tons full load
Dimensions: Length 531.4ft (162m) oa; beam 63.3ft (19.3m); draught 20.3ft (6.2m)
Propulsion: 2-shaft COGOG (4 gas-turbines), 120,000shp total
Performance: Speed 35knots; range 2,500nm at 32 knots, 5,000nm at 20 knots
Weapons: SSM: 2 x 4 SS-N-14 launchers
SAM: 8 SA-N-9 PDMS launchers (64 missiles)
Guns: 2 x 1 100mm; 4 ADMG 630 30mm Gatling CIWS
Torpedo tubes: 2 x 4 533mm M-57
ASW weapons: 2 12-barrel RBU-6000
Mines: Minerails fitted
Aircraft: 2 Ka-25 Helix-A helicopters
Sensors: Radar: 2 Strut Pair (1 Top Plate from third ship) surveillance; 2 Eye Bowl missile control; Kite Screech (100mm) and 2 Bass Tilt (CIWS) gun control; Palm Frond navigation
Sonar: LF active search in bow; variable depth
Complement: 300

Background: The Udaloys are of great interest because they are optimized for the ASW role and are clearly intended to be the anti-submarine component of a mixed battle-group centred on an aircraft-carrier and operating at some distance from its base, probably in the northern and central Atlantic or Pacific Oceans.

The ASW armament is exceptionally powerful: the standard quadruple SS-N-14 launchers abreast the bridge, two RBU-6000 rocket launchers and two quadruple torpedo tubes amidships. The Udaloys also have two separate hangars for their pairs of ASW helicopters and are the first Soviet cruisers to be equipped to operate more than one aircraft, the first four of the class operate Ka-25 Hormone-As, while the fifth and subsequent ships operate the newer Ka-27 Helix. The landing platform is large, but the hangar floor is one deck lower with a ramp for moving the aircraft from one level to another.

The rake of the bow, which is usually sharp, even by Soviet Navy standards, and the positioning of the bow anchor indicate a particularly large low- or medium-frequency sonar dome fitted below, and this is confirmed by the characteristics of the bow wave. There is a VDS at the stem, streamed over the trasom in line with current Soviet Navy practice.

Other weapons are somewhat limited. The single 100mm dual-purpose guns in A and B positions are proven guns, but it is a little surprising that the new twin 130mm mounting is not fitted, as on the Sovremennyy class. There are four 30mm Gatling CIWS, while air defence is provided by eight SAM launchers for the new SA-N-9

PDMS set into the ship's structure, with 6ft (1.83m) diameter cover plates: four on the forecastle, two between the torpedo tubes and two at the forward end of the after deckhouse.

Air and surface surveillance radar antennas seem rather few by Soviet standards. This could well be, however, because the Soviet electronic designers have developed more sophisticated multi-purpose systems, as found in Western ships.

In view of the similarity in dimensions between this and the Sovremennyy class, which appeared at the same time but optimized for the surface warfare role, it is surprising that the two classes do not share a common hull. This certainly would have been the case for most Western navies, as, for example, in the French Georges Leygues class, but the political and economic restraints upon the Soviet Navy are much less severe and they have been permitted to optimize the hull-form. The propulsion form is also different, Sovremenny having steam turbines and Udaloy gas turbines, the latter being particularly suitable for ASW.

These ships are classified by the Soviets as *Bolshoy protivolodochny korabl* (large ASW ships) and by NATO as DDGs, although their size suggests that the description cruiser could be rather more appropriate.

Future: These striking warships are being produced at Kaliningrad (Yantar Works) and Leningrad (Zhdanov Works). Nine are definitely being produced and it would appear possible that a total of as many as twelve might be constructed. Such a building programme, when added to all the Soviet Navy's other construction activities, is indicative of the enormous resources being devoted to expansion of the navy.

Above: A splendid picture of the destroyer Udaloy, name ship of her class. The sharply raked bow and the bow wave pattern are clear evidence that a bow sonar is fitted. The Udaloy class is optimized for ASW and is probably intended to complement the surface-optimized Sovremennyy class in escort groups for the current Kiev class aircraft carries and for the Kremlin class CVNs when the latter become operational in the middle and late 1990s.

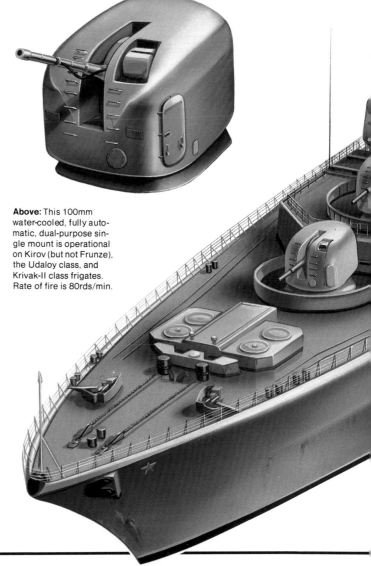

Above: This 100mm water-cooled, fully automatic, dual-purpose single mount is operational on Kirov (but not Frunze), the Udaloy class, and Krivak-II class frigates. Rate of fire is 80rds/min.

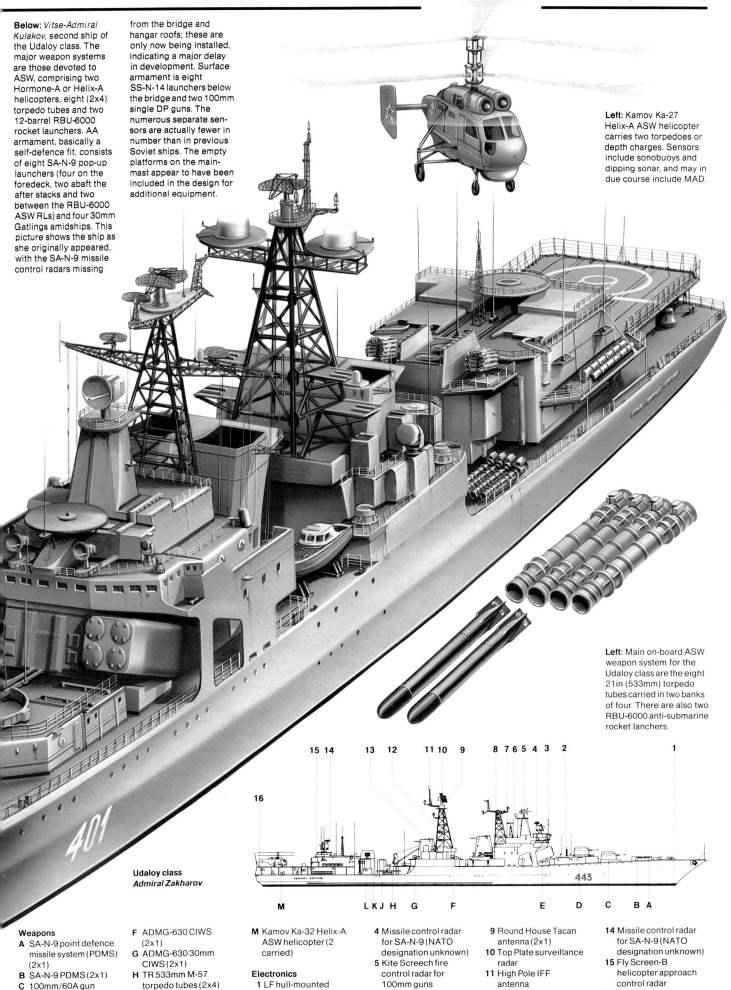

Below: *Vitse-Admiral Kulakov*, second ship of the Udaloy class. The major weapon systems are those devoted to ASW, comprising two Hormone-A or Helix-A helicopters, eight (2x4) torpedo tubes and two 12-barrel RBU-6000 rocket launchers. AA armament, basically a self-defence fit, consists of eight SA-N-9 pop-up launchers (four on the foredeck, two abaft the after stacks and two between the RBU-6000 ASW RLs) and four 30mm Gatlings amidships. This picture shows the ship as she originally appeared, with the SA-N-9 missile control radars missing

from the bridge and hangar roofs; these are only now being installed, indicating a major delay in development. Surface armament is eight SS-N-14 launchers below the bridge and two 100mm single DP guns. The numerous separate sensors are actually fewer in number than in previous Soviet ships. The empty platforms on the main-mast appear to have been included in the design for additional equipment.

Left: Kamov Ka-27 Helix-A ASW helicopter carries two torpedoes or depth charges. Sensors include sonobuoys and dipping sonar, and may in due course include MAD.

Left: Main on-board ASW weapon system for the Udaloy class are the eight 21in (533mm) torpedo tubes carried in two banks of four. There are also two RBU-6000 anti-submarine rocket lanchers.

401

Udaloy class
Admiral Zakharov

Weapons
- **A** SA-N-9 point defence missile system (PDMS) (2x1)
- **B** SA-N-9 PDMS (2x1)
- **C** 100mm/60A gun mounting (1x1)
- **D** 100mm/60A gun mounting (1x1)
- **E** SS-N-14 ASW missile launcher box (2x4)
- **F** ADMG-630 CIWS (2x1)
- **G** ADMG-630 30mm CIWS (2x1)
- **H** TR 533mm M-57 torpedo tubes (2x4)
- **J** SA-N-9 PDMS (2x1)
- **K** SA-N-9 PDMS (2x1)
- **L** RBU-6000 ASW rocket launcher (2x12)
- **M** Kamov Ka-32 Helix-A ASW helicopter (2 carried)

Electronics
- **1** LF hull-mounted sonar
- **2** DF loop
- **3** Eye Bowl missile control radar for SS-N-14 (2x1)
- **4** Missile control radar for SA-N-9 (NATO designation unknown)
- **5** Kite Screech fire control radar for 100mm guns
- **6** DF loop
- **7** Palm Frond navigation radar
- **8** Palm Frond navigation radar (2x1)
- **9** Round House Tacan antenna (2x1)
- **10** Top Plate surveillance radar
- **11** High Pole IFF antenna
- **12** Salt Pot ECM antenna (2x1)
- **13** Bass Tilt fire control radar for ADMG-630 (2x1)
- **14** Missile control radar for SA-N-9 (NATO designation unknown)
- **15** Fly Screen-B helicopter approach control radar
- **16** Variable depth sonar housing

Virginia (CGN 38) class

Origin: USA
Type: Nuclear-powered cruiser
(CGN)
Built: 1972-1980
Class: 4 in service
Displacement: 8,523 tons light;
9,473 tons full load (CGN 38); 10,000
tons full load (CGN 39, 40, 41)
Dimensions: Length 585ft
(178.4m) oa; beam 63ft (19.2m);
draught 29.5ft (9m)
Propulsion: 2-shaft nuclear (2
General Electric D2G pressurized-
water-cooled nuclear reactors;
two geared turbines), 100,000shp
Performance: Speed 30+ knots
Armament: SSM: 4 twin Harpoon
launchers
SAM: 2 twin Mk 26 launchers for
Standard SM-2(MR)
Guns: 2 single 5in/54 Mk 45; 2
40mm Mk 11 saluting guns
ASW: Asroc
Torpedo tubes: 2 x 3 Mk 32
Aircraft: 2 SH-2F LAMPS I
helicopters
Sensors: Radar: SPS-48A 3D air
search; SPS-40B air search; SPS-55
surface search; SPG-51, SPG-600,
SPQ-40A fire control; LN-66
navigation (CGN 39, 41 only)
Sonar: SQS-53A bow-mounted
Complement: 473

Background: The four ships of
the Virginia (CGN 38) class were
originally classified as guided-
missile frigates (DLGN), but this
was changed to guided-missile
cruiser (CGN) prior to the
commissioning of the first of class.
Their layout is similar to that of
their two California (CGN 36) class
predecessors, but with some
modifications, the most significant
of which are the replacement of
the Californias' single-arm Mk 13
launchers by the later Mk 26 twin
Asroc launcher forward and the
provision of a helicopter hangar in
the stern.

In earlier guided-missile cruisers
and destroyers booster-assisted
missiles such as Terrier were
stowed in horizontal magazine
rings and shorter missiles like
Tartar in cylindrical magazines.
The magazine associated with the
Mk 26 launcher, however, has a
continuous belt feed system with
vertical stowage and is capable of
accommodating a variety of
missiles. This has removed the
need for a separate Asroc
launcher, and the Standard
SM-2(MR) surface-to-air missiles
and Asroc rounds are carried
together in the forward magazine.
The resulting elimination of the
Asroc launcher and its associated
reloading deckhouse enabled the
hull to be shortened by 11ft
(3.35m).

The helicopter hangar measures
42ft by 14ft (12.8m x 4.3m) and is
served by an electro-mechanical
elevator covered by a telescopic
hatch. This arrangement in a ship
other than an aircraft carrier is the
first since the Des Moines (CA 134)
class cruisers of the mid-1940s.

The electronics outfit is similar
to that on the California class, but
the more advanced solid-state
SQS-53A bow-mounted sonar has
replaced the SQS-26, the Mk 116

digital ASW fire control system has
replaced the older analogue Mk
114, and the introduction of the
Standard SM-2(MR), which needs
target illumination only in the
terminal phase, enabled the three
forward SPS-51 tracker/illuminators
to be eliminated, reducing top
weight. Since these ships were
first commissioned they have all
received Harpoon at refits, and
they are scheduled to receive
Tomahawk and two Phalanx CIWS
guns at future refits.

The original plan to procure 11
ships of this class, in combination
with CGNs of earlier classes,
would have provided each of the
projected CVNs with four nuclear
powered escort vessels. However,
after four units had been laid down
further orders were suspended
while consideration was given first
to a Strike Cruiser (CSGN) concept
and then later to a Modified
Virginia (CGN 38) design fitted with
the Aegis system. The construction of
the Modified Virginia cruisers
was cancelled in January 1979,
and the proposal was resurrected
in March 1981 only to be cancelled
once again (almost certainly for
the final time) in February 1983. All
these projects have been abandoned
in favour of the conventionally
powered Ticonderoga (CG-47) class
now under construction, and there
are no current plans for any
further nuclear powered cruisers
to be built.

Virginia (CGN 38) and *Mississippi*
(CGN 40) serve with the Atlantic
Fleet, and *Texas* (CGN 39) and
Arkansas (CGN 41) with the Pacific
Fleet. Each pair acts as part of a
nuclear powered task force centred
on a CVN.

Future: The four cruisers of the
Virginia class will be modified
and updated at future refits.
Current proposals include the
fitting of Tomahawk cruise missiles
in Mk 143 armoured box launchers,
and the installation of two
Phalanx Mk 15 20mm CIWS in each
ship. Funds for a proposed fifth
member were not authorized.

Above: USS Virginia serves as
an escort in the Atlantic Fleet,
using her Standard and Asroc
missiles to defend the nuclear
powered aircraft carriers which
form the focus of task forces.

Right: There are two of
these Mk 26 Mod 1
launchers for Standard
SM-2(MR) (shown here)
and Asroc missiles on
each Virginia class
cruiser. Mk 26 launchers
are also being fitted to
nuclear cruisers (Mod 1),
eight Arleigh Burke class
DDGs (Mod 3, Mod 4) and
four Ticonderroga class
cruisers (Mod 5). Modu-
lar design means maga-
zines of 24, 44, or 64
rounds can be fitted.

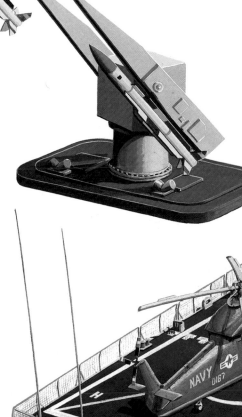

Right: The Kaman SH-2F
Seasprite LAMPS I heli-
copter has equipped the
US Navy's front-line ASW
helicopter force for some
years, and is only now
being supplemented by
the Sikorsky SH-60B
Seahawk. The SH-2F
carries more than two
tons of special equip-
ment, including the
powerful chin-mounted
Canadian Marconi
LN-66HP surveillance
radar, DIFAR and DIS-
CASS sonobuoys, Texas
Instruments AQS-81
towed MAD gear, ALR-66
ESM receiver, navigation
and communications
equipment, and Mk 44 or
Mk 46 torpedoes. Some
190 early model SH-2s
were delivered; all were
upgraded to SH-2D stan-
dard in the early 1970s
and will be further
upgraded to SH-2Fs in
due course; 88 new
SH-2Fs were manufac-
tured in the 1970s, and in
1981 the production line
was reopened to produce
another 18 SH-2Fs.

Below: The US Navy's single 5in/54 Mk 45 was developed by the Northern Ordnance Division of the FMC Corporation. It is mounted in Virginia, California and Ticonderoga class cruisers, Spruance, Kidd and Arleigh Burke class destroyers and Tarawa class amphibious assault ships. It needs a crew of only six men, none of whom is in the mounting itself, and with a total mount weight of 21.7 tonnes is the lightest of its calibre in any navy. To achieve the desired simplicity and reliability certain compromises had to be made and maximum elevation is limited to 65°; rate of fire is 20 rds/min, while maximum ranges are 25,900 yards (23,700m) horizontally and 48,690ft (14,840m) vertically. A laser-guided shell is under development but not yet in production.

Below: USS *Texas* (CGN 39), second of the Virginia class cruisers. These ships are powered by two General Electric D2G nuclear reactors and it is anticipated that they will operate for 10 years on one nuclear fuelling. They are heavily armed for their size, their open weather decks with an apparently small number of weapons concealing large magazines which provide considerable combat capability, which will be further enhanced by the mounting of two armoured box launchers for Tomahawk missiles. The Kaman SH-2F helicopter has a large flight deck on the quarterdeck (fantail) with the hangar below it; the aircraft is brought up to the deck by an elevator.

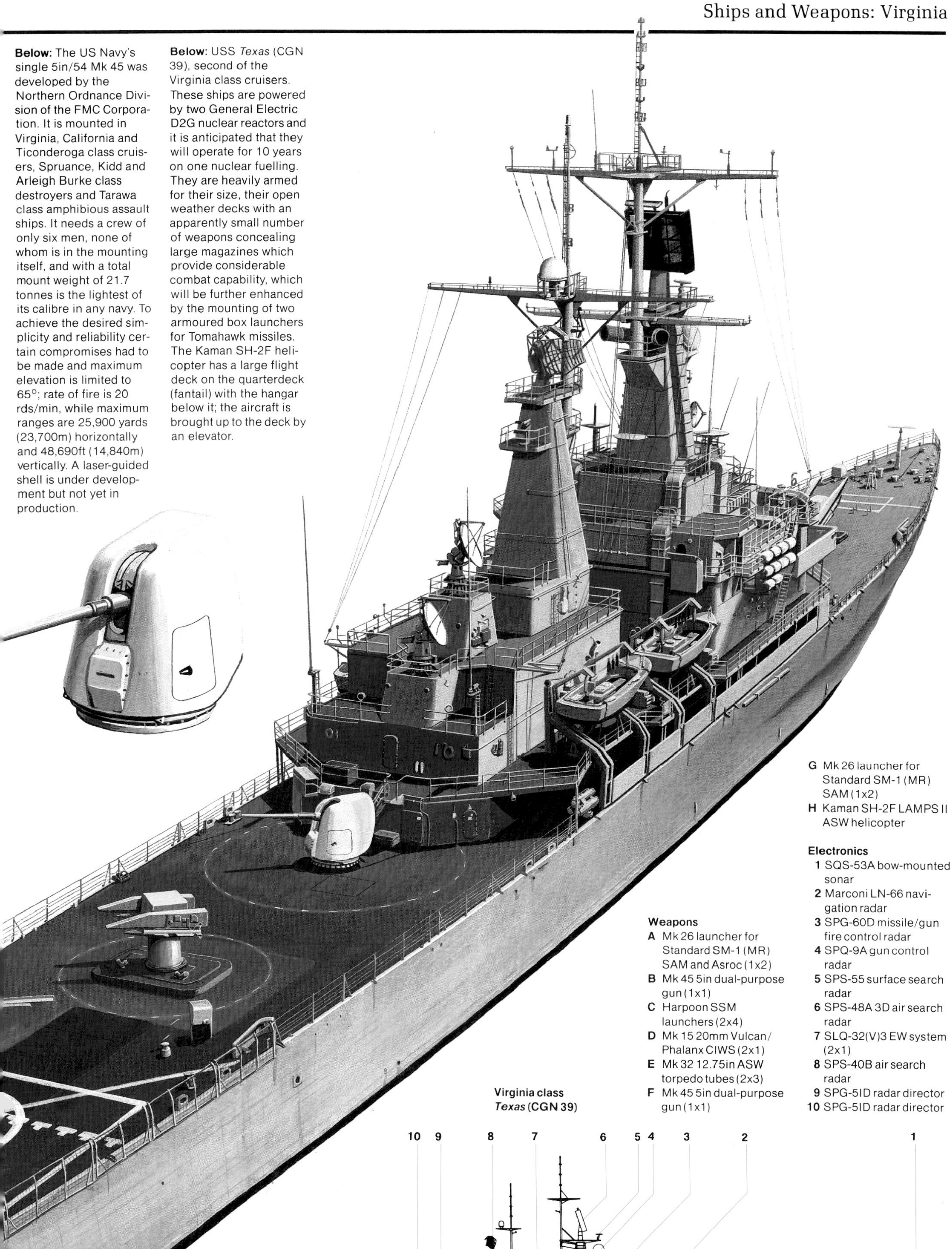

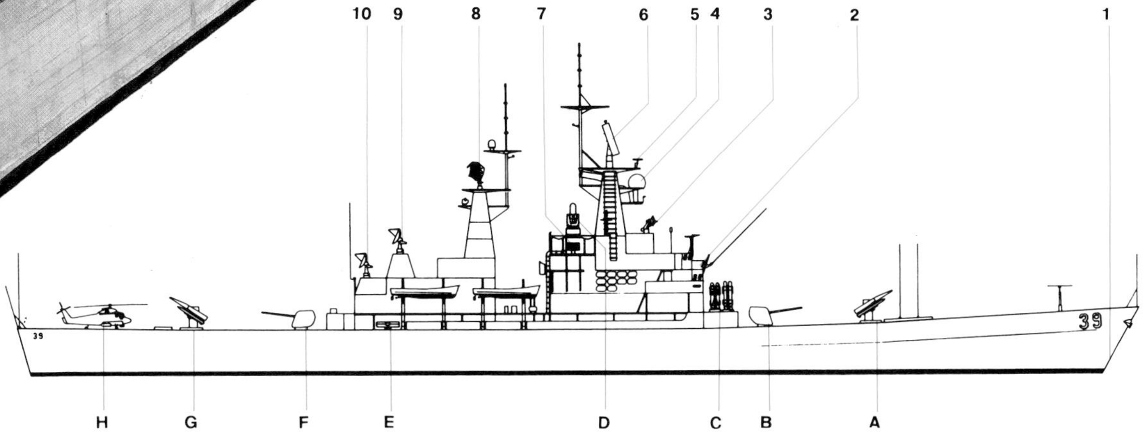

Weapons

A Mk 26 launcher for Standard SM-1 (MR) SAM and Asroc (1x2)
B Mk 45 5in dual-purpose gun (1x1)
C Harpoon SSM launchers (2x4)
D Mk 15 20mm Vulcan/ Phalanx CIWS (2x1)
E Mk 32 12.75in ASW torpedo tubes (2x3)
F Mk 45 5in dual-purpose gun (1x1)
G Mk 26 launcher for Standard SM-1 (MR) SAM (1x2)
H Kaman SH-2F LAMPS II ASW helicopter

Electronics

1 SQS-53A bow-mounted sonar
2 Marconi LN-66 navigation radar
3 SPG-60D missile/gun fire control radar
4 SPQ-9A gun control radar
5 SPS-55 surface search radar
6 SPS-48A 3D air search radar
7 SLQ-32(V)3 EW system (2x1)
8 SPS-40B air search radar
9 SPG-5ID radar director
10 SPG-5ID radar director

Virginia class
Texas (CGN 39)

167

Vittorio Veneto class

Origin: Italy
Type: Light aircraft carrier (CVS)
Built: 1965-1969
Class: 1 in service
Displacement: 7,500 tons standard: 8,850 tons full load
Dimensions: Length 589ft (179.5m) oa; beam 63.6ft (19.4m); draught 19.7ft (6m)
Propulsion: 2-shaft geared turbine (2 Tosi double-reduction), 73,000shp
Performance: Speed 32 knots; range 5,000nm at 17 knots
Weapons: SSM: 4 Teseo launchers
SAM: 1 twin Mk 10 launcher for Asroc/Standard (40 missiles)
Guns: 8 single 76mm/62 (Argo system); 6 twin 40mm/70 (Dardo system)
Torpedo tubes: 2 x 3 Mk 32 for A/S torpedoes
Aircraft: 9 AB 212 or 4-SH-2D
Sensors: Long-range search radar: SPS-40
Air search radar: SPS-52C
Surface search radar: MM/SPS-702
Search radar: SPS-70
Fire control radar: SPG-55C for Standard; 4 Orion for Argo (76mm gun) systems; 2 RTN-20X for Dardo (40mm gun) systems
Complement: 550

Background: The Italian Navy has long been noted for its imaginative and graceful warship designs, whose prime purpose has been to provide the most combat-effective naval units for the unique conditions (both nautical and tactical) found in the Mediterranean. In one stream of this post-World War II development pattern there has been a series of air-capable cruisers, starting with the Andrea Doria class in the 1950s, and passing, by way of the *Vittorio Veneto*, to the new *Giuseppe Garibaldi*.

The first in the series, *Andrea Doria* and *Caio Dulio*, were fairly small (6,500 tons full load displacement) and had conventional helicopter-handling arrangements, comprising a large double hangar incorporated into the after super-structure which led directly onto a flight deck above the stern. Because of their size they could operate only four AB 204 ASW helicopters.

In the *Vittorio Veneto*, which was laid down in June 1965, these arrangements have been considerably modified, with an extra deck aft giving space beneath for a hangar 90ft by 50ft (27.4m x 15.2m). *Vittorio Veneto* was originally designed to operate nine AB 204 ASW helicopters, all of which could be accommodated in the hangar, but these have now been replaced by the improved AB 212, which can also be accommodated in the hangar. The alternative complement of four Sea Kings cannot be struck down, however, as they are too big for the hangar, which is only two decks high; if embarked, therefore, they have to remain on deck.

Four helicopter spots are marked out on the very spacious flight-deck, which is served by a single large centre-line lift immediately aft of the superstructure, and two sets of fin stabilizers result in a steady platform for helicopter operations. There is, of course, no reason why the *Vittorio Veneto* could not also operate VTOL aircraft such as the Sea Harrier although the lack of a forward-facing ski-jump would restrict the aircraft to vertical takeoffs and thus reduce payload/range.

Like the Soviet Navy with its air capable designs (the Moskva and Kiev classes), the Italian Navy has ensured that its ships have an effective armament of their own. As completed, *Vittorio Veneto* had a cruiser armament similar to that of the Andrea Doria class, with a Mk 10 twin SAM launcher forward and single 76mm guns disposed in a symmetrical fashion around the superstructure. She underwent extensive modernization during the years 1981-84 in which the Terrier system was upgraded to fire the Standard SM-1 (ER) missile and the single 76mm gun was replaced by three 40mm/70 Breda compact mountings with Dardo fire control systems.

Future: With the advent of the *Giuseppe Garibaldi* it is clear that no more ships will be built to the *Vittorio Veneto* design. However, the *Vittorio Veneto* will remain an effective and capable component of NATO's Mediterranean fleet for many years to come.

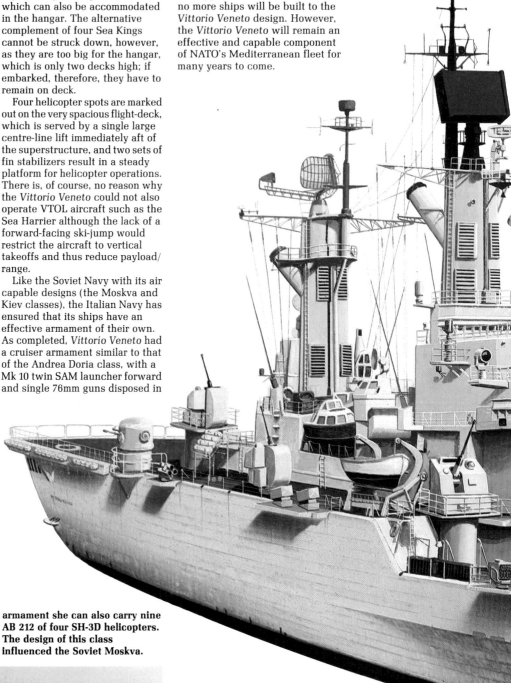

Below: Vittorio Veneto (C 550) is of conventional design forward but has a large flight deck aft. As well as her heavy AA and anti-surface armament she can also carry nine AB 212 of four SH-3D helicopters. The design of this class influenced the Soviet Moskva.

Left: The OTO Melara Otomat Mk 2 (also known as Teseo) sea-skimming anti-ship missile has an active radar homing head. Range is 80nm (150km), but to reach targets over the horizon external target destination is necessary.

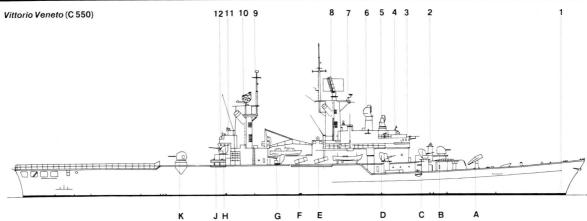

Below: Vittorio Veneto showing her substantial weapons fit, which includes eight single OTO Melara 76mm/62 dual-purpose guns (Argo system), twin-arm Mk 10 launcher for Asroc ASW missiles and Standard SAMs (Aster system), and four Otomat Mk 2 (Teseo) SSM launchers. The two large radars above the bridge are SPG-55C for SAM direction, and the planer array on the forward mack is the antenna for the SPS-52C long-range 3D air surveillance radar.

Vittorio Veneto (C 550)

Weapons

A Mk 20 Mod 7 Aster launch system for Asroc and Standard missiles
B Breda 40mm gun component of Dardo CIWS (1x2)
C 76mm OTO Melara dual-purpose gun mounting (2x1)
D 76mm OTO Melara dual-purpose gun mounting (2x1)
E OTO Melara Otomat Mk II (Teseo) SSM launcher (2x1)
F OTO Melara Otomat Mk II (Teseo) SSM launcher (2x1)
G 76mm OTO Melara dual-purpose gun mounting (2x1)
H 76mm OTO Melara dual-purpose gun mounting (2x1)
J 324mm ILAS-3 ASW torpedo tubes (2x3)
K Breda 40mm gun component of Dardo CIWS (2x2)

Electronics

1 SQS-23G hull-ounted sonar
2 Selenia RTN-20X fire control radar for Dardo CIWS
3 SMA 3RM7 surface search radar
4 Selenia RTN-10X fire control radar for Albatros system
5 SPG-55C SAM control radar
6 SPG-55C SAM control radar
7 MM/SPS-768v1 target designator
8 Hughes SPS-52C long-range surveillance radar
9 URN-20A Tacan antenna
10 RAN-20X air search and surveillance radar
11 Selenea RTN-10X fire control radar for Albatros system
12 Selenia RTN-20X fire control radar for Dardo CIWS system (1x2)

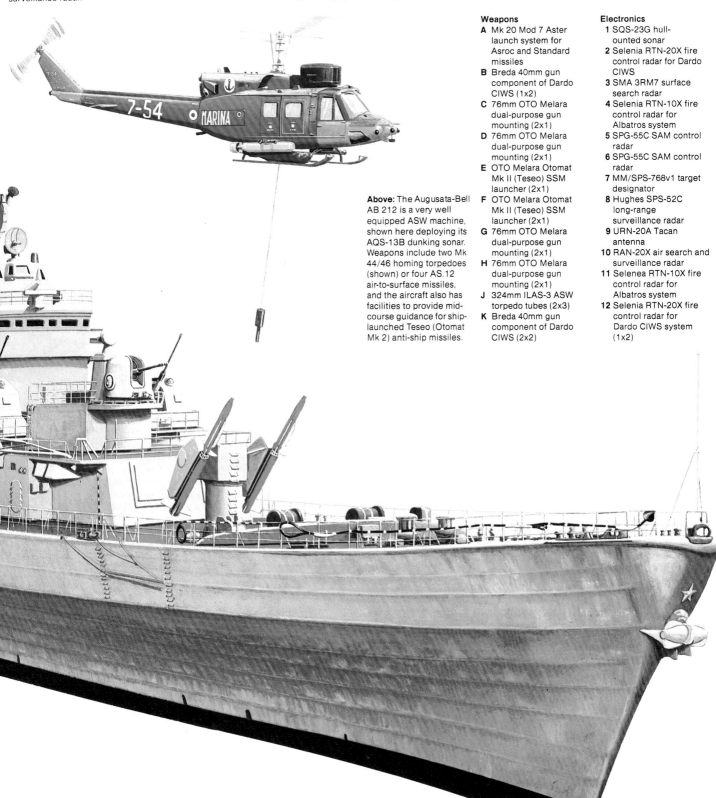

Above: The Augusata-Bell AB 212 is a very well equipped ASW machine, shown here deploying its AQS-13B dunking sonar. Weapons include two Mk 44/46 homing torpedoes (shown) or four AS.12 air-to-surface missiles, and the aircraft also has facilities to provide mid-course guidance for ship-launched Teseo (Otomat Mk 2) anti-ship missiles.

Walrus class

Origin: Netherlands
Type: Patrol submarine (SS)
Built: 1979-1987
Class: 2 building
Displacement: 1,900 tons standard; 2,450 tons surfaced; 2,800 tons submerged
Dimensions: Length 223.1ft (67.7m) oa; beam 27.6ft (8.4m); draught 21.6ft (6.6m)
Propulsion: 1-shaft diesel-electric (3 SEMT-Pielseck 12 PA4-V200 diesels, 6,910hp; 1 Holec electric motor)
Performance: Speed 13 knots surfaced, 20 knots submerged
Weapons: Torpedo tubes: 4 x 21in (553mm) for Mk 48 torpedoes, encapsulated Sub-Harpoon and mines; 20 torpedoes or missiles carried.
Sensors: Sonar: Thomson-CSF Radar: Decca navigation
Complement: 50

Background: The Netherlands has a reputation for innovative submarine design — it was, for example, a Dutch naval officer who invented the schnorkel tube in the mid-1930s — so it is not surprising that the Dutch came up with an unusual concept for its first post-war class of four boats, the Dolfijn/Potvis class, three of which are still in service. The outstanding feature of this class is that they have three interconnected

pressure vessels in a 'treble-bubble' arrangement, surrounded by a non-pressurized streamlined outer casing: the large upper hull contains the crew and most of the equipment, while two smaller hulls side by side below it contain machinery and stores. Although structurally very successful the Dolfijn/Potvis design proved to be cramped and complex and incapable of high underwater speeds, and the formula has not been repeated.

The next class, the Zwaardvis (two built), was completed in 1972 and featured an Albacore-type teardrop hull. In fact, due to technology transfers within the NATO framework, the Dutch were able to utilize many features of the contemporary US Navy Barbel design. The Zwaardvis class replaced two ex-US Navy Guppy submarines in Dutch service. Two Improved Zwaardvis submarines have been ordered by Taiwan, but a repeat order for another two was frustrated by political pressure from the Chinese government.

By the late 1970s the Royal Netherlands Navy was having to consider the replacement of the Dolfijn class in the mid-1980s. A tentative plan for a collaborative programme with the Royal Navy having come to naught the Dutch set about producing an updated

Above: The Walrus is prepared for launch at the Rotterdamsche Droogdok Maatschappij (RDM) yard on October 28, 1985, with the second boat of the class, Zeeleeuw, under construction alongside. The most obvious change compared with the preceding Zwaardvis class is the adoption of X-plane after control surfaces, while new machinery and a five-bladed propeller were also specified for the new class.

Walrus class

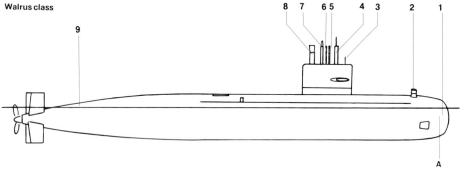

Weapons
A 21in (533mm) torpedo tubes for Mk 48 torpedoes and Sub-Harpoon

Electronics
1 Thomson-CSF active sonar
2 Thomson-CSF passive sonar
3 Periscope
4 ECM mast
5 Periscope
6 Decca radar
7 Radio mast
8 Schnorkel
9 Type 2026 towed sonar array

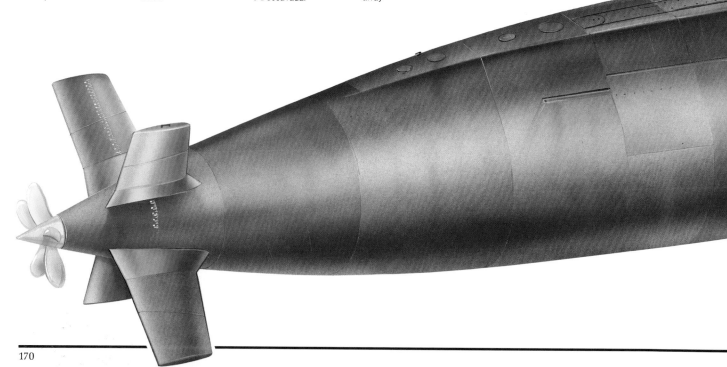

Zwaardvis design, but there are now so many differences that the new Walrus boats are considered a separate class of their own. The most significant external difference is the fitting of X-planes, which give maximum fin area without projecting below the keel, easing operations near the seabed. The interaction of the four fins, which combine stern plane and rudder functions, is so complex that computer control is necessary.

The diesel generators, which are very similar to those of the Dutch Kortenaer class frigates, are sited alongside each other at the broadest part of the hull, and are mounted on a false deck to cut down vibration transference to the hull.

These boats are constructed of French Marel high tensile steel and the number of welded joints and hull apertures has been reduced to the absolute minimum. As a result the naval operational requirement to increase the diving depth by 50 per cent over the

Zwaardvis class has been met. Only four torpedo tubes are fitted, but these are capable of firing Sub-Harpoon missiles as well as conventional torpedoes, and the spaciousness of the torpedo room facilitates rapid reloading.

Considerable efforts have been devoted to improving the control systems and many functions have been automated. As a result the crew has been reduced from 67 in the Zwaardvis boats to just 50 in the Walrus class.

Future: The Royal Netherlands Navy has announced its intention to order two more of this class to replace the last two of the Potvis/Dolfijn class, and it is probable that further units will be ordered to replace the Zwaardvis class.

However, the fire which caused extensive damage to *Walrus* in August 1986 is likely to have an adverse effect on the delivery dates of the remaining three boats already ordered, *Zeeleuw, Dolfijn* and *Bruinvis*.

Above: Following her launch, Walrus was fitting out in a floating dock at the RDM yard when a fire broke out in the upper midship area, causing extensive damage. Already the most expensive warship ever built for the Royal Netherlands Navy, the Walrus had been estimated to cost around £136 million, and repairs may add as much as another third to that figure, as well as delaying her commissioning, originally scheduled to take place in the early part of 1987, by several months at least.

Below: The artist's drawing shows the clean lines of the Walrus class; this is *Zeeleeuw* (S-803). The forward hydroplanes are mounted high on the fin, but the after hydroplanes are of cruciform configuration (known as X-planes), which improves manoeuvrability and means they do not project below the keel, though the interaction between the four planes is so complex that a computer is required to control them. The massive tubular device on the fin is the snort induction mast, a Dutch invention.

S803

Above: The Walrus class boats are armed with four 21in (533mm) torpedo tubes, and the normal weapon load is a mix of Mk 48 torpedoes, Sub-Harpoon and tube-launched mines. Sensors are French (Thomson-CSF sonars) and British (Type 2026 towed array), and are controlled by the Dutch SEWACO VIII (Sensor Weapon Command and Control) system built by Hollandse Signaalapparaaten. The US Mk 48 torpedo, designed for use by submarines against surface and sub-surface targets, has a range of some 50km and a speed in the region of 50 knots. It can either be wire-guided or use its on-board active-passive homing systems.

Wielingen (E 71) class

Origin: Belgium
Type: Frigate (FF)
Built: 1974-1978
Class: 4 in service
Displacement: 1,880 tons light; 2,283 tons full load
Dimensions: Length 349ft (103.4) oa; beam 40.3ft (12.3m); draught 18.4ft (5.6m)
Propulsion: 2-shaft CODOG (1 Rolls-Royce Olympus TM3B gas turbine, 2 Cockerill CO-240 V-12 diesels), 28,000/12,000bhp
Performance: Speed 29 knots; range 4,500nm at 18 knots, 6,000nm at 16 knots.
Weapons: Missiles: 4 MM.38 Exocet SSM; 1 NATO Sea Sparrow octuple SAM launcher
Guns: 1 100mm/55 Mod 1968 DP mounting; 1 20mm Goalkeeper CIWS to be fitted
Torpedo tubes: 2 x 1 L5
ASW weapons: 1 six-barrel Creusot-Loire 375mm launcher with Bofors rockets
Sensors: Radar: HSA WM-25 surface air surveillance; HSA DA-05; Raytheon TM 1645/X navigation
Sonar: Canadian Westinghouse SQS 505A hull-mounted
Complement: 160

Background: The Belgian Navy acquired eight ex-Royal Navy Algerine class warships for use as fleet minesweepers and ASW escorts in 1949-1953. These were due to be withdrawn by 1969, and the Belgian Navy staff formulated a requirement for a replacement class which would "provide, in close cooperation with Allied naval forces, protection of the Allied and national merchant shipping in the North Sea, the English Channel and its Western Approaches". The units were to retain a full ASW capability and be equipped with limited anti-aircraft and anti-surface weapons.

To keep this undertaking to manageable proportions the Belgian Navy applied three principles: to provide only those features essential to the escort mission and self-protection; to utilize only weapons, sensors and other equipment standardized (or at least evaluated) by other NATO navies; and that the ships must be constructed in Belgian yards.

This was a formidable task. The programme was approved on June 23, 1971, design studies were completed in July 1973 and the order was placed in October of that year. France and the Netherlands assisted in the design task, while those nations providing armament and sensors helped in the construction phase. Two ships were built by Boel at Temse and two by Cockerill at Hoboken, with the first ship from each yard commissioned in January 1978 and the second in October of the same year. This was a remarkably smooth and efficient programme, especially when it represents by far the largest warship programme ever undertaken in Belgium.

The Wielingen class is a compact and well-armed design, with as good a combination of anti-air, anti-surface and anti-submarine

Above: Wielingen (F 910), name ship of a very successful class of four Belgian-designed and -built ASW frigates. The octuple NATO Sea Sparrow launcher can be seen here, but at the time this picture was taken the four MM.38 Exocet launchers had not bee fitted.

capabilities as could reasonably be expected on a hull of this size. The only major tactical deficiency is the lack of an ASW helicopter, although it would have required a somewhat larger (and much more expensive) hull to accommodate such a weapon system. Clearly, modern conditions demand a close-in weapons system (CIWS) for protection against incoming missiles: the Belgian Navy decided to adopt whatever system was chosen by the Netherlands and the Goalkeeper system selected by the latter will be fitted to the four Wielingens in due course.

The Belgian Navy can be proud of these ships, which compare very favourably with other ships of the same size such as the Vosper Thornycroft frigates and the MEKO designs.

Future: The four ships of the Wielingen class—*Wielingen*, *Westdiep*, *Wandelaar* and *Westhinder*—will be updated at periodic refits. They will have to be replaced in the late 1990s, but all current Belgian Navy funding is being poured into the Tripartite Minehunter/Sweeper programme on which Belgium, France and the Netherlands are collaborating. The first Belgian vessel, *Aster*, was commissioned in 1985, and it is envisaged that a total of 15 will be built in Belgium; the Netherlands and France were also to build 15 each, though the latter reduced its order to 10.

Above: MM.38 Exocet missiles and containers. After a target fix from the ship's radar, MM.38 is launched at a 15° angle and, following a boost phase, achieves sustained flight at an altitude of 10-50ft (3-15m). It uses inertial guidance and radar terminal homing.

Below: *Wandelaar* (F 912). Among the most comprehensively equipped and armed ships for their size in any navy, the Wielingen class are the first modern warships to be designed in Belgium. Shown clearly here are the NATO Sea Sparrow SAM launcher and the four launcher/containers for MM.38 Exocet. Between the Exocets and the unusual funnel is the HSA DA-05 air/surface surveillance radar. Forward of the bridge are a Creusot-Loire ASW rocket launcher (not visible from this angle) and a 100mm DP gun turret. It is intended to fit the Dutch Goalkeeper CIWS in due course, but the position of the mounting is not yet known. Two launchers for French L5 ASW torpedoes are fitted; one door can be seen in the starboard quarter. Power is provided by two Cockerill 3,000hp diesels and one Rolls-Royce Olympus TM 3B 28,000hp gas-turbine in a CODOG arrangement, giving a maximum speed of 28 knots.

Below: The Wielingen class is one of a number of ASW types to mount the Creusot-Loire launcher for Bofors 375mm ASW rockets. The sextuple mount features automatic loading (in the vertical position) and fires either salvoes or ripples at a rate of one rocket per second. The Bofors 375mm rockets have various warheads and three types of rocket motor to give different range brackets. The missiles follow a flat trajectory to minimize flight time and reduce the target's evasion possibilities and fuzes have proximity, time and impact devices. Range brackets covered are: 388-930 yards (355-850m); 716-1,790 yards (655-1,635m); and 1,730-3,965 yards (1,580-3,625m). Sonar imputs on target location and rate of change of position are fed into a computer.

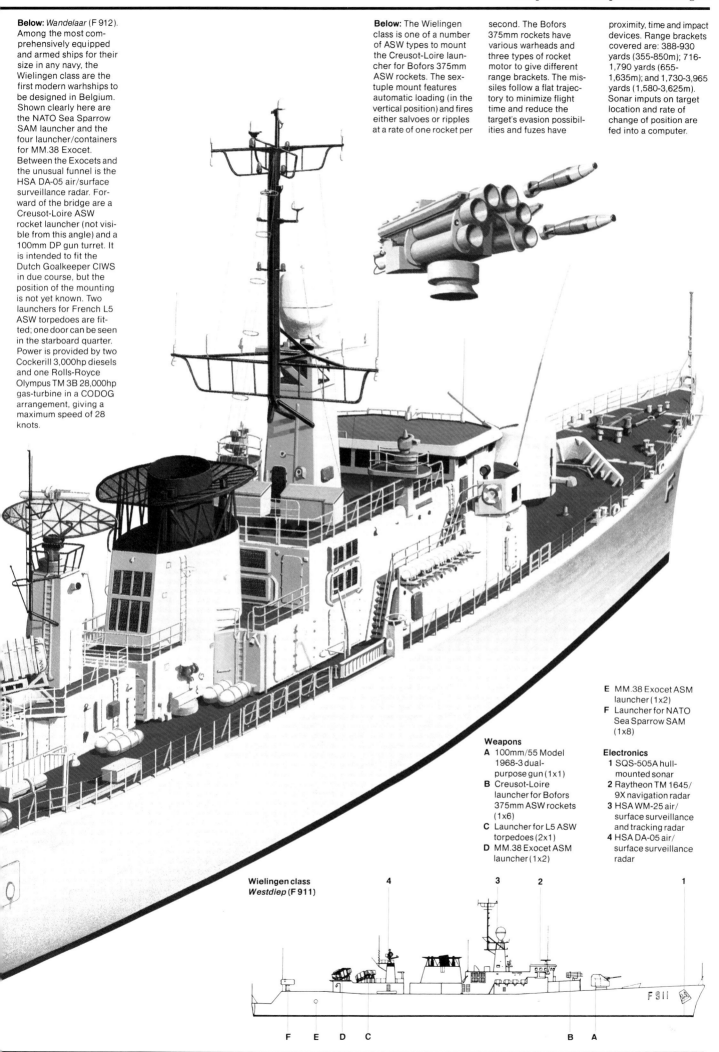

Weapons
A 100mm/55 Model 1968-3 dual-purpose gun (1x1)
B Creusot-Loire launcher for Bofors 375mm ASW rockets (1x6)
C Launcher for L5 ASW torpedoes (2x1)
D MM.38 Exocet ASM launcher (1x2)
E MM.38 Exocet ASM launcher (1x2)
F Launcher for NATO Sea Sparrow SAM (1x8)

Electronics
1 SQS-505A hull-mounted sonar
2 Raytheon TM 1645/9X navigation radar
3 HSA WM-25 air/surface surveillance and tracking radar
4 HSA DA-05 air/surface surveillance radar

Wielingen class
Westdiep (F 911)

Naval Combat Tactics

Introduction

The oceans and seas of the world cover 71% of the earth's surface, and the three major oceans—Pacific, Atlantic and Indian—encompass over 124 million square miles (320 million square kilometres). In their physical characteristics the three oceans differ from one another, especially in terms of temperature and salinity, which vary both horizontally and with depth, producing layers in the sea that can distort sound and provide protection for submarines from the searching sonars of surface ships and aircraft.

The seabed itself changes shape rapidly, especially near land, where numerous shallows caused by shoals and rocks provide a constant hazard to the mariner. And depth of the sea varies. Continental shelves extend for some 40nm from the land masses and here the water averages less than 425ft (130m) in depth. This area, however, includes only about 5% of the world's ocean, and seaward of the shelf is the continental slope, a zone where depth increases rapidly from 425ft (130m) down to about 6,500ft (2,000m). Beyond this again, the continental rise begins a slow descent to depths of 13,000-19,500ft (4,000-6,000m). Known, misleadingly, as the abyssal plain, this area is marked by a rugged and complex topography.

Even here there exist trenches up to 36,000ft (11,000m) deep, where the temperature may be as low as −2°C and the pressure as great as 30 tons per square metre. It might be thought that man would be unable to visit such an environment, but on January 23, 1960, a manned submarine piloted by Jacques Piccard and Lt Donald Walsh, USN, dived to just

Above: A Charles F. Adams class destroyer meets heavy weather. The sea can be a hostile environment for men and for their equipment, but both must maintain a state of constant readiness.

Below: This view of an A7-E Corsair, taking off from the deck of USS Saratoga in January 1986 somewhere in the Mediterranean, conveys something of the vastness of the world's oceans.

short of this depth in the bathyscope *Triste*. A modern SSN such as the Soviet Alfa class is estimated to have a diving depth of 2-3,000ft (610-915m), and depth performance becomes an increasingly important tactical consideration as ASW techniques grow more sophisticated.

The oceans are continuously on the move, affected both by daily tidal movement (caused by the gravitational attraction of the moon and the sun) and by the currents and gulf streams, some of which move as fast as 136 miles (250km) per day. Currents flow at all depths, though they are generally at their strongest near the surface, and their circulation actually occurs in three dimensions, so that a current at any depth may have a vertical component as well as a horizontal one. The main cause of surface currents in the open oceans is the wind.

Superimposed on all this, climatic conditions vary from the extremes of tropical storms and water spouts to the completely calm. The height of waves can change within hours from only a few centimetres to 25-30 metres with wind speeds of over 100mph (160km/h). Likewise, visibility can be as far as a man can see from the bridge of a ship at one moment and reduced to zero by fog or storm the next.

This, then, is the environment in which man has fought some of his bloodiest battles for some 5,000 years, and in order to understand better the tactics of today's sophisticated fleets, it is important to appreciate the evolution of naval warfare over the centuries. For all the advances in technology, it is very likely that the concerns of Admiral Woodward, the

British commander in the 1982 Falklands War, were similar to those of Nelson or many admirals before them. In particular, two thoughts have dominated: the whereabouts of the enemy and the demands of the environment itself.

In general, it should be borne in mind that the sea and the warship have their own unique characteristics which give naval operations specific features, two of the most important being geographic and legal. The most distinctive feature of the sea's geography is the uniformity of its surface: there are no hills and valleys, no areas of dense human population, no frontiers and no roads; friends and enemies can go where and how they like.

The law of the sea is determined mainly by convention. There are considered to be both national and international rights at sea, but in reality, because of the vastness of the area, they are difficult to enforce if challenged. Unimpeded passage on the high seas, an accepted and sometimes jealously guarded privilege available to all, is one that permits great freedom of action and has led to the principle of establishing "habitual usage" as a valid legal precedent. It also means that naval forces can be deployed during peacetime to all parts of the world without necessarily provoking any reaction, and such deployments have long been a common practice of most of the large navies.

It can be seen, therefore, that forces can clash at sea without escalatory consequences that a similar action on land would have. The boundaries between peace, crisis and war are far less clear cut.

Vertical temperture distribution

Temperature (°C)

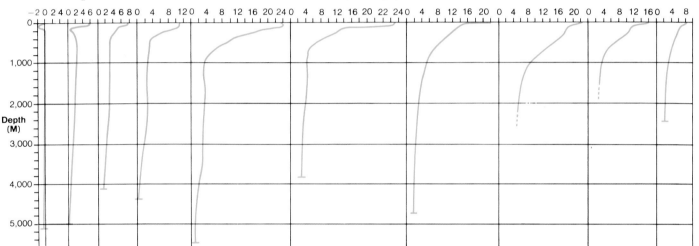

Above: The vertical temperature distribution at a series of stations along a meridian in the Atlantic. This trace clearly shows the changing temperature as the depth increases. Close to the surface solar radiation heats the water, though it can be seen that this effect varies widely, and below the surface layer the temperature falls with depth in layers, some as small as 2-4 inches (5-10cm), until it reaches the thermocline, where it falls more rapidly until it stabilises and slowly decreases to the seabed. These changes have a major influence on ASW as they affect the velocity of sound and distort sonar transmissions.

Left: For the direct measurement of sound velocity, instruments like this Expendable Sound Velocimeter (XSV) are used to obtain sound profiles for ASW operations.

Right: The Trident armed Ohio clas nuclear powered submarine USS Georgia returns from a patrol. For 90 days she will have been invisible in the ocean depths.

The Evolution of Naval Tactics

Since the dawn of history states have realized the importance of trading with each other and that a desire for ever-increasing wealth demands the ability to pass unhindered across the sea—what is known in today's strategic jargon as maintaining the sea lines of communication (SLOCS). The first recorded use of warships occurred some 5,000 years ago on the river Nile: in about 2,900 BC the Pharaoh Snafru sent 40 armed ships to Byblos to buy cedar wood. Another 1,700 years were to pass before ships were designed specifically to attack others. Known as biremes, these were the forerunners of the galley, which was to dominate naval warfare for 2,000 years.

Though ships from the earliest times carried soldiers, the first significant weapon employed was the ram, intended to strike an enemy vessel at its most vulnerable point, on or below the water line. The tactical employment of these weapons was dominated by two major considerations. Firstly, a matter of metres separated ramming and being rammed. In the height of battle the power of manoeuvre and the skills of seamanship were at a premium. Secondly, too often the impact of ramming could be as damaging to the attacker as to the defender, a possibility exaggerated by the design of the ships which, because they needed to be fast and to accelerate quickly in order to produce the necessary kinetic energy for a successful ram, were lightly built with shallow keels.

Ramming has continued to be used throughout history, and until the beginning of this century warships were still being built with bows designed specifically for this purpose. During World Wars I and II there were numerous instances of ships resorting to ramming their opponents, especially during attacks on submarines or when the firepower of the defender was judged to be greater than that of the attacker and it was believed that more damage could be caused by a controlled and premeditated collision than by gunfire, even if the likely outcome was the destruction of the ramming ship.

As recently as 1976, the confrontation between the UK and Iceland over the fishing rights within the Icelandic government's declared 200-mile Economic Zone—the so-called 'Cod War'—was fought out between the respective navies without a single shot being fired, but with considerable damage being inflicted on the vessels of both sides by deliberate collisions.

1571: LEPANTO

The tactics of fighting galleys were essentially an extension of land warfare practice, and in their last great battle, in 1571 at Lepanto, the fleets met like two armies. Their formation was rigid, the commands were military, and while the sailors initially positioned the ships it was the generals and the soldiers who conducted the battle. The day was won for the Christians by their skilful use of 35 Spanish galleys held in reserve until the height of the fighting, and by the deployment of six galleasses, galleys that differed from the standard design in one important aspect: each had sixty cannon arranged broadside. Their guns battered the Turkish fleet and set up the condition for victory, which was to board and capture the enemy's vessels.

This development emphasises an all-important aspect of naval tactics over the centuries, namely the constant search for technological innovation in order to gain tactical advantage. In naval affairs progress has tended to be slow, perhaps due to the natural conservatism of the mariners.

The use of guns mounted either side of a vessel, coupled with the introduction of sailing ships, led to tactics which were employed for the next 300 years. The method of fighting ships changed from line abreast formation to line ahead. This was designed to ensure that a man-of-war could open its field of fire before joining action, though the inaccuracy of the earliest guns

Below: During the 1976 Cod War between the UK and Iceland the opposing navies resorted to the tactic of ramming. Here the Icelandic gunboat Baldur swings her stern against HMS Diomede.

The Battle of Lepanto, 1571

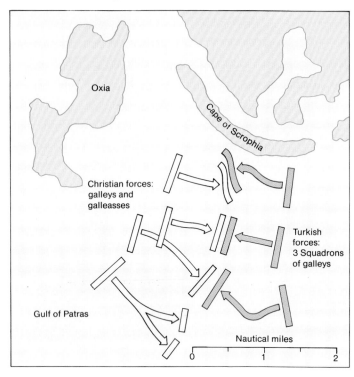

Above: At dawn on October 7, 1571, the most powerful forces that had ever met at sea came within sight of each other at the entrance to what is now called the Gulf of Patras, to the west of the larger Gulf of Corinth. The Christian Navy won the battle through the skilful use of armed galleasses.

and their limited range made it necessary to open fire at virtually point blank distances. Since sailing ships were normally captured by boarding parties in the end, these tactical requirements were complementary to each other.

The advent of sailing ships brought with it a particular benefit which profoundly affected both strategy and tactics: they were the first true ocean-going vessels. While galleys had been restricted to relatively calm waters and normally even spent the hours of

Below: The damage caused after Baldur had rammed HMS Diomede can be clearly seen. For political reasons, no shot was fired by either side in this conflict. Diomede returned home for repair.

darkness in port, the sailing ship had endurance, but at a price, since unlike the galleys they were dependent on wind and tide. This dependence, together with the short range and limited arc of fire of the smooth-barrel cannon, demanded increasing skills in seamanship, with the result that the sailor had to take the initiative from the soldier in the art of marine combat.

Until the end of the nineteenth century the design and size of European warships were virtually standard. There was not even any substantial speed differential to confer a specific tactical advantage on the ships of one nation over another, so the ability to sail as close to the wind as possible and thereby gain a superior position was considered essential. There were, however, disadvantages to being up-wind, since the leeward line of vessels always had the option to turn downwind and run from the action, and days were spent in manoeuvres before battles even commenced. The established naval tactics of the day, normally known as 'Fighting Instructions',

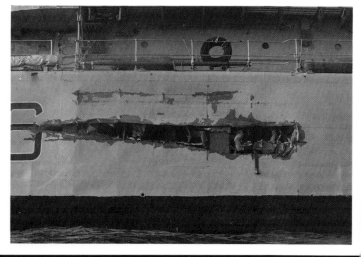

demanded that ships were fought in straight lines, but in practice, this was too rigid a concept. On numerous occasions when it was adhered to throughout an engagement there was no decisive outcome. Indeed, it seemed to be only when ranks were broken and the enemy pursued into a general mêlée that overwhelming victories were secured.

Despite experiences that demonstrated to the contrary, the line formation persisted as tactical doctrine until its ultimate use, with indecisive results, at the Battle of Jutland in 1916. Naval commanders were finally forced to abandon the idea by the advent of air power, and it seems ironic that it took over a hundred years for European navies to learn the tactical lessons which Nelson had so clearly demonstrated.

1805: TRAFALGAR

Trafalgar, generally considered the greatest of all battles between sailing ships, began on the morning of October 21, 1805, when Nelson's fleet engaged the French and Spanish ships under the command of Admiral Villeneuve. Nelson had anticipated—correctly, as it turned out—that the enemy fleet would be found in single line ahead, and his plan was to form the British fleet into three squadrons, leading the windward one himself with the leeward squadron under his second in command, Collingwood. Each of these two he considered should have 16 ships, while an advance squadron of eight of his fastest ships should form the third prong of the attack.

His plan entailed a high concentration of force at the centre of the enemy's line where he expected their commander's vessel to be situated: what actually happened is typical of how tactical plans must be often radically modified by the sea commander to suit the circumstances that actually prevail at the time battle is joined. Instead of the hoped for 40 ships in his fleet, Nelson only had 27. He was therefore unable to deploy the first squadron, whose role would have been to engage the front of the enemy line and prevent the ships there from doubling back to assist their commander.

The fight itself, like the other great battles for which Nelson is famous, was a bitterly contested gun battle with heavy casualties on both sides. The exchanges lasted four hours until finally, with 18 ships taken and one, the French *Achille*, blown up, it was reported to the dying Nelson that victory had been secured in what proved to be the last great sea battle of the sailing ship era.

In naval terms, the arrival of the steam engine restored independence of the sea and wind, enabling ships to sail against prevailing head winds and greatly increasing tactical mobility. And the introduction of explosive shells, together with the rifling of gun barrels and the development

Below: During the eighteenth century naval tactics had become very inflexible and often resulted in drawn out and indecisive sea battles. Nelson's plan at Trafalgar to attack the enemy's line in two places simultaneously was novel and daring, and the element of surprise led to his victory.

Above: A scene on the deck of HMS Victory during the height of the Battle of Trafalgar. At about 1.15 in the afternoon Nelson was hit through the shoulder by a bullet fired by a sniper high in the rigging of the French 74-gun ship Redoutable. The close proximity of the enemy ship is apparent.

The Battle of Trafalgar, 1805

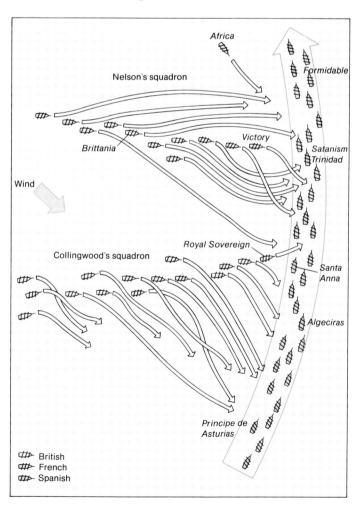

Africa
Nelson's squadron
Formidable
Victory
Brittania
Satanism
Trinidad
Wind
Royal Sovereign
Collingwood's squadron
Santa Anna
Algeciras
Principe de Asturias

⇇ British
⇇ French
⇇ Spanish

of armour to protect against them, led by the late nineteenth century to the building of the first of the modern warships.

A significant new tactic was now developing. While the cannon used at Trafalgar required engagements to be at minimum range (a 32lb shot had to be fired at point blank range to pierce 18in (46cm) of oak), the new ships were able to fight at ever increasing ranges. At the Battle of Manila Bay in 1898, during the Spanish-Prussian war, battle ranges had been 250yd (273m); by May 1905, when the Japanese heavily defeated a supposedly superior Russian fleet which had sailed half way around the world to challenge them at the Battle of Tsushima, the initial engagements took place at 7,000yd (6,400m). Another factor that tended to increase ranges was the rapid advance of the torpedo, which even in 1905 could be fired accurately at a range of 4,000yd (3,600m).

Increased ranges inevitably led to new tactical ideas. Control of gunnery, in particular, was becoming more and more difficult, since firing over a distance of several miles made judgement of the fall of the shot difficult. Consequently the concept of building ships with guns of uniform size gained in popularity. To provide the required range the guns had to be big, and uniformity of size meant uniform time of flight for a salvo, making corrections to the bearing and the elevation of the guns easier to calculate.

In 1906 HMS *Dreadnought*, the world's first all-big-gun battleship, introduced a totally new era in warship design. *Dreadnought* had ten 12in guns and a displacement of 17,900 tons: only 35 years later the Japanese Navy launched the 72,000-ton *Yamato* and *Musashi*, each with a main armament of nine

18.1in guns. *Dreadnought*'s guns could fire 800lb shells 12,000yd (10,900m): *Yamato*'s 3,000lb shells could be fired 27 miles (43.5km). Yet, these great battleships of World War II, like their US, British and German counterparts, were to be the last of their line. The reason was the advent of the aircraft carrier and the rapid advances in naval aviation.

1916: JUTLAND

The great sea battle of World War I took place in the North Sea off the coast of Jutland on May 31, 1916. This was to be the last of the big battles in which the gun was paramount (although airships, seaplanes, submarines, mines and torpedos were all at or near the scene of encounter, none played a major role), and the tactics employed were entirely traditional. Some 250 ships were involved altogether, formed into long battle lines on both sides. Neither side had the advantages of radar, and the battle developed as a series of incidents as the ships came into

sight of each other, the lasting tactical lesson being the spectacle of both sides turning away as soon as they were attacked. The ships were too valuable to be risked or lost.

More controversial than any other battle in naval history, Jutland saw both the British and the German commands apparently missing numerous opportunities to inflict lasting damage on the other. Overall the Germans suffered the greatest damage, though only ten of their ships were lost while the British losses included three battle-cruisers, three cruisers and eight destroyers.

Overall command of the British fleet was exercised by Admiral Sir John Jellicoe, and it is generally recognized that he lost the tactical advantage three times during the battle, starting with his initial deployment of the Grand Fleet into six parallel columns of dreadnoughts, with battle-cruisers ahead and the Queen Elizabeth class battleships at the rear—a moving wall of 35 battleships, 7 miles (11.3km) long, steaming

across the bows of the German High Sea Fleet.

The German Commander-in-Chief responded with an 180° turn of all his ships, a manoeuvre that Jellicoe failed to recognize, perhaps due to the Germans disguising their intentions by a simultaneous torpedo boat attack which forced the British to take evasive action.

Below: The British 1st Battle Squadron in the North Sea; the battleship Royal Sovereign leads HMS Resolution and Revenge. This close line ahead formation dated back to the days of sailing ships and typifies the lack of tactical imagination that led to the indecisive and controversial battle off Jutland in 1916.

The Battle of Jutland, May 31, 1916: the battle-cruiser action

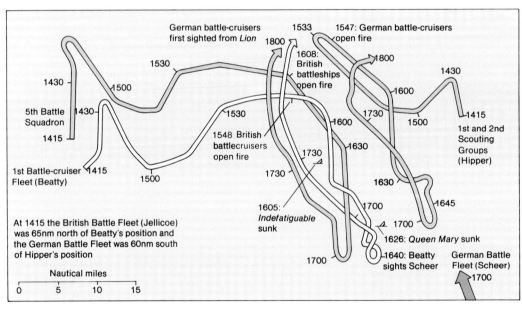

Left, below left and below: The Battle of Jutland can be divided into three phases. The battle cruiser action started with a chance encounter between the opposing forces; the British pursued the German cruisers, which turned south towards their own battle fleet, and the first shots were exchanged at 1547. At this stage the two battle fleets were still 90 miles apart, but the British fleet, under the command of Admiral Jellicoe, and the German fleet, commanded by Admiral Scheer, closed each other unseen at a combined speed of 40-50 knots. Finally, in the late afternoon, the British deployed in a line ahead battle formation. The German fleet steamed into this trap and at 1817 the British opened fire. Using smoke and a torpedo attack as a screen, the German fleet turned away. During the night, though the battle sporadically continued, the German fleet escaped.

Jutland: the battle fleet action

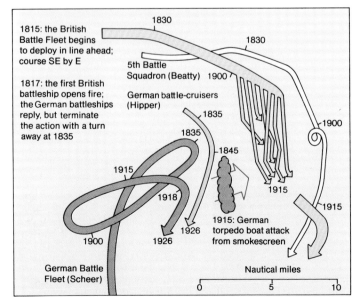

Jutland: the night action

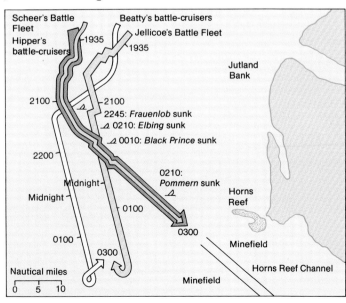

Half an hour later the Germans turned back again and, though the battle continued, the confusion caused in the British command by these two manoeuvres, quickly followed by another, allowed the Germans to escape into the darkness of the night.

The last chance for the British was to manoeuvre themselves during that night between the retreating German fleet and their home base. Jellicoe, however, chose to disregard advice that the Germans would make for the Horn Reef and the safety of the Elbe to the southeast of the battlefield; instead, he anticipated—wrongly — that they would go south to Heligoland and Wilhelmshaven. Over and over again in the history of naval tactics the guesswork of a commander, based too often on flimsy intelligence, has succeeded or failed by the narrowest of margins.

1942: MIDWAY

The great battles of World War II ranged from the conventional, as at the River Plate, where three British cruisers took on and defeated the German 'pocket battleship' *Graf Spee*, to the great amphibious landings in North Africa, Normandy and the Pacific, which depended for their success on control of both the sea and the airspace above it. It was in the Pacific, however, that the big set piece battles took place, and of these the battles of Midway in 1942 and Leyte Gulf in 1944 are probably the most important. These were the first engagements between aircraft carriers, and the range of engagement was decided by aircraft rather than guns.

At Midway, the Japanese fleet of nine battleships, including the *Yamato*, and four carriers, plus cruisers, destroyers and transports with some 2,000 troops, was under the command of Admiral Yamamoto. His intention was to seize the Western Aleutian Islands and the island of Midway and so draw the US fleet out. His complicated plan was dependent on perfect timing. The Americans could only deploy three fleet carriers and 13 cruisers, commanded at sea by Admiral Nimitz, Commander-in-Chief of the US Pacific Fleet at Pearl Harbor, though there was also a strong force of aircraft stationed at Midway.

Most importantly, the Americans had intelligence of the Japanese intentions and were therefore able to concentrate their striking power at the most vital point. They launched their initial attack against the Japanese transports on June 3, but it was not until the following day that the Japanese could themselves bomb the Midway base. At this stage they were still unaware of the presence of the US carriers, a lack of intelligence that was to prove to be Yamamoto's undoing.

As chance would have it, only 13 minutes after he had ordered the reserve attack aircraft to swap their torpedoes for bombs for a

Below: Bombs explode in the water around a frantically manoeuvring Japanese heavy cruiser under attack from US Navy carrier based aircraft. Soon after this photograph was taken the ship was hit and sunk, just one example of how air power completely transformed naval operations during the course of World War II.

second strike against Midway, information arrived revealing the presence of the US fleet. Confusion ensued as new orders were issued to reload the torpedoes. In the meantime, land-based US bombers sent to attack the Japanese carriers suffered heavy losses without inflicting any damage. At the same moment, however, the

first waves of US carrier-based aircraft were on their way from the USS *Enterprise* and *Hornet*, while *Yorktown*'s bombers were just being launched, and they caught the Japanese in the middle of changing weapons.

Although the US squadrons had difficulty in coordinating their attack they managed in less than an hour to put out of action three of the four carriers. The surviving carrier, *Hiryu*, did manage to launch a counter attack which completely disabled the *Yorktown*, but *Hiryo* was soon found by the Americans and sunk by the *Enterprise*'s dive bombers. There was further misfortune for the Japanese when two of their cruisers, *Mogami* and *Mikuma*, collided while trying to avoid an American submarine attack. They instantly became targets for every enemy aircraft, one ship being sunk but the other escaping. This battle marked the end of Japan's naval power.

1982: THE FALKLANDS

The latest significant use of naval power was the British deployment

The Battle of Midway, June 4, 1942

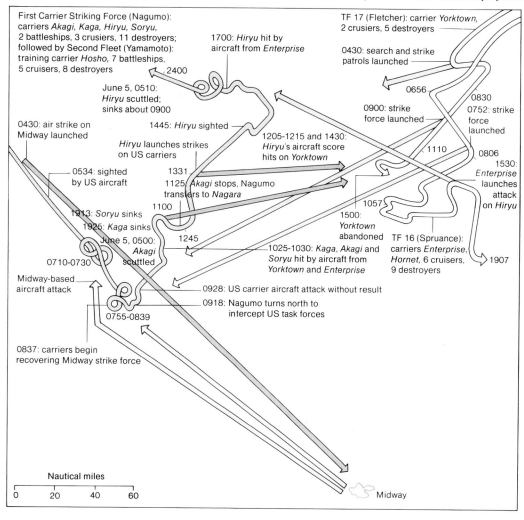

Above: The Battle of Midway, fought on June 4, 1942, marked the turning point of the war in the Pacific. It also signalled the end of the battleship as the supreme weapon afloat, the eleven Japanese battleships of Admiral Yamamoto's fleet then at sea never entering the action, and during the course of the battle the opposing ships never came in sight of each other. The battle unfolded as a series of strokes and counter-strokes illustrating the part played by luck in war: the first US attack failed to locate the enemy, but there followed a number of attacks by American dive-bombers and torpedo aircraft with the US pilots suffering heavy casualties. Between 1025 and 1023, however, a dive-bomber group from USS Yorktown fatally damaged the Japanese carriers Kaga, Soryu and Akagi. This strike was to win the day for the Americans, and end Japan's Pacific dominance.

to the South Atlantic in April 1982. The ensuing action is most notable in that it represents the only major naval battle involving weapon systems developed in the years since World War II. These systems were to prove remarkably effective in the limited, conventional warfare that developed. The issue was one of territorial rights, and the dispute, 7,850 nautical miles from the United Kingdom, involved all aspects of war at sea including the transportation of troops, naval gunfire support, a mass troop landing and action against both naval and air forces.

Many of the tactics employed by both fleets will be discussed, but it is important to note that those employed by both British and Argentinian forces were products of the modern weapon systems involved. As such they were, exercises aside, completely unproven in the heat of battle. In the event, the British achieved all their objectives, a most important prerequisite for which was that they should safeguard, at all costs, their two aircraft carriers, *Hermes* and *Invincible*. While undoubtedly many lessons were learnt, the tactical deployment of the British ships was highly successful.

The basic military plan for the Falklands campaign had four main objectives:

1: The establishment of a sea blockade around the islands.
2: The repossession of South Georgia.
3: The gaining of sea and air supremacy around the Falklands.
4: The eventual repossession of the Falklands.

The small British island of Ascension was established as the so-called 'forward base' for the Task Force, though the term 'forward' was only relative: it was still 3,415 nautical miles (6,325km from the Falklands. Nevertheless, it was to prove to be a critical asset, British control allowing grouping of the naval forces, stockpiling of stores and, most importantly, an area where the United States could actively but discreetly support the British without compromising the US role in trying to achieve a peaceful settlement through diplomatic means.

The Task Force arrived in the vicinity of the Falklands in three separate groups, entering the Maritime Exclusion Zone—the area 200nm from the centre of the Falklands in which Britain had declared all Argentinian ships would be attacked after April 12 — at 01.30 on May 1, 1982. The first group, Task Unit 317.8.2, composed of *Brilliant*, *Sheffield*, *Glasgow*, *Coventry*, *Arrow* and the tanker *Pearleaf*, had been despatched

Right: The Argentinian cruiser General Belgrano, formerly the Brooklyn class USS Phoenix. She sank on May 2, 1982, after being hit by two torpedoes; 321 of her crew were lost.

Above: Elements of the British Task Force gather under the protective shores of Ascension Island. This forward base was an invaluable staging post.

ahead of the main force in order to establish a presence as far south as possible, in case diplomatic moves imposed a freeze on military units in the Falklands area. The second group, Task Unit 319.9 (*Antrim*, *Plymouth* and the supply ships *Tidespring* and *Fort Austin*), had been sent to repossess South Georgia, a plan known as Operation Paraquet. The third and final part was the main battle group which initially consisted of the aircraft carriers *Hermes* and *Invincible*,

with their 20 Sea Harrier aircraft, the destroyer *Glamorgan* and the frigates *Broadsword*, *Yarmouth* and *Alacrity*; the supply ships *Olmeda* and *Resource* were in support and the Battle Group was designated Task Group 317.8.

The Argentinian Navy had three groups at sea and in their preplanned positions by April 20, two days before the British arrived. The aircraft carrier group TG 79.1 and 79.2, commanded by Rear Admiral Allara aboard the *Veinticinco de Mayo*, escorted by the destroyers *Santisima Trinidad* and *Hercules*, was stationed to the northwest of the islands. A second group, TG 79.4, composed of the frigates *Drummond*, *Guerrico* and

Granville, lay some 150nm to the west of the Argentinian strike force. To the south of the Falklands was TG 79.3, composed of the Exocet cruiser *Belgrano* and two former US Sumner class destroyers,

By May 2 the Argentinian carrier groups were in a position to launch an attack on the British. On the previous evening one of the *Veinticinco de Mayo's* reconnaissance aircraft had located the British group some 300 miles to the southeast of the Argentinian ships, which therefore closed during the night until they were approximately 120nm away, and just before dawn the carrier's A-4Q Skyhawks were ordered to a maximum state of deck readiness, fully fuelled and loaded with 500lb bombs, while the crews sat waiting in their confined cockpits.

The British had three SSNs in the area, *Spartan* and *Splendid* to the north and *Conqueror* to the south, but although *Spartan* had located the frigate group TG 79.4 on April 29 neither submarine could find the carrier. It was a Sea Harrier flying a routine night Combat Air Patrol (CAP) that first detected the approaching threat. The British Task Force turned away, anxious to put as much distance as possible between themselves and the Argentinians, and numerous Harrier patrols were sent out in the direction of the enemy carrier to intercept the expected Skyhawk attack.

Meanwhile, 180nm to the southwest of the British naval commander embarked in *Hermes*, *Conqueror* was reporting the manoeuvres of the *Belgrano*. In the early morning of May 2, as the attack from the north appeared to be imminent, the *Conqueror* reported that the Argentinian cruiser had abruptly changed course and was following an aimless zigzag just outside the Total Exclusion Zone and only a short distance from the relatively shallow waters of the Burwood Bank.

If the cruiser were to separate from her escorts and make a dash across this bank, *Conqueror* would be placed at a distinct disadvantage, with her freedom to manoeuvre inhibited by the area of shallows, and in only a few hours, as the imminent Argentinian air attack shaped up in the north the *Belgrano* could be close enough to the British to fire her Exocets (surface range 22nm). In addition, the *Belgrano* had been observed refuelling from the tanker *Puerta de Rosalies* during the earlier part of May 1. To the British command all the signs were that she was about to close on their force in coordination with the enemy group to the north: the classical pincer movement. The British government immediately agreed to a request to change the rules of engagement allowing an attack on both the *Belgrano* and the *Veinticinco de Mayo*.

As dawn broke the Argentinian carrier turned into what little wind there was, but even at her top speed of around 24-25 knots she

Argentinian naval operations, April 29-May 2, 1982

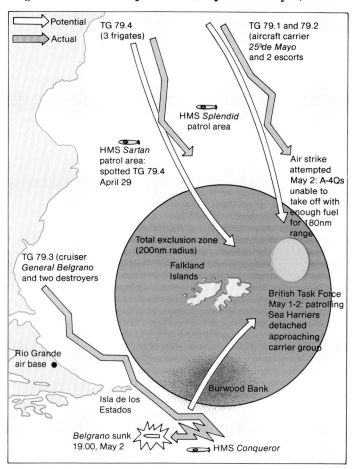

Potential

Actual

TG 79.4
(3 frigates)

TG 79.1 and 79.2
(aircraft carrier
25*de Mayo
and 2 escorts

HMS *Splendid*
patrol area

HMS *Sartan*
patrol area:
spotted TG 79.4
April 29

Air strike
attempted
May 2: A-4Qs
unable to
take off with
enough fuel
for 180nm
range

Total exclusion zone
(200nm radius)

Falkland
Islands

TG 79.3 (cruiser
General Belgrano
and two destroyers

British Task Force
May 1-2: patrolling
Sea Harriers
detached
approaching
carrier group

Rio Grande
air base

Isla de los
Estados

Burwood Bank

Belgrano sunk
19.00, May 2

HMS *Conqueror*

Above: With the Argentinian carrier and surface action groups to the northwest armed with Skyhawk aircraft and Exocet and Sea Dart missiles—surface-to-surface ranges 40nm and 22nm

was unable to create sufficient wind over the deck to launch the fully fuelled and armed Skyhawks. At the same time, reconnaissance had revealed that the distance between the two fleets was opening and had already increased to 180nm, and if the aircraft were

range of 1,400yd (1,300m) on the cruiser's port beam, the submarine fired a salvo of three Mk 8 torpedoes. The Argentinian destroyers commenced a submarine search pattern immediately after the torpedoes struck the *Belgrano*, carrying out several depth charge attacks, while *Conqueror* withdrew to the east. At 19.45 the now abandoned *Belgrano* sank.

This event ended the only surface engagement of the Falklands war, one in which tactics were a mixture of the modern and the traditional. The sinking of the *Belgrano* appeared to break the morale of the Argentinian Navy. TGs 79.1, 79.2 and 79.4 withdrew to the north, the remains of TG 79.3 returned to port, and although the *Veinticinco de Mayo* remained at sea for a further seven days, on May 9 she berthed at the Puerto Belgrano naval base and her flights disembarked; the A-4Qs were redeployed to Rio Grande Naval Air Station, where they continued to operate until the war's end.

The remainder of the Falklands conflict centred on the anti-warfare environment, but it should be added that the Argentinians were also known to have three submarines at sea, two German-built Type 209s, the *Salta* and the *San Luis*, and the large Guppy-class *Santiago del Estero*, whose existence forced the British to be continuously on their guard against possible submarine attack.

Endless zig-zagging of a force is tiring on all concerned. In addition, each possible submarine contact has to be fully investigated and the main body of the fleet turned away, probably adding hours to its intended passage towards its objective. During the early part of May 1, for example, when *Glamorgan*, *Arrow* and *Alacrity* were closing the land near Stanley to carry out a shore bombardment, their ASW screen, provided by *Brilliant* and *Yarmouth* and several Sea King helicopters, detected a

possible submarine. The subsequent search and eventual attack took all day, during which numerous depth charges were dropped and, at one stage, oil was seen on the surface. One Argentinian submarine, the *San Luis*, later reported making a torpedo attack on a British ship during the course of this particular day. During the war no submerged Argentinian submarine was known to have been destroyed, though during an ASW action on April 25 the *Santa Fe*, while on the surface, had been attacked by Royal Navy helicopters and forced into Grytviken. She was captured by the British later the same day when they returned to South Georgia.

THE LESSONS

Examination of these five great sea battles, the first and last of which took place 400 years apart, serves to demonstrate that while tactics have of necessity been modified to make the use of the available weapon systems, the two great imponderables for the naval commander remain. Firstly, where is the enemy and in what form will he attack? Secondly, will the environment in which he has to operate act to his advantage or his disadvantage?

A naval action is transitory and fleeting, involving highly mobile forces in situations which can and do change rapidly under constraints which in themselves are peculiar to naval operations. Geography does not limit the number of options open to the enemy and the role of intelligence gathering therefore has paramount importance. Early warning of the enemy's whereabouts is essential to ensure success, and it is impossible to prepare precise operational plans in advance as, for instance, the general would do on land. And since the distances involved can be immense, good, flexible communication facilities are essential, as is extensive logistical support, aspects clearly demonstrated by the operations in the South Atlantic in 1982. Lastly, it is essential to deploy your naval units early to make up for the relatively slow speed of surface ships.

These characteristics—the enormous dimensions of the potential area of battle; the transitory aspect of operations; and the heavy burden of constraints such as intelligence gathering, operational planning, communications, logistical support and slow deployment of forces—together remain constant amid the continual evolution and development of warfare at sea. With them in mind, some specific details of modern tactical ideas can now be considered.

respectively—and the Belgrano group to the southwest armed with Exocets, it is easy to understand why the British naval command wanted the rules of engagement changed to allow attacks on them.

to dump fuel to reduce take-off weight, they would have insufficient to reach the British fleet. Admiral Allara, turned his ships away to the north.

Meanwhile, some 500nm to the south, *Conqueror* manoeuvred to attack the Belgrano. At 18.57, at a

Left: HMS Conqueror, the submarine responsible for the sinking of the Belgrano, returns to Faslane at the end of her protracted patrol during the South Altlantic War.

Surface Warfare

Locating and positively identifying the enemy is an essential element of surface warfare, but while various intelligence-gathering media are available to the naval commander, from satellites and reconnaissance aircraft to merchant vessels and shore-based operatives, it should not be assumed that, even today, this is a precise and all-embracing art. Despite all the facilities available to the British and Argentinian surface groups in the South Atlantic, for example, they still had considerable trouble in locating each other, and numerous recent naval exercises by both NATO and Warsaw Pact fleets have been marked by similar difficulties. It is important also to note that positive identification is essential, and it has been seen that a particular phenomenon of twentieth-century naval engagements has been the increasing distance between belligerents.

The Soviet captain on the *Kiev*, before firing his SS-N-12 missiles at a range of up to 340nm, will want to be convinced not only that his target is beyond question an enemy warship but probably which ship it actually is. He will therefore rely on information being reported from surveillance units such as Tu-16 Badger-F maritime reconnaissance and elint aircraft, Hormone-B helicopters or forward-positioned submarines. His dilemma, however, is that because these units will have to close the enemy to identify it, they will in their turn be vulnerable to detection, forewarning his target of enemy activity, since the defending naval commander, must assume that detection of a Badger, for example, represents a high possibility that a major Soviet missile armed naval unit is nearing or within firing range. The attacking naval group, therefore, has to balance the need for information against the requirements of covert operations, at least until it believes itself to be established in a position of tactical advantage.

Radar is probably a warship's primary source of target information. A vessel's own surface search radar will normally have a range capability of 40-60nm, and to increase this range it is necessary either to use AEW aircraft or to place other ships further along the line of a possible attack (commonly called the threat axis). Target acquisition information can then be fed, via data links, back to those units with long-range missiles. The positioning of units within a task force is therefore an important tactical consideration.

The inability of radar to positively identify a vessel provides an obvious opportunity for deception: the placing of relatively low-value units such as large supply vessels in positions where an attacker may assume a main body to be may risk the loss of such vessels but will help the primary ships. Similar ruses can also be employed on a larger scale. It is common tactical practice to form two or more task groups in order to give the enemy the problem of deciding which contains the vessel or vessels that represent the greatest threat. As the British task force initially approached the Falklands, for example, the guided missile destroyer *Glamorgan* was placed well to the east to transmit radio and radar signals as a decoy to the shadowing Argentinian reconnaissance aircraft, which were believed—correctly—to be feeding information back to their own aircraft carrier group.

Electronic countermeasures (ECM) can also be used to deceive the enemy or to deny essential target information. Chaff can distort the apparent positioning of

Above: A Kanin class DDG with the cruiser Udaloy in the background illustrate well the sophisticated radar systems of these Soviet ships. Each has a comprehensive fit of surveillance, weapon control and navigation radars.

Below: The 45,000-ton USS New Jersey at sea surrounded by her protective screen of escort destroyers and frigates. Note the speed and courses of the other ships as they vigorously patrol their sectors.

Soviet anti-ship missile threats

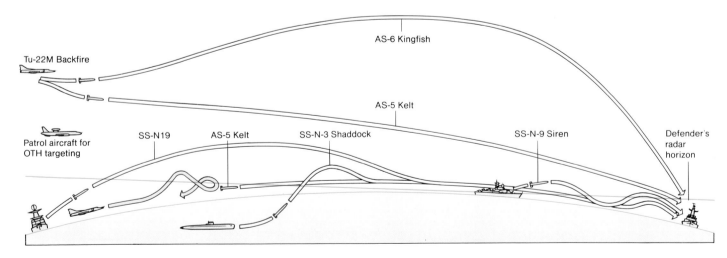

Above: The Soviet anti-ship missile threat to a NATO warship appears at first sight to be overwhelming. It ranges from the aircraft-launched AS-5 and AS-6 through ship-launched missiles, including SS-N-19s fired from Kirov at an estimated range of 310 miles (500km)—though at such a distance the firing ship would require another vessel or aircraft to provide target acquisition data—to submarine-launched missiles such as the SS-N-9 with its 70-mile (110km) range. The hazard for the defending ship is compounded by the growing number of missiles that use the sea-skimming mode to minimize the radar warning time. Also apparent here is the effect of the earth's curvature on a ship's radar horizon. This is of particular benefit to attacking aircraft, allowing them to approach below the lobe of the defender's radar. NATO navies have developed a number of weapon systems to counter these threats, and a rapid response air defence missile system, preferably supplemented by a gun-based close-in weapon system is a vital element in a modern warship armoury. The threat will be further compounded when new-generation supersonic missiles are deployed.

a fleet, while jamming on an opponent's radar frequency will deny essential range information, but there is a price to be paid. The use of electronic systems, whether radar or ECM, gives away a great deal of information, and knowing the operating frequencies of an enemy's radars is an essential weapon in the naval commander's armoury. Once a radar contact has been made, detection of a particular transmission on that bearing can immediately confirm the identity of the target.

In all naval operations a balance has to be established between covert and overt policy. The most difficult and complex problem occurs when, faced by a powerful enemy who has sufficient means to take the initiative in several spheres of action at the same time, a commander is forced into a defensive position with relatively limited means, though with any military engagement, initiative, innovation and surprise can provide an advantage to even the weaker opponent. Too rigid an adherence to established practice will present no unforeseen action to the enemy, who will expect certain manoeuvres, having followed closely all exercises in peace time, but will not expect the unrehearsed or the undetected.

The major operational consideration in war is the deployment of naval units, and this is determined by the resources available and by the task. It is important to have a navy at sea, since ships in harbour are obviously particularly vulnerable to attack. Traditionally, warships have been formed into battle fleets, and even today similar principles apply, so that task forces are composed of ships which offer mutual protection. The makeup of a particular combination depends on the military aim, as well as the

Task force sector screen

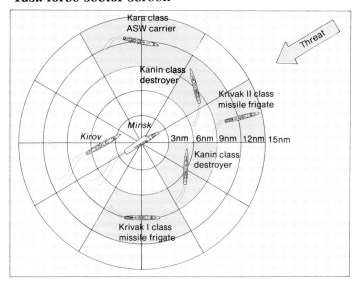

enemy's potential.

An obvious case is where one of the preliminary choices is to attack enemy territories with carrier-borne aircraft. The main body in this case will be one or more aircraft carriers together with their necessary ASW, AAW and AEW support, a principal fighting force akin to the battle groups of earlier eras. Such a force could engage air or surface targets or attack commercial assets at sea. Conversely, if the enemy were known to have such a force in being, it would be necessary to form a similar group to oppose it. Likewise, a powerful task group can be formed by missile-armed ships linked to long-range surveillance and search units, and this again would require sophisticated escort protection. Lastly, while either of the above groups could also be supported by SSNs, it is equally possible to create a battle group solely from this type of submarine, provided

they can be linked with the necessary communications and are armed with weapons whose range is sufficient to allow engagement with the enemy at a far enough distance to minimize the risk of counter-attack.

Once at sea, a task force has to protect itself against several sources of attack, and protective screens can be created around a main body, with ships positioned so that the characteristics of their weapon system can be used to the advantage of the whole group. Spacing between the ships is determined by two main factors: the range and capability of their detection and weapon systems; and the likelihood of a nuclear attack, since the closer the ships

Below: A major group of the Falklands task force returning to the UK. Though the escorts are not in a tactical screen the size and composition of the group is typical for two carriers.

Left: Typical disposition of a Soviet task force. The main body of the force—the aircraft carrier Minsk with her accompanying missile cruiser—acts as the guide, changing course every few minutes to reduce the threat posed by submarines, while the outlying escorts are allocated patrol sectors of 60-72 square miles (155-185km^2) which they patrol constantly to guard the main body against air or submarine attack. Such a group would be able to advance at relatively high speed toward its objective, even though alterations of course in an ASW environment would be frequent. The positioning of the escorting ships would be determined by the capabilities of their detection and weapon systems. If one ship has to be released, the sectors of the remaining ships can be adjusted.

are to each other the greater the risk of several being lost during a tactical nuclear exchange. Ships are allocated sectors to patrol relative to a guide at the centre of the screen. Normally this is the main body, though in order to disguise the formation other units may be placed in the centre.

The routing of a force will take account of the objective and the latest intelligence reports on enemy activity. Detection of an unidentified surface unit will result in immediate action to establish the intruder's identity, either by air reconnaissance or by detaching one or more escorts temporarily formed into a Surface Action Group (SAG).

Air cover for the task force is essential. Ever since the Battle of Leyte Gulf, aircraft have had to be considered the primary weapon at sea. They allow long-range reconnaissance, as well as pursuit of the all-important aim, the destruction of the enemy before he can achieve a position inside the range of his own weapon systems.

It should be noted that in this age of highly sophisticated naval vessels, replacement of lost ships is a lengthy process. It is perhaps more important than may have been considered necessary in the past to sink the enemy's warships rather than just disable them. It should also be borne in mind that due to the hit probability for a missile being far greater than was previously the case with conventional gunnery systems, the tactical advantage must lie with the force that fires first.

The missile's high degree of accuracy, together with its range, highlights a new tactical development: whereas in the past the manoeuvring of a warship was all-important to ensure that its weapons could be brought to bear on a target, as the range of weapons increases this ceases to be a major consideration. A naval gun firing 12nm gives an area within which it is possible to strike at an enemy of 453nm^2, but a missile with a range of 124nm gives an area of 48,325nm^2. In other words, as the

firing range of weapons increases by one order of magnitude, the area in which it can be targeted increases by two orders of magnitude. While manoeuvring of ships will still be important, the task in relation to engaging the enemy should, at least in this respect, become simpler.

The navies of the Western Alliance devote a large proportion of their warship expenditure to equipment that aids command and control. (The present state of the art is to be found in ships such as the US Navy's Ticonderoga class destroyers equipped with the Aegis system.) Such money is well spent. The modern combat environment is extremely complex, with attacks likely to be both random and multi-directional as an attacker aims to saturate a defender's capabilities. Any task group will have both strengths and weaknesses, and the task of the naval commander is to achieve an effective interaction between his forces to exploit the former and to cover the latter. The speed of attacking missiles, coupled with the possibility of not detecting the attack until it is well under way, demands rapid analysis of the threat and instant response with the most suitable weapon system. Command and control in this type of environment is obviously essential. It must be computer-aided to the extent that reactions, even the firing of defensive weapons, are automatic. It is no good having the most sophisticated missile system, if you are denied the opportunity of deciding to use it.

NUCLEAR ATTACKS

It has been recogized for some time that the use of tactical nuclear weapons at sea is a distinct possibility: both the Soviets and the Americans have missiles armed with nuclear warheads, nuclear shells and nuclear mines,

and the attraction of their deployment in the maritime environment is that ther use would not necessarily escalate into a full-scale nuclear battle, since both the explosion and the resulting fallout are only likely to affect the military units. In fact, most modern warships are designed to cope with this threat. Their superstructures and hulls are constructed as sealed units in which a positive pressure can be maintained to prevent the ingress of contaminated air, and they are fitted with pre-wetting systems to wash any radioactivity from exposed surfaces, while the crew have full protective clothing. Having survived an attack, the ships of a fleet can clear contaminated areas using prewetting. They can also plot the fallout pattern with reasonable accuracy using pre-planned charts, the choice of chart depending on the size of the weapon. And having plotted the danger area the ships

Above: USS America makes a dramatic sight as her pre-wetting or water washdown is fully activated. Such systems are designed to wash radioactive contamination from the exposed

are able to manoeuvre around it or, if necessary, to cross it, calculating when they need to start and finish and taking suitable precautions.

NAVAL GUNFIRE SUPPORT

A major role of naval vessels is in the support of troops during or after amphibious operations. Naval gunfire support can provide invading forces with a major advantage—the 16in guns carried by the US Navy's Iowa class battleships, for example, are able to fire a 2,700lb projectile a range of 25 miles (40km). Tactically, however, the manoeuvring of ships during such operations can make them extremely vulnerable.

Because of the ranges involved it is essential if accuracy is important to have spotters placed at forward positions to correct the fall of shot. This can be achieved either by putting ashore specially trained personnel who work their

surfaces on the upper decks, allowing ships to transit safely through fallout areas. The line of sprays forward of the island structure is designed to wash down parked aircraft.

way into a position from which they can see the target, or by using a helicopter as an observation post, though the latter can itself be vulnerable to counter attack.

The spotters must report back to the bombardment ship the position in which shells land relative to the target, normally by giving grid references. In turn, the command in the ship has to correct the bearing and elevation of fire. The geometry of the problem is complicated by the movement of the ship, though most modern gunnery systems can lock on to an artificially created target in their computerized control systems (it is unlikely that the ship's radar will be able to see the target on land).

In order to keep the solution as simple as possible, ships normally maintain a steady course, but this in turn exposes it to counter attack. On June 12, 1982, for example, the British destroyer *Glamorgan* was carrying out nightly bombardments against Argentinian positions on the south of the Falkland Islands. The Argentinians improvised a temporary MM38 Exocet battery mounted on the back of an army truck, and by using an American-built TPS-43 radar to provide target information were able to fire a missile at the ship. The Exocet hit *Glamorgan's* side near the stern, causing a groove along the deck before exploding opposite the hangar doors. Ships in the naval gunfire support role are not only vulnerable to attacks from the shore, but also to aircraft and submarines.

FAST PATROL BOATS

The tactics of fighting Fast Patrol Boats (FPBs) are in many respects far removed from those associated with major units. They rely on their small size for concealment from visual or radar detection, as well as on their speed, and over the last 20 years they have become

Tactical avoidance of nuclear fall-out areas

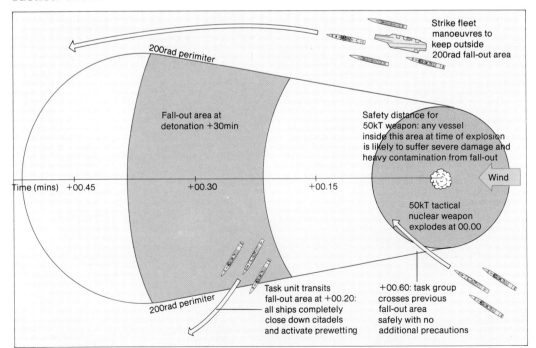

200rad perimeter

Strike fleet manoeuvres to keep outside 200rad fall-out area

Fall-out area at detonation +30min

Safety distance for 50kT weapon: any vessel inside this area at time of explosion is likely to suffer severe damage and heavy contamination from fall-out

Time (mins) +00.45   +00.30   +00.15

Wind

50kT tactical nuclear weapon explodes at 00.00

200rad perimeter

Task unit transits fall-out area at +00.20: all ships completely close down citadels and activate prewetting

+00.60: task group crosses previous fall-out area safely with no additional precautions

Left: There is every likelihood that in a major conflict between East and West tactical nuclear weapons would be used at sea. Not only are they an effective method of striking a group of ships with a single weapon, but because military units only would be involved, their use would not necessarily lead to an all-out nuclear war. Both NATO and Warsaw Pact navies exercise in simulated fallout conditions. The position of a nuclear explosion can be plotted and depending on the estimated size of the weapon a fallout pattern can be predicted using standard charts. In the area immediately around the explosion the damage to ships is likely to be severe. As the fallout travels downwind and dissipates, ships will be able to transit through the contaminated area, continuously washing down their exposed decks and supertructures and completely sealing off their internal spaces. The diagram illustrates a typical plot of a fall-out pattern.

Naval gunfire support

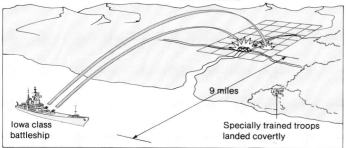

Spotters judge fall of shot and advise ship by radio using superimposed grid for corrections

Ship's helicopter

9 miles

Iowa class battleship

Specially trained troops landed covertly

Above: Ships capable of firing large shells several miles are ideal support for attacking ground forces. Often unable to see the target, the ship requires guidance from a spotter either on the ground or in the air. Corrections are made by reference to a grid.

Below: A full broadside: the nine 16in guns of USS Iowa fire simultaneously during her deployment off the Lebanon—nine 2,700lb shells fired at distances of up to 27 miles (40km) at targets on shore which the ship will probably never see.

increasingly sophisticated. The sinking by an Egyptian Osa class missile boat, armed with the Soviet SS-N-2 Styx system (range 20nm), of the Israeli destroyer *Eilat* in October 1967 marked the beginning of a revaluation of this type of vessel. The Egyptian Osa was one of two, both of which maintained cover in the entrance to Alexandria harbour during the course of the attack.

The Soviets, especially, have been quick to realize that fast missile-armed boats can be considered a strike force in a modern fleet. They are, of course, best suited to operations in coastal waters, where their shallow draught gives them the ability to move between islands and to lie close alongside the coast, and the Scandinavian navies in particular are adept at camouflaging their FPBs either by painting or by covering the entire boat with netting and appropriate foliage.

Normally working in teams, FPB crews will lie in wait for the opposing forces to come within range. If movement is necessary they will manoeuvre as close to the shore as possible with the intention of merging with the coastline on an enemy's radar picture, and if they have to close the opposition they can take advantage of the radar blind arcs created by islands and headlands. They also practise merging with fishing fleets, often drifting for hours among groups of trawlers, and they can be concealed by a transiting merchant ship, again manoeuvring virtually alongside the larger vessel's hull to gain radar cover.

In the waters of the North and Norwegian Seas vessels of this

type using such tactics represent a very real threat to a NATO strike force. A Soviet Nanuchka class vessel of only 900 tons displacement, for example, carries six SS-N-9 missiles, each with a range of 70nm, and while this is beyond the Nanuchka's radar horizon, target information could be passed to it from a far more humble vessel, such as a fishing boat.

There are also several classes of FPBs armed with conventional torpedo systems. Again, if they can close a task group without being detected they present a formidable threat. Once they feel confident to expose their positions they will run in for an attack at 40-50 knots. At only a few miles' distance and at high speed they make a particularly difficult target to engage.

There can be no hard and fast rules established for counter tactics against FPBs, but it is essential to recognize their capabilities and for a naval commander to be aware of their potential threat, since once they have begun their attack the missiles they launch have to be countered in a similar fashion to any other. Their strength lies in remaining undetected, so every effort must be made to find them before they can achieve a firing solution. It is interesting to observe that most NATO navies have acquired helicopter-mounted ASM systems, such as the Royal Navy's Sea Skua, specifically to deal with this threat. Many of the smaller navies in the world have acquired Fast Patrol Boats, a high percentage of which are missile armed, and these vessels represent an offensive capability quite out of proportion to their size.

Below: A Spica II of the Swedish Navy fitted with the new multi-purpose Sea Giraffe radar makes a high speed run during a simulated attack. Armed with six wire-guided torpedoes and a single 57mm

Bofors gun capable of firing at a rate of 200 rounds per minute, this 190-ton vessel has an impressive capability for its size. Used skilfully, FPB's are a serious threat to much larger warships.

Anti-Submarine Warfare

The modern submarine has two main roles: to search for and destroy enemy naval and merchant ships; and to attack other submarines. To achieve these ends effectively it must be capable of remaining at sea for prolonged periods without support; fast; able to operate at various depths; have detection systems able to locate its target at as great a distance as possible; and, most importantly, be able to destroy its enemy with minimum risk to itself. All these qualities contribute to the submarine's greatest asset, its ability to remain undetected.

The relatively recent parallel developments of nuclear power and the Albacore-shape hull have made submarines so hard to find that there are serious doubts about the ability of surface units to detect a nuclear submarine before it attacks, and have led to the tactical use of nuclear submarines in support of surface forces. The most effective anti-submarine weapon is another submarine that works and fights in the same environment and is able to take advantage of the unique peculiarities of the sub-surface world.

The aim of anti-submarine warfare must be to deny the enemy effective use of his submarines. This can be achieved either by destroying those vessels or by adopting tactics and manoeuvres that inhibit their operations. Of all the types of modern naval warfare, it is the anti-submarine battle that most occupies the thinking of the strategists and tacticians. New weapon systems are being developed all the time, and most of today's navies devote the lion's share of their expenditure to this discipline.

Above: A US Navy Raleigh Class LPD lies close to the snow-covered Norwegian coast while her landing craft ferry troops ashore. NATO amphibious forces frequently exercise in these waters.

Traditionally, especially in World War II, captains of ASW ships during hunts for submarines appeared to place great store on identifying with the thoughts of their opponent—almost an attempt at mental telepathy between the attacker and the defender. Great stress was placed on knowing how submarines were fought, and even on the particular strengths and weaknesses of individual submarine captains and their use of techniques such as the settling of the boat on the sea bed, the use of layers to avoid sonar detection and the release of oil and clothing through a torpedo tube to simulate damage.

In a modern ASW action it is unlikely that this type of mental battle will be so significant. In the comfort and warmth of a modern operations room, surrounded by electronic plots, digitized radar displays, the glow of subdued red lighting and the constant chatter of voice nets on headsets, it is difficult to imagine a captain projecting himself into the mind of the submarine commander. Nevertheless, it is still important to try. Submarines still use some of the old techniques, especially those that are enhanced by the speed of modern boats, such as the sprint and drift tactic that allows a nuclear submarine to make a high-speed dash, albeit noisily, followed by a long period of total silence as the submarine drifts down towards its targets. "Know your enemy" is a philosophy that still serves the military command well. Except in exercises, however, few commanders at sea in any navy have had the experience of actually hunting a submarine in a hostile environment.

The main area of conflict in any future hostilities between NATO and Warsaw Pact marine forces will probably be the North Atlantic and in particular the Norwegian Sea. Norway is of extreme importance to NATO strategy, stretching as it does northward toward the Soviet Union's main Atlantic naval base inside the Kola Inlet at Murmansk. Norway is also likely to be a prime Soviet target, since control of this area would allow the positioning of ships and aircraft that could easily harass transatlantic support for the Western Alliance. NATO strategy therefore calls for rapid reinforcement of the single Norwegian brigade which is confronted by seven Soviet divisions, and control of the Norwegian Sea, which measures approximately 1,000nm by 800nm, is likely to be, in a World War III scenario, one of the major areas for naval engagements, since naval forces will have to secure the lines of communication across it in support of land forces ashore.

Tactically, this could be done in two ways: either by saturating the area with aircraft and ships and

Below: ASW ships of the Standing Naval Force Atlantic, each from a different NATO country, in line abreast. Their ability to work together ensures close coordination in time of war.

Soviet naval exercise, April 1980

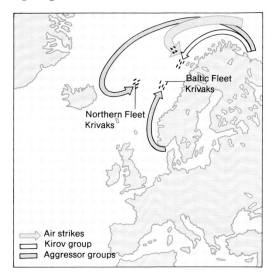

Simulated air-to-surface strikes in transit

ASW action with 3 submarines

Krivaks depart Baltic

Kiev in transit to Northern Fleet

- Aircraft
- Kiev
- Krivaks (3)

Springex 84

Baltic Fleet Krivaks

Northern Fleet Krivaks

- Air strikes
- Kirov group
- Aggressor groups

Summerex 85

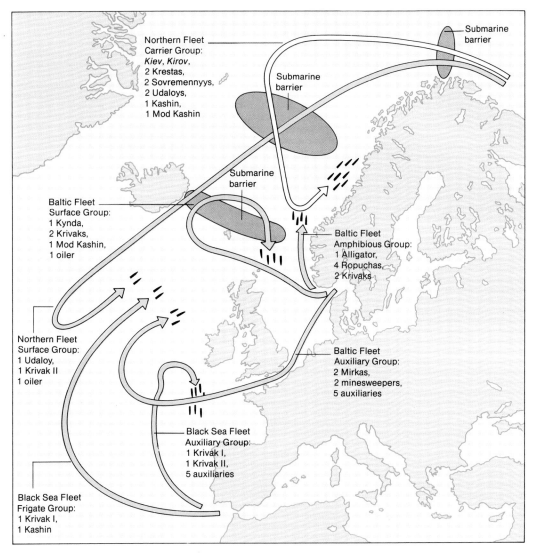

Northern Fleet Carrier Group:
Kiev, Kirov,
2 Krestas,
2 Sovremennyys,
2 Udaloys,
1 Kashin,
1 Mod Kashin

Submarine barrier

Submarine barrier

Baltic Fleet Surface Group:
1 Kynda,
2 Krivaks,
1 Mod Kashin,
1 oiler

Submarine barrier

Baltic Fleet Amphibious Group:
1 Alligator,
4 Ropuchas,
2 Krivaks

Northern Fleet Surface Group:
1 Udaloy,
1 Krivak II
1 oiler

Baltic Fleet Auxiliary Group:
2 Mirkas,
2 minesweepers,
5 auxiliaries

Black Sea Fleet Auxiliary Group:
1 Krivak I,
1 Krivak II,
5 auxiliaries

Black Sea Fleet Frigate Group:
1 Krivak I,
1 Kashin

Above: Since 1980 the Soviet Union has carried out a series of increasingly ambitious naval exercises in the Norwegian Sea, the Iceland-UK gap and the waters to the west of the UK. These exercises are designed firstly to rehearse the Soviet Navy's ability to operate out into the North Atlantic against NATO forces and secondly to practise their response to the deployment of a UK/Netherlands amphibious force which would be the initial NATO seaborne reaction to a crisis in the northern flank. The first of this series of exercises, in April 1980, was a relatively modest affair based on a Kiev class ship and three Krivak frigates as the carrier transited North from the Mediteranean to the Northern Fleet. In 1984, in the Springex 84 exercise, the Soviet Navy conducted a large-scale deployment to the Norwegian Sea consisting of half the Northern Fleet's major warships and many of its submarines. Two groups of Krivaks simulated the enemy NATO forces, while air activity included attacks by Backfire bombers and submarine barriers were deployed in the Norwegian Sea. The 1985 exercise was bigger still, 50 warships, over 30 submarines and 25 auxiliaries taking part; NATO's monitoring of the activities involved 90 ships and more than 100 aircraft sorties.

accepting the consequent set-piece battle; or by attempting to disrupt the enemy's plans for concentration by keeping forces widely dispersed with greater latitude for manoeuvre, a course which is more likely to avoid a battle and to result in a series of engagements. The size of the Norwegian Sea would demand two or possibly three carrier battle groups, probably in support of amphibious forces, and demands on the control of such a dispersed attacking force would be considerable, but there would be distinct advantages in terms of anti-submarine warfare. Detection of enemy submarines is paramount, and a fast-moving and constantly manoeuvring task force would more easily confuse and deceive the enemy and might well force him into unwanted manoeuvre and therefore possible exposure. Such forced errors are the key to this type of warfare.

It is important to consider how a large task force would proceed. The concept of the protective screen around the main body is all-important: by advancing in such a manner the specialisation of each unit, both surface and aircraft, can be exploited to the full. In the inner zone of protection would be the active-sonar frigates and helicopters. To allow control and to ensure that the area was fully sanitized, each vessel and helicopter would be given a sector of defence, normally some 60-72nm² in area, and each ship would manoeuvre continuously to deny attacking submarines the information they need to set up a firing solution for their weapons. Ships would use mainly hull-mounted sonars, and the larger units in particular would tow noise makers to decoy any possible torpedo attack.

Outside this inner zone, the next area would be patrolled by ships and aircraft using passive sonar devices. This is the most likely area for vessels with towed arrays such as the American TACTAS system. It is also here that the hunter-killer nuclear submarines are most likely to be deployed in support of the task force, well away from their own surface units, free to manoeuvre and removed from the noise of cavitating propellers, where their commanders can assume that any movement detected is an enemy.

With the main body carrying out a zig-zag course astern of it, restricting its speed of advance to probably 10 knots or so, the SSN is able to make the most of its speed advantage to cover large areas of sea, though this has to be balanced against the restriction that higher speeds involve greater noise from the submarine and increase the possibility of its own detection by the enemy. Helicopters in this area would be more likely to use sonobuoys because of their passive capabilities and their ability to cover wider sectors than dipping sonars.

Beyond this screen is the outer

zone. Here, well in advance of the main body, will be the LRMP aircraft, utilizing the full range of their detection devices—radar, both non-directional and directional sonobuoys, MAD and the Mk I eyeball—to feed constant information into the aircraft's computer system. Such aircraft are also armed with torpedoes and depth charges for prosecuting an attack if a submarine is detected.

With such a screen around him, the task force commander will proceed towards his objective. He must constantly be aware of all the information available to him, both from his own forces and from external sources including satellite surveillance and intelligence reports. Detections of possible submarines near to the main body will demand instant reaction. Attacks can be carried out by a variety of weapons depending on the distance from the fleet. Submarines at more than five miles will be attacked either by helicopters using homing torpedoes or possibly by ships released from their sectors to form a coordinated and independent attack unit. Such attacks will more than likely proceed according to general preplanned tactics, with each ship operating within a designated sector based around the submarine's suspected datum. The modern frigate in this situation would launch its helicopter armed with torpedoes.

It is essential to remember that positive sonar contacts of submarines are notoriously difficult to establish. Ships can search in vain for hours, either because the contact was spurious in the first place or because the enemy submarine has managed to slip away undetected; its commander is, after all, more interested in

Countermeasures to torpedo attack

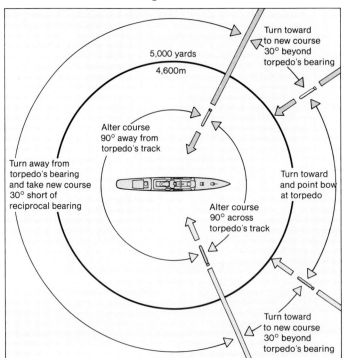

Above: Once a torpedo is detected, a ship must take immediate action if it is to have any chance of avoiding being hit: the time available will be extremely short, and all the manoeuvres shown must be carried out at full speed—indeed, they must be virtual reflex actions. Their aim is to present a narrow profile to the approaching weapon while simultaneously displacing the ship's position as rapidly as possible. Note that the manoeuvres are slightly different if the torpedo is first detected at a distance of less than 5,000 yards (4,600m), when the time available is naturally

much shorter. The one exception to these tactics is when a ship is towing a noise-maker, when to turn might place the ship between the decoy and the torpedo. Recent developments in torpedo technology are making evasion by surface ships increasingly difficult. The US Navy's Mk 48 torpedo is capable of operation in wire-guided, active or passive acoustic, and non-acoustic modes, and the British Tigerfish has a similar capability, together with an on-board computer which will take over the final run into the target, using the torpedo's own sonar for terminal guidance.

attacking the main body than the patrolling frigates.

As soon as a submarine contact is made by any unit in the task force, the main body will turn away from the estimated position of the enemy vessel, and at all times zig-zag plans will be maintained. Normally these plans are predetermined, though they can also be established by the local commander: either way, based on the desired course to be made good, they will allow the ships of the group to alter course together without any further signal or communication. Plans can be drawn up to take account of the estimated capabilities of particular types of enemy submarines, and while vessels out in the screen are unlikely to follow a preset zig-zag pattern, they need to know the manoeuvres of the main body in order to maintain their correct station.

Torpedo attacks can normally be detected by a warship due to the high noise of the fast running weapon. While the modern homing torpedo makes evasion difficult, certain countermeasures can be taken. Manoeuvring the ship to present as narrow a profile as possible and simultaneously, at high speed, opening the bearing relative to the torpedo, can result in the weapon passing its intended target. Also, as already mentioned, towed noise makers can decoy a torpedo, causing it to overrun.

Of course, the force commander cannot afford to take evasive action every time a submarine is detected whatever its position from the force, though the speed of SSNs greatly restricts his options. Nevertheless, he will normally have to establish areas of danger relevant to the main body based on the estimated capabilities of the

Task force reaction to submarine contact

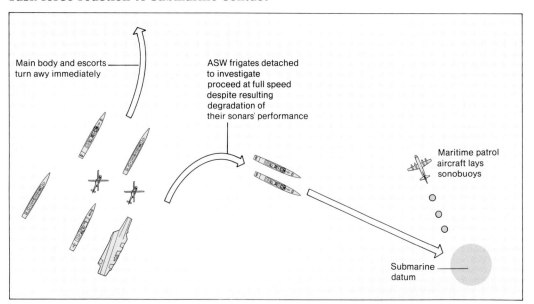

Above: A submarine contact discovered near enough to a task force that it could represent a future threat must be fully investigated and, if possible, destroyed. On receiving such a report, a force commander would

turn his main warship group away from the direction of the threat while at the same time detaching suitable ASW units—ships or aircraft—to proceed at full speed toward the enemy submarine's estimated position.

Right: The Royal Navy's Type 22 ASW frigate HMS Broadsword during an anti-submarine exercise. Alterations of course need to be virtually continuous in an ASW environment in order to deny an enemy the chance to attack.

enemy's submarines. Even a nuclear submarine will prefer to be in front of the target when preparing for an attack, and any submarine will have to close its target to within range of its weapons. These two considerations define its area of manoeuvre. The surface commander can estimate this area, normally referred to as limited lines of submerged approach, and within these lines can be estimated the torpedo danger zone (TDZ). Though it is obviously a risky decision, he can now plan certain defensive actions for each of these areas if a submarine is detected. Unless he is to manoeuvre his ships all over the sea, the naval commander often has little option but to make informed guesses.

The development of the nuclear submarine with its high-strength Albacore-type hull has led to demands for weapons more powerful than the light torpedo, which by its very nature is not big enough to carry a particularly large warhead, so the nuclear powers have developed nuclear depth bombs (NDB). Capable of being carried by ship-borne helicopters, such weapons need only be dropped in the vicinity of the submarine to produce a kill, and being small and exploded under water they produce little or no fall-out. Their use, however, is likely to be restricted by political considerations as well as by the commander's more immediate concern for the safety of his own submarine.

STRATEGIC BARRIERS

The anti-submarine battle in areas such as the Norwegian Sea will be fought using strategically placed barriers. These are independent of

the operations described so far in that they are used to detect and destroy submarines and are not necessarily related to what a surface force is attempting to use the sea for. Perhaps the most famous barrier is the one established by NATO to cover the gaps between Greenland, Iceland. the Faroes and the United Kingdom, the main exit routes for Soviet submarines to the North Atlantic. It would also be possible to establish barriers further to the northeast in the North Cape/Bear Island gap, as well as further south in the entrance to the Mediterranean.

In total, there are considered to be sixteen such choke points around the world, where barriers can be established using various detection systems and weapons, such as bottom arrays, submarines, LRMP aircraft and mines. In the Iceland/Faroes gap and across the top of the North Sea NATO has the much-publicized SOSUS system of fixed detectors in place, while to the north of Iceland a Captor minefield could be laid quickly and backed up by submarines and aircraft to make a formidable screen.

Limiting lines of submerged approach

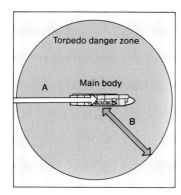

Left: Task group commanders have to be prepared to make instant decisions on whether or not a detected submarine poses a threat to their force—they cannot always afford the time to alter course—and it is possible to establish some rules for assessing a potential threat. These are normally thought of as the limiting lines of submerged approach, and while they are illustrated and can in practice be used as an overlay on a plotting table, they can also be computerised readily so that an assessment can be available instantly on a commander's attack information screen. The first step is to plot an advanced position based on the centre of the main body and allowing for the effect of an attacking torpedo's running time (A). Around this advanced point a circle is created called the Torpedo Danger Zone; its radius (B) is the range at which it is anticipated that torpedoes would be fired, and it can now be imagined that this circle moves along with the main body.

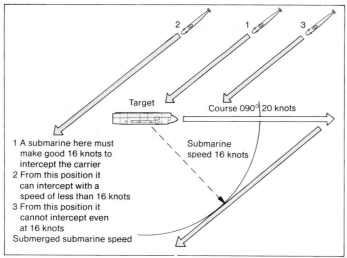

1 A submarine here must make good 16 knots to intercept the carrier
2 From this position it can intercept with a speed of less than 16 knots
3 From this position it cannot intercept even at 16 knots
Submerged submarine speed

Left: To assess whether a detected submarine can actually intercept the main body, some assumptions have to be made about the submarine. Although the speeds of different types of submarines vary, during an attack a submarine will always proceed as slowly as possible to minimise noise and so reduce the risk of detection. Once the speed has been estimated, an arc with this speed as its radius can be drawn (16 knots in this example), and at the same time the main body's course and speed can be plotted (090°, 20 knots). A line drawn from the 20nm mark as a tangent to the arc of the submarine's speed will give the relative course the submarine must make good at 16 knots.

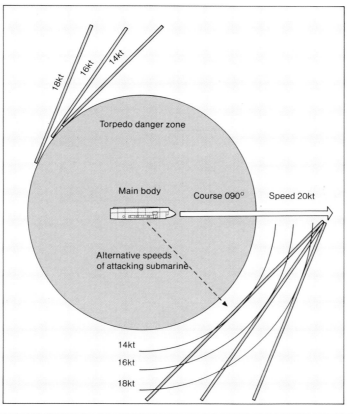

Left: In reality, the submarine does not have to directly intercept the ship in order to reach an attacking position—it needs only to manoeuvre itself within the range of its torpedoes. In practice, therefore, the first and second diagrams are combined as shown here. In addition, several realative courses can be prepared to cover differing submarine speeds—in this example 14, 16 and 18 knots—and instead of drawing the submarine's relative course direct to the aircraft carrier at the centre it can now be drawn to the periphery of the Torpedo Danger Zone. It can be seen that any detected submarine with an estimated speed of less than 18 knots and a position to the right of the relative courses drawn represents a threat to the carrier. (It is important to note that the submarine tracks shown are relative rather than true courses.) It is also possible to estimate the limitations on the courses a submarine would have to steer from its detected position to close the carrier, enabling the force commander to decide with some accuracy where to place his airborne units for protection.

Such screens do have some inherent weaknesses. To begin with, the land bases of sea bed detectors are vulnerable to attack, as is any cabling involved. The airfields in Iceland, Scotland and Northern Europe are also vulnerable, since most LRMP aircraft are based on medium to large civilian aircraft and therefore require substantial runways and maintenance support. Only Argentina, Brazil, France, India and the United States operate fixed-wing anti-submarine aircraft from carriers. The tactics of the Soviet submarines can also weaken the effectiveness of a barrier, and many are continuously deployed south of the main barriers in case of a sudden escalation in tension. Submarines can avoid detection by transiting SOSUS areas in close packs or by seeking cover from their own surface units, and it has been estimated that in the face of such tactics there would be less than 30% attrition in the choke points.

The great value of barriers is to give vital intelligence of enemy submarine movements, allowing immediate reaction. In the modern naval battle scenario, where every piece of information is vital to the naval command, the critical consideration is control and communications. With large numbers of ships, aircraft, submarines and a diversely spread enemy, it is easy to lose the ability to coordinate a sea-going force with the result that its weapons and detection devices are reduced in effectiveness.

CONVOY PROTECTION

The protection of merchant shipping against submarine warfare is also of vital importance, particularly to the Western Alliance. Over 99% of the world's trade is still carried by ships: every day around 120 ocean-going ships

US Navy strategic underwater surveillance

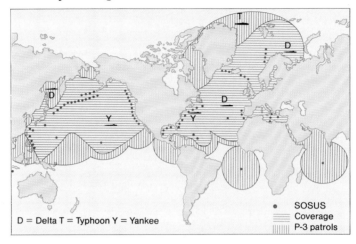

D = Delta T = Typhoon Y = Yankee

- • SOSUS
- ||| Coverage
- ||| P-3 patrols

Above: In order to be fully prepared for war it is essential that both East and West attempt to keep track of each others SSBN's. The US and its allies have a wide coverage of the world's oceans in their quest to detect Soviet submarine activity, and this map shows just the USN's own capability, using its static submerged systems of sonar arrays (SOSUS) and its large fleet of P-3

arrive in Western Europe to discharge three million tons of cargo, and approximately 30 million tons a month of crude oil is delivered to Europe and America. It is estimated that in a major conflict in Western Europe, a thousand ship loads a month will be needed to meet the minimum civilian and military requirements, in addition to which 500 ship loads of military stores, equipment, ammunition, fuel and men would have to cross the Atlantic.

The traditional method of protecting merchant shipping in a war environment is to form the vessels into convoys to facilitate

Orion ASW patrol aircraft. Also shown are the known deployment areas for Soviet SSBN's. The survivability of static arrays in waritme is questionable as it must be presumed that the Soviet Navy has a reasonable knowledge of where they are. Nevertheless, if they do nothing more than show changes to normal deployments, they will have fulfilled a valuable strategic function.

control and coordination and allow the defending forces to make efficient use of their limited resources. Many question if in this age of nuclear weapons and fast merchant ships convoying is still viable, but it is perfectly possible to plan for convoys which are spread out over a very large area of sea. Thirty or forty ships spaced at five-mile intervals, while still forming a coherent and controllable group, would cover $750nm^2$ of sea area, and it would take nine or ten 5MT tactical nuclear weapons, all precisely placed, to destroy such a convoy.

Increasing the space between ships also makes the attacking

submarine's task considerably more difficult. After any attack on one ship, the submarine commander would have to transit several miles before he was in a position to start setting up a new fire control solution. Moreover, having attacked the first vessel, he would know that the defending forces were aware of his location and hunting for him. During World War II it was usual to space ships in a convoy at half-mile intervals, and it can be calculated that doubling this distance reduces the risk of loss to about one quarter, but only enlarges the defence area for the escorts by half. Again, increasing the space to two miles decreases the risk of loss to one sixteenth, but only increases the convoy perimeter by two and a half times.

There are two main ways that a convoy can be protected: providing it with its own dedicated escorts; or sailing it through areas already occupied by supporting groups. The latter is the most likely to be used in a modern war, since it allows a more efficient use of limited naval resources and, most importantly, permits passive sonar operations in quiet areas of sea before the fast-moving and therefore noisy merchant vessels arrive. Such support groups would include ships with towed arrays, helicopters and hopefully LRMP aircraft; ideally, each group would have a nuclear submarine in support.

Convoys should be routed to impose the maximum confusion to the enemy and thereby minimise the risk of exposure. Long-leg zig-zags, each course being some 10-12nm long, with 30-40° alterations in course, for instance, make it particularly difficult for an attacking submarine to get into the grain of a convoy. The route should also allow the maximum protection from support groups, who would advance their position as necessary, and such groups

The GIUK gap: NATO's ASW barrier and the Soviet response

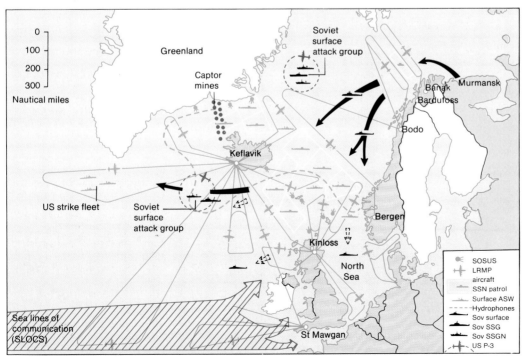

Left: In the event of conflict Soviet ships and submarines, both SSNs and SSGNs, will be expected to break out into the Atlantic and the North Sea through the Greenland-Iceland-United Kingdom (GIUK) gap. In addition, both submarines and surface vessels will exit into the North Sea through Skagerrak from the Baltic. Both areas are considered to be choke points in NATO terminology, and a great deal of effort has been put into attempting to seal these sea passages. They will be covered by a series of layers involving ASW aircraft, fixed monitoring devices such as SOSUS and patrolling submarines, both SSNs and SSKs. In addition, during periods of increasing tension US and European strike fleets can be expected to enter the area. This map, taken from Soviet sources, shows the possible disposition of forces. Note that NATO LRMP aircraft are not only having to cover the choke points but are also supplementing strike fleets, shadowing Soviet surface action groups and patrolling SLOCs.

Convoy support groups

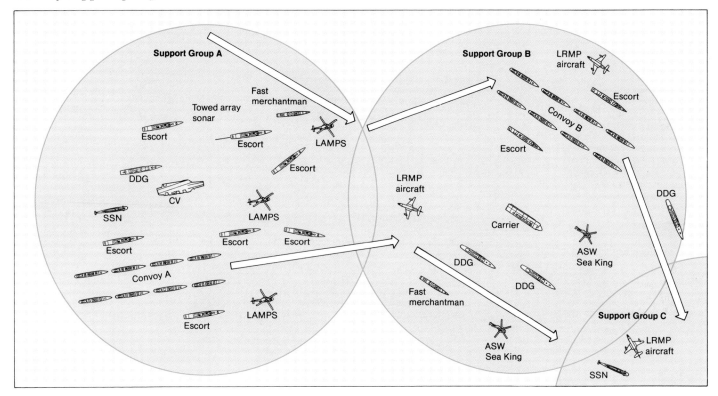

Above: The routing of convoys in a modern war would have to make the optimum use of relatively limited naval resources, since navies no longer have ocean going

escorts available in the sort of numbers used to support convoys during World War II. This diagram shows the use of support groups to sanitise areas in advance of

transiting convoys. The merchant vessels would require a minimum number of escorts to accompany them and might even have only ASW helicoptears based on a

merchantman. The support groups for their part would only be dedicated to a convoy while it passed through their areas before being released for other duties.

should have their own air cover with the particular aim of destroying any shadowing aircraft. It is vital to deny the enemy as much information as possible and thereby force him to reveal his whereabouts.

In order to reach a firing solution, the submarine captain has to sort out what is going on on the surface. His shore authority will pass him intelligence information based on satellite and air reconnaissance, but this is

bound to be historical in nature, and his sonar information may well also be confused, since fast-moving convoys make a good deal of noise that can be augmented with acoustic deception equipment, so the submarine may have to use its radar; it will certainly use its periscope. Use of radar should be detected by the defending forces' ESM detection equipment and will provide a bearing on the submarine's position extremely quickly,

while either radar or periscope could be detected by the radar of an LRMP aircraft.

If a submarine has to transit at high speed to close a convoy, again he increases the risk of detection. In the last war submarines enjoyed a speed advantage ratio of 16:6 over the typical convoy, but only when the submarine was on the surface. Today that advantage is approximately 30:17 with the submarine submerged, but while

17 knots is a speed easily sustained by a modern merchant ship, a submarine transiting submerged at 30 knots would be very vulnerable to detection.

THE MISSILE THREAT

Torpedo-firing submarines are only one type of threat. Convoys are also liable to attack from missile-firing submarines, such as the Soviet Echo Class, which will utilize target information from satellites or reconnaissance aircraft. The range could be as much as 300nm, but the submarine would have to surface before it fired and would therefore make itself vulnerable to detection. On the other hand, the Soviet Charlie class boats are able to fire missiles while still submerged, but their range is only one third of that of the surface-launched weapons. Nevertheless, such threats should be more easily containable in the support group type of convoy screen, since point defence systems such as Sea Wolf can provide cover in case of missile attack.

The essential principle of tactical defence of a convoy involves confusion of the enemy, in the hope of forcing him to show himself, and once detected, a submarine should be destroyed before it can attack.

Left: A Soviet Echo II SSGN would have to surface to fire its SS-N-3 missiles, making itself vulnerable to detection. Nevertheless, these 25-year-old boats are still a serious threat to the West.

Naval Air Warfare

The first sea battle to involve exclusively non-contact combat operation of ships was the engagement off Midway Island on June 4, 1942. This was a battle dominated by carrier-borne aircraft, with the ships of the two opposing sides, the United States and Japan, rarely closing nearer than 100nm to each other: in the space of a single day it was demonstrated that the battleship had become obsolete. Today these figures could be greater, though it is interesting to note how the Argentinian Navy's operations were restricted by bomb and fuel load, as described in the discussion of Surface Warfare. Sea battles will in future be fought over enormous spaces, imposing a significant restraint on naval commanders as they seek to keep touch with the developing action and making satellite and airborne surveillance systems an essential tool in the modern naval environment.

The threat from the air can take several forms: attack or reconnaissance aircraft, and missiles launched from the air, from other ships or submarines, or possibly from land. All these weapon systems are limited in range, though aircraft can extend their endurance significantly by the use of in-flight refuelling. In addition, the naval commander has to consider scenarios involving multiple air attacks with both aircraft and missiles having to be engaged simultaneously. The Soviet Naval Air Force, for example, is known to practise attacks involving waves of 19 Tu-22M 'Backfire' bombers at a time. The task force commander must, therefore, have a comprehensive and flexible command and control system to coordinate his defensive weapons.

An accurate assessment of the threat is essential. The naval task force must take account of the air weapons that could be deployed against it and the capabilities of those systems, and the tactics of the enemy's missile launch platforms, whether aircraft, ships or submarines, should be familiar to the defender. In the modern environment this knowledge is not so readily available as it may have been in the past, since tactics are necessarily designed to exploit the particular advantages of a specific weapon system. Naval guns in the early twentieth century were relatively standard in all navies, and tactics were correspondingly similar, but modern weapons proliferate, and as the frontiers of technology continue to be rolled rapidly back, so the tactics of different forces grow increasingly unpredictable. It is essential, therefore, that the manoeuvres of potential enemies are examined in peacetime, and indeed that careful note is taken of the actions of an enemy in the opening stages of a real conflict.

Having determined the strength and size of the threat, the commander should then consider the likely direction and form an attack might take. Obviously, good

Above: Today's navies constantly prepare for war with exercises that are as realistic as possible. Here a US Navy bomber aims off as a Charles F Adams destroyer refuels from the LPH USS Guam.

intelligence information is essential, while incorrect or non-existent information can be disastrous. For instance, it was known that Argentina possessed six Super Etendard naval strike aircraft and that a similar number of AM39 Exocets had been delivered from France, but the British were assured by the French that the Argentinians would not be able to connect up the complex firing circuits; an incorrect assessment that, for HMS *Sheffield*, was to prove disastrous.

DEFENCE IN DEPTH

It has already been seen that the positioning of ships in a task force must take account both of the threat and of the strengths and weaknesses within the force to ensure the maximum protection for the main body. Normally the major unit is an aircraft carrier with the escorting ships forming a screen to provide protection against air, surface and sub-surface attack. Good positioning of the ships will make the most effective use of their individual weapon systems in support of each other.

AAW tactics are based on the concept of defence in depth, beginning with an outer air battle and continuing through successive combat regions with engagement of approaching missiles and aircraft taking place in each. This attrition of the intensity of an attack is

Air defence of a task force

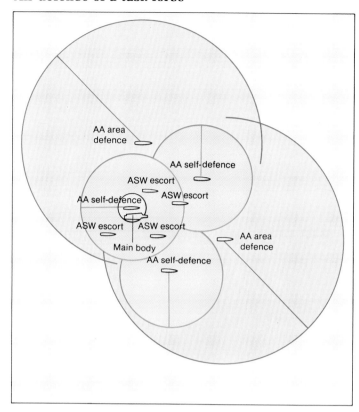

AA area
defence

AA self-defence

ASW escort

AA self-defence   ASW escort

ASW escort   ASW escort

Main body

AA area
defence

AA self-defence

Above: The positioning of the air defence ships in a task force will be determined by the range of their missile systems. Here the main body is a carrier with an esorting cruiser which would use its point defence systems—guns, short- **range missiles and CIWS—to supplement those of the carrier. Further out, beyond the screen of ASW escorts, are air defence ships with medium-range and area defence SAM systems to provide defence in depth.**

designed to reduce it to manageable proportions by the time it reaches the inner point defence zone. Ideally, the weapon carrier itself should be destroyed far from the battle group, before it can compute a weapon launch solution.

Electronic warfare plays a significant part in this air battle, providing targeting inputs to SAM systems and vectors to defending interceptor aircraft. EW can also degrade threat air targeting as well as provide electronic decoys to the homing missiles. Jamming or deception of a threat acquisition radar will force the enemy pilot to close his target much nearer than he would otherwise wish, making him more likely to encounter the air defence umbrella and increasing the chance of his destruction with his weapons still on their racks.

In the point defence zone itself individual ships protect themselves, though escorts can be positioned close alongside larger vessels, such as carriers, to provide mutual defence. Systems such as Sea Wolf, close in weapon systems (CIWS), EW and decoys must be closely coordinated to ensure a last-ditch protective cover.

Air protection for the fleet at sea is essential. European nations appeared for a time to be turning to land-based aircraft to provide air support for their fleets, and although the introduction of the Invincible class returned fixed-wing aircraft to the Royal Navy in the shape of the STOVL Sea Harrier, and the French have

maintained a small but effective carrier force of two vessels, NATO generally has chosen to rely on the US Navy's 14 big carriers. The Soviet Navy has only in the last few years received fixed-wing aircraft carriers, and their Yak-36 Forger aircraft have a strictly limited capability to defend their parent ship against the attack squadrons of a US Navy strike group.

Missile and gunnery systems, together with fixed-wing aircraft cover, can be used to form an air defence umbrella over a fleet at sea. It is a basic rule of naval tactics that the enemy should be engaged as far as possible away from the main body, and aircraft can be positioned ahead of the force or in the direction of the threat at distances of 100nm or more. They are then well positioned to engage attackers before the latter can reach a firing position for their own air-to-surface systems, as well as contributing to the early warning capability of the fleet.

EARLY WARNING

Early warning of air attack is vital, and military intelligence reports, satellite surveillance, AEW aircraft, fighter aircraft and radar picket ships positioned ahead of the fleet can all help to provide it. Of these sources, the first two provide good and useful information, but are unlikely to give warning quickly enough once an enemy attack is under way. AEW aircraft, on the other hand, are invaluable. The US

Left: A US Navy strike force presents an awesome display of fire power—the carrier alone has more than 85 aircraft embarked. In support of an amphibious group or as a base from which to launch a strike deep into an enemy country, **such a force is a considerable threat, well able to defend itself against all forms of air, surface or sub-surface counterattack. Soviet Navy units continually practise defending themselves against such a group.**

Above: The rapid expansion of the Soviet Navy in the last 25 years into a full ocean going force has necessitated the development of sophisticated procedures for replenishing ships at sea. Here a Kiev class carrier and a Kashin **destroyer refuel from the fleet auxiliary Berezina while a Kresta II manoeuvres alongside the tanker's starboard side prior to connecting up hoses and jackstays for passing solid stores such as food and ammunition.**

Navy's E-2C Hawkeye, flying at a height of 30,000ft (9,000m), can increase the radar surface coverage of a force out to 260nm—a three million cubic mile surveillance envelope—and can track up to 800 targets and control up to 40 intercepts simultaneously.

The lack of such an aircraft was a severe handicap to the British forces in the Falklands. The Gannet AEW aircraft had been phased out with the scrapping of the carriers *Eagle* and *Ark Royal*, and the Royal Navy, preparing essentially for battle in the North Atlantic, had turned to the land-based Shackleton as a stop-gap while waiting for the introduction of the AEW Nimrod. Even the Nimrod would have been incapable of operating for significant periods in the Falklands area, though ASW Nimrods were deployed south from Ascension Island using in-flight refuelling. So strongly did the British forces feel their consequent vulnerability that a crash programme was instituted to equip Sea King helicopters with a modified AEW version of the Searchwater reconnaissance radar used by the Nimrod MR.2.

The positioning of a radar picket ship can also usefully extend a task force's radar horizon. This task calls for a ship equipped with a medium to long-range high-definition radar such as the British Type 965R system, the US SPS-40 or the Soviet Top Pair, positioned on or near the edge of the battle group's radar horizon, though if the main direction of a likely attack is predictable a force commander may wish to send such a vessel further toward the enemy.

The ship's detection range will be limited by the characteristics of its radar. A radar emission can normally be considered to be lobe-shaped: detection range is longest at the centre of the lobe, and the lobe itself is incapable of following the curvature of the earth to any significant extent.

HMS *Sheffield*'s radar, for example, had a surface range of approximately 60nm and an air range of about 200nm, though the latter is particularly susceptible to climatic conditions. The Argentinians would have been fully aware of the characteristics of this type of radar having the same system in their own Type 42 destroyers, *Hercules* and *Santisima Trinidad*, so that, by approaching the force at a selected height, an Argentinian Super Etendard pilot would be able to utilize his own radar advantage to set up a firing position.

The first Exocet strike against the British battle group during the Falklands war is a good illustration of the tactics involved in both an air attack and a task force's defence against it. The surface

Right: An AEW Sea King fitted with a Searchwater surveillance radar flies protectively over HMS Illustrious. AEW support was to prove vital for the British during the Falklands operations.

actions of May 2, 1982, have already been related, culminating in the sinking of the *Belgrano* during the early evening of that day. For the next 48 hours the British battle group, TG 317.8, manoeuvred to the southeast of the Falklands with small groups of ships and aircraft closing the islands to bombard or carry out reconnaissance missions.

The British were aware that their enemy was equipped with the Exocet AM39 missile, but considered the threat unlikely due to the Argentinians' lack of expertise and their supposed lack of experience in the techniques of in-flight refuelling, and it was hoped that the bombing of the Stanley runway by Vulcans and Harriers would deter the Super Etendards, the Exocet launch aircraft, from using this facility.

The British commander, meanwhile, had to optimize the location of his ships. On the one hand he had to be close enough to the Falklands to conduct operations; on the other he had to keep as far out of range as possible of the Super Etendards flying from the mainland. This restricted the British aircraft carriers to an arc east and south of the islands, within which the only flexibility was to move from one section to the next.

On the early morning of May 4 a small group of Royal Navy vessels was picked up on the radar of an Argentinian Lockheed P-2H Neptune conducting a maritime reconnaissance misson some 100nm south of the Falklands. The

Above: This combination of Super Etendard attack aircraft and AM.39 Exocet missile proved to be a devastating threat to the British Task Force during the 1982 conflict with Agentina.

Argentinian Navy's four operational Super Etendards (a fifth was cannibalized for spares) were stationed at the Rio Grande air base: for some time they had been practising attacks on their own Type 42s, even taking it in turns to embark their pilots in the ships so that they could observe for themselves the best approach pattern and the moments of possible radar detection. At 0940, alerted by the Neptune, two aircraft were scrambled. At the same time a KC-130H Hercules took off and at 1000, 150nm from

the mainland, the tanker refuelled the two Exocet carriers.

The vessels of the British fleet were deployed to give the maximum protection to the carriers, forming five layers of defence. The outer defence zone was provided by two Sea Harriers and the 40nm range Sea Dart systems of the Type 42s stationed 20nm ahead of the main body along the threat axis. Eight nautical miles ahead of the carriers, formed in a sector screen, were four general purpose frigates. Between them and the main body, three supply ships, each establishing a significant radar image, provided a missile decoy barrier. The carriers themselves were being protected by the Sea Wolf-equipped Type 22s *Brilliant* and *Broadsword*. It was, in today's state of the tactical art, a classic

defence with two exceptions: the first was that the British lacked an airborne early warning aircraft; the second, that they believed it to be unlikely that the enemy would attempt the kind of attack that was already under way.

Successfully refuelled, the Argentinian aircraft flew directly toward the targets reported by the Neptune, and before entering the detection range of the British surveillance radars they dropped down to wave-top level (the forward vision of the pilots even became blurred by the salt spray building up on their cockpit windscreens). The aircraft climbed momentarily to 500ft (150m) and swept twice with their on-board Agave radars, but detected nothing; however, the Neptune had already established direct contact with

Above: Photographed by an amateur photographer on HMS Coventry, this scene vividly demonstrates the speed with which an A-4B Skyhawk passes over the ship on its bomb run.

them and updated their target information.

At 11.00 the Super Etendards climbed once more. On their radar screens appeared several small and one large contact. Each pilot immediately chose his target and locked on the attack computers: the range was 27nm; the time 1104. The missiles were launched. The aircraft turned away without waiting to see the results of their attack.

One of the Type 42s in the outer defence screen had detected a possible emission from a Super

Above: During a well executed Skyhawk attack aginst the British destroyers Coventry and Broadsword both ships were bombed. Here Coventry suffers one of the fatal direct hits.

Etendard radar, probably during the attacking aircraft's second and final look. The ship had fired chaff and gone to action stations, while the remainder of the force was alerted on the air warfare communications net. Soon after, the same ship momentarily detected two radar contacts, but quickly lost them, possibly as the aircraft turned away. In the Anti-Aircraft Warfare Coordination room in HMS *Invincible* they had received the reports, but due to early reporting of what turned out to be spurious contacts, were doubtful

of the new signals' authenticity.

Accordingly, AAW Co-ord requested confirmation, but it was too late: the Exocets were locked on. HMS *Sheffield* was at the south end of the forward air defence screen and was in fact transmitting on her SCOT satellite communications system clearing signal traffic for the task force. Though this is a rapid evolution, it had the effect of blotting out a possible detection by the ships EW equipment of the radar frequencies of both the Super Etendards and the Exocet. The flight time of the Exocet, at supersonic speed, was two minutes. The missile was detected for the first time visually, allowing no time for effective countermeasures. At 1751 that day, just under seven hours after being hit, the ship was abandoned.

The Exocet attack on HMS Sheffield, May 4, 1982

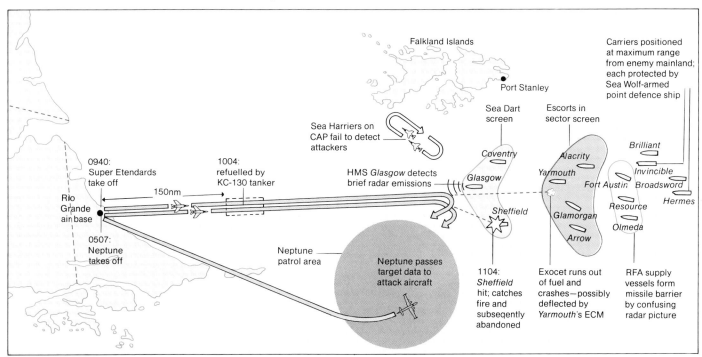

Above: The classic tactic in all successful military operations is surprise, and on May 4, 1982, two Super Etendards of the Argentinian Navy achieved this essential element. Alerted by a P-2H Neptune carrying out a maritime

reconnaisance flight some 100 miles (185 km) southeast of the Falklands, the two attacking aircraft took off from the Rio Grande airbase at 0940. At 1004 they refuelled from a KC-130 tanker and descended to wave height for

their approach to the Task Force. The British command had had several false alarms that morning and when one of the ships in the forward positioned Sea Dart screen reported a momentary radar contact they were already too late:

the attacking aircraft fired their Exocets, and HMS Sheffield was fatally hit. Had the two pilots waited to identify the carriers as their targets before launching their missiles the outcome of this war might have been very different.

The other Exocet had continued toward the main group of ships, but eventually fell into the sea either due to lack of fuel or possibly after being deflected by electronic countermeasures taken by HMS *Yarmouth*, positioned in the inner sector defence screen.

This episode has many significant tactical lessons. On the British side, the Royal Navy had been caught technically unprepared for a new development in air power. On the other side, the Argentinian pilots had failed to press home their attack. Had they waited even one or two more minutes they could have detected the carriers and exploited even further their tactical advantage (the *Sheffield*, though a significant loss to the battle group, was soon replaced). Such considerations, and the details of the attack overall, highlight the difficulties of modern naval warfare. Technology would appear at first glance to load the dice in favour of one side or the other. This is evidently not necessarily the case. Surprise and knowledge of the enemy are still essential prerequisites for success.

TACTICS DURING AIR ATTACK

When considering further the response of a fleet to an air attack it is essential to remember that the enemy almost invariably formulates his firing solutions using radar, and is unlikely to have been able to positively identify his target, while task force's defence policy relies on counterattack and perhaps more importantly on deception.

Defence in depth is essential to a task force and can be considered in terms of range from the centre of the fleet. The first line of defence is the responsibility of the carrier's fighters. Flying combat air patrol (CAP), at least two aircraft will normally be placed 100nm or so down the line of the enemy's most likely direction of attack, where

they may be controlled by the carrier itself, by an AEW aircraft or by a radar defence picket.

The role of the CAP is to destroy an attack before a missile launch can be achieved by the enemy aircraft. Enemy forces may include reconnaissance aircraft such as a Soviet Badger-F or even, as in the case of the Argentinians during the Falklands conflict, a civilian registered Boeing 707. Again, such aircraft should be destroyed. Note also the vital role played by the Argentinian Neptune during the Exocet attack which destroyed HMS *Sheffield*.

The secondary line of a force's defence will be designated to the area defence systems, and it is important to remember that an incoming attack may not have been detected in time to attempt a fighter response. If the attacking

Below: An F-14 Tomcat of the US Navy's Fighter Squadron 111 returns from a combat air patrol to its mother-ship, the nuclear powered aircraft carrier USS Carl Vinson visible below.

Above: May 25, 1982: stationed at the north end of Falkland Sound to engage Argentinian aircraft approaching the beach landing area, HMS Coventry was herself attacked, capsized and sank.

aircraft are able to approach at low level and fire their missiles while still below the defending ship's radar patterns there may be little or no time for a successful fighter interception, and the area defence missile zone may be the first area in which an indication is given of enemy activity. The third and inner area is the point defence zone and is protected by rapid-response weapons such as the French Crotale or the US Navy's 3,000rds/min Vulcan Phalanx.

Absolute command and control of these three zones of defence is essential. The boundary between one zone and another is likely to be infringed by friendly aircraft on occasions, during an air battle, for example, and confusion on the command's local air picture plot could too easily lead to the force engaging them. In addition,

returning CAP aircraft have to enter the missile defence zones to land on their carriers. Strict rules of approach must be enforced, possibly by the creation of narrow, missile-tight lanes through the zones themselves.

DECEPTION

Deception, and the confusion it can cause either in the mind of an attacking pilot or in the homing device of a missile, is an essential aspect of maritime defence. Radar detection is the primary and often the only means of pinpointing the intended target, but an enemy still has to identify which of the many contacts he is looking at on his radar is his designated priority. The first possibility available to the naval commander, therefore, is to form his ships in an unorthodox pattern.

In the discussion of sector defence it was seen that the usual practice is to place the main body at the centre of a defensive screen. On the pilot's radar picture, which normally views a surface force in

Task force air defence zones

Aircraft defence zone

Area missile defence zone

Point missile defence zone

15nm

5nm

100nm   40nm   35nm   60nm

Above: Air defence in depth is essential for a task force at sea, when the aim must be to destroy the enemy at as great a distance as possible from the main body of ships before a missile attack can be launched. A carrier group would therefore move inside an air defence zone some 100nm deep with area and point defence missile zones ensuring terminal protection from missiles.

Below: The return of the Falklands Task Force. The auxiliaries Olmeda, Fort Austin and Tidepool are escorted by HMS Apollo, Birmingham, Ardent and Avenger. Note the identification flags.

only two dimensions, the pattern or disposition of a fleet is fairly easily discerned, and the pilot expects to see a large target such as an aircraft carrier in the centre of several smaller contacts. If he is approaching at low level and has to increase height momentarily in order to obtain a radar picture of his target, he must make quick decisions on the identity of the carrier.

The task force commander has the option to place the carrier in the screen itself and replace it with another vessel considered more expendable. The *Atlantic Conveyor* was probably in such a position when she was lost during an Exocet attack on the British task force. It is interesting to note the great confidence the Argentinians had, after this successful attack, that they had sunk HMS *Invincible*.

Another primary source of deception is to confuse the radar picture of a fleet's disposition by the use of chaff. This is normally a cloud of light metal strips, fired by rocket, which blooms in the vicinity of the defending vessel. Several rockets are fired simultaneously. Because of the lightness of the material it will float in the air for some time, though moving downwind. It is therefore essential for the vessel firing the chaff to turn downwind and match the wind's speed in order to stay within the pattern it has created. Though obviously of great value during an air attack, such an action makes ships extremely vulnerable if there is also simultaneous enemy submarine activity. It was reported during the Falklands campaign that helicopters were used to fly close to their parent ships and distribute chaff in order to decoy incoming missiles.

Lastly, confusion can be caused by electronic warfare. Jamming on an attacker's radar frequency can deny him essential information, particularly on range. In a similar manner a missile's acquisition radar can be jammed, though once a missile has locked on it is normally extremely difficult to deceive it. Again, various attempts have been made to alter a ship's infra red signature, which shows as intense areas of heat around the funnel and machinery room areas. The British experimented with a special paint treatment vertically along the line of the funnel of some ships during the Falklands campaign as a method of dissipating the intense heat, and this can be seen on some of the photographs of HMS *Sheffield* after her fire.

Defence against air attack is a complex operation and a major concern for a naval commander. At the present time both Soviet and Western navies depend on a complex mixture of weapon systems giving defence in depth. As with the surface and sub-surface battle however, the key to success is to detect the enemy at as great a distance as possible from the force, combined with an ability to effectively control and command the defensive systems available.

Mine Warfare

The final area of tactics to be considered is mine warfare. This is of manifest importance, providing the attacker, or the defender, with an opportunity to effectively neutralize areas of sea and restrict or deny access to a foe. It also demands efficient counter-measures, since the maintenance of clear access to ports and anchorages is an obvious necessity. The technology of mines has advanced considerably in recent years, though mainly in their use in greater depths of water, rather than in the basic principles of their design, and the Soviet Navy in particular has carried out a great deal of research into deep-water mines.

OFFENSIVE MINELAYING

The most interesting aspect of mine warfare is its use in the offensive role. Mines can be laid either overtly by aircraft or covertly by submarine: both NATO and the Warsaw Pact have these capabilities and practise their use on a regular basis, and the US Navy used mines extensively during the Vietnam war. Originally the Americans attempted to prevent the passage of stores and munitions by the North Vietnamese and their allies along the coast and up into the numerous inlets by using ships and aircraft in endless patrols. This policy was unsuccessful, and on May 9, 1972, they turned to the extensive use of mines. During a single night, aircraft launched from carriers sowed mines in the approaches to all the ports as well as along the inland waterways, whereupon the North Vietnamese, lacking a minesweeping capability, became greatly restricted in their water-borne logistical support.

The Americans have developed a useful weapon system for deployment from submarines, the Submarine Launched Mobile Mine (SLMM) Mk 67, which allows a submarine to plant mines in shallow water in depths of up to 330ft (100m). The submarine itself does not have to approach too close to the intended area as the mine can be launched through a torpedo tube and will then propel itself to reach waters inaccessible to its mother ship. The Soviet Navy has a similar system.

The water depths in the sea areas adjacent to most of north-western Europe are generally 200ft (60m) or less. The entire North Sea, the English Channel and the Atlantic approaches to the UK and France lie above the shallow continental shelf, and in many areas sea traffic is confined to restricted waters due to shoals and banks. It is therefore an area ideally suited to offensive mining; it is also the very area that NATO must use in order to resupply land forces active on the European mainland. By laying a variety of sea bed mines and floating mines, especially in key areas such as the approaches to SSN and SSBN bases (ie, the sea passages through the Minches and into the Clyde)

Minelaying

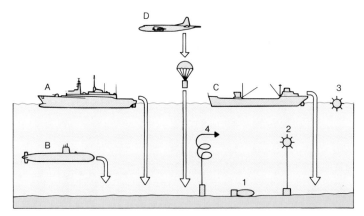

the Warsaw Pact could severely restrict use of these harbours.

A useful spin-off of such activities is that the defenders have to commit both precious manpower and machinery to clearing the mines. When World War II started, for example, the British had 75 minesweepers: within a year this had risen to about 700, and by 1945 they had 274 fleet minesweepers and 443 smaller minesweepers. Including all trawlers and auxilliaries, as many as 1,500 vessels were involved, and 14,300 mines were cleared. Despite this, 534 ships, a total of 1,406,000 tons, were lost to mines, nearly all of the losses being suffered in home waters and

Above: Mine warfare is a relatively cheap yet effective method of neutralizing large areas of sea. Mines can be laid by warship (A), submarine (B), merchant ship (C) or aircraft (D), and all these methods can be used covertly. The mines can lie on the seabed (1), be moored to float at a pre-set height (2), float on the surface (3) or be launched automatically from a seabed capsule (4).

Below: Minesweepers of the NATO Standing Force Channel exercising together. The Channel and North Sea ports could be rapidly mined by an enemy and maintenance of mine clearance expertise is vital.

Above: An RH-53D airborne mine countermeasures helicopter towing a sled to clear magnetic influence mines believed to have been laid by the Libyans to harass shipping in the Red Sea in 1983.

Below: The outer case of a Captor mine being recovered. This weapon would be deployed in deep water, generally in the vicinity of strategic routes travelled by enemy submarines.

more than 50% being incurred in the first 16 months of war.

Mines are also used in an anti-submarine role. Here they will be laid at much greater depths, the US Captor system being operational down to depths of 2,000ft (600m). Such weapons are obviously ideal in the choke points used by the Soviets for moving their SSNs and SSGNs into the Atlantic or Pacific, and like shallow water mines they can be laid by aircraft, ships and submarines. The great danger of such a system is that the torpedoes they fire are not selective. There is no IFF capability, and since they fire automatically a homing torpedo with an estimated range of 3,000ft (1,000m), friendly submarines need to keep well clear.

DEFENSIVE MINELAYING

Used in a defensive role, mines are laid to protect entrances to harbours and waterways, pre-

planned exits being formed through the fields to allow safe passage to the defender's own shipping. Such minelaying is designed especially to protect ports against incursion by submarines, to protect the flanks of ground forces against attack from the sea and in support of amphibious landings. The new Soviet wire-controlled mines would be particularly useful in such applications, as they can allow passage of their own vessels and are activated only in the event of enemy attack.

Mine warfare is not an end in itself, but its great effectiveness and relative cheapness make it an essential part of the modern armoury, and defence against it becomes increasingly difficult as their sensitivity increases. The best defensive tactic is to detect and destroy the delivery system—aircraft, ship or submarine—before it can release its load.

Offensive and defensive use of mines

Below: The remotely controlled submersible of the French PAP 104 minehunting system being launched. The increasing sophistication of Soviet mines has led to the development in the West

of minehunting techniques which minimize the risk to both men and equipment. This French system allows the remote placement of a disposal charge alongside a mine located by the control ship.

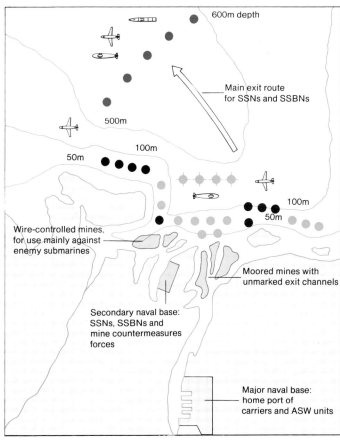

Above: There are considered to be 16 choke points around the world, through which shipping passes; each could be mined. In addition, every port is vulnerable to mining, and in the early stages of a conflict every effort would be made to pin down an enemy in his own harbours. Mines are also used defensively to protect a port against possible enemy submarine intrusions. This diagram shows how the various types of mine might be used, with Captor, quick strike and submarine-launched mobile mines used offensively and moored, antenna contact and wire-controlled mines protecting main and secondary bases.

Offensive minelaying

Captor mines

Quick-strike minefields

Submarine-laid mobile mines

Surface minelayer

Minelaying aircraft

Minelaying submarine

Defensive minelaying

Anti-submarine antenna contact mines

Minefields

Conclusion

The battle has always been and remains the main means of solving tactical tasks. For a long time sea battles were the sole form of naval combat, but nowadays the navy forms an integral part of the operations of other branches of the armed forces, and with the development of modern weapon systems the distance between combatants has increased. During World War II battles exceeded the range of optical visibility: in future it can be anticipated that naval engagements will take place over enormous spaces, but given both the increase in destructive power of the weapons and the consideration that naval forces will already be at sea by the outbreak of hostilities, the moments of combat are likely to be short. Nevertheless, the elements of tactics are likely to remain constant. They are to seek out the enemy, to achieve tactical deployment of forces and to deliver strikes as soon as the weapon platforms have achieved target solutions.

It must be emphasized that although tactics, for the sake of clarity, have been described in the three main divisions of surface, air and anti-submarine warfare, in reality all three should be anticipated simultaneously by a naval task force. Of the three, undoubtedly, command of the air is the most essential prerequisite for success. The British in the South Atlantic won the air battle, but it was a close-run thing, and any future war between the Warsaw Pact and NATO would involve extensive air hostilities.

NATO strategy calls for reinforcement of the Western European flank by sea, while strike fleets will have to operate in the Norwegain Sea and the Eastern Mediterranean in support of amphibious forces, and the Soviets are well prepared for this eventuality. Their main tactic is to swamp their enemy's defences with coordinated aircraft, missile and submarine attacks. Every form of naval warfare should be expected in these circumstances including the use of tactical nuclear weapons.

In many respects, however, the basic tactical rules will be the same as in the past. It is essential, first of all, to locate and track the positions of the enemy's forces, and while this will not be too difficult given modern satellite surveillance techniques, only the SSN will really be able to retain the element of surprise. The environment itself will be the same as ever. The weather will still play its part. Weapon ranges will obviously remain important, and the ideal situation is still to be within range of the enemy, but outside the range of his weapons.

In other respects the battle will be different. It will take place against a background of strategic deterrence, with the location of SSBNs a constant worry to both sides. Actual knowledge of the enemy's technical ability may be more restricted than in the past. Missiles are more accurate than guns, so the advantage will lie with the ship which fires first. And battles will be fought in an electronic environment, so effective and subtle ECM will be all-important.

All these considerations lead to several conclusions which can be summarized as follows:

Above: Anti-submarine warfare is a constant preoccupation: the threat must be sought constantly and the means to neutralize it always available. Here an Asroc from one of the carrier's escorts detonates in the distance.

Below: Tactical decisions on deployment can be matters of life and death: detection of air attack in Falkland Sound during the British landings at San Carlos was difficult, and HMS Ardent was one of those to pay the price.

Above: The rapid deployment of naval units is vital both for the successful prosecution of a mission and to keep the adversary guessing: here the carrier USS America transits the Suez Canal between the Red Sea and the Mediterranean.

Below: The cruiser Long Beach demonstrates the constant changes of course that both the main bodies of task groups and their escorts must make if they are to minimize their chances of falling victim to an attack by enemy submarines.

1: Deception plays a major part in modern naval warfare. Ship formations, decoys, feints, chaff, jamming, electronic deception, all have a part to play. Even the sudden fast transiting of a task force after the pass of a surveillance satellite can provide confusion.

2: If possible, forces should stay outside the enemy's range. If the objective prevents this, then it must strike first.

3: Maximum protection should be provided for the main bodies, especially if they include carriers, and air cover for a task force is essential. Optimization of the positioning of ships to provide the most effective supporting cover from long-, medium- and short-range missile systems—the so-called defence in depth—is vital.

4: Long range airborne radar coverage is indispensable.

5: Coordination of SSN forces in support of a surface group is necessary to take advantage of the submarine's unique ability to maintain an element of surprise.

6: It will be more important than ever to sink the enemy, not just cause damage, since naval losses are hard to make good. Equally, structural design and damage control will be of the utmost importance in order to ensure that a ship is not necessarily lost as a result of only one missile hit.

7: Mine warfare will play a key role.

8: The resources of a fleet, a battle group, a task force or a task unit must be balanced to provide as wide a range of capability as possible.

9: For all the relative slowness of moving major naval groupings, speed is nevertheless important. Its value could even increase, since it can provide an ability to carry out swift actions to the disadvantages of an opponent.

10: Command and control of naval forces to ensure coordinated responses to enemy attacks are a critical requirement. Good interaction between units is essential in order to exploit their strengths and to cover their weaknesses.

11: The use of nuclear weapons at sea must be expected and ships should be deployed to take account of this threat.

12: Good communications and logistical support are essential.

13: The role of a single naval unit, such as a missile-firing submarine, can have a significant impact, given its ability to destroy a major naval unit without warning and perhaps even single-handed.

14: For all the preplanning that must be done before a naval battle, covering aspects such as whether to attack or defend or the selection of priority targets, it has to be stressed that at sea the unexpected will often occur, and many decisions will have to be made in the heat of battle. Indeed, history has shown that the naval commander who does the unexpected, who breaks the accepted rules the day, will more often than not emerge the victor.

Glossary

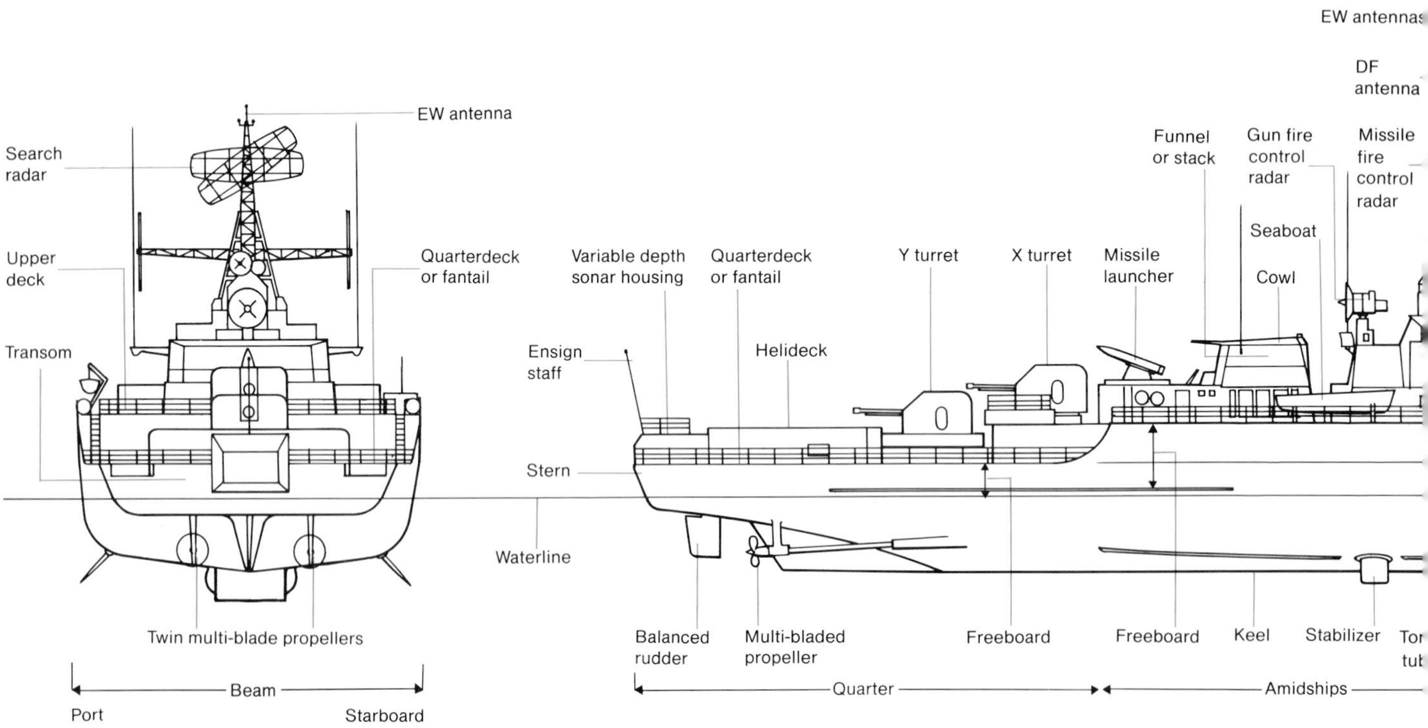

Search radar
Upper deck
Transom
EW antenna
Quarterdeck or fantail
Twin multi-blade propellers
Port — Beam — Starboard

Variable depth sonar housing
Ensign staff
Stern
Waterline
Balanced rudder
Multi-bladed propeller
Quarterdeck or fantail
Helideck

EW antennas
DF antenna
Funnel or stack
Gun fire control radar
Missile fire control radar
Seaboat
Cowl
Y turret
X turret
Missile launcher
Freeboard
Freeboard
Keel
Stabilizer
Torpedo tube
Quarter — Amidships

Index

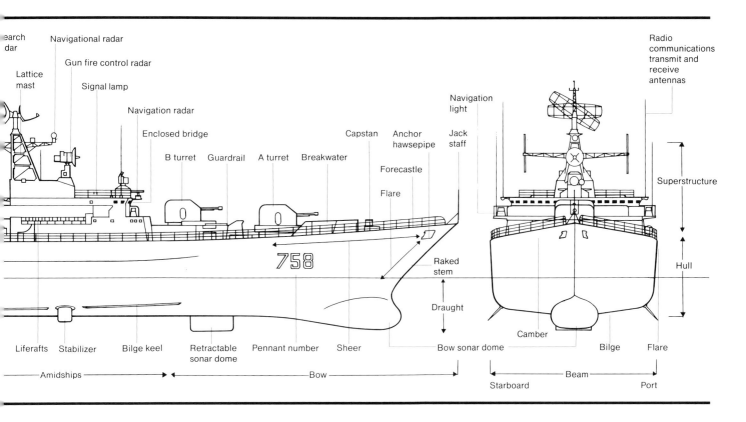

Picture Credits

Endpapers: Hughes Aircraft **Page 1:** Mod-Navy **2/3:** US Navy **4/5:** US Navy **6/7:** US Navy **8:** MoD-Navy **9:** (top) US Navy; (bottom) MoD-Navy **10/11:** Ericsson **12:** (left) Vosper Thornycroft; (right) US DoD/Mitsuo Shibata **13:** Canadian Forces **14/15:** (top left) US Navy; (top right) US Marine Corps; (bottom) Royal Navy **17:** (top and centre) US Navy; (bottom) Royal Australian Navy **19:** (top left and right) US DoD; (bottom) Royal Netherlands Navy **21:** (top and bottom) US DoD; (centre) US DoD/Mitsuo Shibata **22/23:** (bottom centre) MoD-Navy; (remainder) US Navy **24:** (top left) Vickers; (top right and bottom) US Navy; (centre) MoD **25:** (centre) MEKO/MARS; (bottom right) US DoD; (bottom right) MEKO **26:** (top) Cammell Laird; (centre) US DoD **27:** (both) MoD-Navy **28:** US Navy **29:** (top left) US Navy; (top right) Rolls-Royce; (bottom) Hughes Aircraft **30:** (top left and bottom) US Navy; (top right) Paxman **31:** Vosper Thornycroft **32:** (top) US Navy; (bottom) US DoD **33:** US Navy **34/35:** (all) US Navy **36:** DCN **37:** (top left) HDW; (top right) Stone Manganese **38:** US DoD **39:** US Navy **40:** US DoD **31:** (top left) RDM; (top right) US Navy; (bottom) Vickers **42:** (top) US Navy; (bottom) Dassault-Breguet **43:** US Navy **44:** (all) US Navy **45:** (top) Aerospatiale; (bottom) US DoD **46/47:** (right) US Navy; (centre) General Dynamics; (top and bottom right) US DoD **48:** (top) ECPA; (bottom) Aerospatiale **49:** (top left) Matra; (top right) MBB; (bottom) McDonnell Douglas **50/51:** (bottom left) Matra; (centre right) OTO Melara; (remainder) US Navy **52:** (both) US Navy **53:** (top left) Hollandse Signaalapparaten; (centre right) DCAN **54:** (both) US Navy **55:** (top left) ECPA; (top right) Boeing; (bottom) Goodyear Aerospace **56:** (top) Aerospatiale; (bottom left) US Navy; (bottom right) Marconi **57:** (top) Aerospatiale; (bottom) US Air Force **58:** Thomson-CSF **59:** (top and bottom right) US Navy; (bottom left) Hollandse Signaalapparaten **61:** (both) US Navy **62:** EDO **63:** (top) EDO; (centre) Agusta **64:** (top) US Navy; (bottom) Jet Propulsion laboratory **65:** (top) MoD; (bottom) US Navy **66:** (top) Grumman; (bottom) MoD-Navy **67:** (top) Thorn-EMI; (bottom left) Lockheed; (bottom right) British Aerospace **68:** NATO Channel/Eastlant **69:** McDonnell Douglas **71:** (both) British Aerospace **72:** (top left) Indal Technologies; (bottom right sequence) McDonnell Douglas **73:** (top) Lockheed-California; (centre) Sikorsky; (bottom) Westland **74:** (top) Westland; (centre) NATO Channel/Eastlant; (bottom) Aerospatiale **75:** (top left) British Aerospace; (top right) Grumman; (bottom) Dassault-Breguet **76:** (top left) US Navy; (top right) Panavia; (bottom) Dassault-Breguet **77:** (top and bottom left) US DoD; (centre) MoD; (bottom right) British Aerospace Dynamics **78/79:** (left) Marconi; (centre) Boeing; (right) Elisra **80:** (upper left) Raytheon; (lower left) Hughes Aircraft; (right) Hollandse Signaalapparaten **81:** US Navy **82:** (top left) US Navy; (top right and centre) Irvin; (bottom right) Plessey **83:** (top left and right) US Navy; (bottom) Sperry **84/85:** US Navy **86/87:** (both) US Navy **88:** US Navy **90:** Stato Maggiore Marina **92:** Plessey Marine **94:** ECPA **95:** SIRPA-Marine **97:** US DoD **98:** (both) SIRPA-Marine **100:** SIRPA-Marine/MARS **102:** Fincantieri/MARS **104:** JMSDF **106:** MoD-Navy **107:** Swan Hunter/MARS **108:** US Navy **110:** US DoD/Mitsuo Shibata **113:** US DoD **114:** MoD PR **116:** US Navy **118:** NATO **120:** US Navy **122:** DCN **123:** DCN **125:** US Navy **126:** MEKO/MARS **128:** (both) US Navy **130/31:** US Navy **132:** Vosper Thornycroft **134/35:** (both) US Navy **136:** US Navy **138/3:** (both) US DoD **140:** Reportabegild, Stockholm **142/43:** (both) Royal Navy **145:** (both) SIRPA-Marine/MARS **147:** MoD-Navy **148:** US DoD **149:** US Navy/Royal Norwegian Air Force **150:** (both) US Navy **152:** (both) US Navy **154:** US Navy **157:** US Navy **156/57:** (both) MoD-Navy **158/59:** (both) HDW **163:** US DoD **164:** US DoD **166:** US Navy **168:** Italian Navy **170:** RDM **171:** Royal Netherlands Navy **172:** Royal Belgian Navy/MARS **174/75:** (both) US Navy **176:** (top) NATO; (bottom) US Navy **177:** (left) Sippican; (right) US Navy **178:** (both) MoD-Navy **179:** National Maritime Museum **180:** Imperial War Museum **181:** US Navy **182:** (top) MoD Navy; (bottom) R Scheina/MARS **183:** MoD-Navy/TRH **184:** (both) US Navy **185:** MoD-Navy **186:** US Navy **187:** (left) US Navy; (right) Ericsson **188:** (top) US Navy; (bottom) NATO STANAVFORLANT **190/91:** MoD-Navy **193:** US Navy **194/95:** (all) US Navy **196:** (top) Aerospatiale; (bottom) MoD-Navy **197:** (both) MoD-Navy **198:** (top) MoD-Navy; (bottom) US Navy **199:** MoD-Navy **200:** MoD Navy **201:** (top) US Navy; (centre) Goodyear Aerospace; (bottom) DCN **202:** (top) US Navy; (bottom) MoD-Navy **203:** (both) US Navy **Back jacket:** (top left and centre) US Navy; (top right) MBB; (bottom left) SIRPA-Marine.

Above: The Spruance class destroyer USS John Young.